45 911 349 2

Hertfordshire

Renewed 22 MAY
2016

Please renew/return this item by the last date shown.

So that your telephone call is charged at local rate,
please call the numbers as set out below:

	From Area codes 01923 or 020:	From the rest of Herts:
Renewals:	01923 471373	01438 737373
Enquiries:	01923 471333	01438 737333
Textphone:	01923 471599	01438 737599

L32   www.hertsdirect.org/librarycatalogue

D1355649

A QUIET COURAGE

Also by Liane Jones

Flying High

Liane Jones

A QUIET COURAGE

BANTAM PRESS

LONDON · NEW YORK · TORONTO · SYDNEY · AUCKLAND

TRANSWORLD PUBLISHERS LTD
61-63 Uxbridge Road, London W5 5SA

TRANSWORLD PUBLISHERS (AUSTRALIA) PTY LTD
15-23 Helles Avenue, Moorebank, NSW 2170

TRANSWORLD PUBLISHERS (NZ) LTD
Cnr Moselle and Waipareira Aves,
Henderson, Auckland

Published 1990 by Bantam Press
a division of Transworld Publishers Ltd
Copyright © Liane Jones 1990

British Library Cataloguing in Publication Data
Jones, Liane, 1958-
     A quiet courage: the story of SOE's women
     agents in France
     1. World War   2. Army operations by Great
     Britain. Army. Special Operations Executive.
     Women officers
     I. Title
     940.54′86′410922

     ISBN 0–593–01663–7

Printed in Great Britain by
Mackays of Chatham, Chatham, Kent

For the women of F Section

CHANNEL

Dunkerque
Calais
Boulogne
Lille

BELGIUM

Dieppe
St Quentin
MUSICIAN

LUXEMBOURG

GERMANY

Cherbourg
Le Havre
SALESMAN
Rouen
SILVERSMITH
Reims
Nancy

Caen
Paris
Châlons-sur-Marne

St
Malo
SCIENTIST (2)
Chartres
SCIENTIST (1)
MINISTER

HEADMASTER
Le Mans
HISTORIAN
Joigny
Troyes
TINKER

CLERGYMAN
Orléans
DONKEYMAN
Auxerre
YONNE
SCHOLAR

Nantes
Tours
MONKEYPUZZLE
Blois
Cosne
Dijon
Dôle

SOLOGNE
INDRE
Nevers
ACROBAT
SWITZER LAND

WRESTLER
Châteauroux
HECKLER

Poitiers
Chalon-sur-Saône
St Amouri

ARTIST
VIENNE
Montluçon
FIREMAN
Vichy
MARKSMAN

ATLANTIC
Angoulême
Limoges
VENTRILOQUIST (2)
Clermont Ferrand
PLANE
Lyon
SPINDLE (2)
Annecy

CORRÈZE
St Étienne
PIMENTO
Grenoble

Périgueux
FREELANCE

Bordeaux
DORDOGNE
DRÔME

Agen
Avignon
JO CKEY

Condom
GERS
Toulouse
MONK
Marseille
SPINDLE (V)
Cannes

Pau
Tarbes
Toulon

STATIONER
Perpignan

MEDITERRANEAN

MAP OF OCCUPIED FRANCE
Showing The Réseaux Of F Section's Women Agents

Contents

Acknowledgements   ix
Introduction   1
 1 *First Contacts*   16
 2 *'The Organization': The Workings of F Section*   24
 3 *Agents in Training*   32
 4 *Going In*   46
 5 *Prosper and the Great Hope*   50
 6 *An Agent in Poitiers*   68
 7 *Odette's Mission*   80
 8 *The Weaving of the Net*   98
 9 *The Net Closes on St Jorioz*   115
10 *The Net Closes on Prosper*   129
11 *The End of the Intrigue*   142
12 *Missions Under a Shadow*   151
13 *Developments South of the Line*   163
14 *The South-West, 1943-4*   178
15 *Early 1944: Eliane, Yolande, Elizabeth*   193
16 *France Mobilizes*   210
17 *Lighting the Fuse*   237
18 *Fighting into the Open – D-Day and After*   260
19 *Arrested in Paris*   276
20 *Liberation*   285
21 *On the Other Side of the Wall*   292
22 *Captivity*   309
23 *The End of SOE*   325
Epilogue   329
Bibliography   346

Acknowledgements

I have so many people to thank and so many debts of gratitude and recognition to pay, that I can't begin to organize my acknowledgements. The women agents who talked to me at such length – Lise de Baissac, Yvonne Cormeau, Odette Hallowes and Didi Nearne – know what I owe them; Francine Agazarian gave me no less in the letters she wrote. It is self-evident that the book could not have been written without these women: they are the book's *raison d'être*. I have tried to pass on something of their characters and spirit, as well as their adventures; it was a presumptuous exercise to start with, and I can only thank them for letting me attempt it and apologize to them for those places where – they will see only too clearly – the book falls short of the reality.

Vera Atkins has been an inspiration, a teacher, a conjuror of names, addresses and invitations, and a friend. When I fell into fits of confusion and doubt I would apply to her and would get encouragement (not always the gentle kind). Maurice Buckmaster has also been generous with his time and hospitality, and opened the world of 64 Baker Street to me with his descriptions of its people and atmosphere.

I am deeply grateful to Francis Cammaerts, Maurice Southgate, René Clément, John Farmer, Monsieur and Madame Bastelica, Renée Bernet, Brian Stonehouse, Robert Maloubier, Jacques Bureau and Geneviève Mathieu for talking to me about their experiences in occupied France, and about the people they worked with. They helped give me a better understanding of what it meant to work in the Resistance. Some of them are mentioned only briefly in the narrative, or not at all, but they were all important to the writing of the book.

I'd also like to thank Yvonne Burney (formerly Yvonne Baseden), Pearl Cornioley (formerly Pearl Witherington) and Nancy Forward (formerly Nancy Wake). Although they didn't want to give interviews they gave their permission for me to write about them and suggested sources of information about their SOE work.

I owe an enormous debt to the work of M.R.D. Foot, especially his book *SOE in France*, for which he was allowed the unique privilege of access to French Section files. This book is an invaluable source of information and I have drawn extensively on it. My thanks are also due to the following people: Peter Lee, Paddy Sproule and the staff of the Special Forces Club; Christopher Woods, Gervase Cowell and Ursula Thomas of the SOE Archives; Geoffrey Hallowes, André Watt, Maurice Chauvet, Annick Burgard, the staff of the Imperial War Museum (especially the Reading Room staff), Jerry Kuehl, Sara and Philippe Ward, Hugh Jones, Madame Southgate, the late Mrs Buckmaster, Geoffrey Chandler, Hugh and Caragh Hanning, Robert Marshall, and Rachel Huson, all of whom helped me with my research in ways as various (everything from document translation to dog-sitting) as they were valuable.

I want to thank Sara Fisher, my agent, for her help with my research, my plans, my writing and my morale (which seems to have been making quite a few demands on her during these two years). Similarly, thanks to Heather Holden-Brown who first gave me the idea of writing the book and whose continued interest in it has been a great encouragement, to Kate Parkin, who commissioned the book and helped me a great deal in the early stages of writing it, and to George Morley who took over from Kate as my editor and with whom it was actually fun to work on the (so-called) completed manuscript. My thanks also to Alan Earney, Sally Gaminara, Broo Doherty and Liz Laczynska of Bantam Press for their interest, help and ideas. And to Tom Graves for his picture research.

Thank you to my parents Eve and Alan Jones for their many different kinds of help and interest; to my family in Wales for the same; and to my friends, especially Deborah Wolfson for all her encouragement and willingness to listen to my moans.

Finally, my thanks to Siobhan Kilfeather for things she understands without my listing them, and above all to Jamie Buxton. I can never thank Jamie enough for everything he's given me and everything he's put up with in the last two years, but at least he must be pleased that the book is finished.

Introduction

France, 1941: one year had gone by since German troops had swept into the country from the north-east, and the Third Republic of France had fallen. It was one year since the old marshal Pétain, hero from the First World War, had signed the armistice with the invading Germans. Now France was physically divided in two: German forces occupied the northern half of the country, and the Atlantic coast; south and east of that was land governed by Pétain and his ministers. The northern part was known as the 'occupied zone'; the southern part as the 'unoccupied zone' or as Vichy France, because it was governed from the spa town of Vichy. The border between the two, the 'demarcation line' was hard to cross: one needed a special permit to make the journey. But then, one needed permits and licences for many things in France now.

French people needed permits to drive vehicles, ration tickets for food, special permission to cross the demarcation line. They had to carry identity cards and papers wherever they went. And there were things they simply could not do: they were not allowed into certain cafés, restaurants, cinemas and clubs in the occupied zone – Germans only. They were not allowed to drive petrol-powered cars unless on official business. In Vichy France, they were not allowed out after curfew. They were not allowed to listen to the BBC radio broadcasts, on which Churchill and de Gaulle sometimes spoke. They were not allowed to carry maps or compasses. They were not allowed to own printing materials. The restrictions proliferated with every month, and varied according to the region of France and the authority in control.

To live in the occupied zone was to be under German rule. German troops were garrisoned across northern France; a Paris-based German administration made the laws and enforced them through the French police force, backed up with German soldiers and the Gestapo. The Gestapo was a security force connected to the Nazi party's intelligence and counter-subversion organization, the SD. There was also the Abwehr, the intelligence wing of the German army, and this had its own operatives, but to the French they all tended to be identified as a particularly ruthless body of special police, known as the Gestapo. The Gestapo was feared and hated by the French; the sight of Gestapo officers going through hotel registers or raiding an apartment was a potent symbol of France's subjugation, as well as its instrument.

Life in the occupied zone was restricted and difficult. The German administration was determined to stamp out resistance as it arose, and so laws were passed to make French people carry elaborate identity cards and to register with local authorities when they moved about. Almost immediately, people here and there managed to get hold of rubber and ink and make duplicate official stamps; with these they made duplicate identity cards. The Gestapo began raiding houses where they suspected such activities were taking place: it was illegal to own printing materials; people convicted of it faced long sentences of imprisonment and forced labour in Germany.

Certain journals were banned, and so were printed and circulated clandestinely. With an eye on the more liberal conditions in Vichy France, the German administration made it very difficult for inhabitants of the occupied zone to cross the line. It was not enough to seek permission on the grounds of visiting family or friends. Permits were usually given only for people travelling on some kind of official business. The Germans did not want people from the occupied zone going to and from Vichy France, perhaps sending information to the British or the Americans, perhaps smuggling things back into the occupied zone – guns, explosives, money, food.

The shortage of food and clothing was a preoccupation with German occupiers and French people alike. In the occupied zone, the best of the produce went to the Germans, as did most of the clothing materials. Fuel stocks and petrol were also taken by them: French people had to convert their petrol-powered cars into '*gazogenes*', vehicles which ran slowly and erratically on charcoal burners. French factories – of which there were many in the industrial north-east – were requisitioned to make parts for German military equipment.

In the unoccupied zone, the regulations governing life were slightly freer, but the lack of food and materials was just as bad. In fact, in some districts, it was worse. Vichy France was largely rural and agricultural, and the Germans saw it as a source of food for the German population at home and for the enormous German army. The best of the produce

was requisitioned from large farms and smallholdings and sent east
to Germany. Already in 1941 there was not enough left to feed the
people of Vichy France. Finding enough food for their families was
a constant worry; farmers with livestock were hard put to keep them
alive and healthy.

Administration-wise, the Vichy government was independent in
name but in fact it had to do everything it could to appease the
powerful Germans. It promised to check the possibility of insurgence,
and to do so it formed its own Vichy police and security force. Vichy
police were to the local gendarmes of the south what the Gestapo
were to the gendarmes of the north: they undertook to hunt down
would-be subversives, and called on the help of the gendarmeries
to do it. They did not always get the co-operation they wanted –
some local gendarmes were more inclined to the Resistance than to
Vichy, and the more lenient sentences for crimes such as carrying or
issuing false papers made resistance seem more possible. Moreover,
there was the Mediterranean coast, from which small craft could and
did smuggle fugitives out of the country; the Pyrenees also offered an
escape route into Spain, albeit a hard one.

But in 1941, there was little active Resistance at work. The people
of France were shocked at what had happened to their country and
they were divided, physically by the demarcation line and ideologically
by different political beliefs. The disagreements ran very deep: many
people, remembering the First World War and recognizing that France
was utterly unequipped to take on Germany, thought that Pétain's
armistice had saved France from annihilation and should be preserved.
Others thought that the armistice should be repudiated and that the
French should join together and rise against the Germans.

Many people on the right were opposed to throwing out the
Germans because they believed it would allow the Soviets to lead
in the Bolshevists. Conversely, many communists were reluctant to
rise against Germany initially, because it would put them at odds with
the Soviet Union, which had signed a non-aggression pact with Hitler.
In June 1941, when Germany attacked the Soviet Union, the French
communists threw their weight behind the resistance once and for all,
but the divisions continued to split would-be resistants into different
groups – in Vichy France, three main groups emerged: '*Libération*',
which contained many trade unionists and socialists, '*Combat*', which
was politically more right-wing, and the *Francs-Tireurs et Partisans*,
known as the FTP, which was communist. And there were many
more groupings besides: but what they had in common through this
first year of the occupation was that they could actually do very little.
They concentrated mainly on putting out underground journals and

circulating them. Anti-German posters appeared on walls overnight and were torn down by German soldiers the next day. Printing presses were seized by the Gestapo and new ones would be set up a few weeks later, producing new issues of the Resistance press. People who wanted a false identity card, or a travel permit, might be able to hear of an address which dealt in them. But it was a little here and there; the occupation was too new and too powerful, the French people still too unsure of their new condition, for resistance to make much impact.

Yet many French people were already learning clandestine ways of getting things done – they had to, to feed their families. The black market, strictly illegal on both sides of the line, flourished. People grew used to buying eggs or milk from a small, hidden store in the outhouse of a nearby farm; they learned how to ask a shopkeeper if there might not be something available later on that day. They began to recognize the shops and the travellers who had ways of getting produce from other regions – even from across the line.

And as the black market throve, so did the clandestine routes across the demarcation line. People who wanted to get into the other zone to see family or friends, to carry out work, to do a little buying for the black market, could approach certain tradespeople who would smuggle them over in their goods vans. Or there were enterprising 'scouts' who would organize transport to an ill-guarded spot and then pass on their passengers to a guide willing to lead them across the dangerous ground on foot. It was like an underground travel agency, and many ordinary people used it. They had to – if they were denied a permit (and most were) there was no other way across.

So, in the summer of 1941, early resistants rubbed shoulders with otherwise law-abiding citizens as they threaded their way through the many obstacles and restrictions of life in occupied France.

And into France in 1941 came the very first SOE agents, to work with these early subversives and fan the flames of the Resistance movement.

SOE was conceived in the summer of 1940, when Churchill – head of Britain's coalition government – and the chiefs of staff were reckoning Britain's position anew. In recent months, France had fallen and the British Expeditionary Force had been evacuated from Dunkirk. The new maps of Europe showed the Germans spread east into Yugoslavia, west to the French Atlantic coast and north into Norway. Dislodging them from these territories, they reasoned, could not be done entirely from the outside. Britain would have to get in touch with the people of the occupied countries, help them arm and organize themselves, so that they could loosen the Germans' grip. The German occupation of Europe would have to be destabilized from within.

So, in the summer of 1940, SOE – the Special Operations Executive – was born. It was a top secret organization, so secret that no one outside it was to know it existed. Its job was to find people who had knowledge of the occupied countries, and recruit and train them as undercover agents.

These agents would be trained in clandestinity so that they could elude the authorities; they would be taught the resistance skills: organization, sabotage, silent killing, weaponry. They would be issued with false identities and papers. Then the agents would be smuggled into the countries by boat, or parachuted from aeroplanes at night. Once there, under their false identities, they would gradually contact local Resistance groups, recruit their own, and keep in touch with London through contacts in neutral embassies and international offices and, wherever possible, through coded radio transmissions. In time London would send them arms and explosives, parachuting them at night onto pre-arranged spots. As the agents equipped and trained the Resistance groups, so the uprisings could begin. The aim of SOE was, in Churchill's words, to 'set Europe ablaze'.

During the rest of 1940 and early 1941, SOE was established in headquarters in London, and was split into sections, each one dealing with a different country. While the French struggled to recover from the arrival of the Third Reich in their own country, SOE's newly-formed French Section struggled to acquire information, contacts and recruits. And by the end of 1941, the first agents were infiltrating France.

Who were these agents? Their recruitment was a clandestine business, relying heavily on introductions and having only one clear criterion: that the agents be able to pass as French civilians. Some were French people who had left when the Germans invaded and made their way to England; some were British people or people of other nationalities who had lived in France and knew it well. They came from all kinds of backgrounds: from careers in industry, commerce, diplomacy, show business; from more and less monied and educated backgrounds. Some were in their twenties, some in middle age.

And some of them were women.

France was marked out from the beginning as one of SOE's most important countries. Across the Channel she lay, a potential stepping-stone to Britain for the Germans, or – one day perhaps – the first stage of a counter-attack against the Germans by the British. Because France was so important, several different sections were to

develop within SOE, all working with agents in France. A section
called 'DF' was set up to support clandestine escape routes out of
France. A small section was created to work with expatriate Poles in
occupied France. When it became obvious that the young General de
Gaulle, now in London trying to raise an army of 'Free French', had
a fair amount of support among the people of France, 'RF' Section
was created to work in direct co-operation with de Gaulle and the
Free French, sending in Gaullist agents to promote the idea of
resistance and encourage subversion and sabotage.

But the biggest section at work in France was not tied to any one
leader or political idea: 'F' Section was in business to provide practical
help to the French Resistance, and once in France its agents would
work with anyone who was ready to respond. The agents' missions
were to recruit and organize resistants, to teach them the skills of
sabotage and weaponry, and to arrange for arms and explosives to
be parachuted in to them so that they could put these skills to use.

Once they were in France, the agents of these different sections
would often encounter one another and work together. But back in
England, their headquarters were kept strictly separate with their own
staffs and offices. Confidentiality, and sometimes rivalry, ensured that
their operations were independently run.

F Section's headquarters were at 64 Baker Street, and here all its
planning was done. From here F sent over 400 agents into France
and thirty-eight of them were women. Some other country sections
also used women: French women were often recruited within France
to work on escape lines and just before and after D-Day RF Section
sent out thirteen French women agents. But only F Section recruited,
trained and sent women into France as a deliberate policy, from the
beginning of the war through to its end. Only F Section, because of
its London roots and its apolitical nature, gathered such a cross-
section of women, of British, French, American and other nationalities, from unworldly secretaries to sophisticated diplomats; from
middle-aged hotel managers to young escaped resistants; from house-
bound mothers to roving journalists.

This book tells their stories, and through them the story of
F Section's work in France.

I came to these women by a roundabout route. In the mid-1980s I
was reading Martha Gellhorn's writings, when I came across her war
journalism. I have always been uneasy with war writings – so many
of them are self-consciously unflinching on the battlefield and yet
prone to emote plangently at the sight of a burnt-out family home
or a wounded child. The destruction of homes and families, the

maiming and killing of children and civilians are an intrinsic part of warfare. Repeatedly to express surprise and horror when the fighting affects civilians seems to me to be a blindness on the part of the correspondents, a clinging to the notion that there is such a thing as an honourable way of fighting wars.

Martha Gellhorn's was the only war journalism I had read which showed implicit acceptance that wars are 'total' and directed against the lives of ordinary, non-military people. This recognition pervaded all her pieces which I read, whether they dealt with bombarded civilians in Madrid in 1937, a young bomber crew on an outing in the 1939–45 war, or the authorities of San Salvador in the 1980s. They consistently showed that in war, as in peace, each person has to take sole responsibility for the way she or he lives, in small matters as well as large.

That thought took my mind back to the women I had heard about when I was a child: heroines like Violette Szabo and Odette Churchill who had volunteered to leave safe lives in Britain and go into Nazi-occupied France as agents of the Resistance. Why had they done it? It was an unexpected thing for a woman to do in those days; it ran counter to popular attitudes, which held that women must stay at home and 'smile on through'. It was against the spirit if not the law of the Geneva Convention. I began to wonder what circumstances and attitudes had borne on the women as they weighed up their decisions and what it had been like for them once they were in France, working with the underground.

I was brought up on stories about these women, but like most people I had only a hazy idea of who they were or what they did, based mainly on the film *Carve Her Name With Pride* about Violette Szabo, and the film *Odette* about Odette Churchill. When I decided to get hold of the books on which the films were based and read them, I discovered the existence of SOE and F Section. And the books whetted my appetite, not so much by what they told me as what they didn't. Both books were written in the decade after the war as part of a popular movement to establish gallant, pure war heroines. The pictures they painted of the two characters and their resistance work were highly coloured and dashing; they contained little reflection and very few of the insights which I sought. The stories were told in a very conventional way, and yet the facts which they related were anything but conventional. Both books, significantly I felt, were written by men. I felt sure that if the women themselves had told their stories, I should have read something quite different.

I was not after revelations or denunciations. It was just that I knew that in the early 1940s, women and men in Britain (and in France) did not stand in the same relation to the war. Quite simply, men expected to go on active service while women did not. The education of girls and boys had been different in this respect; the two sexes had been trained up to fulfil complementary roles. Inevitably, a woman who went into France as an SOE agent would not be prepared for it in the same way as a man; she might have all the same SOE practical training behind her but her mind-set would be different. She would notice other things from those which a man might notice; she might have to make different adjustments. Some things would come more easily to a woman, others would take more conscious thought. I did not want to prejudge any of these differences, but by now I was intrigued, verging on the fascinated. I read the book which is the reference volume for everyone interested in F Section, M.R.D. Foot's *SOE in France*,[1] and discovered that there were about fifty women agents sent into France by SOE. I made some tentative enquiries about where I might learn more and was given the address of something called the Special Forces Club in Knightsbridge, London. I wrote to the club with a list of the F Section women agents, copied from Foot's book, and asked if the club could put me in touch with any. A reply came back naming six of my long list of women, offering to pass on my letters to them. It was less than I had hoped for but, as the club pointed out, it was over forty years since the end of the war and in that time many of the women had let their club membership lapse, others had moved and left no forwarding address; recently a number of them had died. I sat down to write to the six women named, and also to two people mentioned frequently in the books and memoirs about SOE which were now my staple diet: Vera Atkins and Maurice Buckmaster. I explained to all of them that I was hoping to write a book which told the stories of some of the women agents from the women's own point of view, and of the six women agents, four agreed to talk to me and help me with the book: Yvonne Cormeau, Didi Nearne, Odette Churchill (now Odette Hallowes) and Lise de Baissac (now Lise Villameur). Vera Atkins and Maurice Buckmaster also agreed to see me. And so I began the research for *A Quiet Courage*.

This book is about what it was like to be a woman agent in F Section; what it was like to go into France undercover and to work with the people of the French resistance. There are four women at the heart of the book, the four who have told their stories to me in person. Their stories are told in detail, as the women themselves remember them, and each story is quite distinct from the others, being shaped both in action and in telling by the personality of its

[1] *SOE in France*, M.R.D. Foot, HMSO, 1966.

protagonist. These four women have strong personalities; I suspect that had I been able to trace all thirty-seven or so women agents, I should have found that they were all similarly striking. But I could not trace them all, not even all the survivors, and had I done so I could not have told all their stories at equal length.

In these pages are the stories of thirty-seven agents. The qualifying 'or so' in the last paragraph refers to the fact that the exact number of official F Section agents is disputed. In his book, M.R.D. Foot puts the number of F women agents at thirty-nine and of RF agents at eleven. I decided early on that the RF agents, recruited late on in the war through de Gaulle's Free French channels, and mainly sent into France after D-Day, lay outside the scope of my book. I also began to come across difficulties with some of the names listed as F Section women agents. SOE archives are closed to the public, although one can (and I did, often) write in with specific questions about the organization. No one, not even the SOE archivists, know exactly what material is in the archives, filed under which heading. And it isn't always possible to trust implicitly in such documents as are found: many were written up in haste at the end of the war, based on reports from returning agents and at some distance from the events themselves. A number of people who came to work for F Section as agents were first recruited in France by agents already there; some of these are listed in the archives as F Section agents, others not. In trying to decide who to include in this book, I've been guided by Vera Atkins, whose memory is renowned, by the archive information available to me, and by my own sense of what this book is about.

For this reason, a few women sometimes listed as F agents are absent from these pages, and three others are included briefly, with a question mark. The two absent women are Giliana Gerson and Ginette Jullien: the latter Vera had never heard of; the former was sent into Vichy France in 1941 to collect information on travel routes, but she travelled there openly, as a Chilean national, and six weeks later returned to England for good. She was not an agent in the same sense that the other women were.

The three women who are included only briefly are Yvonne Fontaine, Madeleine Lavigne and Krystyna de Gyzicka (often known as Christine Granville). Vera Atkins claims that the first two were recruited in the field and never became official F Section agents; however, I have included them because they were both brought to Britain during the war and subsequently re-entered France to work with F Section *réseaux*. Krystyna de Gyzicka was recruited by SOE Cairo and therefore was not an official F Section agent, but she went to France to work in an F *réseau*, and so she too is in here.

Vera Atkins also insists that Virginia Hall was never an F Section agent: that she first appeared in France, where she made contact with F Section agents, and that when she returned in 1944 on her second mission she was an agent of OSS, the American secret service which worked in conjunction with SOE. SOE archives support the fact that she was an OSS agent on her second mission, but they furnish quite detailed information as to how she was recruited for F Section in London in 1941 by F Section Officer Nicolas Bodington. I believe that Bodington 'made an agreement' with Virginia Hall in January 1941 and did not bother to mention the fact to Vera Atkins or Maurice Buckmaster when they joined the Section a month later. He was a secretive person, as the book will show. But in either case I should give Virginia Hall a prominent place in this book: she did so much important work for F Section that she cannot be omitted. Indeed, the first chapter is about her and her work.

The other women in this book are fairly and squarely in the F Section canon. Their stories are told in varying degrees of detail: the four women who worked with me on the book are its main characters, of course. But also, while I was reading up on the other women and talking to their fellow agents and colleagues about their missions, certain of those now dead or untraceable reached out and caught my imagination. I decided that I would develop their stories in the same way as I was developing the stories of the four women I knew. I would try to recapture their characters and their adventures as well as I could from the archives and from talking to those who had known them, and then the portraits of them would stand not only as a record of these women but also as a symbol of the other women who did not come back from the war, or who have since died or been forgotten.

So, besides the stories of Yvonne Cormeau, Didi Nearne, Odette Churchill and Lise de Baissac, I have also written at length about Andrée Borrel, who was executed in a concentration camp, Jacqueline Nearne, who died in the early 1980s, and Peggy Knight, who I believe is still alive but whom I cannot trace.

I hope that my account of these women will illuminate rather than overshadow the other, more briefly told stories.

For me, the personalities of the four central women agents are a living presence in this book. I hope they are as vivid for the readers. I have met these women and talked to them at length; I have had numerous telephone conversations with them and we have written to one another as my work on the book continued. They have helped me enormously, each in her own way.

The first I met, and the one I see most frequently, is Didi Nearne. Didi is not her real name: it was her nickname at the time she joined F Section and all her SOE friends still call her that. She asked me to use it in preference to her real first name as she wished to guard her privacy.

Didi is the youngest of the four, now in her mid-sixties. She is naturally independent and enjoys solitude. After the war she worked as a nurse; now she lives in the London flat that used to belong to her sister Jacqueline and apportions her time between F Section friends, friends in France with whom she shared captivity and whom she visits quite regularly, and people outside the SOE circuit. Didi likes to attend F Section dinners and reunions: for instance, she almost always goes to the Bastille Day dinner which takes place on 14 July every year.

Didi has not told her story before, as her experiences in German captivity left her badly traumatized. But when she received my letter she answered at once, and seemed quite keen to see me. She suggested meeting at the Special Forces Club, which is where she goes regularly to meet friends and keep in touch with the people of F Section. Almost all our meetings since then have taken place there, under the rows of framed photographs which show the agents as they were in the war, captured in black and white youth.

Didi still lives with the things that happened to her in France. She tells her story forcefully and vividly, and is anxious that her emotions as well as the historical facts should be accurately recorded. Her work as a radio operator and above all her behaviour under German interrogation is a matter of great pride and importance to her. She speaks in a jumble of images, eager to convey what she means. She has an enthusiastic and determined manner: she likes to be active; she knows what she wants. Now that she is telling her story, she is pursuing a number of avenues into her past: as I write she is trying to trace a copy of the statement she made to the Gestapo when she was under interrogation. The search for it has taken her months and still continues.

It is impossible not to be captivated by the way in which Didi tells her story: she is extraordinarily compelling. One of my most vivid impressions of her is from the Special Forces Club: she is standing at the bar a few feet away from me, having absolutely refused to let me get up from my seat and order us drinks. I am rather feebly drinking mineral water; she, dressed in bright pink trousers, pink sandals and a yellow top, is just taking a large glass of sherry for herself. She is talking cheerfully at me all the time in her loud, sing-song cadences, describing her interrogation by the Gestapo.

Yvonne Cormeau, by contrast, has a cool manner. She is now in her mid-seventies and when I first spoke to her it was in her London flat. Since then she has remarried, become Mrs Farrow and gone to live near Derby. The change of surname makes little odds in SOE circles where she is still widely known by her code-name *Annette*.

Of all the women, she keeps the closest links to the people she worked with in France. Since the war ended she has gone back to visit them every year; she feels deep bonds with them and yet she talks about them in a matter-of-fact, almost clinical way. Yvonne Cormeau is not a sentimentalist: her approach is analytical and careful but also unselfconscious. She is not worldly or cynical; she simply likes to think about things. She is also an organizer – it is she who arranges the Bastille Day dinner each year.

She gives magazine and newspaper interviews every so often now; her voice sounds distinctively through the various house styles, in the sharp little portraits of this person or that, and in the observations which come off the main subject of discussions at a tangent. She likes to gossip and debunk: during our first telephone conversation she told me with restrained glee that in basic military training, she had been well treated as a WAAF. 'The officers preferred us to the FANYS. They were known as la-di-da-workshirkers behind their backs.' She also has a taste for scurrilous anecdotes – at least, the anecdotes sound scurrilous but then again they might well be true. And all the while decorum is beautifully maintained: decorum with teeth.

I met Odette in her husband's club: I saw a small woman in her seventies with bobbed blonde hair and a designer jumper: she looked fashionable and extremely French. Odette is famous – in some people's interpretation notorious – for having a strong personality and very definite opinions. Within a few minutes, this side of her was made evident in a few quiet, self-composed comments. But she was also charming, very charming, and unexpectedly thoughtful.

At that meeting as in all my other conversations with her, I was seduced by her voice. She talks beautifully: the rhythms and figures of her speech are quite hypnotizing in their ability to bring alive not only scenes but emotions. That first afternoon we talked for much longer than we had planned and in the months that followed she telephoned me every so often to talk some more: usually she called when an event or meeting had started her thinking about her war-time experiences, and sometimes she sounded haunted by the memories.

Odette has been a celebrity ever since the war. Once she had been made famous by the book and the film of her story, the mechanisms of fame simply went on working. She often regrets this but it is too late for her to reverse the process. Forty years after her name became known, she still receives letters from strangers – many of them from schoolchildren doing projects on her. Last year she and many other former agents went to an SOE memorial service; the national press reported on it, mentioning Odette by name. She understands why it happens – the journalists want a well-known name on which to hang the story, and hers fits – but she is uncomfortable with it. She knows that other agents may feel slighted; she feels also – and this is important to her – that her name is sometimes used to eclipse the agents who died, rather than to honour them.

But she can handle the publicity well. Odette has handled many things in life and continues to do so. I never speak to her without getting a clear picture of her as she must have been in occupied France: determined, self-willed and quite indomitable.

Lise de Baissac, since married and widowed as Madame Villameur, lives in Marseille. Her flat was once the studio of her architect husband: it overlooks the Vieux Port, now a harbour filled with pleasure boats. Lise Villameur has left the world of her resistance work far behind; one of the first things she said to me was, 'I tell you frankly, I no longer have any interest in talking about the war. But if you are interested in it and in finding out what I did, I'll be glad to help you.'

She helped me in fact quite unstintingly, not only answering all my questions but also by keeping me with her all day, and taking me on a tour of Marseille as a kindness to a stranger at a loose end. The drive round the city was unforgettable: sitting behind the wheel of her Deux Chevaux and peering through rather than over it ('I was five foot six during the war and quite robust; age has shrunk me more than most'), Madame Villameur took us along a route of her own devising, blithely ignoring traffic signs and one-way systems, nudging the car horizontally across traffic jams, and at one terrifying moment turning out of a side street into a six-lane dual carriageway, chugging slowly and erratically across the stream of cars so that we could do an illegal left turn on to the far carriageway. I can still see the astonished faces of the drivers as they swerved to avoid us.

By these means, I saw the old quarter of Marseille, which the Nazis had 'evacuated' in January 1943 in an attempt to stamp out Resistance. Then we drove along the Corniche and back inland to the cathedral of Notre Dame de la Garde, high on a hill. The back wall of the cathedral is scarred with bullet holes from one of the liberation battles; inside the church plaques commemorate the resistants who fell there.

When we returned to the flat, Lise Villameur had a rest while I read through her annotated copy of *SOE in France* and made more notes about the doings of Lise de Baissac. Then we talked some more about her resistance work. In Lise Villameur's memory more than in most, her own activities are far less vivid than the people she worked with. When she spoke of the Gateau family, who had been her good friends and comrades on her first mission; or of Mary Herbert, who had worked with her brother Claude; or of Andrée Borrel or Claude himself, I could almost see them.

Yet she's far from iconizing these people. Equally important to her are the friends she has today: and there are many of them, nothing to do with her time in SOE. She has a sharp appetite for life, not expressed flamboyantly but manifested in her various activities and interests. After I had done some more research into the archives, I discovered from an F Section report that Lise had been considered perhaps rather 'touchy' and 'ambitious', observations which amused her greatly. At the same time, the author of that report also acknowledged that she was greatly loved by the French people in her area. The combination of the two expresses, however clumsily, something of Lise de Baissac.

Other personalities stalked the writing of this book, though they are perhaps less evident to the reader. Vera Atkins is one: other people's books and memoirs have already recorded her astuteness and her considerable personal presence. I found out for myself her wit, her generosity and the strong mutual affection which still binds her to the agents of F Section, women and men alike. She is in touch with scores of them, and knows what happened to scores more. I was referred over and over again to Vera when I was seeking information on this or that; she could almost always help me.

She lives in London and in Winchelsea, has a social life crammed full with engagements (by no means all SOE-linked), and is extremely good company. She can certainly seem formidable and I have no doubt she could be 'difficult' to great effect if she wished, but she was never so with me, even when I pestered her for information. After our first – long – interview, she met me several times in the club, to talk about the agents and events, to see how my researches were progressing and to drop into those researches illuminating – and often wickedly funny – opinions and titbits of information. Vera does many things and has many friends, but she is deeply committed to the people she met in F Section and she is perpetually ready to help and protect them if need be.

Then there is Maurice Buckmaster, who invited me to meet him and his wife (who, sadly, has since died), and who was so obviously full of affectionate memories of the agents that the scenes at Orchard Court suddenly came alive for me.

There is Maurice Southgate, who entertained me all day at his home near Sarlat; a man of irreverent humour and enormous determination, he made me understand that there was fun in the Resistance as well as struggle. He is a big man both physically and in character: he told me he had been very strict with the resistants in his *réseau*, and then immediately picked himself up for being proprietorial: 'I'm talking silly now.' I left him wishing I could start another book at once, all about him.

Francis Cammaerts, the agent *Roger*, I met only once, but his intelligence, integrity and independence of mind encouraged me down new avenues in the way that I thought about the French Resistance war.

Lastly, there is Francine Agazarian. Vera put me in touch with her, and although I have not yet met her, we write fairly regularly. Francine is a survivor of one of the great F Section disasters: she worked in a *réseau* which was broken by the Germans and almost all her comrades, including her husband, were executed. She has long been working to come to terms with what happened and to find adequate ways in her own life of honouring those who died. Her kind of courage is not what I was thinking of when I chose the title of this book, but her letters have made me realize that living on as a survivor is just as important and as relevant, just as much a part of the women's work in France as the events and sacrifices of the time. For me, Francine Agazarian embodies the courage of remembering, and refusing to forget.

ONE

First Contacts

In August 1941, a tall American woman with a limp arrived in the town of Vichy and attached herself to the office of the newspaper, the *New York Post*. She was, she said, an American journalist and as a citizen of a neutral country she was entitled to move unhampered round Vichy France and file her reports.

Her name was Virginia Hall and she would probably have been an excellent correspondent for the *New York Post* if she had chosen to write regular reports. But in fact she wrote very few – she spent much of her time in Vichy making friends in high places, notably with one or two people in the Vichy police force, and then she seemed to get bored of Vichy and moved on. When she reappeared, it was in Lyon, the largest city in Vichy France, and her new friends here were a curious mixture.

She was on good terms with the staff at the American consulate, calling in there frequently to discuss the international situation and the post from America. She mixed socially with journalists, some businessmen and a doctor. She had also struck up a friendship with a woman named Germaine Guérin, who was an enthusiastic black marketeer and had an owner's share in a brothel, and through her Virginia had soon met a fugitive RAF pilot, several people who worked for an escape organization known as '*Les Files de Calais*' (The Calais Line), and a number of helpful prostitutes. Virginia Hall was turning into someone who would become known as *Marie* to some, as *Philomène* to others: a resistante, a universal aunt, a fixer and a point of contact for dozens of resistants and SOE agents. She was to be a linchpin of the early development of SOE in France.

*

She was also an enigma, and remains one even today. She died a few years ago, having always refused to talk about the work she did in France, just as she refused to discuss what she later became – a CIA operative. It is in the memories of other people that one can trace her in France: from summer 1941 to winter 1942 she came and went in the lives of agents and resistants, meeting them at a station or an hotel; opening her door to provide a night's shelter; vanishing on an errand to find a new radio crystal or ration ticket. She appears in cameos in other people's stories, confident and mysterious. She was a striking figure: tall, red-haired and with a pronounced limp, she was not quickly forgotten by those who saw her. But she was discreet and skilful all the same, and always stayed one step ahead of the authorities trying to close in on her. In these early days of SOE's endeavours she flickered through the streets of Lyon and the lives of F Section agents, an eminence rouge.

When Virginia Hall arrived in Lyon in autumn 1941, she found the city already peppered with Resistance groups. There were a number of escape organizations at work in Lyon: these picked up fugitives, like shot-down RAF pilots and wanted resistants, and passed them along a network of helpers to the Mediterranean coast or the Swiss border, where they could be smuggled out of the country. There were also clandestine presses and forging operations in the city. And, beginning to appear in Lyon, and knock on her door, there were SOE agents.

Who was Virginia Hall? She was thirty-five, from a wealthy Baltimore family, and she had been following a diplomatic career in embassies and consulates around Europe until 1939. Comments from people who knew her then indicate that much of her real work was in intelligence. She was clever, incisive and socially confident. A few years before the war she had lost half a leg in an accident – even at the time, there were conflicting stories of how it had happened: some people said it had been a hunting accident; others that she had run for a tram and slipped beneath it. Now she had an artificial leg, which she referred to in a companionable way as 'Cuthbert'.

She had come to France in 1940, driving ambulances during the fall of France. She had had to leave after the armistice, but she had been determined to return. First she went to England and there, in January 1941, she met one of F Section's staff, Nicolas Bodington. Bodington – as this book will show – had his own intelligence contacts and the two almost certainly met through these channels. At the time F Section had some agents in training and it planned to send them into France that spring. Bodington discussed with Virginia Hall the ways in which she might be able to help those agents; he then helped her to get a cover as an accredited journalist on the *New York Post*. In summer 1941 Virginia Hall made the roundabout journey through Spain into France travelling as an American citizen. By autumn she was in Lyon. She had American intelligence work to do there; she had also agreed to be a liaison person for F Section's agents, ready to help them if and when they called on her.

The first SOE agent arrived in France in May 1941. He was a Frenchman, Georges Bégué, and he was parachuted just south of the demarcation line with a radio set, so that he could transmit coded information back to London. He was followed by another Frenchman, Pierre de Vomécourt, who immediately recruited his two brothers, Philippe and Jean, as well. They all now began making contacts, trying to start separate resistance groups, which would all report back to London. And so it was beginning: by autumn there were over a dozen agents in France, and they were settling in different parts of the country, trying to start independent 'circuits', or '*réseaux*' as they were known in French.

Most of the *réseaux* were in Vichy France, although there was already a promising collection of resistants gathering round Pierre de Vomécourt in Paris, forming a *réseau* code-named Autogiro. It was important for the agents in charge of these *réseaux* to keep apart from one another as much as possible. They were not supposed to go visiting each other, and yet they needed to have ways of getting in touch. How would a new agent, dropped by parachute into the dark countryside, know where to find his *réseau*? How could an agent in Antibes, who heard rumours of an impending search in Limoges, warn the agent in Limoges? Where could an agent go to get a new set of identity papers immediately?

The answers to all these questions and more were provided by Virginia Hall. From autumn 1941 until November 1942, when the Germans would march across the demarcation line and occupy the whole of France, the progress of SOE's early *réseaux* was inextricably linked to this woman. In November 1941 she wrote a letter to SOE, giving her address as the Grand Nouvel Hotel in Lyon. The letter was smuggled to Britain via Switzerland; the information was probably also sent over one of the two SOE radio sets now in France. By January, not only were agents hearing about her on the grapevine and finding their way to her for advice, help and contacts, but SOE in London was sending new agents to France with instructions to go to the Grand Nouvel Hotel and make contact with her.

Virginia Hall was also in regular contact with one particular agent based in Antibes: his name was *Olive* and besides organizing a *réseau* down there he worked with Virginia to gather information on all the resistance groups in the region, so that they could produce a report for SOE.

These were F Section's beginnings and Virginia Hall made a peculiar and unique contribution to them. The real story of the women agents does not begin until July 1942, when women began to be infiltrated into France secretly. Virginia Hall was not like these women: she lived in France under her own name, protected to a certain degree by her status as an American, and her work was not like the work of the other women. She was no less important – on the contrary, she was instrumental in getting SOE *réseaux* established in France – but she was different. Her adventures in Lyon deserve a whole book to themselves – or they would if one could unearth the information about them, now visible only in tantalizing glimpses through the adventures of others. In this book she appears again later – in 1944 – infiltrated this time clandestinely, and with an official mission comparable to the other women. Then we'll hear more of her: meanwhile, her Lyon adventures are a window through which to view the ups and downs of SOE's early operations in France.

The story of the SOE *réseaux* in these early days is a chequered one. The 1941 agents were pioneers; they struggled to organize *résaux* but for months there was only one radio set among them, hampering liaison with London. Autogiro flourished but by winter 1941 many of the agents south of the line had been arrested. Then, in early spring 1942, SOE sent out a new agent, a young man named Peter Churchill, to look into a large resistance organization which had been rumoured to exist, centred round a contact of *Olive*'s in Antibes. The contact was an artist named André Girard, who had given himself the code name *Carte*. This was also the name of the organization, which he claimed was a huge network of people ready to resist, stretching right across Vichy France and into the occupied zone, and including highly placed people in Pétain's Armistice Army. Peter Churchill – who was helped on this mission by Virginia Hall – returned to Britain and gave an optimistic report on *Carte*. But before anything could be done about it, and while new SOE agents were just starting to be infiltrated in the early spring, there was a disaster: Autogiro was smashed.

There were few of the 1941 agents left free in France now. But new ones were infiltrated; new *réseaux* began and during the spring and summer of 1942 Virginia Hall, now living in a flat Germaine Guérin had found for her, gave shelter to numerous arriving agents;

connected up radio operators with radio sets; passed messages, provided ration tickets and identity cards; kept her ear to the ground and warned agents to get out of town when she heard they were under suspicion; and patiently pumped her contacts in the Vichy police for news about agents who had been arrested, seeking some way of bribing or otherwise arranging their release.

She was incessantly busy. One agent, Ben Cowburn, later reported of her: 'If you sit in her kitchen long enough you will see most people pass through with one sort of trouble or another which she promptly deals with.'

These comings and goings brought danger with them and at least one agent, Henri Le Chêne, thought the set-up unhealthy. Le Chêne was a Frenchman in his fifties; arriving in France that spring he made his way to Lyon and inevitably to Virginia Hall. At the time, accommodation was desperately hard to find in Lyon and so Virginia was allowing a radio operator to transmit from the flat, while other agents and resistants made rendezvous there. The evening on which Henri called, the flat was full of people, while the entire passageway was festooned with over seventy feet of radio aerial. Le Chêne, a cautious man, was horrified by what he saw: he left, never to return. A few weeks later, he moved into the country west of the city and started *Plane*, a propaganda *réseau*. It was to do well, surviving the sporadic arrests of that spring and summer, and in the autumn a woman agent would arrive to join the *réseau*, Marie-Thérèse Le Chêne, Henri's wife.

During these spring and summer months, Virginia Hall frequently had to cut corners and carry on her liaison work in a way which would have horrified the official SOE training schools – yet the fact is that her flat was never raided, and throughout all the upsets and terrors of 1942, she continued to work unscathed. Several agents were to remark on her talent for survival, but it was a talent she worked at: she cultivated her contacts in officialdom well, and she kept in close touch with the American consulate, gathering its protection around her. She was a highly trained intelligence operative and F Section benefitted from her skills.

There was need for caution as well as urgency: the flurry of new agents coming in, and the stepping up of resistance work – more radio transmissions, more couriers carrying messages, even, as spring 1942 wore on, a few night-time parachute drops of arms in different parts of the country – all increased the chances of being caught. Counter-resistance forces were on the alert: north of the line the Gestapo, here in the unoccupied zone the Vichy police, launched surveillance operations to winkle out resistants. 'British agents' were the greatest prize of all, and frequent controls and spot checks were carried out in trains, on main roads, and in hotels, to trap those with false papers. If the papers were in order – and forged identity cards and passes were already being made to a very high standard – then there was still the possibility of trapping resistants into errors under interrogation. Where were they going? What were they going to do there? What was in that bag? What was written on this folded paper?

Such controls were especially frequent near the demarcation line and in the big cities. In Lyon, police checks were becoming regular events, and several times Virginia had to leave hotels or cafés, where she was waiting to meet an agent, because she was warned that there were police checks going on in the area.

One morning she went to the Grand Nouvel Hotel and ordered a coffee. She was due to meet an important new agent here, but as she sat, reading a newspaper and listening to the conversations going on round her, she overheard some disturbing news. The whole town was apparently talking about two parachutists who had come down the previous night. They had been seen descending by the police: one had been captured immediately but the other had got away. Virginia asked the barman if he knew anything about it: yes, he said, it was supposed to be true. At this very moment other hotels were being searched by the police, and they were expecting them at the Grand Nouvel soon. Virginia paid her bill and left: she had no desire to be under police scrutiny.

The agent she was there to meet was the one who had got away and he did eventually meet her. By autumn he was building up a *réseau* in Lyon itself. But other agents were less lucky: there were many arrests in the summer months, and many *réseaux* were broken up.

On the other hand, some agents now escaped from prison. In August, eleven agents, who had been arrested in 1941, managed to suborn a guard in a Vichy concentration camp on the Dordogne, and escape. The escape had been carefully planned: the wife of one of the prisoners had found out about the plan, had sent messages through to Philippe de Vomécourt, who ran a large *réseau* Ventriloquist centred near Limoges, and had arranged with him for a lorry to be hidden in the woods near the concentration camp. The dates and times were settled and when the agents escaped, they were carried swiftly off in the lorry to hide out in the countryside. After that, they made their way to Lyon in small groups, where Virginia Hall passed them on to escape lines. They all got safely out of the country.

At about the same time, a new agent arrived in Lyon: a radio operator called Brian Stonehouse. Virginia helped him find shelter, but it was very difficult to get a place from which he could transmit. At the beginning of September, someone arrived who took over that job from Virginia: it was another woman agent, Blanche Charlet.

Blanche Charlet was one of the new generation of agents, the generation which included women. Her story could be told along with that of the other women – were it not that it was over so soon. Blanche arrived at a very dangerous time. So many more agents had come in during the last three months and Lyon was becoming known as a Resistance centre, focusing police attention on it. What was more, restrictions on the Vichy French population were tightening: the Vichy government – at the behest of the Germans – was beginning to conscript fit young men into work parties bound for Germany. To enforce conscription, '*rafles*' (round-ups) were already taking place in the streets of Marseille. Curfew was enforced with growing rigour. It was much harder for people to move around without attracting attention.

The effect on agents and resistants was severe. 'Safe' addresses were discovered and blown; people were caught with incriminating messages at spot checks. One arrest usually led to many more as captured resistants had information beaten out of them and as their regular haunts were watched; suspicion and capture could be infectious, like a disease.

Ben Cowburn had been in France since autumn 1941, travelling between zones, recruiting resistants and assessing the potential for new *réseaux* in different regions. He often called on Virginia for help. Writing in his memoirs, he described how, that spring, his meetings with resistants would almost always be shadowed by someone's arrest:

'I would ask after another friend. "Oh yes! I was forgetting, he has been arrested too. Do you know, I saw him only the day before and *he had the look of one who is going to be taken*." Yes, I understood, I knew that look – it was a curious thing, too curious to believe unless you had seen it.'

Virginia Hall saw many of her fellow agents catch the infection. They would leave her flat to go about their secret work and then bad news would come. The infection was to strike Blanche Charlet and Brian Stonehouse within two months: on 24 October, detector (D/F) vans picked up Brian's radio signals while he was transmitting, and tracked him to his house. He was arrested at his set, and a few minutes later Blanche arrived to see him and she was arrested too. Although Blanche's colleagues from training were only just arriving, her mission was already over. She was to spend the next year in prison.

Virginia Hall's mission was drawing to a close too. The pace had not slackened, far from it, but she was about to be overtaken by events. At the beginning of November, the Germans marched over the demarcation line and occupied the whole of France.

The first impact on the Resistance was to threaten many of its groups. In the first week of November, a large number of resistants and some SOE agents fled their territories and hurried down to the Pyrénées, keeping just ahead of the advancing Germans. Virginia Hall was among them, and after a few days' delay in Perpignan, which was now swarming with fugitives, she and a small party of fellow escapees made the gruelling forty-eight-hour climb over the winter mountains into Spain.

In autumn 1942, Virginia Hall's time in Lyon was over. The eminence rouge, the red-headed woman with the artificial leg and the catholic mix of friends, was no longer there to help resistants and agents who came calling. And coinciding with her flight, the first phase of SOE's French operations had also ended.

The very early, pioneering days of SOE agents were over. At SOE French Section headquarters in London, staff were putting into action some co-ordinated plans. These were designed to begin where the pioneer agents left off, picking up on contacts and building them into new ambitious Resistance networks for the future. Women agents were very much a part of this future.

TWO

'The Organization':
The Workings of F Section

The women and men who F Section was sending into France had only a scanty idea of the organization behind them. They called it just that, 'The Organization', and from their first interview with the recruitment staff, through their training to the night of their departure, they saw the members of staff irregularly, for an assessment here, a briefing there.

Nor did they meet these staff officers in the Baker Street headquarters. As a security measure, agents were not told where the F nerve centre was; instead they met staff and prepared for their missions in a special flat kept by F Section in Orchard Court, Portman Square, just a few streets away.

In fact, the F Section staff team was small and it was quite possible for most of its officers to be in the Orchard Court flat at once, talking to different agents in the privacy of the six separate rooms. One agent might come in through the main entrance of Orchard Court, give her code-name to the doorman, Park, and be directed to a room where a small, poised woman of about thirty waited, dressed in civilian clothes. This was Vera Atkins, the intelligence officer, there to discuss with the agent her proposed cover story, asking the agent all kinds of questions about her background and her knowledge of France, to see how well the cover and the person suited. In another room, the French briefing officer, Jacques de Guélis, might be giving another agent his operational instructions, poring over maps of his future territory. Nicolas Bodington, deputy head of F and a debonair man in his early thirties, might be testing a third agent on her cover story and her instructions, making her recite them and answer quick-fire questions on them. In the two rooms next door, two different agents due to leave together might be trying on the 'French' clothes supplied by SOE's tailors, complete with French labels sewn in, French train tickets in the pockets and hidden money belts. Behind another door Gerry Morel, signals officer, might be taking a radio operator through his codes. Even the bathroom, fitted with a large, exotic black bath, might be occupied: a tall man with a long-featured face and an air of compressed vitality might well be discussing the task ahead with a fifth agent. The tall man was Maurice Buckmaster, head of F Section from the end of 1941, and neither he nor anyone else in F Section could afford to stand on ceremony.

These were the F Section officers who the agents were most likely to meet. There were others too – Robert Bourne-Patterson was planning officer, for instance, and in the overall SOE coding section a young man, Leo Marks, devised codes for agents of many countries, including France. But for the agents of F Section, these discreet meetings and interviews in Orchard Court, when they might be hurried down the back stairs to avoid meeting another agent at the front, provided their contact with the staff of F Section. This was the extent of their knowledge of the people who would soon be on the other end of the airwaves, trying to respond to their cryptic messages, to advise and support them when they were out in the field.

Although the meetings between agents and staff were limited, they were as full as they could be, and often they left the agents and staff with strong impressions of one another. Vera Atkins and Maurice Buckmaster in particular seem to have inspired trust and affection in many agents: partly it is because they were constantly in F Section from 1941 until the end of the war; partly it is because their work involved them in many aspects of an agent's briefing and mission; but also it's a reflection of their own interest in the agents, and commitment to them. Today they are both still in touch with very, very many of them.

Buckmaster was a young man for so senior a post, in his late thirties, and a charismatic figure. Physically he was eye-catching: tall, with a loose frame and a long-nosed face. In photographs taken at the time he looks pleasant and malleable, but in the flesh he made a stronger impression. Many agents came to talk of him as someone authoritative, even inspirational. He also knew France and loved it in the same way as the agents, and perhaps that too communicated itself.

He has been criticized since the war for some of the troubles which befell F's agents and he is still reluctant to believe the extent of the intrigues which caused many of them. He was not a plotter; he did not have the mentality of a spy and in some instances this allowed him – and his agents – to be manipulated. But if he lacked some of the finer skills of double-dealing, he had qualities that were ultimately more valuable to the work of Resistance: he had commitment, energy and imagination.

Vera Atkins, intelligence officer, is the other figure who appears and reappears throughout the stories of F Section's women. She had joined F Section at the same time as Buckmaster in early 1941 and worked as part of the team, researching into conditions in France so that agents would get the right cover stories and documents, discussing new recruits and their training records, helping with final briefing sessions. Her work cut across a number of areas and often brought her into contact with the agents. Where Buckmaster was outgoing and enthusiastic, Vera was self-contained and formidably astute. She was a shrewd judge of character and had an incisive, occasionally combative manner. She joined in the discussions on agents' characters and their suitability for certain missions; she was involved in teaming agents with one another and Buckmaster was ready to listen to her suggestions and intuitions. She was part of F Section mythology even at the time; some people were slightly in awe of her strong personality, but agents soon found in her a perceptive helper and friend.

Vera knew and worked with almost all the women whose stories are told in this book. She was often involved in the final stages of agents' preparations for the field and at these times the agents would often confide in her their worries – they might want to know more about their destination; they might be unhappy with their cover stories. In each case Vera would work with them to overcome the difficulties. She also performed an important service for many agents by undertaking to keep in touch with their families in England. Agents relied on Vera and trusted her in more than just her formal capacity.

When the agents left for the dangers of life in occupied France, Maurice Buckmaster, Vera Atkins, and the others, monitored their progress anxiously from the Baker Street offices.

By mid-1942 the clear objective of F Section was to build up a network of Resistance circuits or *réseaux* all over France, and keep them in readiness for a future Allied invasion. Each *réseau* would have at its core a small team of F agents, who would liaise with Baker Street by radio and who would receive supplies of arms and explosives, dropped by parachute at night. The agents would arm their Resistance contacts, train them in weaponry and sabotage techniques, and reconnoitre the sabotage targets in their region. They might carry out attacks against specific targets at London's request; they might indulge in some harrying of the occupying forces; but mainly they would hold themselves in readiness for the invasion. When it came, all the *réseaux* in France would receive the signal to act: the Resistance fighters would go into action, blowing up communications, blocking German reinforcements, attacking the troops; all across the nation shadow armies would rise to support the invading Allies and throw off the occupation.

To say that the staff at Baker Street worked to this plan is to over-simplify. It's truer to say that they struggled to devise ways of meeting this objective, as the ground shifted constantly beneath their feet. For one thing, it was a continual struggle to get aircraft allocated to them for supply drops. They needed bombers and Bomber Command was extremely reluctant to risk pilots and craft on what it saw as dubious exercises. Why risk planes to arm amateur Resistance groups when they could be dropping bombs directly on the factories and power stations of France?

Baker Street's planning also had to go in step with events in the existing *réseaux*. If there were arrests going on in one area, a new neighbouring *réseau*, however desirable, might have to wait a few months. If an entire *réseau* was broken, and all the agents and chief resistants were arrested, new contacts had to be found before it would be safe to send out a replacement team. If conflicting reports came in, casting doubts on this or that agent, or sometimes even on the security of whole *réseaux*, they had to be assessed and a contingency plan put into effect. Agents might have to be recalled to make progress reports. They might have to be given a swift passage out of France to prevent arrest. The day-to-day practicalities of supervising the agents' progress, at such a distance and with only partial contact, interfered at every level with the strategic planning.

The single most important thing for Baker Street was to receive regular information from the agents. Among the circuits there was always a shortage of radios and agents who could use them, and the staff waited anxiously for each message from each circuit. For the agents out in France, sending the radio messages was highly dangerous, as the Gestapo had detector (D/F) vans and patrols which could locate the illicit transmissions. So agents were given schedules or 'skeds' – times at which they would be expected on the air. The messages were coded by the agents in special personal codes and then keyed into the sets as morse signals. They were received by SOE's signals stations; these stations – staffed largely by women – received transmissions for all SOE's country sections and, using their specially provided keys, decoded them, transcribing them into 'clear'. A teleprint of the transmission in clear would then be driven up to the Country Section HQ.

These messages were the life-blood of F Section. They carried top secret information about the progress of Resistance, reported on German counter-activity, described sabotage targets, requested arms drops and reinforcements, gave details of dropping grounds, safe houses and contacts for new agents to use. In Baker Street the staff, led by Buckmaster, worked incredibly long hours – sometimes literally round the clock – to keep up to date with these messages and to send back replies and further instructions – often urgently requested by the agents.

The difficulties of transmission and reception often mangled the messages so that they arrived on Buckmaster's desk making little sense. They had to be puzzled over, sent back for rechecking and, if that made no improvement, the staff would have to interpret them according to their best judgement, and decide on a response. Every message was potentially a matter of life and death for agents and Resistance groups; the pressure never let up.

If the message required a complex response, it would have to be sent on a sked to the individual radio operator. Sometimes, however, simple messages could be sent over the BBC public airways, on a slot known as the *Messages Personnels*. This method of getting simple messages to agents and resistants had been invented by Georges Bégué, F's first radio operator, in 1941. He had noticed that most French people listened to the BBC French Service on their household wirelesses: although it was forbidden by both the Germans and Vichy, almost everyone did it and, as the authorities found the ban impractical to enforce, the risks involved were quite low. People listened to General de Gaulle's rallying addresses to the French population, and to Winston Churchill's; they also listened to the *Messages Personnels* which were broadcast at regular times, including 7.30 p.m. and 9.15 p.m. These 'messages' were sent in to the BBC by people wishing to contact friends or families separated from them by war, and they were short messages giving news of people's whereabouts, of births and illnesses, making pleas for information or return messages. Georges Bégué suggested that F Section could send coded messages out on the programme, which would mean nothing to anyone but the agents of a certain *réseau*. The method was used from late 1941 onwards, with great success. It was especially useful for signalling that an arms drop, or the parachuting of agents to a reception committee, would or would not go ahead. The *réseau*'s radio operator would transmit a request for an arms drop, suggesting a place and date. Baker Street would transmit in return that it was being organized and the message to listen for would be *'L'hibou n'est pas un éléphant'* (The owl is not an elephant). On the night in question, the agent and the reception committee would tune in to the *Messages Personnels* and listen for the nonsensical message. If they heard it, the drop would take place; if not, then it wouldn't and they need not go to wait for it.

It was clear to the Germans and to the Vichy government that these were coded messages, but there was no way of interpreting them. Sometimes dummy cryptic messages were put out as well, to fool the Germans into thinking that there was a large operation on, or to raise false alarms and disguise the fact that a large operation would be taking place in a few nights' time. The *Messages Personnels* also came to be used for all sorts of pre-arranged messages, such as telling an agent that his wife had given birth to a daughter – *'Clémentine ressemble à sa grand-mère'* (Clementine looks like her grandmother). Vera Atkins was regularly involved in devising these messages and getting them to the BBC's Bush House on time – often a matter of vital importance.

Besides the all-consuming mechanics of keeping in communication with the agents and sending instructions and responses, the staff continued throughout to recruit, train and assess new agents.

Recruitment

Being recruited by F Section was an utterly unexpected event for most of the women. As a secret organization, SOE had to recruit by stealth, which meant by word of mouth and by some gentle subterfuge in official channels. Under wartime conditions, the people of Europe filled out endless forms. When they registered for identity cards; when they applied to join the services; when they crossed national borders – on these and on many other occasions people were required to write down information about themselves and their backgrounds. In Britain SOE did what it could to tap this great pool of documentation. Working through the War Office, it secured agreement from the RAF and the WAAF (Women's Auxiliary Air Force) that they would pass on details of personnel with connections to occupied countries. British customs agreed to do likewise.

A large proportion of the women agents came from the services eventually, but the procedure took some time to work – in fact it wasn't until 1943 that the first WAAF came to F Section. The other ways of arriving at F Section were by entering the country as a fugitive from France and having one's name passed on by immigration, by personal recommendation, and by responding to one of the many vaguely-worded appeals or advertisements for people who spoke French to contact the War Office. So, in these different ways, the women came under consideration by F Section staff.

Once the decision had been taken, at F's inception, to use women agents, their recruitment was just the same as the men's. Early on it was extremely informal but by 1942 most potential recruits were passing before a man named Selwyn Jepson, in a shabby interview room in the War Office.

Few of the women knew the purpose of the interview they attended. Most had received rather uninformative letters, asking them to present themselves for an official interview in connection with possible war work. Even those who had been introduced through personal contacts had only a vague idea that they were interviewing for high security work. They did not imagine what they were to be asked: in the 1940s, with the British government using the preservation of family life, wifely and motherly duties as tools of propaganda, it simply wasn't imaginable that the same government was sending women on armed missions behind enemy lines. When the women, having navigated the corridors of the War Office building, entered room No. 321, they took in the dingy decorations, the wash-basin with a board balanced on it, the trestle-table and two hard chairs, and the quiet-looking middle-aged man behind a pile of papers, and wondered why they were there.

The middle-aged man was Captain Selwyn Jepson, an author and the mainstay of F's recruitment policy throughout 1942 and 1943. Buckmaster and his colleagues had a high regard for Selwyn Jepson's skills; they reported that he was 'far ahead of anyone as a talent spotter'. His job was to size up the potential recruit, and to decide in the very first instance whether she or he could make a good agent. He had little to go on other than the interview itself: through questioning the interviewee about her or his past and present life, he had a chance to observe attitudes and responses. The substance of the personal history might prove some guide: from it he could tell how worldly a candidate was, how sheltered or experienced, but experience itself would not necessarily be a qualification, nor lack of it a bar. The agent would have to pass as French so a markedly British appearance was a drawback; so was a markedly Jewish appearance, given the persecution of Jews by both Germans and Vichy. But then appearance could be disguised to some extent, so at this stage he would be unlikely to disqualify a promising candidate on appearance alone.

The ability to speak fluent French was a must. A perfect French accent was preferable, but sometimes an accent could be explained away by a clever cover story – the agent supposedly having Swiss origins, say, or French colonial ones.

Knowledge of France itself was desirable. And while living relatives and close friends in France could prove a security risk, the agent could always be sent to a different region.

Like so much in F's clandestine work, it came down to a matter of character and instinct. Selwyn Jepson used the interview to gather an essential impression of the candidate. If his gut feeling was good, he broached the possibility of going to France.

He did not give them a sales pitch. He explained very briefly that the work would be dangerous and hard, that their chances of coming back were about 50 per cent, that if they were caught they might be tortured and could expect no help from England. Were they interested?

The succession of women who sat in that office, listening to that proposition, heard it with a range of emotions. They were in different situations – some were single; some were married, with children; some were widowed, with children. Some were temperamentally adventurous; others cautious and uncertain of how they would cope with such work. Some were too stunned to think. A number of them asked for time to think it over. Selwyn Jepson watched their responses carefully. He was wary of over-enthusiasm, of a romantic or headstrong approach. F Section needed people who could keep their heads and bear long periods of inactivity and strain. He was also prepared to take time and trouble with the women who were initially reluctant to accept; if they changed their minds after careful thought they might turn out to be very valuable recruits.

Not surprisingly, all the women who spoke to me could remember very vividly their first interview. This was the moment when they took their first, irreversible step away from the familiar world and towards that of Resistance. From now on they were travelling inexorably towards an adventure which would play itself out in an occupied country, in conditions of danger and hardship, under the constant shadow of arrest and death. For all except a very few French refugees, it would be their first contact with the forces of occupation and Resistance. For all of them, even those who had already worked with the Resistance, they were committing themselves to a life more lonely and dangerous than any they had known.

THREE

Agents in Training

Accepting the challenge was a significant moment for the agents – but it did not mean that they would definitely go to France. It meant only that they would begin a long, gruelling training programme, to see if they were suitable agent material. The entire training programme could last months and took the prospective agents to a sequence of 'schools', mainly in country houses scattered around Great Britain. Wanborough Manor in Surrey was one of the principal houses, and there were a series of others around Beaulieu in Hampshire, where agents received the final stages of their training in lush, peaceful settings. 'What does SOE stand for? Stately 'Omes of England,' went the training school joke.

SOE training was a curious procedure. In 1940 when SOE was founded, there existed nothing like it in the country. MI6 training programmes covered some similar ground but were geared for intelligence work, not subversion and sabotage. SOE had to develop its training from scratch, and swiftly. Through 1940 and 1941 it set up schools to teach different aspects of the agents' work. There was basic physical training; more advanced paramilitary and survival training; radio training; weaponry and explosives; coding and ciphering; background on German uniforms and ranks; clandestine and security techniques. The schools served all the Country Sections; courses were arranged so that the different Country Sections took it in turns to use the different schools.

The courses were developed and modified as the war continued and agents came back from the field with their own experiences to add. In 1941, some of the courses were fairly rudimentary; by 1942 most of them had reached a high level of theoretical and practical teaching. F Section's courses had, by this time, the benefit of several agents' experiences. As time went on, they began to use not only the experiences of the agents but the agent themselves: a returned agent would be assigned to a group of trainees as their 'conducting officer'. He or she would go through the whole training programme with the group, offering advice and encouragement, bringing the trainees up to date on conditions in their destination country, and supervising progress. The 'conducting officer's' reports would then be added to those of the various training instructors, to be considered at the end of the course by the Country Section staff.

The schools were odd places, bringing together people who knew nothing about one another and who knew very little about their future work other than that it would be highly dangerous. The groups mixed people of differing ages and backgrounds, men and women together, and imposed on them the conditions and disciplines of boarding school. Inevitably they produced something of a boarding school atmosphere: in the memoirs of some of the male agents, tales of japes and pranks flourish.

But within this structure, the work was serious and hard. Supervision was constant as well, and the instructors filed reports on the trainees at all stages. No records were kept of how many trainees were rejected and at what stages, but the assessments were tough and most courses would see a few members drop out or be removed. They would usually be sent to other training courses for different work and intensively trained for something else, to drown out any sensitive information they might have picked up. If they were still considered a security risk they would then be sent to a posting somewhere distant and insignificant – there was a village, Inverlair, in the Scottish Highlands where 'workshops' were staffed by such unfortunates.

The first women agents to go through the training schools went in the spring of 1942: the last went in the spring of 1944, by which time the pressure was on for D-Day, and some of these last women had time only for the briefest of training before they were dropped. As the needs of France and the Resistance changed, so the training was adapted to fit. But most courses followed a broadly similar pattern, with a little more emphasis here, less there.

The preliminary course, usually held at Wanborough Manor in Surrey, lasted two to three weeks. Here trainees were put through physical training – lots of early morning runs and exercises – and basic military and firearms training. Theoretical classes were usually conducted in French; both they and the practical exercises were closely supervised by instructors. Trainees were known by code-names, as a confidentiality measure and to instil a sense of security in them from the start. They were not supposed to talk indiscreetly about their outside lives or their expectations, and during their free time instructors watched them to gauge their reliability. Sessions in the school bar or the local pub were sometimes staged to see how the trainees behaved under the influence of alcohol.

The instructors made regular reports on their trainees and the school's commandant passed them on with his comments to Baker Street. Buckmaster had weekly – or more frequent – meetings with the commandant, and other Baker Street staff often went down to the school to see how the trainees were doing. At the end of the course, the school made its final reports, recommending some trainees, making negative reports on others, and the Baker Street staff met to discuss the findings. They did not always agree with them; where Baker Street felt an agent had promise, she or he was sent on to the next stage of training.

The next stage might be different, depending on the job which Baker Street had in mind for the agent.

Each *réseau* would require a small number of agents at its heart: an organizer, to be in overall command; a courier to liaise between the organizer and the different groups within the *réseau*; and a radio operator to keep up communications with Baker Street. Those three agents were the minimum for effective running of a *réseau*; to these might be added a sabotage and firearms specialist to train the French Resistance groups, and as the group grew, another courier and radio operator and perhaps an assistant to the organizer might be needed.

The demarcation between the various jobs sounded greater in the training than it was in the field. Once in France, most agents were to find that all hands and minds were needed all of the time. When they were not transmitting, radio operators were frequently busy making contacts, carrying messages and sorting out difficulties with the local groups. Couriers were emphatically more than the name suggests: they not only took messages but worked closely with radio operators, finding them safe houses, providing them with look-outs and arranging for the transport of their sets from place to place; they also deputized for the organizer in dealings with the French groups, helped organize the reception of arms drops – and in many cases they were fully involved in sabotage work. Sabotage experts also organized and liaised; organizers spent much of their time travelling to carry messages, give instructions, consult with radio operators, give arms training to resistants.

But in order to do this work and have a fair chance of survival, each agent had to have a clear place in the team. Each one was to be a jack of all trades and at the same time a specialist.

Women tended to be trained either as radio operators or as couriers. France in the early 1940s was a nation led by men, even more so than Britain. French women did not have the right to vote; they were certainly not expected to take charge of anything but the kitchen and nursery. The Resistance groups F Section hoped to arm and co-ordinate were likely to be predominantly male, not to mention self-consciously masculine. They might agree to take orders from a British or Anglo-French envoy, especially if he provided them with weapons – but from a woman?

Moreover, women were seen as being especially fitted for radio operator and courier posts. To be a radio operator, you had to be patient, careful, manually deft, and to have the steady temperament and courage to bear long periods of tension and inactivity. A radio operator was at risk from D/F vans all the time she was transmitting and receiving; she would be in possession of valuable and incriminating evidence while she transcribed and memorized messages; to be found at any time with the radio set would mean certain arrest. It was an extremely dangerous job and one which had to be endured without the relief of action. Women were used to waiting and to fulfilling repetitive tasks quietly. They were also, many of them, practised in dexterity, through typing, sewing, even – as in Yvonne Cormeau's case – playing the piano.

As couriers, women had many advantages over men. Men in France were the natural suspects of the occupying Germans; what was more, from the summer of 1942 onwards, youngish, fit French men began to vanish from France as they were conscripted into work parties and sent to Germany. A man between the ages of eighteen and thirty-five became a conspicuous figure and could expect to be stopped and questioned, perhaps even arrested. It became increasingly difficult and dangerous for men to travel, and male agents had to get themselves excellent false documents explaining their freedom, or else travel out of sight of police and troops. Women agents, on the other hand, were able to blend in with all the other women now carrying on the daily business of French towns and villages. The Germans were less ready to suspect women of Resistance involvement – the Vichy paramilitary, the feared and hated *milice*, were more streetwise but they too concentrated on searching for men. Meanwhile, women had many opportunities to pass messages in shops, cafés, post offices, and their regular presence in these places would raise no eyebrows at all.

Trainees who were to become couriers followed the standard

process of training. After the preliminary course they were sent up to the west coast of Scotland, to be trained to cope with the rougher side of Resistance. They went on survival expeditions, where they had to improvise shelter and food for themselves in the hills, and find their way home with compasses. They learned to handle different weapons – notably Sten guns and the larger Bren guns; they were taught to handle the safe, plastic explosives which would be dropped into France, to make fuses and lay charges; they did practical exercises when they had to blow up targets and carry out ambushes. Their physical training continued, with endurance exercises and rock climbing, in case they had to escape over the Pyrénées; self-defence and the techniques of silent killing for times of extremity. They also learned elementary morse code for use at drop receptions and in emergencies.

Everyone went through this course. Trainees who were going to be radio operators also had to go through their own special, lengthy course of radio instruction. This took place sometimes before, sometimes after the Scottish course, at radio centres in the Midlands and the Home Counties. It was extremely taxing training and lasted a minimum of six weeks. In the field, the entire *réseau* would be relying on the operator's ability to get through to England; the course was designed to make each operator into a dedicated, highly-skilled expert.

The radios the agents used were modified during the war, but basically they came in three or four parts, which, although heavy, could be carried together in a small suitcase. The parts included a receiver and a transmitter and about twenty yards of aerial, which had to be spread out when the set was operating. As already mentioned, the agent would have a schedule of times at which to come on the air; and at each of these scheduled times or 'skeds', the agent had to assemble the parts, put up the aerial and insert into the set a crystal, which would allow the set to operate on a certain frequency. She (or he) also had to plug the set into the mains electricity current or attach it to another source of power like a car battery.

Once the set was assembled and the frequency found, the operator would contact the home station by pressing a single key and sending morse signals. The signals would convey not a straightforward message but a coded one – the operator's personal signing on code. The receiving operator at the home station would normally be expecting the transmission; once it was heard and identified an acknowledgement message would come back over the agent's receiver, again in code, telling the agent to proceed.

The agent would key in her coded messages, as fast as possible without jeopardizing the clarity of the signals. Operators were not supposed to be on the air for more than fifteen or twenty minutes but in reality they often had to spend longer in order to complete their messages, and interference might force the home station to ask for a repeat of certain parts.

Once the transmission was complete, the agent might have to stand by to receive and take down a stream of messages from England. In the early years of the war, agents transmitted and received on the same skeds; in the spring of 1944, though, skeds were rearranged to split up the two tasks, cutting down the time an agent had to spend on the air without a break.

Radio operators had, therefore, to learn morse code so that they knew it instinctively; they had to be able to encode and decode both accurately and swiftly. They had to learn how to commit messages to memory so that they did not endanger themselves and their information by keeping written copies.

They had to learn to maintain and repair their sets and to improvise when they found themselves in poor transmitting conditions.

They also had to learn not only how to operate their sets under pressure and in haste, but how to observe stringent security precautions all the while. Much of the illegal radio traffic between France and England could be monitored by the Germans; even when they could not locate the set, they could intercept and record signals. It was vital therefore that the messages be coded in a way that could not be penetrated by anyone but the key-holders. Each operator had a personal code in which she or he communicated: early on in the war, these codes were based on a word or a sequence of numbers; in the middle years they were based on a phrase or saying or short poem which meant something personal to the agent but would not occur to anyone else. By the end of 1943, in addition to having a personal code, each agent was issued with a pad of silk slips, and each silk slip was printed with columns of letters and figures. Using the columns and rows in different sequences, the agent could have a continually changing code, and home station could identify the code for each sked from its own duplicate pad. Once all the combinations on a slip had been used, the agent burned it and moved on to the next.

The correct use of codes was a complex business; the process of coding and ciphering tedious and exhausting. There were also security checks. Each agent had a check, which might be a certain kind of error included in every message – a transposition of the letters S and T, for instance – and which would reassure home station that it really was the agent transmitting freely. The reason for these checks was that if an agent were captured with her set and codes, the Germans would not be able to take her place on the airwaves without being detected. As an extra precaution against the Germans extracting the security check, agents had two checks, one a 'bluff' check they could tell their captors under duress and the other a secret 'true' check, which home station would continue to look for.

It was not always so easy to stick to these guide-lines in the field. Conditions sometimes made it difficult for transmissions to be properly completed; codes and checks changed with successive security scares; under pressure of time some agents left out their checks from regular transmissions and when others who had been captured deliberately left out theirs as a warning, home station sometimes assumed it was just a mistake.

But these were all difficulties to be faced later in the field – in training, the agents were expected to practise until they got it right, every time. At the end of the weeks of training, radio operators were sent with their sets on clandestine exercises: they would have to go to a certain area, find somewhere from which to transmit and send certain messages to the home station. They were often sent to places where mountains or buildings played havoc with transmission; sometimes they were trailed by SOE training officers and had to lose them; sometimes the police were issued with a description of them and told that they should be pulled in for questioning if spotted. The exercises were made as difficult as they could be, to test the trainees' resourcefulness and skill. Radio operators ended their course with no illusions that the job would be easy.

Radio operators and couriers alike, along with all the other trainees, then went into detailed security and clandestinity training in the Beaulieu schools.

Here they learned what it would take to live behind enemy lines. They learned about the current state of France's two zones, the role of the demarcation line and the various restrictions which attended everyone's movements. They were instructed in the importance of false documents and cover stories, and of looking, thinking and being French. There were dozens of French habits and characteristics they would have to adopt: ways of greeting people, ways of wearing clothes, the observance of new wartime conditions – under new rationing laws, for instance, women were not entitled to cigarettes. There were certain commodities that were simply not available in France, and trying to buy them would attract attention. Often the 'conducting officer' agents would pass on tips from their recent spells in France. 'Don't go into a French restaurant and ask for pastry,' was the advice of newly-returned agent Ben Cowburn in 1943, 'always travel in second class or go *only* in first class – it depends on what you look like and what you're doing; don't have shiny shoes.'

The Beaulieu schools instructed trainees in the hierarchies of the German occupying forces, and taught them to recognize the various uniforms and understand the authority they represented. There were many divisions within the German forces in France, but the main bodies were the Abwehr, the security and military intelligence wing of the German army; and the Sicherheitsdienst or SD, the security force of the Nazi party. Both operated to crush subversion and Resistance: but the SD, working in tandem with the SS and under the leadership of Himmler, was the more formidable and its methods were more ruthless. Himmler was also responsible for the Gestapo, the security police who hunted down agents and resistants, and the SD and the Gestapo worked in close co-operation. From the point of view of agents in the field, the Gestapo and the SD were one. Their headquarters were near one another in Paris; if agents were arrested they might be taken first to Gestapo headquarters, on Rue des Saussaies for interrogation; or if they were known from the start to be agents they would probably go straight to SD headquarters, three grand old houses at numbers 82, 84 and 86 Avenue Foch. There were special 'interrogation' rooms where torture was used at both headquarters.

Besides the Abwehr and the SD, there were also various different levels of French police and Vichy security forces. The exact relationships and activities of the forces changed as the occupation progressed, and each batch of trainees learned the latest that was known about them. Up until November 1942, while Vichy France was still free of Germans, the Vichy police were responsible for security there. Then, after the Germans crossed the line and occupied all of France, the Gestapo operated in the south as well as in the north. In 1943 the Vichy zone, still unoccupied in name though very much occupied in fact, also saw the birth of a new force: the *milice*. This was a volunteer counter-subversion force, made up of French civilians and bitterly hated by the Resistance. The *milice* was dangerous because its members lived in the local communities, had access to local gossip and were able to spot Resistance fermenting where the Germans missed it.

The local French gendarmerie, on the other hand, was very often sympathetic to Resistance. It was a bewildering subject and F Section gave its trainees what help it could: some general knowledge, much drilling on the recognition of uniforms, and good wishes.

Against this background, the trainees now learned the skills of clandestine work. They were taught the mechanics of making contacts, passing messages and keeping rendezvous. They were taught the overriding importance of organizing their *réseaux* on a cell structure, using 'cut-outs' whereby people knew only one or two others in the chain, so that arrests in one village would not lead directly along the line of contacts to bring down couriers, radio operators, organizers.

A cut-out was a deliberate break in a chain of contacts. An organizer might be working with a Resistance group thirty kilometres away: rather than meet regularly with the group's leader, he would send messages through his courier – this was the first cut-out. The courier would also use a cut-out: instead of taking the message directly to the group leader, she or he would meet an intermediary at a neutral spot and pass on the message to be taken to the leader. If urgent business arose which meant that the organizer had to meet the group's leader face to face, one would not go directly to the other but couriers and intermediaries would arrange a rendezvous for them, some way from either of their bases. It was time consuming but it was vital for safety. At Beaulieu, trainees had it drummed into them that not only must they do this with their Resistance contacts and with their meetings with one another, but they must train the French resistants to use the same method amongst themselves. F hoped that each team of agents would eventually be in touch with hundreds, even thousands of resistants. If the resistants were in direct contact with one another, they could not possibly survive arrests or infiltration by the Germans.

The use of cut-outs was basic, essential security. Alongside that, the trainees learned the nuts and bolts of undercover work. Using cut-outs, for instance, meant that agents – especially couriers – would often be keeping rendezvous with strangers. To identify them, they would have to use passwords. Beaulieu taught the trainees how to formulate passwords which would not be noticeable to casual listeners: there was the use of questions and answers. One large Paris-based circuit used a fixed password for a while: '*Ou peut-on trouver l'essence à briquet?*' asked the first person (Where can I find some lighter fuel?). The second came back: '*Du carburant, vous voulez dire?*' (You mean petrol?). It sounded innocent enough to anyone listening in, and if the second person were not a group member, he or she would find nothing odd in such a question. But passwords like this in common use were not ideal – as more people knew of them, the chances grew of the enemy getting hold of them, and Beaulieu encouraged trainees to create new passwords or signs for each occasion. This might mean carrying a newspaper open at a certain section; or the courier saying, '*A quelle heure part le train pour Bordeaux?*' to which the contact would respond, '*C'est à dire l'express?*'; or if the meeting-place were somewhere where there was general company, like a café, the verbal sign might be indirect: for instance, the courier might order a drink using a certain form of words; the contact might then place an order using another pre-arranged phrase. This method of recognizing and acknowledging contacts could be used if the two were due to go on elsewhere – to a safe house perhaps, or to meet a third person. It meant that they did not have to approach one another in front of others; they could leave separately and meet up outside, making sure they were not being followed.

Couriers were encouraged to memorize information and carry verbal messages whenever possible; anything written down was dangerous, as it might be found at a police or German control. Sometimes, however, the information was too long and complex to be memorized. It might be a series of messages for a radio operator to send; it might be a detailed description of a new landing ground; or instructions for a planned sabotage expedition; or important warnings about suspected traitors. Some aspects of the agents' work would require absolute accuracy and attention to detail and so had to be written down. The trainees learned how to write in tiny handwriting on small slips of onion-skin paper. These slips could then be rolled up and hidden, perhaps on the agent's person or perhaps disguised in an object – putting them in a cigarette and offering it to the contact was a popular device but one which women could not easily use given that French women did not smoke in public. But there were creative gadgets available – a clothes brush with a secret compartment; a hollow wine cork; a briefcase with a false lining. These could be used for carrying messages, though they did not facilitate the passing of them. That had to be done usually with some sleight of hand – wrapping a message into a newspaper or magazine and handing it over was a favourite and simple manoeuvre. Another method was to code the message into the newspaper or magazine itself by picking out certain letters in the text with pin pricks or ink marks.

So agents were taught the bizarre and deadly serious techniques on which they would have to rely. They were taught how to recognize if they were being watched, how to lose followers by taking sudden detours, and how to find unofficial exits out of stations and shops.

They were put through practice interrogations by instructors and by Baker Street staff; sometimes they were called out of bed in the middle of the night to undergo rough questioning on their cover stories; their responses were carefully monitored and noted.

At the end of the course they were sent off on a practical exercise. It varied according to their intended job in France. They might have to find out information about some installation or base, or gain access to some guarded place and leave an object there. They might have to travel to a distant town, make contact with people known only vaguely by description and bring back certain information; for radio operators the exercise would again involve making radio contact. Their 'targets' were real; the obstacles they had to negotiate and the forces of law ranged against them were also in earnest. The exercise usually lasted four days and was a gruelling test.

This was the last stage of the training for most agents. Some now took short specialist courses, such as the course in industrial sabotage which lasted three weeks and which would equip them to direct sabotage operations on factories and power plants in France. But for most agents this was the time of reckoning, when the course was over and Buckmaster and his colleagues at Baker Street were making the final decision on whether or not to send them to France.

How did they decide? There were the obvious things to be considered – fitness, technical skills, the trainees' achievements or failures in the tests. The trainees had all been monitored throughout the courses, and the Baker Street staff had received reports from the instructors and from conducting agents. Usually, Buckmaster and his fellows had visited the schools themselves and formed their own impressions.

But there was not always a consensus: often there were discrepancies and divergences of opinion. A trainee might have impressed one instructor and fallen foul of another. Sometimes the overall report on a trainee might be discouraging, yet someone from Baker Street would have a strong belief in that same person. How much of this belief could be justified in the face of adverse training reports? If a trainee fell short in certain skills, the extent of the problem could be gauged and quite likely remedied with extra training. But much of the school's report was to do with character, and how was one to decide between conflicting assessments?

The answer was that in this, as in most things, the Baker Street staff trusted their own instincts. They knew the sort of qualities they were looking for; the most important was, in Buckmaster's words, 'essential guts'. If they felt that a trainee had the guts and the singleness of purpose for the job, they were prepared to override the schools' reports, however unpromising. They knew that all this training was no more than an approximation to what awaited the agents in France. Out there, quite other qualities might be required – and if the Baker Street staff thought an agent possessed the 'inner glow', they would let her or him go.

It was just as well Baker Street did this, for many of the instructors erred on the side of convention. They looked for the qualities which would do a man well in the regular forces – leadership, force of personality, dynamism. The subtler qualities sometimes passed them by – they recommended against Francis Cammaerts, for instance, a man who was to organize a massive, secure *réseau* in the south-east of France and inspire thousands of French resistants. He came to the schools in his twenties, a pacifist and a schoolteacher, and the final report on him from the Beaulieu school bewailed the fact that he was 'lacking in dash' and 'not suitable as a leader'.

Women trainees often provoked a welter of confused responses in these instructors. The idea of training women for active service was peculiar enough to some of them; and in SOE archives lie a number of instructors' reports which show a mingling of resentment, impatience and sheer mystification in their dealings with the women.

Of Yvonne Cormeau, a self-contained, thirty-two-year-old woman with one daughter, whose husband had recently been killed in action, the commandant of the first school wrote:

> At present much the most capable female member of the party. Very friendly with No. 14 with whom she exchanged eternal girlish confidences about the rather mediocre gentlemen of the party. Too friendly with No. 4 for me to hold her in much respect. . . . Represented as doing this for 'love of France'; real motive obscure.

This is a curiously snide report, given that its subject was acknowledged as so capable – and incidentally, went on to become one of the longest-serving agents of the war. This commandant certainly spent a good deal of time watching Yvonne Cormeau's movements and imagining what she was saying. Yet he seems to have been determined to read the worst into everything, and viewed in the light of later events, his assumptions look somewhat wide of the mark. For instance, the No. 14 he mentions was almost certainly Yolande Beekman, who was later to work in one of the most dangerous regions of France and to leave behind her a reputation as a steady, dedicated radio operator. She and Yvonne did spend a good deal of their free time talking, but they weren't appraising the male trainees – on the contrary, Yvonne remembers how the conversation centred around Yolande's impending marriage to SOE training instructor Captain Bateman, and how it might affect her chances of going to France. Who No. 4 was I don't know – presumably a man, since the commandant found his friendship with Yvonne so unsettling, but then what, in the commandant's mind, counted as 'too' friendly? Or was it just something about Yvonne Cormeau herself which disturbed him, and made him suspect even her 'real motive' for joining SOE?

Perhaps there's a clue in the rather cryptic comment added to the end of this report – either by the commandant or someone else: '. . . Is the only member of the party who seemed to have sex appeal for the male members but it was exerted in a very quiet way.' It sounds rather as though the commandant felt it himself, and resented it.

Four months later, another training officer in a different school felt no such unease. He evidently saw little reason to conjecture about the trainee's sexual interests and habits; moreover, he had had little difficulty in sounding her 'real motive':

> There seems to be plenty of strength of character in this student. She is the sort of person who takes some time to make a decision of any importance, but would not go back on it, once it was taken. She told me in private conversation, for instance, that she found great difficulty in making up her mind to take the job on, entailing as it does the separation from her five-year-old daughter. The conflict of duties and responsibilities was solved in the end by the thought that she was doing more for her child in this way, on the long view, than by affording her the normal mother's care. She has, moreover, deep personal reasons for hating the Boche – the smashing up of family life, the loss of husband, and her mother in a concentration camp. All this, and the job of managing her own affairs, have given her strength and independence of character.

It wasn't unusual for women to have mixed reports of this kind. Quite often, their qualities seem to have been increasingly recognized as the course went on – and perhaps as they gained confidence. But there were some who, like Lise de Baissac, a woman in her mid-thirties and of very independent mind, impressed the schools from the start. This is the report from her preliminary training:

> Intelligent, extremely conscientious, reliable and sound in every way. Is quite imperturbable and would remain cool in any situation.
> In both practical exercises and theoretical problems she has shown a capacity to sum up a situation, make a decision and stick to it without becoming flustered. A considerable experience of the world has built up for her a very high degree of self-confidence.

All they said about Lise de Baissac was true, and more. But it was her evident experience and self-confidence which helped them recognize it so quickly. The Baker Street staff were delighted to have their impressions so strongly endorsed and soon after her training was completed, they sent Lise to France on a particularly lonely, taxing mission. But the decision to accept an agent was not always so easy to make. There was frequent agonizing in Baker Street about the schools' reports; but the last word was Buckmaster's and a number of women finally became agents in defiance of the training schools, because he personally believed in them.

FOUR

Going In

By parachute, by small aircraft, by boat; these were the three
clandestine routes into France. In the early days, agents could
use only two of them: they could 'drop' by parachute or land by
boat; in 1943, Lysander and Hudson aeroplanes were able to land
on secretly prepared fields, taking agents in and picking up fugitives
for the return journey.

In all cases, the journey had to be made at night, and had to
coincide with certain phases of the moon: planes had to fly without
lights to get past German defences, so parachute drops and aircraft
landings needed bright moonlight for navigation. Agents going in by air
had to wait for the 'moon period': the series of nights in each monthly
cycle when the moon was full or nearly full. On the other hand, boats
were vulnerable as they approached a hostile shore, so landings from
the sea took place on moonless nights, using the darkness as cover.
Aircraft and boats alike were at the mercy of the weather: departure
dates were scheduled for the suitable moon periods, but there was
never any guarantee that they would take place. There was also
the matter of arranging 'receptions' for the new agents – contacts
who would meet them and take them to a safe house – and such
arrangements might go wrong at the last minute. Going in to France
was an uncertain business and agents often waited in readiness night
after night, only to find that conditions stopped them leaving and that
it would now be another three weeks before the moon favoured them
again. Between now and then they would have to stay in one of F
Section's 'holding houses', with other agents whose real names they
would not learn, waiting.

Before agents reached this point of departure, they had already gone through a preparation process. Once they had completed their training and been formally accepted by Baker Street, they had to be fitted out for their future life in France. SOE tailors made them clothes in French styles and, when possible, in French fabrics. French labels, cut out of other clothes, were sewn into these new ones. Clothes had to be carefully chosen as the agents could take few changes of clothing in with them: they usually went out with just one principal outfit and some accessories. Shoes could not look too new; neither could money. All agents had to take out some French money, and many took a great deal in order to pay the costs of a new *réseau* – they would have to keep themselves in food and shelter, find transport for future arms drops, pay wages to full-time French recruits, have money ready to smooth their paths in black market payments and bribes. French bank notes had to be allocated to agents with care so that their serial numbers were random and not suspiciously consecutive. They also had to be distressed: there were occasions when Buckmaster and his staff had to throw new notes on the floor and trample on them to give them a suitably tattered look.

Agents were shown how to cut and arrange their hair in typically French styles. They even had their teeth checked for signs of British dental work: each agent had to go to the SOE dentist and have any suspicious fillings removed and replaced with the gold used in France.

Once the Baker Street staff had decided on an agent's mission, a suitable cover story would be worked out and false papers made. Male agents had to have a cover which explained why, if they were of service age, they were not in service. They were given 'jobs' such as travelling salesman for a firm involved in producing war materials – in many cases the firm would be a real one which had agreed to co-operate and issue an employment certificate. Or they were given professions such as a mechanic or an electrician and provided with a cover story to explain that they had been bombed out of their home towns. Women agents could more easily be given identities as refugees or war widows, and needed no special exemption from service, but they shared with the men the need for identity cards which would stand up to checking. The names of parents had to appear on the card, and the place and date of birth; also the *mairie* (town hall) where the non-existent birth had been registered. The possibility of discovery through a check of the birth register was a serious one; to get round it the documents department chose as places of birth towns where the *mairie* had been destroyed by bombs, or else towns in French colonies which lay safely beyond the reach of the telephone.

Agents had to learn their cover story, steep themselves in it so that they could answer a barrage of questions on it without stumbling.

Their false identity cards were made, giving descriptions of them and incorporating all the stamps and information in demand at that time in their destination region of France. This was no easy matter to ensure as identity paper requirements were continually changing – forged papers were widespread in France and both the German and the Vichy authorities were tireless in their efforts to eradicate them. Agents in the field would try to keep Baker Street in touch with all the changes, sending information over the radio and giving returning agents examples of new cards and papers to take back. The communications system was very good, sometimes it was even too good – there are several stories about new agents arriving with the correct papers while everyone in the area still had the old ones.

At this late stage in the preparations, the agent received his or her mission. For security reasons it was left to the end, but the briefing was as intensive as Baker Street could make it. With the agents, the staff studied maps and indicated the intended area of operation. They pin-pointed landing grounds and dropping grounds which had already been found; they identified sabotage targets and the whereabouts of local Resistance groups. They gave them the names and addresses of such contacts as were available, and filled them in on the local travel conditions.

The amount of information Baker Street was able to provide varied according to the region, the stage of the war, and the number of agents who had managed to get information out. From 1942 onwards, staff at headquarters were able to rely increasingly on the reports of agents coming back from the field.

These final preparations and briefings took place in Orchard Square, in an atmosphere of concentrated improvisation. The use of the bathroom as an office rapidly became an organization joke: it struck a liberating note of comedy into what was inevitably a tense time for the agents. Besides all the practical details of the missions which lay ahead, the agents and the staff also had to deal with arrangements for the agents' families. Agents were not allowed to tell their families about their work, and of course they would not be able to contact them from France. Vera Atkins took on many tasks to lessen the agents' sense of isolation and worry: she arranged to write occasional letters to parents or dependents reassuring them that the agent was well; in the case of women leaving behind children she helped organize their schooling and care.

Once all these matters were in hand, the agents had only to wait until the call should come. However they were going to enter France, their journey would almost always begin by aeroplane. Those going in by boat would fly to Gibraltar, where they would board a submarine or boat for the seaborne stretch of the journey to the south of France. Those going in by parachute drop or by a clandestine aircraft landing would fly directly across the Channel and northern France to their destination.

When the call came, the agents had to pack and be ready to go within hours. An F Section car, carrying one or more members of the Baker Street staff, picked them up and drove them out of London, through the afternoon or evening traffic, to Tempsford airfield in Bedfordshire, or to Tangmere airfield in Sussex.

At the airfield, as darkness fell and deepened, a routine got underway which was familiar to the staff but strange and memorable to the agents: the agents were taken through their cover story again; they had a last-minute check through of clothes and belongings to see that they had all that they needed, and that no incriminating evidence such as British cigarettes or bus tickets lurked in their pockets. Then they were given two things: one was a good luck gift – a cigarette case, cuff-links, a piece of jewellery – it was to be a reminder of Baker Street's good wishes and an object to pawn or sell on the black market if necessary. The other was a cyanide pill, which the agents were free to take in extremis: the Catholic church, they were told, had given special dispensation for them to do this.

Agents who were going to drop by parachute underwent a final check of their parachute harness, to make sure it was correctly fastened. Then they were taken across the grass and tarmac to where the aircraft waited, its engines already running. They shook hands with the staff, heard from them the traditional French valediction – *'Merde!'* – and climbed aboard.

FIVE

Prosper and the Great Hope

On a dark July night in 1942, Yvonne Rudellat was landed by felucca on a deserted stretch of shore on France's Mediterranean coast.

Two months later, on 24 September, Andrée Borrel and Lise de Baissac dropped from the cockpit of an aeroplane high above the Loire valley and floated silently down through the night air.

All three of them were bound for destinations in the occupied zone: they were part of SOE's great hope for Resistance in northern France. Although they now separated and went their own ways, each was to play her part in what became known as the Prosper story.

Prosper was a huge *réseau* which grew up in the occupied zone between autumn 1942 and summer 1943. It took its name from its organizer, SOE agent Francis Suttill, code-named *Prosper*. *Prosper* was not yet in France when the three women agents arrived; as Andrée Borrel and Lise de Baissac made their jump, he was still undergoing his final briefing. His mission was an important one, for the staff at Baker Street were relying on him to take operations in France on to a new, organized level. He was being charged with the mission of building a new *réseau* in Paris, to replace the shattered Autogiro. He was also to oversee the setting up of Resistance groups in other parts of the occupied zone. F Section now had a list of the Carte contacts in the occupied zone, provided for them by *Carte* himself; using these contacts as a starting-point, *Prosper* was to recruit small teams of resistants from different regions in the occupied zone and report back on them and their potential. Soon afterwards, other agents would go out and take over as chiefs of the *réseaux* in the zone; arms and explosives could be dropped to the resistants once they were organized and *Prosper* and his fellow agents could undertake the necessary training of them. It was an ambitious plan but F Section staff were looking anxiously to the prospect of an invasion of France: most people expected the Allied troops to go into France within twelve months and that would necessitate a co-ordinated network of armed fighters, trained and ready to rise in mass support. There was no time with which to play.

With this aim of preparing France for the Allied landings, the Prosper *réseau* was born. And these three women agents were involved in it, from its very first stirrings.

Yvonne Rudellat was a French woman who had been working in London when SOE recruited her. In her late forties, she was older than most of the women agents: she had married an Italian and lived with him and their two daughters in London until they had separated. When the war began she worked in a small London hotel as a receptionist/manageress and it was one of the hotel guests who introduced her to SOE. The accounts of her from those days are scanty but those which do exist all refer to her as cool and efficient, someone well able to organize and keep her nerve.

She was the first woman agent to go into France by undercover means. Whereas Virginia Hall had entered the country as a free citizen, protected by her 'neutral' nationality, Yvonne Rudellat had to be smuggled in secretly. In the summer of 1942 the southern half of France was still an officially 'free' zone; the Mediterranean coast was only patchily guarded by the Vichy forces and illegal craft made frequent trips to and from its shores. Yvonne Rudellat was carried to these shores by felucca and set down there. Her code-name was *Jacqueline* and her instructions were to go north to the town of Tours and make contact with an agent who had been there since June, known as *Gaspard*. Her mission would be to work as a courier, first for *Gaspard* but soon for an important organizer due to follow her out: *Prosper*.

Yvonne reached Tours, a thriving town near the confluence of the Loire and Cher rivers, in August and made contact with *Gaspard*. But things did not go well. *Gaspard* (in real life an Englishman named Flowers) was finding it hard to get his *réseau* started. His radio operator was keeping only one jump ahead of the direction finding vans and he did not seem particularly pleased to see Yvonne. They worked together briefly, along with another new arrival to the *réseau*, a dedicated French resistant, Pierre Culioli. Unfortunately neither Yvonne nor Culioli got on with *Gaspard* and their work was hampered by disagreements and what the other two saw as *Gaspard*'s inefficiency. Yvonne and Culioli began work closely together: in September and October they organized several receptions for the arriving Prosper agents and by December they had co-operated with them in many ways. Then an incident took place which forced Yvonne to leave Tours: one day she came into her rented room to find that someone had been there in her absence and offloaded on to her a mass of incriminating evidence, including a radio set and code sheets. She could not be sure that her landlord had not seen the things and she had no choice but to flee.

With the help of Pierre Culioli, Yvonne hid the evidence and got herself out of town: she went eighty kilometres south to Poitiers where she lay low. This was the end of her and Culioli's partnership with *Gaspard*: from now on the two of them would work together as an autonomous team in the Sologne, south of Paris, their *réseau* Monkeypuzzle becoming part of the Prosper network.

Yvonne Rudellat was a brave, resourceful woman: that much would become clear through her actions. But she did not survive the war and though she worked with Pierre Culioli for the next nine months, and was instrumental in building up the Prosper *réseau*, it is hard today to form a picture of the woman herself.

Andrée Borrel is a different matter. She was being dropped into France with instructions to work alongside *Prosper* as his courier and lieutenant. *Prosper* would need her; in fact, Baker Street knew that *Prosper* would need all the help he could get. Whereas Yvonne Rudellat would now work within *Prosper*'s orbit but on a separate patch (her and Culioli's *réseau* was known as Monkeypuzzle), Andrée Borrel would be the organizer's right hand. She was now being dropped, under the code-name *Denise*, one week ahead of *Prosper* to prepare some contacts for his arrival.

There are many brief snippets about Andrée Borrel to be found scattered in the various books and archives. They are slender on facts about her time in France but we know that she worked alongside *Prosper*, at the heart of the *réseau*, and so the story of the Prosper *réseau* is itself in many ways that of her life in the field. What the comments of her colleagues and acquaintances provide is the impression of a vivid, determined, resolute character. A very 1940s word, 'gallant' seems to hover round her figure as it emerges from the backward glances.

When she dropped on to the banks of the Loire, Andrée Borrel was just twenty-two years old. She was French and working class; her father had died when she was young and she and her sister had been brought up by their mother, going to school at Louveciennes near Paris. Andrée had left school and worked for several years as a sales assistant in a Paris boulangerie; in 1939 she had travelled south with her mother and, volunteering as a nurse, had been stationed near

Toulon. In 1940, after the Germans had marched into the northern half of France, she had been approached by one of the doctors and asked to help with an escape line and so her involvement with the Resistance had begun.

For two years Andrée Borrel had worked on the escape line – it matured into the famous PAT line which smuggled over 600 members of the Allied forces out of France – and then in 1942 she and other members of the line were denounced. She fled through Spain and managed to get to England and there, through Resistance contacts, she was recruited into SOE.

According to her sister she had always been '*un garçon manqué*'.[1] She was physically strong and energetic; she loved action. Taking risks did not terrify her; after the war her sister spoke of Andrée carrying explosives out of Paris in a rucksack. She believed that Andrée had found her *métier* in the Resistance.

Another Resistance agent who trained with Andrée Borrel said she was 'not of great education, and she was entirely wonderful, cool, calm, brave always, a good comrade for men, an excellent friend, but nothing more, you understand.'[2]

Andrée was on the left politically, believing and hoping that the working people of France would join together to drive out the Germans and transform the country. She had a particularly close and straightforward relationship with her organizer *Prosper*. Some of the SOE women agents fascinated their colleagues; *Prosper*'s reference to his courier in a report from the field has in it nothing of fascination but everything of respect and admiration and another kind of love: 'Everyone who has come into contact with her in her work agrees with myself that she is the best of us all.'

But on the night of 24 September, Andrée Borrel had not yet met *Prosper*. She arrived in France as his herald.

The agent who landed with her, Lise de Baissac, had her own instructions. Her mission was linked to the Prosper *réseau* but was to be geographically apart; her story is told in the next chapter. From Andrée Borrel's point of view the small, reserved woman in her mid-thirties was both a comrade and a stranger: they had in common the danger of their positions, the risks that lay ahead, but they had to keep their plans to themselves.

The two women were met out in the dark fields by Yvonne Rudellat's and Pierre Culioli's local helpers. They were taken to a nearby house and hidden away and there they stayed for a day or

[1] *Death Be Not Proud*, Elizabeth Nicholas, Cresset Press, 1958
[2] Ibid

two, learning about the ways of life in occupied France in 1942 and preparing for their next moves. Andrée Borrel was to go north to Paris, Lise de Baissac south to Poitiers, respectively the heart and the edge of the occupied zone. They did not talk much to one another: they were both reserved, self-contained people and wary of knowing too much about one another's mission. But they spoke a bit about their lives before the war and discovered, oddly enough, that their paths had crossed in those normal pre-occupation days: Lise de Baissac's local *boulangerie* on the Avenue Kléber, where she had used to go every day to buy her bread, was the one in which Andrée Borrel had worked.

Lise de Baissac had not known Andrée Borrel in training and after these few days together she saw her only once or twice, when Andrée brought her information. But what she says of her echoes every other testimony: 'She was a girl of the people. She was *formidable*, Andrée Borrel, *vraiment formidable*. Very courageous, very prepared.'

When Andrée Borrel left the valley of the Loire she went straight to Paris and immediately began to prepare the ground for the new *réseau*. She had been given a contact: two sisters, Germaine and Madelaine Tambour, who worked with the Resistance and lived with their mother in an apartment at 38 Avenue de Suffren. In fact, these sisters were members of Carte, the large network of contacts built up by Andre Girard or *Carte* himself, from his base in Antibes. He had given their names to Baker Street to use. Andrée went to the Avenue de Suffren and met them; she also looked up her sister who was living at 23 Rue de Caumartin and enlisted her help in the work ahead. A few days later, on the night of 1 October, she went to a landing ground near Vendôme where, with Yvonne Rudellat and Pierre Culioli, she received her organizer, *Prosper*.

Prosper in civilian life was Francis Suttill, a thirty-two-year-old Anglo-French man. His father was British, his mother French and he had been born near Lille in north-eastern France. Until the outbreak of war he had been an international lawyer. His French was good but accented (F Section decided he could pass for a Belgian) and he had no experience of the Resistance, but his SOE trainers had been impressed by him: he was by all accounts a charismatic man, strong, capable and able both to inspire and manage others.

A photograph of *Prosper* taken around that time shows an unlikely face for a Resistance hero: he looks younger than his thirty-two years, thoughtful and fine-boned; there's a complete lack of swagger, instead there is a concentrated vibrancy. The photographs which survive of the male SOE agents are mostly more glamorous than those of the women – the women often look stiff, especially in uniform, or wary, whereas the men frequently look dashing, staring confidently at the camera. *Prosper*'s photograph, however, shows a man neither dashing nor overtly confident yet he is glamorous, with the uneasy mystique of the very private person.

He was dropped with another agent, a French man called Jean Amps who was briefed to be an assistant and the newly formed group – *Prosper*, Jean Amps, Andrée Borrel, Yvonne Rudellat and Pierre Culioli – immediately took cover locally and made plans. *Prosper* was impatient to start work at once: he and Andrée Borrel decided that they should set out as soon as possible on a series of trips into the countryside around Paris; there they could sound out contacts and start recruiting for the *réseau*. They would soon be receiving a radio operator, he told them: Baker Street was sending a man, code-named *Archambaud*, in the next moon period. Would Yvonne Rudellat and Pierre Culioli arrange *Archambaud*'s reception?

Prosper was impressed by the energy and competence of Yvonne and Culioli. The omens looked good and when *Prosper* and Andrée took leave of their comrades to begin recruiting, they were optimistic of success.

Andrée Borrel had found *Prosper* an apartment near her own in Paris but they scarcely saw the city during the next few weeks for they spent all their time travelling. Together they went to the areas of Blois, Orléans, Romorantin and Chartres to the south-west of Paris; Melun to the immediate south-east and to Beauvais, Compiègne and St Quentin in the north and north-east. They had contacts in these places, supplied to them by Baker Street; these were mainly Carte contacts, people whom Girard (*Carte*) and his followers had approached and enlisted as willing to help. The pair looked up these people, sounded them out and recruited them. Principally they were seeking farmers willing to receive drops of arms and explosives on their land: together with their new recruits they scouted for suitable fields for receptions, and for suitable barns or buildings in which the arms could be stored. They explored the possibilities of transport for getting the arms to Paris – could they be smuggled through in farm trucks or vans, or hidden in bulky farm packages sent by train? They took down the co-ordinates of the dropping grounds for transmission to England.

Their cover while they were travelling was as a brother and sister team, he a salesman in agricultural products, she his negotiator. It was a good cover in rural France where women traditionally did the bargaining and it was a necessary precaution because *Prosper*'s accent was too striking for comfort. Andrée, in her role as hard-nosed French sister, would do all the initial talking with the contacts until they could be sure they were with friends.

These travels took *Prosper* and Andrée through October and into the winter months. Meanwhile, south of Paris, Yvonne and Pierre began to receive more agents bound both for the Prosper *réseau* and for others. On the night of Hallowe'en, 31 October, the promised radio operator *Archambaud* dropped with another agent on to the ground at Nouan-sur-Loire. The other agents moved on rapidly, down to Bordeaux where a strong *réseau* was growing up; *Archambaud* was eagerly awaited in Paris.

The Prosper *réseau* – named after its organizer – was now beginning to build up. Meanwhile *Prosper*'s and Andrée's tireless recruiting was counterpointed by the arrival of new agents from Britain who had missions to organize other new *réseaux* in the occupied zone. These would be independent of Prosper, though there would be lines of communication which linked them.

On 17 November, Michael Trotobas, one of the agents who had escaped from Mauzac, dropped to a Monkeypuzzle reception with a radio operator Staggs. The two of them set off for Lille to start a *réseau*, Farmer, there.

A third agent, Gustave Biéler, who dropped with them that night injured his back when he landed and had to stay put for a few weeks, but then he too left, for St Quentin in the north-east where he started the *réseau* Musician.

On the next night, 18 November, a Madagascan businessman, France Antelme, dropped to a reception near Poitiers, organized by Lise de Baissac. She put him in touch with a contact in Paris where his mission was principally an economic one: he was to approach business contacts with plans for the future funding of supplies for the Allied invasion, whenever it came. He also had instructions to contact any non-Gaullist Resistance groups he could find and to see if they could work with F Section towards the same longed-for invasion.

The rest of November went by without any more incoming agents in the north – though on the ground the agents themselves were recruiting and finding houses and arranging lines of communication. The new *réseaux* of the north were establishing themselves: so was one other *réseau* of the occupied zone which had started up in the south-western extremity of the zone, around Bordeaux. This was Scientist, led by Claude de Baissac, Lise's brother. Like his neighbours further north, he too now had lines of communication to the Prosper organization.

So already, before the end of 1942, an 'infrastructure' was in place north of the demarcation line; F Section had – it hoped – the skeleton of a vast underground Resistance force. Soon it could begin to send in arms and supplies, along with still more agents, and start the co-ordinated preparations for action.

It's crucial to an understanding of the Prosper story to realize that in 1942 everyone involved in the French Resistance knew that an invasion would come and that no one knew when. Almost everyone thought it would come much sooner than it did: they expected it in the spring of 1943, or the summer; they hoped they would not have to wait till the autumn. At the end of 1942 the occupation had already lasted over two years with all its privations and fears, and these were growing greater not less. The people of France had long been carrying a heavy burden. For these people in 1942 who were risking their lives to pass messages or to house radio sets and agents – let alone for the agents themselves, hunted on all sides – it was unimaginable that this kind of life could be sustained for eighteen months. Had they known they would have to wait until June 1944 for the invasion they would have despaired, and they would have had reason to do so. The truth was that it was simply too long, much too long, for them to last. The Germans were vigilant against the growth of Resistance forces and none of the *réseaux* in place in 1942 would survive intact to 1944. But then in 1942 no one involved in them – either in France or in Baker Street – dreamed that they would have to.

For radio operators around Paris, Bordeaux and Lille were now sending to Baker Street news of new recruits and contacts, areas opened up to SOE, dropping grounds available for use. And in Baker Street ambitious plans were being laid to make them operational.

In November the Allies had invaded North Africa and the German forces had marched over the demarcation line into southern France, destroying all but the last illusions of Vichy independence. In the last few months of the year the much hated '*Service Travail Obligatoire*' or STO – conscription of French men to Germany to work - was beginning to bite. The French population was restive: in some places young men were taking to the hills to avoid STO and forming the early groups of *maquis* resistants; it seemed that France was heading inevitably for crisis. What was more, thousands of German troops were now tied up on the eastern front, fighting Soviet troops, with winter threatening them. From London it looked as though the tide was turning; stretched in every direction, Germany would surely find it harder and harder to keep a grip on France in the months to come. The time to strike might soon arrive.

Everyone was looking ahead, nerved up for action. As 1942 became 1943 a very significant addition was made to F Section's agents in France, an addition which Baker Street believed would make all the difference to Prosper and its associated *réseaux*. He was a new agent, Henri Déricourt, whose mission was to organize clandestine flights in and out of France for any agents who needed them.

Since the Germans had gone into the southern half of France, the Mediterranean coast was guarded and felucca trips had had to stop. Baker Street was anxious to find other ways of bringing agents out of France quickly; the staff were also keen to find new ways of taking them in, more exact than dropping them and less likely to damage precious radio sets. Parachute drops were perfect for one-way traffic but what was needed now was a system of undercover aircraft landings and pick-ups. Henri Déricourt was a Frenchman and a pilot: he was introduced to SOE at the end of 1942 and after swift, intensive training he was dropped blind into occupied France on the night of 22 January 1943. His mission was to start a small *réseau*, Farrier, which would be responsible for organizing landings and pick-ups. It was an exciting development: the vast and ever-spreading Prosper network, and emerging *réseaux* as far away as Marseille and the Jura, would be relying on his services in 1943.

Paris in 1943

Paris in 1943 was a bewildering city. On the one hand life seemed to go on much as before the war. German soldiers patronized the cafés and bars; officers from the army, the security services and the administration provided custom for restaurants, theatres, night-clubs, 'spectacles'. Businesses operated. The metro ran. Shops sold merchandise. There were even races at Longchamps. People coming to the capital from other parts of the country were often astonished to see the variety of Parisian life.

But on the other hand the shops were often empty of stock. Food available legally was scarce: it was the black market which flourished and its marketeers throve. In June 1943 two kilos of butter cost 876 (old) francs – which was the total of what the average person had to spend for a whole month. Whereas in the country many people were able to supplement their official rations with a few eggs or some milk or some wheat from a neighbouring farm, in Paris such things were wildly expensive. People made extra-ordinary savings and sacrifices to be able to afford one or another of them every few weeks. Shopping had become a sub-culture: people queued for hours, and paid other people to queue for hours on their behalf, for a loaf of bread. The shortage of food and of other commodities like shoes, fabric and soap was more acute than ever.

In Paris as everywhere else, the getting of life's staples obsessed the whole population.

The occupation was imposing other hardships on the Parisians too, eating away further and further at their civil liberties. The Jews had been the first to suffer: since the previous summer all French Jews in the occupied zone over the age of six months had to wear a large yellow star. Thus marked out, they had had one right after another taken away: by 1943 they could not have telephones, carry on businesses, read in libraries, buy stamps, eat in restaurants or cafés, bathe in swimming pools or attend races. They could shop only during certain hours – usually between 3 p.m. and 4 p.m. when most shops were shut or else already sold out. On the Paris metro they were allowed to ride only in the last carriage.

These were the conditions imposed on the Jews who remained. Thousands had been deported; the deportations, which had begun in 1941, were continuing and growing larger. In June 1942 the Paris police had rounded up 13,000 Jews and sent them east to Germany and – ultimately – the concentration camps. Many Jews were now fleeing from Paris and the occupied zone; in November 1942, in the wake of the Germans marching into the south, the Italians had taken over the administration of some of the southern and eastern parts of France and they treated Jews very much better than did either the Germans or the Vichy administration. In the first half of 1943 thousands of Jews fled from Paris and other parts of France into Italian-occupied territories.

Now non-Jewish French citizens too began to find their rights curtailed. STO had been imposed towards the end of 1942 – first it applied only to factory workers, then, as the labour shortage in Germany continued to be acute, it was extended to a few other categories of fit, young men, then to some more not so young men. By the beginning of 1943 almost any healthy man – merchant, civil servant, shopkeeper, student, farm worker – might be conscripted, usually with only one day's notice given before he was packed into a train and sent to Germany.

Not surprisingly hundreds, thousands of men were soon evading these orders. So measures were brought in to force these 'réfractaires' into the open. By March 1943, French men aged between eighteen and fifty had to carry a work certificate signed by their employer. Then they needed official work cards to collect letters from the post office. Men found without a card could to go prison for a month; a false card could get them three years. The penalty for making false cards was indefinite forced labour. By June French civilians had to register with traders to buy rationed produce. Simply going out into the streets of Paris and other cities had become dangerous: periodically the police would round up men and put them on an east-bound train within hours. These round-ups were known as '*rafles*'.

Demonstrations by the French, usually held at the stations, had no effect. Men prepared bolt-holes for themselves should the letter of conscription arrive. They learned to check the streets they entered for police or barriers, signs of an impending *rafle*. In country areas some of them took to the woods, sleeping in barns or empty farmhouses and going raiding for food: this was the very beginning of the *maquis*.

So in 1943 in Paris, beneath the surface appearance of a city running as usual, there were all sorts of forces at work. The Parisians were being pulled ever more strongly in opposite directions. Like any capital city under occupation, Paris attracted collaborators and profiteers. But now it was also seeing a growth of sympathy for the Resistance.

The Prosper agents based in Paris were not short of helpers.

It is not easy to find resistants who worked in Prosper: so few survived the war. But one who is still at large is Jacques Bureau who worked as Prosper's radio expert. Jacques Bureau had become involved in resistance work in 1942; like most people, he was brought into it by a friend. This friend had been recruited by André Girard for Carte and was working with the Tambour sisters. At that time their work consisted mainly of listening to broadcasts from London and passing on messages and this was where Jacques Bureau found his *métier*: he was an electronic technician and he helped adapt and maintain household wirelesses for receiving the BBC broadcasts.

Then Andrée Borrel made contact with the Tambours and in October Germaine Tambour introduced Jacques to *Prosper* and *Archambaud*. He liked *Prosper* immediately and agreed to work with him, helping to maintain *Archambaud*'s radio set and, as the *réseau* expanded, to service other sets and do what he could to keep open the airwaves to London.

Now he had a stroke of luck: he was offered a senior post in a government ministry electronics centre. He worked in a well-equipped laboratory, full of electronics parts and he was able to take parts of agents' radio sets into work with him to repair. Moreover, he was able to drive an official van which was also used – in these petrol-scarce times – to supply food to the ministry canteen. 'So it was ideal; I could hide the transmitters under vegetables, under the carrots.'

His seniority protected him from unwelcome investigations. As head of a service in a ministry, he had good relations with the authorities. What was more, he found that he was by no means the only resistant in government employ: through contacts he discovered that organized recruitment was going on and that there even existed a list of officials who were ready to work with the British. 'The list had been drawn up to show who specialized in what so that if you needed a doctor willing to work with agents, for instance, you could look up the names on the list.' It was a kind of Resistance Yellow Pages.

He also had useful contacts with the city's mental hospitals. Being on good terms with one of the medical directors, he sometimes stored his Prosper equipment – sets, spare parts and crystals – in unlikely cupboards and cellars of mental wards and hostels. Driving into an asylum in his ministry van, who would stop or question him? And who would think to conduct a search in such places?

As he worked steadily at his job and on Prosper equipment, seeing *Prosper* about once a week, Jacques Bureau, like most other resistants, was in touch with many very different currents of the life around him. He had his social friends, his Resistance comrades, his acquaintances at work and in the authorities. His secret work gave him glimpses of other bizarre underground channels: he came across a doctor who would take in people hunted by the Germans, certify them as insane and hide them in the asylums. He also valued the usefulness of the 'wrong' kind of friend: to be well in with Vichy officials or police gave one useful protection against suspicion.

For as 1943 arrived, the Germans and the collaborationist French authorities were on the alert for signs of Resistance activity. Paris was not only full of Parisians, Germans, petty criminals and profiteers; it contained a growing number of paid informers.

Action

It was into these conditions that F Section now began pouring arms, explosives and supplies. In the early months of 1943 Prosper became suddenly and dramatically operational.

The night-time drops began in January. On nights when the weather conditions were favourable and the moon was bright, planes could be heard flying overhead. Out in dark fields, in the freezing cold, people who were defying the curfew saw the aircraft they were expecting fly over, turn and come back and discharge into the night dozens of shapes which first plummeted then floated down towards them. As the containers hit the ground – in a specific field if they were lucky, but often drifting away into other fields, trees or ponds – the people rushed to gather them in, carrying them to the carts and trucks, loading them on, and then when they were all there the convoy would lurch off through the darkness to hide the illegal stores in a barn or shed, until they should be needed.

The dropping grounds which *Prosper* and Andrée Borrel had found, and others which their recruits had found for them, were certainly being put to use. Arms and explosives were dropped on to Prosper grounds north, south-east and west of Paris, and they went on being dropped, through January, February, March and April into spring; through May into summer. The rate of activity was high: by the end of May the various grounds of the Prosper *réseau* would receive between them 240 containers.

They were also receiving extra agents. On 22 January *Prosper* and Andrée Borrel received Jean Worms near Chartres. He went off with another agent, Jacques Weil, to the Chalons-sur-Marne area, where the two of them set up Juggler, a sub-*réseau* of Prosper. From within France came Octave Simon who had worked with Philippe de Vomécourt: he went north-west to the Sarthe where he too organized a sub-*réseau*, Satirist, which received a lot of arms. In March an agent called François Garel, another escapee from Mauzac, was dropped blind with a radio operator Marcel Rousset: they went to the Sarthe as well, to set up another sub-*réseau*, Butler, which concentrated on sabotaging railway targets with the newly-dropped explosives.

New agents also arrived to be added to the Prosper nucleus, based in Paris. Jack Agazarian had come out at the very end of 1942 as *Prosper*'s second radio operator. His wife, Francine, was landed by Lysander on the night of 17 March and she joined the Parisian group as well. This meant that there were now five agents at the heart of the operation, working together in Paris: *Prosper*, Andrée Borrel, *Archambaud*, Jack and Francine Agazarian.

The only one who would survive the intrigues and disasters ahead was Francine Agazarian, and when I asked her if she would talk about those days she said she couldn't: being the only one to survive, and with the knowledge of what the others went through after their arrest, makes the subject too close to her and too painful. But she wrote to me, describing her sensations and hopes at the time and opening the door for a moment on to the way that the Prosper agents worked, separately but in partnership, through these months:

> Although in the same network, my husband and I were
> not working together; as a radio operator he worked alone

and transmitted from different locations every day. I was only responsible to *Prosper* (whom we all called François). He liked to use me for special errands because, France being my native land, I could get away from difficulties easily enough, particularly when dealing with officialdom.

François was an outstanding leader, clear-headed, precise, confident. I liked working on his instructions, and I enjoyed the small challenges he was placing in front of me. For instance calling at town halls in various districts of Paris to exchange the network's expired ration cards (manufactured in London) for genuine new ones. Mainly I was delivering his messages to his helpers: in Paris, in villages, or isolated houses in the countryside. From time to time I was also delivering demolition material received from England. And once, with hand-grenades in my shopping bag, I travelled in a train so full that I had to stand pressed against a German NCO. This odd situation was not new to me. I had already experienced it for the first time on the day of my arrival on French soil, when I had to travel by train from Poitiers to Paris. A very full train also. I sat on my small suitcase in the corridor, a uniformed German standing close against me. But, that first time, tied to my waist, under my clothes, was a wide black cloth belt containing bank-notes for *Prosper*, a number of blank identity cards and a number of ration cards; while tucked into the sleeves of my coat were crystals for Prosper's radio transmitters; the crystals had been skilfully secured to my sleeves by Vera Atkins herself, before my departure from Orchard Court. My .32 revolver and ammunition were in my suitcase. The ludicrousness of the situation somehow eliminated any thought of danger.

In any case, I believe none of us in the field ever gave one thought to danger. Germans were everywhere, especially in Paris; one absorbed the sight of them and went on with the job of living as ordinarily as possible and applying oneself to one's work.

Because I worked alone, the times I liked best were when we could be together, François, *Denise* [Andrée], Gilbert (*Archambaud*), Jack and I, sitting round a table, while I was decoding radio messages from London; we were always hoping to read the exciting warning to stand by, which would have meant that the liberating invasion from England was imminent.

*

By early spring 1943, the Prosper organization had spread over a massive geographical area and had contacts, direct and indirect, with many other *réseaux*. Francine remembers her regular trips to the countryside; Andrée Borrel's sister recalls Andrée repeatedly travelling, going out to country areas where arms had been stored and helping to bring them in to Paris. *Prosper* had made contact with a number of communist groups in and around Paris and they were some of the earliest resistants to use Prosper-dropped supplies in attacks. Even as Francine settled in, a newly returned agent was reporting back to Baker Street: 'Germans are killed daily in the streets of Paris . . . and 90 per cent of these attacks are made with arms provided by us, e.g. to the Communists.'

But the arms traffic was not only one way from the countryside into Paris; in these early months of 1943 the Prosper agents were also helping to prepare sabotage units out in the country areas.

It's not difficult to see how Andrée Borrel must have spent this time: travelling to meet people, to take information from them about their needs and intentions, to pass on instructions; working through contacts to set up transport systems; arranging rendezvous and hand-overs; liaising with *Prosper* about who was to have what; liaising with *Archambaud* and Jack Agazarian about messages sent and received on the radio; meeting now and again in the small group of five 'round a table' to discuss progress. Her sister says that often Andrée and *Prosper* would rendezvous in her flat in the Rue de Caumartin to exchange notes.

There was also the matter of training the people they recruited. As the arms and explosives began to arrive, *Prosper* and Andrée had to coach their helpers in the use of them. Through Jacques Bureau they found a secure room for their teaching sessions: he was a jazz enthusiast and connected to a famous jazz venue, the Hot Club in Montmartre; here, above the booking offices, tucked away in an upstairs room which no casual passer-by would have reason to know existed, Andrée and *Prosper* would instruct their French helpers in weaponry.

Yet there is a peculiar difficulty in trying to capture the essence of the Prosper agents' lives. In the circles which know or care about SOE, or about French Resistance, people have taken sides. For in the summer of 1943 the Prosper *réseau*, across all its extent, would suffer a devastating series of arrests – no one knows for sure, but it's estimated that 1,500 people were captured. All the central Prosper figures were to be among them and all were to be killed in the prisons or camps.

And ever since then, fellow resistants, agents and people with various interests in the story have been debating how it happened and who to blame. Inevitably, through these years of debate and speculation, the picture of the agents themselves has become unclear. They are not here to defend themselves against the accusation that they were careless.

Were they careless? Some people believe they were; they point to the fact that they met socially in Paris, had meals together and talked in cafés. There is certainly evidence that they had regular cafés where they were known: one was the Bar Lorraine in the Place des Ternes. There is also evidence that they met together: in the Tambour sisters' flat, in Andrée Borrel's sister's flat, in the home of Monsieur and Madame Guerne, Parisian resistants who worked with them, out near Versailles in the home of the principal of the *Ecole Nationale d'Agriculture* where they had a number of contacts. But was this really so rash? In every *réseau* there were places where members met to pass messages and hold meetings. Cafés and restaurants were very widely used for this. And agents had to eat, to talk about their worries, to relax: where better to do this than safe in the home of a fellow resistant? Francine's description of the meetings makes it clear that they were low-key affairs, very much concerned with the work in hand.

So much of how we interpret the agents' actions depends on hindsight. It is easy, years after the Prosper *réseau* was smashed, to look back at meetings like this and decide that they must have been arranged carelessly or too frequently. They might have been, certainly, but there is no direct evidence for this.

What does seem to be true is that *Prosper* and his fellow agents did not use the system of cut-outs in the same security-conscious way that some of the other *réseaux* used them. Whereas in some *réseaux* organizers kept the names and addresses of many contacts to themselves, the Prosper agents seem to have had a large degree of shared knowledge. But even so, they did not share everything by any means. Jacques Bureau says that he saw *Prosper* about once a week through the winter and spring of 1942 and 1943: often *Prosper* came to his house to have dinner with himself and his wife. Yet in all that time, he never met Andrée Borrel. *Archambaud* he met, because as radio operator *Archambaud* sometimes had to work directly with him, but not Andrée Borrel nor Jack or Francine Agazarian, because, he says, *Prosper* took care not to forge unnecessary contacts.

'*Prosper* was very security conscious. He told me that I should not know lots of different people because it was hazardous. So all the time I only knew *Prosper*, *Archambaud*, the Tambour sisters and

Armel Guerne. He was a very careful man.'

Not everyone agrees with him. I have heard rumblings from other former agents that *Prosper* spread his net too wide and too quickly. And to Rémy Clément, a man who came to work in Paris that spring, organizing clandestine landings and pick-ups, *Prosper* appeared 'a dangerous man'.

'His vision was too big. He wanted to be head of all the different groups. He was surrounded by too many people.'

But this is really a different criticism. The Prosper *réseau* was growing incredibly fast – but it was being encouraged to do so by Baker Street. Moreover, Baker Street was using the Prosper radios and communication channels for other *réseaux* too, forcing even more co-operation between *réseaux* than *Prosper* himself initiated. Up in St Quentin in the north-east, the Musician *réseau* was not provided with its own radio operator: from the time that the organizer, Biéler, arrived there in March 1943 he had to rely on Prosper's radios.

In Poitiers, Lise de Baissac had chosen not to have her own radio operator: it was a decision which helped to safeguard the position of herself and her helpers in Poitiers, but it did mean that she had to rely on two other *réseaux* for messages: one was Scientist, the other Prosper.

There was also the fact that agents continued to be sent into France through the Prosper channels and were given contacts from the same source: for instance, Yvonne Rudellat and Pierre Culioli received Ben Cowburn and his radio operator in April, when they arrived *en route* to Troyes. Reaching Troyes, Ben Cowburn's chief contact there proved to be a friend of Octave Simon, the organizer of Prosper sub-*réseau* Satirist. And so it went on.

And there was another factor which linked Prosper with other *réseaux*: the new agent in charge of landings and pick-ups, Henri Déricourt. By March he had met most of the inner circle of Prosper agents – *Prosper* himself, Andrée Borrel, *Archambaud* and Jack Agazarian. His first operation had taken place successfully on 17 March: it was a secret landing of two Lysanders which brought in four new agents and picked up another four. This very first flight of his had directly served the Prosper *réseau*; Francine Agazarian had arrived on it. Moreover, Déricourt had arranged the operation through the Prosper radios. It was to be the start of a long association between himself and Prosper and, had they but known it, this was where many of the Prosper agents' problems began.

Reading through the various second- and third-hand accounts of the Prosper adventures, I found it mentioned a number of times, usually in passing, that Andrée Borrel had been one of the few people not charmed by Déricourt. She never liked him. But they did not meet often and she was too busy with her own courier work for her feelings to become an issue; this was to prove a pity before the summer was out.

SIX

An Agent in Poitiers

Down in Poitiers, a university town just north of the demarcation line, Lise de Baissac was quietly running her own tiny *réseau*. She had no other SOE agent with her; she lived alone in a two-room apartment and was known to a few people in the town as a widow of quiet habits. It was a very different life from that of the Prosper agents, yet her work was vital to their organization and brought her into contact with many parts of it.

Her mission was to set up and run a reception *réseau* for incoming agents. Poitiers was conveniently situated for landing and dropping grounds: the wooded slopes of the Vienne provided good cover; the banks of the Loire, a favourite arrivals zone, could be reached within the hours of darkness. Lise de Baissac's job was to help agents who had just arrived in France and who would be told to look her up. She might have to arrange shelter for them, find contacts to help them on their way to their own *réseaux*, give them initial guidance on life in occupied France – identity requirements, ration cards, travel regulations and so on, 'To help them take their first steps in France,' was the way she described it.

It was a job which meant that she had to stay in one place, where she could be found. And this meant that she had to be absolutely secure, to establish herself in Poitiers without attracting the slightest attention or suspicion. She had to live quietly, so that the agents who passed through her hands went safely on their way, unwatched. She had to keep herself to herself, for if the authorities became curious about Lise de Baissac's activities, they might soon be able to trace the paths of many agents, leading to many corners of the French underground.

Lise de Baissac was thirty-seven when she dropped into France with Andrée Borrel. When I met her she was eighty-three, living in an apartment on the waterfront of the Vieux Port in Marseille. She is a widow now, Madame Villameur; the apartment was once the studio of her husband, an architect. I was taken aback by her appearance when she opened the door – she was so small and fragile, with white hair and a pretty face. I had been expecting someone more formidable. But within a few minutes it was obvious why F Section had chosen her for this job. She is vital but self-contained, generous but cool. 'I tell you frankly that I have no more interest in the war,' she said. 'Since it ended I don't like to spend my time thinking back to it. But I am quite happy to tell you whatever you want to know.' As soon as she began to talk to me, I could hear the Lise de Baissac for whom other people had tried to prepare me. I can't believe she has changed much over the years. Here was no '*garçon manqué*' but someone whose instinct was to do things quickly and well.

Like Andrée Borrel, Lise de Baissac had escaped from occupied France and come to England, but there the similarity ended. Lise de Baissac had been born in Mauritius, which made her technically British, although she had been brought up in France. She spent all her childhood in Paris and describes herself as 'French in feeling and in education'. She was very much a '*jeune fille bien élevée*' and once grown up she had continued to live a fulfilled and independent life in Paris. She was in her mid-thirties when the war started.

The German invasion and the flight of thousands of French troops and civilians from the north shocked her deeply. She watched the turmoil of those spring weeks in 1940, when half the country seemed to take to the roads, and felt that France was crumbling. 'I was very, very unhappy to see the retreat, the flight of large parts of the population – all the people from the north who fled before the Germans. I thought it was wrong to have done that, that one had to fight. It was painful, it was terrible to see the fall of France.' After the armistice she had not wanted to stay in a France half-occupied, half in collaboration with its occupiers. So she had made her way south and asked about the possibility of being repatriated to Britain.

At the same time as Lise de Baissac was making these arrangements and travelling, with many delays, through Spain and Portugal, her brother Claude was crossing the Pyrénées on foot and being imprisoned in Spain. They met up in Gibraltar where they and two thousand other refugees were finally able to sail for England on board a boat built for five hundred.

Arriving in England, they both began to look for war work and one of their cousins introduced Claude to SOE; he in turn recommended

Lise. She was interviewed by Captain Jepson and asked if she would be willing to go back to France as an agent. Lise was not a natural adventurer; as far as she could imagine the danger involved, she feared it. But she did not consider refusing. 'I said yes, why not? I am well qualified to do it. I know France well. I can help. Of course I was frightened of the danger but you know you always thought you would get through it and come out the other side. You always believed that no matter what happened it was others who would die but you, you would never die. Most people are like that; illness is something that happens to others, accidents happen to others. Anyway I found it natural to do what I could. It didn't occur to me to refuse.'

Lise trained in the second batch of F Section's women, with Odette Sansom, Jacqueline Nearne and Mary Herbert, and she was the first of them to go. She was physically petite, in manner calm and reserved, quietly and unquestionably committed to doing what she could.

Lise de Baissac is not one of the well-known heroines of SOE, but hers was one of the names which brought recognition and respect from every agent I spoke to. 'Oh yes! Lise de Baissac!' they would say. 'You must try to speak to her.'

In autumn 1942 F Section already had one de Baissac in the field: Claude had gone out at the end of July to start a *réseau*, Scientist, in Bordeaux. Now, with this underway and the plans for Prosper all ready to be implemented, F Section sent out Lise with instructions to establish herself midway between the two centres of Paris and Bordeaux. So on the night of 24 September she dropped with Andrée Borrel.

She fell through the air, suddenly silent after the noise of the aeroplane, and saw the ground come rushing up beneath her.

Lise wasn't a sentimental person; she didn't like heroics or grand gestures. But when she landed back on French soil, in that field near Mer-sur-Loire, she was moved with an unexpected passion:

'I had lived in France, you know, all my youth and when I was parachuted back into France and set my feet back on the soil of France, the land of France ... I felt a very powerful emotion. I felt something very strong from touching the land.'

She was back, to do what she could to liberate her country.

Where Andrée Borrel's mission in Prosper rapidly swept her up into a flurry of activity, Lise de Baissac's clandestine life was from the beginning careful and solitary. After the first few days in hiding with Andrée Borrel, acclimatizing to occupied France, she set off alone for her destination, Poitiers. She had the promise of a contact to come: one of the resistants who had received her in Mer-sur-Loire had told her of an auctioneer in Poitiers who was well-disposed towards the local Resistance groups. When he could get to Poitiers, he would introduce them; meanwhile, however, she was on her own.

So Lise de Baissac arrived in Poitiers 'all alone, knowing no one and with no local knowledge, with my little case in my hand,' and began to play out her cover story, that of Madame Irène Brisse. Madame Brisse was a widow from Paris who had regretfully decided that life in the capital was now too difficult for her; so she had come to live in Poitiers, attracted by the civilized ambience of the university town and by the fine old churches and buildings in the surrounding countryside, which she planned to visit.

In this guise she went to the *syndicat d'initiative*, the first port of call for all newcomers, and enquired about rooms to let. She was directed to a likely address and here she went through her first few moments of real fear, when her landlady seemed to be scrutinizing her papers with unnecessary attention. 'She looked at me and said "You understand, there are so many false ones about that I have to be very careful." It was indeed false but she thought it was genuine! It was a really unnerving experience.'

Lise settled in to her room and soon afterwards the resistant from Mer-sur-Loire came into Poitiers and took her to meet the auctioneer, Monsieur Gateau. He was a kind man and eager to play his part in the Resistance. And now, discreetly, slowly, Lise de Baissac's resistance life began. Monsieur Gateau helped her find a pleasant two-room apartment which removed her from the inquisitive eyes of landladies and fellow lodgers. He introduced her to a person here, another there, willing to help. She bought a bicycle on which to cycle round the countryside looking for landing and dropping grounds.

But despite Monsieur Gateau and his family, who made her welcome as a friend, she was extremely lonely. She had decided while still in England that she did not want a radio operator with her – she thought it was too risky for an operation as immobile as hers. Nor did she have a courier: instead she was to rely upon the couriers or contacts of other people seeking her out to bring her messages from England, and she would go herself to rendezvous with other *réseaux* when she had information to pass on. It was the safest arrangement, or seemed so at the time.

But now that she had to begin her mission, she found that her isolation weighed heavily on her. The first few weeks, for instance, when she was cycling round looking for landing and dropping grounds, meant miles of solitary cycling through country lanes; hours of fruitless searching. Then, when she found a possible ground, she would embark on a wary conversation with its owners – perhaps on the pretext of trying to buy eggs or milk, or asking directions – gauging their sympathies, approaching the subject of the Resistance, never giving away more than she had to. If the people agreed to let their land be used, she passed the information to another of her local helpers and kept herself at arm's length from then on. She could not afford to be directly involved herself: too much was at risk should she be caught.

It was a slow process, finding people to help her. She was by no means without contacts in northern France: in and around Paris were many people she had known for years. The problem was, how to find those she felt sure would help and at the same time keep out of the way of others? Like other agents, she let her instincts guide her. Her first approach that autumn was a lucky one:

> I met an old friend of mine, Savy, on a train. I knew him very well; I knew what he was like. I said, 'Here I am!' and he said, 'I thought you'd left.' I said, 'Yes, I left and now I've come back; would you like to help?' He said, 'I should think so! For a long time now I've been trying to find out who to go to.' He was very active. He went to England eventually and did very good work.

But it was not always so easy. Nor was it always possible to predict where people from her former life would turn up. Once, sitting in a restaurant in Poitiers, she saw a man she had known in Paris. It was unexpected seeing him there, but he had been a good friend and she trusted him: she decided that she would approach him:

> I sent him a short note via the waiter. He saw me; he was alone and afterwards I went over to his table and told him what I was doing. I said, 'Are you interested?' and he said, 'Definitely not. I have *eight* children to look after, four of my own and four of my brother's who's dead. I can't put them at risk.' I understood – I knew he couldn't help me but I knew he wouldn't do anything to hurt me. It was difficult for people with children and families. They didn't want to endanger their lives.

And then there was always the danger that seeing people from her former life could be positively dangerous. Many, many people in France at this time were ill-disposed towards the Resistance – maybe because they were Pétainistes, maybe because they believed the Resistance to be composed of thugs and gangsters. (Vichy and German propaganda promoted this belief to good effect.) If such a person who had known Lise in the past came across her now, mysteriously repatriated in France and living under a false name, the meeting could prove fatal for her.

Paris was the most perilous place for Lise, with all her pre-war contacts, but she could not avoid going there. Because she didn't have her own radio set, she had to contact London through the Prosper radios in Paris. Later she would use the Scientist radios in Bordeaux but in the late autumn and winter of 1942 she went several times to Paris to rendezvous with contacts and pass and collect messages. As she walked through the streets and waited in cafés she had continually to keep her eyes open for people she knew: if she saw them first, she had a chance to turn away before they recognized her. She was careful but even so she could not guarantee her own safety: one day she saw a boy she knew and realized that he too had seen her. She didn't trust him so she pretended not to recognize him and tried to slip away among the other people but he began to follow her. She quickened her pace; so did he. He began running after her, apparently determined to stop her and, afraid, she ran too, darting in and out of the crowds until she managed to get into another street, away from him. She had succeeded in losing him but the incident left her shaken.

Back in Poitiers she was safer. There, being conspicuous was not her problem. Poitiers was a university town; it was also near the demarcation line and so had long been a centre for German troops. At the beginning of November, of course, the Germans crossed the line into the south, but the two zones still officially existed and Poitiers remained an important centre for travellers. There were many people passing through it all the time and Madame Irène Brisse attracted no one's attention: she was accepted as 'just another woman who had left Paris for the more peaceful provinces. *Bon. C'est tout.*'

So, quietly, with long periods of waiting in between isolated bits of action, Lise de Baissac took her place in the growing network of F Section agents in France.

Her *réseau*, Artist, played its first active part in SOE operations in October. It was not what Lise expected, for instead of hearing that her first agent was on the way she was given a message that F Section intended to make an arms drop in her area. She was not equipped to receive arms drops and she spent an anxious few days alerting all her local contacts and taking out her bicycle again to see if

she could find somewhere suitable to store them. Eventually she found
a farmer who could receive the drop in his field and store the arms in
his farm buildings. Lise was not to be present herself at the reception
– throughout her mission she was to observe strict security and keep
away from the physical operations – so she had to give instructions on
the procedure for reception committees – the security rules of silence
and small numbers, the flashing of the agreed letter in morse, with
a torch, as the aircraft flew overhead; the transporting of arms and
burying of the mini-parachutes which carried them down.

On the night of the drop, Lise was discreetly and blamelessly
at home, waiting anxiously for news. When it came, it was good: the
reception had been successful and the arms were safely stored. So
far, so good.

But receiving arms drops was not Lise's job; receiving agents
was. Now she was brought a message that her first agent was due:
it was France Antelme, a Mauritian businessman who dropped in
November. He was a vivid character – he had already worked for SOE
in Madagascar – and his arrival stands out in Lise de Baissac's memory
from the weeks of waiting and standing by which characterized that
autumn. He came to her flat slightly dazed from his short experience
of occupied France. She took him in and quickly realized that he did
not know France at all. Although, as a Mauritian, he spoke French
very well, the ways of the country itself were foreign to him.

'He had never been to France. He didn't know it at all. He
was a little lost.'

Lise kept him with her for quite a while, coaching him in French
manners and the documentation he would need to understand,
explaining about the exigencies of the occupation and the sub-culture
which arose from them – the intricacies of ration cards and the black
market, for instance. Then, once he was ready, half sorry to see him
go, she passed him on to Savy, the old friend in Paris who had been
her first recruit.

'He looked after him as I had been looked after by Monsieur
Gateau the auctioneer, you understand. One introduced him to
people and then he left because he had to make a start on his
work.'

Autumn became winter and now and then other agents made their
way to Lise's door, directed there by contacts in the field or by Baker
Street. They were looking for various things from her – her advice,
some contacts, perhaps some ration cards or other documents; once
they had them they moved swiftly on towards their destinations.
Sometimes Lise had been told of their coming and helped arrange

their receptions; at other times they were dropped blind and turned up unannounced. None of them stayed long enough to become comrades.

But as 1942 turned into 1943, Lise de Baissac occupied herself mainly by waiting for instructions, alone. Yet the *réseaux* around her were starting to grow and flex their muscles. North and east of her the Prosper *réseau* grew; south of her, around Bordeaux, her brother's Scientist *réseau* was spreading rapidly. Poised in between the two, Lise de Baissac carried and received messages, fed agents to contacts, kept the channels of communication open. Hers was a quiet place in the eye of the storm.

Her life in early 1943 could hardly have been more different from that of Andrée Borrel or Yvonne Rudellat, although her work touched on theirs at so many points. Andrée had *Prosper* and the other agents in Paris as close comrades; Yvonne worked together with Pierre Culioli and small groups of local Resistants. Both of these women, too, were active in a way Lise de Baissac was not: Andrée visited scattered groups, attended night-time drops, instructed resistants in weaponry. Yvonne, come the late spring, would be busy carrying out sabotage raids. They were in the mainstream of Resistance activity: for them, now that more agents were arriving and arms were pouring out of the sky on almost every moonlit night, matters were advancing.

For Lise de Baissac, though, 1943 continued as 1942 had done: she worked carefully and mostly in isolation. The agents she received came and went – they added to other people's *réseaux* but not to hers. Her life in Poitiers was as lonely as that of some radio operators.

'I was very lonely. Very, very lonely. You grew to know very well what solitude was. Because you are alone; you have false papers; you never have a telephone call; you never get a letter.'

Her closest friends were the auctioneer Monsieur Gateau and his family. They lived near her and provided a respite from the solitude and strain of her mission. 'Really, it was as if I were a part of his family. I didn't live with them because it wasn't possible but when, for instance, they had some eggs, they gave me two. That sort of thing helped me a lot and they helped my morale too because you had to talk – at least to those you could talk to. I couldn't tell them everything because I didn't want to risk compromising them but all the same they knew I was there to help the Resistance and so I could talk to them a little.'

She filled her time by taking private Spanish lessons with a professor from the university, a refugee from Franco's Spain. Through him she met another teacher, 'a very nice woman', who also became a friend. But these friends knew her only as Madame Brisse; they knew nothing of her Resistance activities and friendly as they were she had to be on guard when she was with them: she could not relax and let her true concerns show through.

There was an occasional contact, apart from the Gateaux, which combined personal friendship with Resistance work: that was her brother's courier, Mary Herbert. Mary Herbert was an Englishwoman in her thirties who had trained with Lise; she had been landed on the south coast of France by felucca at the start of October and had made her way to Bordeaux to work in Scientist. Now she sometimes came to Poitiers to bring messages to Lise and to carry others from Lise back to the Scientist radio operator, for transmission to London. Lise liked Mary Herbert; her visits were a rare opportunity for Lise to talk to someone who was both a friend and a comrade. Even between these two, however, there were subjects they did not raise for security's sake.

At other times, Lise would herself go down to Bordeaux to take messages to her brother. She usually made her way to a café in which he had a special corner and where he generally passed by every day. The owners of the café were friendly to the Resistance: they knew Lise by sight and they knew she was a comrade of Claude's; keeping their heads down, they never asked for more information. She would sit and wait for Claude, sometimes all day, sometimes even into the night: she rarely left notes for him; it was dangerous and in any case she usually memorized her messages and carried them verbally. Instead she would sit like many other people who were bored or cold or simply enjoyed sitting in cafés, an unobtrusive figure whiling away the hours. It was not, after all, as if she had any great claims on her time.

So this was the rhythm of her days. But in fact the work that Lise de Baissac did as organizer and sole member of Artist had great significance, especially for the fortunes of Prosper. After the new year and the sudden speeding up of activity in the Prosper *réseau*, Lise saw more agents coming in and turning to her for help. And in February she helped the new air movements agent, Déricourt, mount his first landing and pick-up operation. It marked a breakthrough in the way that Baker Street and the agents were able to communicate.

Lise became involved with Déricourt after a rendezvous with her brother Claude, in February, who told her that he and a few others had to return to England urgently to make reports; would she help to arrange it? Lise knew that the new agent Déricourt had been infiltrated into France and was based in Paris; through her contacts she got in touch with him and passed on her brother's request.

Between them Déricourt and Lise organized a double Lysander operation, using Prosper radios to communicate with Baker Street. Déricourt sent his newly-recruited assistant, Rémy Clément, into Lise's region of the Vienne to look for possible grounds. A field near Poitiers was chosen as the landing ground and its co-ordinates passed to London; a date was fixed during the next moon period. Déricourt was to handle most of the arrangements for the landing ground and the aircraft; Lise was to liaise with her brother and other would-be passengers as they prepared to leave, and she was to be ready to receive new agents who would be brought in by the same operation.

It was settled that this first operation would take place on the night of 17 March. F Section would be sending four new agents in to France, using two planes; these would also pick up a total of four others currently in the field and fly them back to England. It was a risky operation: the planes used would be Lysanders, which could take off and land with hardly any run-in. They were quiet too, but they were tiny and could only take two or three passengers at the most, so there would have to be two of them, landing one after another. The operation required a lot of organizing at all levels, to make sure that the agents would be gathered together and waiting to leave at the right time, that the landing ground would be free from obstacles and that the new arrivals could be taken swiftly from the landing ground to safety.

Lise met Déricourt during the course of these preparations. Her contact with him was brief but she took to him; he seemed both efficient and pleasant and she had no misgivings about him.

'I found him very agreeable, Déricourt,' she said musingly, thinking back. 'I liked him a lot. He was very courteous and charming.'

The night of 17 March came and the operation, thoroughly planned and much worried about, was at hand. Listening to her household wireless, Lise heard the cryptic go-ahead message read out on the BBC *Messages Personnels*: the flight was on for tonight. She was staying in her apartment that evening, out of the direct action; she wondered how it would go.

The agents had all converged on Poitiers already and had been taken to meet Déricourt who was running this first pick-up himself. Claude had gone, and with him France Antelme, also returning to London with information. The third agent was slightly known to Lise, too, as she had been given his name as someone to contact when she first arrived: it was *Gaspard*, recalled by Baker Street. The fourth traveller she did not know. Now the operation was in the hands of Déricourt and the pilots.

In the field chosen as the landing ground, Déricourt was preparing the reception. The procedure for guiding in the planes and receiving the passengers was fairly simple, but it relied for its success on accurate timing and a landing ground free of obstacles.

The organizer of the reception – this time, Déricourt – placed a number of bicycle lamps or torches on the ground to form a horizontal line several hundred yards long, and running against the wind. At the far end of the line another lamp (or two) was placed at a 90° angle, and to the right-hand side, to form a short axis. With the bulbs illuminated, the improvised runway could be seen from the air. When the aircraft was heard flying overhead, the organizer went to the start of the horizontal line and turned on a hand torch, directing its beam to the sky. He flashed up a morse letter, pre-arranged over the radio and expected by the pilot. If the pilot did not see this signal, he wouldn't bring the plane down. If he did see it, he flashed back another agreed letter in return; then the organizer and his helpers (usually the agents waiting to leave) turned on the bicycle lamps, illuminating the 'runway' so it could be seen from the air. The pilot brought the plane down, touching down at the start of the horizontal line, taxi-ing along it, turning at the end and returning slowly to the starting-point.

Then the passengers would jump down from the plane; the departing agents would take their places and within minutes the plane would move off again, running down the line into the wind for take-off, climbing steeply from the ground over bushes and trees into the night sky.

This was Déricourt's first operation, and Lise's, and both they and the staff at Baker Street were apprehensive. Clandestine landings and pick-ups had been done before in the unoccupied zone, but this was a complicated one, involving two craft. Moreover, a lot hinged on it: if all went well, a valuable new route in and out of France would be established.

The first Lise knew about the operation's success was when the new agents arrived at her apartment. The two small, bug-like Lysanders had brought in four of them, three men and a woman. They reached Lise's apartment without mishap and she took them in. They were all bound for independent missions and they did not stay long. In Lise's words: 'They settled down with a little bit of comfort and then the next day each one went his own way.' The woman among them went on her way to Paris: she was Francine Agazarian and had come to join her husband Jack and the other agents in Prosper.

It had been a successful operation and an important one. More like it would follow, though Lise would not be involved in them.

With this one over, apparently undetected, Lise resumed her exacting, enforced seclusion. It is hard to convey the boredom and loneliness of her life and yet to keep a sense of the tension and the importance of her work. For it was important – it was Lise's efficiency and continued camouflage which allowed many agents to do their work in the face of the dangers and accidents which befell them.

At the end of March, for instance, three agents, Garel, Rousset and Fox, were dropped blind to start a Prosper sub-*réseau* in the Sarthe. When they landed, Rousset found that he had lost his radio set in the drop. Without it their *réseau* was stillborn. So he went to Lise de Baissac; she got a message through to the Prosper radio in Paris asking for a replacement set to be dropped. Baker Street received the message and rapidly despatched another set by one of the night-time arms drops: by May, the sub-*réseau* Butler was up and running, just beginning to make its sabotage raids on the railways of the Sarthe.

That was typical of the tasks Lise de Baissac undertook: in her way she was like a more discreet Virginia Hall, doing for the new *réseaux* of 1943 what Virginia Hall had done for the unoccupied zone in 1941 and 1942.

And the new *réseaux* were growing fast – thanks partly to Déricourt's operations. For following the success of the March operation, not only were agents dropped into northern France at an ever faster rate, but in almost every monthly moon period a Lysander – or a pair of them – brought in new arrivals, sometimes carrying other agents back in their place. By the end of May, thirteen agents would have arrived this way. Lise de Baissac saw only some of them and then for only short periods before they slipped away. But as she worked quietly and carefully in Poitiers a giant network was spreading out around her – and a trap.

SEVEN

Odette's Mission

Before we move on to unravel the intricacies, plots and double-plots which lie behind the Prosper and Déricourt affair, there is one other woman's story still to be brought in: Odette's.

Odette's story is one of the better-known ones: a book has been written about her and a film has been made. For a generation growing up immediately after the war she was a familiar heroine. The details of her story are less well-known now. When I began my research I recognized her name but that was all: when I met her she was to me just as interesting, no more no less, than the other women I was meeting. In conversation she spoke a lot of the other women – those she trained with, those she met later in captivity – and a lot of the people at SOE in Baker Street. She too had her place in the pattern.

It is not a connection often made, for Odette was working down in the south-east of France far from Prosper in the north. But all the same the fates of her *réseau* and of the Prosper agents were to interlock at several vital points.

Odette's time in France runs concurrent with that of Andrée Borrel, Yvonne Rudellat and Lise de Baissac. She went into France by sea at the end of October 1942. A felucca brought her and four other agents to the Mediterranean coast of France on the night of Hallowe'en, 31 October: it was a moonless night and they put ashore near the harbour of Cassis, some miles east of Marseille.

At this stage in the occupation, the unoccupied zone was still free of Germans – just. Within ten days they would have marched over the demarcation line and the Italians would be flowing in from the east – to occupy the south-eastern regions of France – official retaliation for the Allied landings in North Africa. But at the turn of the month the illusory autonomy of the unoccupied zone still held; the Mediterranean coast was inadequately guarded by the Vichy police and agents were still coming in to southern France and fugitives leaving by sea. Virginia Hall was still in place in Lyon, working her web of contacts, and the agents who F Section had been sending in throughout the spring and summer were scattered across the country, evading arrest and struggling to establish working *réseaux*.

Landing on the almost-deserted shore with Odette on that autumn night were two other women and two men. One of the women was Mary Herbert, who would join Claude de Baissac in Bordeaux.

The other was a French woman in her fifties, Marie-Thérèse Le Chêne. She had instructions to go to Lyon, where her husband, Henri Le Chêne, was running a small *réseau* producing Resistance propaganda.

The men were George Starr, who would start a *réseau* over in the south-western corner of France, and Marcus Bloom, a radio operator bound for Toulouse.

Not that they knew these facts about each other: security had prevented them from discussing their missions or their destinations. They were only travelling companions, more or less anonymous comrades with their minds now turning, as they landed, to their own instructions.

Odette did not expect to stay long in this part of France. The mission she had been given was to go northward, across the demarcation line into the occupied zone and the hill country of the Auxerre, where she was to settle and start up her own *réseau*. The group was now told by the men who came forward to meet them that they were to go first to Cannes; Odette did not suspect that she would be staying there.

Odette Sansom was thirty and had three young daughters back in England. She was French but when she was eighteen she had married an Englishman, the son of an old First World War comrade of her father's, and had gone to live with him in England. In 1942 Odette's husband was away in the armed forces and she had moved out of London and was living with her daughters in Somerset.

She was recruited into SOE by chance. Answering an appeal for people with knowledge of French to contact the War Office, and imagining they wanted translators, she found herself called for interview and listening to the proposition that she return to France for undercover work. Her first instinct was to refuse. She had been told something of the nature of the work and she simply did not think she could do it; besides, there were her daughters to consider. She said no and went back to Somerset.

But from the start of the war she had been haunted by the fact that in France her mother and the rest of her family were once more suffering invasion and occupation. And now as more bad news came from France she began to doubt her decision:

> I thought, Oh I don't know ... I was torturing myself about what's right, what's wrong, and I think – perhaps if I do the training, they will see that I'm not right, and at least I will come back then feeling it's been done and I'm no good, and I will be satisfied.
>
> By that time I knew about the work of course because they had told me more or less what would be expected. I was so sure that I could not do the training anyway and I would be back, able to pass on to something more practical, and that's how it happened.

The training, however, with all its inductions into the French way of life, made her think it might be possible:

> I started thinking I could be useful because I definitely felt I could disappear in France. After all, it was the country of my birth; I could mix with people well. I felt if I could work almost alone I would last for ever. I did; I felt that, I felt I could be useful that way.

At the end of training, Odette agreed to go if she might be given a mission as self-sufficient as possible. She had misgivings about working with a large group, but she believed that on her own she could fit in very well and gather helpers around her without attracting attention.

Now SOE had to decide whether or not to take her. The final report from the training schools advised against it; the instructors found her too self-willed and intractable. Jerrard Tickell, who wrote the 1940s book on Odette, had access to the schools' reports and quotes from one, written in August 1942:

> *Céline* [her training code-name] has enthusiasm and seems to have absorbed the teaching given on the course. She is, however, impulsive and hasty in her judgements and has not quite the clarity of mind which is desirable in subversive activity.

> She seems to have little experience of the outside world.
> She is excitable and temperamental, although she has a
> certain determination.
> A likeable character and gets on well with most people.
> Her main asset is her patriotism and keenness to do
> something for France; her main weakness is a complete
> unwillingness to admit that she could ever be wrong.

This was no one-off impression. You don't have to speak to Odette
for twenty seconds to see that 'a certain determination' is a cool
understatement. And when Maurice Buckmaster decided that despite
these reports she should go to France, it was not because of any
hidden faith in her malleability. All these years later, he speaks with
a mixture of respect and resignation of Odette's 'terrible *managing*
character, her masterly character. She did it her way and that was
it.'

But F Section decided to accept her nevertheless, and to turn her
managing traits to advantage by sending her in to start a *réseau* on her
own: she was to go to Auxerre and begin recruiting people for a circuit
she would then run. Her mission was agreed, including the diplomatic
(and very French) manoeuvre that to save male feelings she would run
the *réseau* at one remove, with a French man as figure-head. She was
provided with a cover story as a war widow, and arrangements were
made for her three daughters to be looked after in a convent school.
Then it was time to leave.

In the course of my researches a number of agents (all male)
asked me curiously what Odette had said about leaving her children. How could she have done it? They seemed to think that her
emotions must have been complex, labyrinthine to allow her both to
love her daughters and to leave them, with only a 50 per cent chance
of coming back. But though the choice was a difficult one to make,
the feelings which attended it were not.

'It's a mistake when people say that in captivity I was courageous.
It wasn't then that I was – it was the day I left this country. I left it
with a broken heart. And I knew that nothing else that happened to
me would ever be that painful; and it never was.'

So, Odette, thirty years old, French born and bred, mother of three,
a determined, quietly wilful character, was on her way into occupied
France to become an agent. The journey by air from England to
Gibraltar, then by sea from Gibraltar to Cassis, lasted days. When
Odette and her fellow travellers finally stepped off the coastal train
at Cannes they were tired, dirty and uncomfortable. They looked an

incongruous bunch as they were taken through the town, for Cannes had kept its holiday character despite the war: in fact, war had filled its streets, cafés and clubs with moneyed refugees from the occupied north. Beauty salons and fashion shops and expensive pâtisseries continued to ply their trade, albeit with some rather strange raw materials in their products. It was through the back entrance of a beauty salon that the agents' guide now led them, into a room where they were met by the organizer of the Cannes *réseau*, a young man called Peter Churchill.

The newly-arrived male agents were soon taken off to another safe house, to be rested and sent on their way. The three women stayed in the rooms behind the beauty salon, having a brief respite before they went off in different directions on their own missions.

Peter Churchill wrote several books of memoirs and in one of them[1] he described his first impressions of the three women. Mary Herbert struck him as frail and very obviously English – he had doubts about her stamina and wondered how she would survive the rigours of underground life. Oddly and ironically enough, she reminded him of a very young male agent who had recently come out to the south of France, and whom he thought too frail for the work as well: in the event both of them would show their resilience in different ways.

Marie-Thérèse Le Chêne he described as a grey-haired woman, full of common sense and humour.

His first impression of Odette seems to have been something of a *coup de foudre*: telling the story not long after the war, by which time he and Odette were married, he wrote lyrically of the determination, self-reliance and sheer force of character which blasted themselves into his consciousness. Poetic licence? Romantic licence in retrospect? Maybe, but there must have been a good deal of truth in the account, because within a few days he had asked Odette to stay and work for him in Cannes.

The situation in the south-east of France was unpropitious for organized Resistance. Down on the Côte d'Azur the towns were full of people who had fled the occupation and were making themselves an alternative, affluent life in the south. The black market was everywhere, providing for those with money; there was constant movement of people in and out of the towns; in the countryside and towns alike, many people were Pétainist while the groups of potential resistants which had formed were utterly disorganized and often embroiled in

[1] *Duel of Wits*, Peter Churchill, Hodder & Stoughton, 1953

fierce rivalries with one another. There had been SOE activity down on the coast ever since the autumn of 1941: in that time *Olive* had built up the *réseau* Urchin round Antibes, and had begun to liaise with the French Resistance organizer *Carte*, in whom SOE were so interested.

The staff of F Section were keen to bring the Carte organization under their control. They had sent Peter Churchill into France in January, on a reconnaissance trip to meet *Carte* himself and assess his network. On his return, Peter Churchill had reported that there seemed to be a possibility of working with the organization. Discussions had gone on repeatedly in Baker Street and in August F Section had sent out its own deputy head Nicolas Bodington, to look further into the potential for co-operation. *Carte* himself had talked to Bodington and assured him that the people working under him were ready to form active sabotage teams, and that eventually he could raise 300,000 active resistants.

So at the end of August 1942 Peter Churchill had been sent back in to France to act as the liaison between the Carte organization and Baker Street. But when he arrived the real difficulties of his mission became apparent. For one thing, *Olive* had just been arrested and Peter Churchill had to take over the remains of his *réseau*; now as well as liaising between Carte and Baker Street he had to make plans for receiving arms and explosives and directing sabotage forays. For another, *Carte* proved very difficult: he gave long messages to the *réseau*'s radio operator and refused to shorten them, despite the dangers of staying on the air for too long. He was jealous of any possible piece of action which might take place in the region and insisted on supervising everything personally. And though he was happy to talk and plan at length, his well-disciplined teams of resistants failed to materialize.

By the end of October, Peter Churchill was frustrated at the delays and worried by the lack of security among *Carte*'s followers. He had found some good local helpers, including a woman known as 'Suzanne' who ran a beauty salon and worked secretly as his secretary. He had also got himself a new radio operator, a young, aggressive man called Adam Rabinovitz and known by his code-name *Arnaud*. But he was still badly in need of a reliable courier, which was where Odette came in.

Perhaps it was inevitable that, being forced to stay a few days in Cannes to wait for some extra identity papers, Odette would end up working with Peter Churchill and *Arnaud*. They were hard pressed: she agreed to do some courier work for them while she waited to leave for Auxerre. But she was not happy with the circumstances she found herself in and she didn't like Cannes. Its population was too transitory and too heedless to make life for Resistance workers secure: the contacts of Peter Churchill's she met in these 'temporary' days were too flamboyant.

Her first task for Peter Churchill proved a sharp contrast to the kind of retiring life she looked forward to in the Auxerre. Agreeing to help him out, she found herself taking a train to the bustling, dangerous city of Marseille. Marseille had been a lively place even in peacetime: besides the respectable residential and commercial areas of the large city there existed the illicit life of a major port, with a flourishing criminal element, brothels, mean streets, minor and major smuggling activities and all the police pressure they engender. In wartime, Marseille's underground life had grown threefold − along with the old illicit trades there was now the black market, the forging of documents and ration cards, escape lines and other Resistance work. There were also informers and people prepared to profit from both sides in any way they could. It was difficult to know who was truly trustworthy; hard to find a channel of communication through this underground that would not deliver you to the enemy. And, of course, now the gendarmes and the Vichy security forces were also the enemy.

Odette's first trip to Marseille involved making contact with a man there and handing over a briefcase full of money. It was dangerous to be carrying money anyway, but when she arrived at the address she had been given the contact was not in. She had to kill hours of time: she went to a cinema and saw a film, sat in cafés, walked around, always with the incriminating case full of notes. Eventually she returned to the address and this time made the contact; she was then directed to another contact at another address, a café. By the time she had finally met the right person and handed over the case, she had missed the last train back and was in danger of being caught by the curfew. She considered sleeping in the station but her contact dissuaded her: he told her that in Marseille the police regularly conducted *rafles* at the stations, arresting people they found there, sometimes even sending them off for deportation to the factories in Germany. He proposed an alternative: he knew of a brothel where she might be able to find shelter.

So Odette's induction into Resistance life in the south went on, very different from the way she had imagined herself settling in to her mission:

> 'It was a house mostly for the Germans,' she remembered.
> 'There was a woman there when I arrived. I said, "Have you
> got a bed?" She looked at me, she said, "Huh! A bed for the

night. Do you know what we are?" I said, "Yes, it's obvious –
Heure du Paradis!" And I said, "Yes I do realize, that's why
I'm here. Can you put me away somewhere tonight quietly?"
And then she realized and she said, "Yes, all right."

'You know funnily enough those women, that type, were
nearly always on our side. They were very good, very very
good. Anyway, there I was. I spent the night there, came
down in the morning, there was a gendarme at the desk! I
thought "Ohh!" because you were supposed to see in the
book who'd been there. But I laughed my way out of it and
it was all right.'

When Odette returned to Cannes, Peter Churchill asked her if she
would consider staying and working with him. She was not keen on
the idea but now the North Africa landings had happened, the Germans had crossed the demarcation line and their Allies, the Italians,
were arriving along the Côte d'Azur. Agents who heard they were
known to the Gestapo were fleeing. The safety of the *réseaux* had
become an even more brittle thing and when *Arnaud* transmitted Peter
Churchill's request to keep Odette working with him, the coded order
came back from England that she was to stay, and work as courier in
Peter Churchill's *réseau*, now given the name Spindle.

So Odette came to be a courier on the Riviera, travelling regularly along the coast to Marseille with messages and codes, carrying
communications to Carte contacts around the 'unoccupied' zone,
bearing messages when necessary for other SOE organizers and radio
operators south of the line. It was work which was difficult to do in
the circumstances of disorganization and fear which now prevailed.
Men were being picked up more regularly – especially in cities like
Marseille – and sent off to Germany; the people of southern France
were uncertain whom to trust. The demarcation line was officially
'relaxed' and some trains began to run once more across it, but
communications between the zones were still difficult.

Odette's time in Cannes was fraught with anxiety and frustrations:

Cannes was not a place which lent itself to that kind of
Resistance work. It's a playground, Cannes, always has been
and so you had to be more careful, because a lot of people
didn't want to be involved.

And really the group, I wasn't happy about the security.
Not at all. There were too many and some of them were too
ostentatious and flamboyant, especially on the French side.

* * *

She did her best to limit her contact with the members of the
group, insisting on using cut-outs in approved SOE style and trying
to avoid meeting certain of the leaders. But it wasn't always possible
– the local resistants were untrained in security and Odette, who had
wanted to work alone, found herself going from one contact to another
and forging links she had no desire to forge.

By contrast, the relationship between Odette, Peter Churchill
and *Arnaud* was very close. They saw a good deal of each other:
Peter Churchill worked closely with both *Arnaud* and Odette; Odette
and he together did their best to keep *Arnaud* in safety and supplied
with food. All three of them knew the frustrations of dealing with the
Carte organization and were thrown back on one another for support
and practical help.

It's evident from the way that Odette speaks about the other
two that there was a dynamic between them. They were by no
means similar personalities: Peter Churchill was an outgoing character who thrived on action; *Arnaud* was an independent, dogged
young man with a violent temper; and there is controversy about
Odette as there is about many of the people whose missions ran
into trouble. Every source agrees on her strength of will and spirit.
But some people see her as the adventuring kind, while she herself
talks continually, almost obsessively, of her longing for anonymity and
security.

Which version is true? Experiences do become altered in the memory
and in the repeated telling, especially over nearly half a century. But
then, Odette was there on the south coast and the people who put
forward hostile assessments of her were not there – they were usually
elsewhere in France, hearing things at second or third hand, often
months or years after the event. Peter Churchill's memoirs present a
fierce Odette, but also a fiercely controlled and conscientious one.

And Odette in her turn is still swift to talk about Peter Churchill
and *Arnaud* as a team she respected and admired:

> I must say I admired the way Peter worked, and *Arnaud*.
> Those two were wonderful. They were both very dedicated.
> *Arnaud* was like me, he couldn't stand the insecurity, but
> there you are, he did his work very well. He and Peter
> were very close to each other.

As for Odette, although her base was with the other two in Cannes,
she was often on the move. Her journeys were long and repetitive,
full of discomforts and dangers. They were also very often thwarted.
Odette's memories of them are bleak: for her they were an endless

compounding of anxiety, discomfort and tedium – run through with
the presence of danger:

> You take a train from Cannes to Marseille for example;
> if you are lucky, your false papers are good enough to pass
> the test when you arrive at Marseille. You always wonder
> if you are going to.
>
> You spent a lot of time waiting for things to happen
> that didn't. You spent a lot of time going to places to
> realize something that you could not realize. I travelled to
> Paris once in the engine of a train because I did not have
> the special permit. I arrived in Paris black from head to
> foot, tidied myself as best I could, and all that for nothing
> because the man I was supposeed to contact never turned
> up. Then you've got to bring yourself back to base.
>
> Then you spent horrible nights in different places, like
> that bordel in Marseille. Again, I was sent to Marseille once
> and I had to bring back some messages for *Arnaud* that had
> to be sent the next day. Well, there wasn't any train to bring
> me back that night. So I knew of somebody who had one
> of those cars that used to work with a special contraption
> attached to them, and we came back through the Esterel
> at night. We were stopped first by the police who asked what
> we were doing there and I said I was rushing to my young
> son who had been taken ill. They said, Oh yes, yes and let
> us go on. Then when we arrived in Cannes we had to stay
> tucked away because we had arrived too early and again we
> could not be seen before the curfew was lifted. It was all
> uncomfortable; it was horrible in a way.

Amid this discomfort, and the insidious tedium which dulled the
senses, moments of acute danger could spring up. It was bad enough
to have to go through a routine papers check with false papers,
but there were greater dangers for a courier who was carrying
incriminating messages – or even worse, a radio set. Being a woman
and physically small, Odette escaped the attention of the *rafles* and
of the security forces on the look out for likely resistants. But she
attracted a different kind of attention which could be just as fatal,
and there was no guarding against this. On the train to Marseille
one day, carrying *Arnaud*'s heavy radio set concealed in its case, she
was noticed by a group of German officers:

> The train was full of Germans, so I was standing in

the corridor near a compartment reserved for German
officers. One of them opened the door and asked me
in and *lifted* that suitcase in the luggage. I thought – my
God, he's going to ask if I am carrying gold! Because the
size of the suitcase did not correspond with the weight! –
and I thought, when we arrive in Marseille he's going to
say to someone, you'd better open that suitcase. So then,
when we arrived in Marseille he took it down again – he
could hardly lift it – and handed it back to me!

Looking after *Arnaud* and his radio set was one of Odette's first
priorities:

I used to have to find new houses for him because he would
use a house maybe, with luck, three days at the most. It was
the limit. Sometimes twice, sometimes once. So to get new
people all the time who would accept him – it was very
dangerous for the people who let him use their house for
sending his messages. So that was almost a full-time job,
finding people.

He also had to be kept fed, despite his official non-existence and
the difficulties of rationing. 'In Cannes it was extremely difficult to
find enough food to feed *Arnaud*. Because Cannes doesn't produce
anything but flowers, you know. *Arnaud* was always starving.'
    So, beset by difficulties and frustrations, Odette and Peter Churchill
and *Arnaud* survived in Cannes through the autumn months and into
winter, and struggled to make some progress with their mission.

This was not easy, for the Carte organization was beginning to
disintegrate under its own internal pressures. Its leader, *Carte* (André
Girard), was quarrelling furiously with his second in command, a man
named Frager who was anxious to move forward into some form of
organized action. The antagonism between the two meant that no real
work was done. Since the unoccupied zone had been overrun, the
Mediterranean coast was guarded: now there was no more possibility
of arms deliveries by felucca. At the end of November the Germans
dismantled the Vichy Armistice Army, and yet another element of the
Carte plan – that important contacts in that Army would one day rise
and fight for the Resistance – became meaningless.
    Besides the tensions within Carte and the pressures of the German
advance, the three Spindle agents had to cope with countless practical
frustrations. Their mission seemed cursed: a few times they tried to

arrange landings or pick-ups, asking the local groups to select fields
for the operations. But almost always when Peter turned up to inspect
them, he discovered that there was a ditch right across the middle or
trees in the way, or a house a few yards away, rendering the ground
useless. Odette observed the behaviour of some of the resistants with
horror: 'They were so irresponsible some of them, and so obviously
resistance you know – short of wearing a label saying "I am Resistance!" – that you felt you didn't want to be with them.'

She dreaded that their slapdash way of doing things would bring
them all down. 'I felt fear. I felt that anything could happen any time.'

But in fact it did not need a major disaster to put the Germans
on to the group; something small had already happened which put
them all in danger. It had happened shortly after Odette's arrival,
in November, when André Marsac, one of the Carte members who
often worked with Peter Churchill, took a train from Marseille to
Paris, carrying information about Carte members and contacts.

This information was no coded, cryptic message. On the contrary,
it comprised extensive descriptions and contact addresses, taken
from *Carte*'s proudly maintained central records. *Carte* had a gift for
gathering information: it was against every rule of security but then
he had not been through SOE training. Since the beginning of his
recruitment drive, he had kept records. They were extensive records,
written on special forms and giving full details of the recruits, including
their name, their address, their skills, their appearance, their temperament – even the telephone number where one existed. These forms
were terrifyingly incriminating. They were not even coded. They sat
for much of the time like a time bomb in *Carte*'s study in Antibes;
sometimes senior members of Carte carried them from one place to
another. On this journey north, Marsac had taken with him more
than two hundred of these forms, carried in a briefcase.

The journey from Marseille to Paris in 1942 took all day; the train
had been crowded and hot, and Marsac had fallen asleep. When he
had woken up the briefcase had gone. He comforted himself with the
thought that it might – just might – have been stolen by someone too
stupid to know what the papers meant or too friendly to the Resistance
to pass them on. But luck was not with them – the thief was an agent
of the Abwehr, the German army security force, and the information
was already on its way to the Abwehr's Paris headquarters.

From November then, this information had been in enemy hands.
It threatened all of them; like the Prosper agents, Odette and her
comrades were working in the shadow of imminent arrest.

There was another link too between the Prosper and the Spindle agents, besides the precariousness of their positions. Since *Carte* had passed on the names of his northern contacts to SOE, there were Carte contacts who were now working in Prosper. In Paris there were the Tambour sisters and Jacques Bureau, at the heart of the *réseau*; out in the country there were many, many more. So far this had not brought the two sets of agents dangerously close, but nevertheless the links existed. Before the summer of 1943 they were to become complicated by other factors.

Christmas 1942 came and went in the south-east. Life became more dangerous for resistants and non-resistants alike as the Germans made their presence felt. In January, German troops evacuated the old port of Marseille, claiming it was full of criminals. Thousands of families were turned out of their homes and sent to refugee camps; from there many went to concentration camps. Much of the old quarter was burned down. The message was clear, not only to the Marseillais but to everyone along the south coast: the occupying forces would gut the cities if they had to, to stamp out Resistance.

Within the Carte organization further east, the new year brought an intensifying of the ill will between *Carte* and his number two, Frager. Frager was as temperamental as *Carte*, though more practically inclined, and early in January things came to a crisis, with each one declaring he could no longer work with the other. Peter Churchill, forced to make a choice between them, backed Frager and sent a radio message to Baker Street explaining what had happened and recommending Frager as the better bet.

Chaos now reigned within Carte. *Carte* himself, understandably, refused to accept Peter Churchill's decision and continued to lead a faction of the group in opposition to him and Frager. In February, the agents arranged a night-time pick-up for him and he was flown back to England to put his case in Baker Street. Shortly afterwards, the message came that Peter Churchill and Frager were to go too, to give their reports on the case. They had to mount another pick-up operation, and this one went spectacularly wrong.

The landing ground they decided on was a disused aerodrome over in the south-west near Périgueux: the RAF had a photograph of it and suggested that they use it. It seemed a good idea, especially after all their problems with grounds chosen by local groups, and Peter and Odette arranged to go to reconnoitre the ground and to meet Frager and another resistant, Jacques, in Périgueux on the day of the operation. So the day before the pick-up was scheduled, Peter and Odette arrived at Périgueux station. They found rooms in an hotel and had lunch and that afternoon they hired two *vélo-taxis*, the small-wheeled carriages pulled by cyclists, and were driven into the countryside, to the village of Basillac. To their consternation, when they arrived at the aerodrome, they saw uniformed men coming out of the buildings. The place was not deserted after all.

They paid off the *vélo-taxis* and walked round the aerodrome, pretending to be young lovers out for a stroll. The field next to the building was suitable for a landing, but the place where they would have to wait for the aircraft was uncomfortably close to the buildings. And who exactly was in the buildings? To find the aerodrome inhabited was a blow, but Peter was getting desperate to straighten out the *réseau*'s affairs. If he and Frager didn't get back to England on this operation, they would have to make the 800-kilometre trip back to Cannes only to reorganize the pick-up for another night. Provisionally, they decided to go ahead.

They walked back to Périgueux and Odette telephoned *Arnaud*, telling him in an innocuous-sounding phrase that they would be carrying out the operation. Now he would send the message to London.

The next day, in the afternoon, they met Frager and Jacques in Périgueux. Jacques told them that he had already cycled to Basillac and actually gone into the aerodrome grounds. He had talked to one of the men there, who seemed to be connected with the French Air Force, but he had not been able to establish whether they were Resistance-minded or not. Peter and Odette were perturbed to hear that he had spoken to someone, but they all felt that they should go ahead. If the plane was going to come, they could at least try to receive it.

That evening Peter borrowed a radio from the hotel and took it to his room, tuning in to the *Messages Personnels*. The message he needed – '*Les femmes sont parfois volages*' (Women are sometimes fickle) – came through the crackling. He went down to reception and paid for his room, then went to a neighbouring hotel where Odette, Frager and Jacques were having dinner, and told them that the pick-up was on for tonight. Frager settled his bill (Jacques was staying in a small café) and they all set off to walk to Basillac. If all went according to plan, only Odette and Jacques would come back along the road, perhaps with a newly-arrived agent.

They reached the aerodrome at about 10 p.m. and went cautiously into the field. They had three lamps with them, and they set them out to make a runway. Then they retired into the shadow of a bank, behind which a river ran, and waited.

Too early, they heard the sound of an aeroplane engine. It flew directly overhead, a Lysander, and Peter flashed up his morse letter. But there had been a communications mix-up – the letter he flashed up was not that which the pilot expected, and the plane flew on. While they took shelter again, wondering what had happened, they froze: two men were walking out of the buildings across the field. They came nearer; they passed by, apparently noticing nothing in the misty darkness.

Shortly afterwards, they heard the sound of the Lysander coming back. They prepared to flash at it again but suddenly from the aerodrome buildings a bright light came on and then a voice began shouting that it was too early; the light should be turned off. There were Germans in the aerodrome – they knew the resistants were there and were laying a trap!

As the Lysander, alerted, flew off, Odette and the others scattered, running for cover. They had the advantage of darkness but they could hear men rushing out of the buildings after them. They could also hear tracker dogs. Odette, separated from the others, was running through a patch of trees towards the bridge over the river when she realized one was on her scent. She swerved away from the bridge and ran through the undergrowth to the river itself. She waded straight in: the water rose to her waist and left her breathless with its icy chill, but it had covered her scent. She heard the dog moving away. She waited a while, but no one pursued her to the river and eventually she heard the voices of the Germans grow fainter. She dragged herself across to the opposite bank and made for the road, where she saw Jacques. He too was soaking wet; they made their way back to the town, staying in the shadows and shivering in their sodden clothes, until they could reach Jacques' café and slip into his room.

It turned out that the entire party had been extraordinarily lucky: Peter and Frager had got away too and all four of them rendezvoused the next day, uncomfortable, tired but alive. They left town at once, heading back to what they thought of as the relative safety of Cannes.

But when they arrived back things were in turmoil. What Odette had always feared had happened: the group had been blown. During the last two days members had been arrested and now those still free were urgently packing up their belongings and preparing to leave. Odette, Peter and *Arnaud* would have to go too, at once. But where?

They would go, said Marsac, to Haute-Savoie. Marsac's mother lived in a village 300 kilometres north of Cannes as the crow flies, high up in the mountains of Haute-Savoie: it was good Resistance country up there and it offered immediate refuge. It seemed a good course of action. Peter Churchill got new identity cards made for himself; Odette had medical papers forged certifying that she had to live at an altitude of 5,000 feet for her health; *Arnaud*'s radio set was given to a courier, and they set off for Haute-Savoie.

The village of St Jorioz lay on the shore of Lac Annecy, ringed by mountains. It was a quiet place: the nearest town was Annecy, fifteen kilometres away; the village was served by a local bus and had the usual village shops and cafés and an Hôtel de la Poste with rooms to let. Farming land spread back from the lake shores and forests covered the lower slopes of the mountains: it was not a place which outsiders had much need to visit. Peter and Odette made this village their new base.

Things came together quickly in St Jorioz. Peter and Odette moved into rooms at the Hôtel de la Poste, and soon found that the proprietors, Jean and Simone Cottet, were friendly to the Resistance. In supposedly general discussions, the Cottets told them that there were many resistants in the surrounding towns and villages; there was even a *maquis* group hiding out in the forests. It all boded well. The most urgent priority, though, was to find a house from which *Arnaud* could transmit. The mountains which encircled the lake protectively were a terrible obstacle for *Arnaud*'s transmissions. He needed not only a safe house but one which faced a gap in the mountains, and a northward gap at that.

While their comrades from Cannes settled in to villages around St Jorioz, and – through Madame Marsac and others – made contacts with the local resistants, Odette spent her days cycling on the roads around Lac Annecy, up and down the tracks leading to the hill hamlets and villages, looking for suitable houses for *Arnaud*. When she found a likely place, she would approach the owners cautiously, feeling her way. She felt much happier here in the mountains than she had done in Cannes; the people she met from the local Resistance groups seemed steady and reliable, and she felt that now she was separated from the Cannes group she could at last 'disappear'. Here in the quiet of the mountains she felt she could work in her own way.

> I had a great asset – I was a French woman in France and I don't care what anybody says, you can never put in a person the same feeling of roots ... you see there are waves, little things that you understand just by looking at a person. You don't have to put it into words: I knew at once the mind of the person I was talking with. I could feel it better ....

The group was gathering again, much smaller this time, but also more secure. The local resistants Odette met impressed her.

There was a very strong resistance movement in Savoie.

There was especially a group in the mountains; the chief
of that group was Anton Morel – a wonderful man – and we
were anxious to be more associated with these different type
of men. They were much more – with their feet on the
ground; much more dedicated in a way and you felt much
safer with them.

It was a local resistant who finally solved *Arnaud*'s problems and
found him a house for his transmissions. It was a few kilometres
south of the lake, some way above a large village called Faverges.
From Faverges you took an uphill road to the hamlet of Les Tissots
and here, facing north-west across a gap in the mountains, was an
empty villa, owned by the forest warden. It had all the requirements
for *Arnaud*: it was isolated and safe and the gap in the mountains
lessened the interference in his transmissions. He stayed in a house
in Faverges village and went back and forth to Les Tissots to meet
his skeds.

From now on, Odette often made the trip from St Jorioz down
the western shore of the lake to Faverges, or to Les Tissots itself, to
take messages to *Arnaud*. She also liaised between Peter Churchill and
Anton Morel – known to his resistance friends as *Tom. Tom* Morel, in
everyday life a Vichy policeman, ran a large group of resistance and
maquis in the area. (Already in 1943 he was enormously respected
and loved: today there is a memorial to him on the Annecy-Thones
road where he led a battle in March 1944 before being killed by the
milice.) It was agreed that Peter Churchill and *Tom* Morel should not
come into direct contact, so Odette was the liaison and often cycled
along the lake shore to see him and his wife.

The group seemed to have won a reprieve, even to be set fair to
build up another *réseau*. There was a house near the Hôtel de la
Poste, called '*Les Tilleuls*' and this became the group's meeting
place. But now a newcomer arrived to join them, a man named Roger
Bardet.

Bardet came to the agents through their local Resistance contacts.
He was apparently a dedicated resistant who had just escaped from
a camp in Germany. He had come to Annecy and had contacted the
Resistance there and made it known that he was willing to work with
the British agents. So he was introduced to them.

From the agents' point of view, the newcomer's experience of the
Germans and his resourcefulness in escaping made him valuable to
them. On the other hand, security dictated that people who had been
in German custody were always suspect. There was always the risk
that the escape wasn't genuine, that the person had been released by

the Germans and had made a deal to report back to them.

As so often, the final decision had to be made on instinct. And here the agents had different feelings. Peter Churchill and Frager both felt that Bardet was genuine. But Odette had a different reaction to him:

> I was told one day that I was going to meet someone in Annecy, a man who would be a great asset to the group because of his past, because he had escaped once as a prisoner from Germany, because of this and that. I met this man and I said to Peter, 'Well, I shall never trust him.' And he said, 'Why not? He's got everything that we can wish to have. I mean he's got contacts, he's got this, he's got. . . .' I said, 'I don't know. I just shall never trust him.' He said, 'Oh you would call that feminine intuition I suppose.' I said, 'Well, call it what you like, that's the way I feel.'

With the arrival of Bardet into the group, Odette began once more to feel insecure. And when *Arnaud* met Bardet he too disliked him.

The personal chemistry among the group around Lac Annecy had grown extraordinarily intense by now. There was the mutual closeness of Peter Churchill and *Arnaud*; there was the three-way friendship and interdependence of Peter Churchill, *Arnaud* and Odette, and there was the romantic love growing between Peter Churchill and Odette.

According to Peter Churchill's memoirs it was now, in Haute-Savoie, that their love came into the open. Years of polite skirting round the issue in books and interviews have made it impossible to know when and how they stopped being close comrades and started being lovers. But what is sure is that by now there was not much time left for them to be either.

Bardet's entry into the group had altered the equation of trust and loyalty. In March, Peter Churchill and Frager finally managed to leave by a night-time pick-up for England, to give their side of the *Carte* story and to discuss their future missions. They did not know it but in their absence the scenario on the lake shore was to change: the threads which now began to twitch led all the way to Paris and back and were ready to pull in their prey.

EIGHT

The Weaving of the Net

By August 1943, disaster had visited the agents in Paris and in St Jorioz. Odette, Yvonne Rudellat and Andrée Borrel were in captivity along with most of their comrades, Lise de Baissac and her brother were hurriedly picked up from their disintegrating *réseaux* and the ripples were still spreading outwards, destined to bring down many more agents before the year was out.

It was known as the Prosper affair and it was thought to be the worst disaster to befall the French Resistance, one of SOE's darkest hours. There have been many attempts to investigate it since it happened and these usually have one of two premises: one is the theory that the Prosper agents were careless and over-ambitious and by their own mistakes brought about the collapse of their *réseau*. The other is that Henri Déricourt was a double agent in the pay of the Germans, and systematically betrayed his SOE comrades. During a French trial of Déricourt shortly after the war strong circumstantial evidence emerged against him; indeed he admitted giving information to the Germans though he said that it was done under duress and not as a deliberate act of betrayal. Various Germans testified that there had been a double agent in Paris at the time but the German intelligence officers immediately involved were by then dead or missing and there was no one to swear that Déricourt was the man. And then the case was thrown into even greater confusion when an F Section staff officer entered the witness box and said that F Section had known all along about Déricourt's contacts with the Germans and sanctioned them.

Déricourt was acquitted. Since then many people have tried to unravel what happened during the six months that the Prosper agents and Déricourt worked together. It is a difficult task because so much happened – and depending on the angle from which you view them, the events can suggest different things. What's more, the role of Baker Street in all this has long been under a shadow. Did Buckmaster and his staff know what was going on with Déricourt and Prosper or didn't they? Shortly after the war Buckmaster was still defending Déricourt vigorously; when I saw him recently he was more circumspect, admitting that Déricourt had betrayed people, hinting that Baker Street had realized the fact towards the end.

Many people connected to the affair have hinted, over the years, that there was more to it than has ever been proved. Some people who for a long time were unwilling to speak about it have now disclosed the way it looked to them. One is the late Harold Sporborg, who was deputy chief of the whole of SOE at the time. (He died in the mid-1980s.) Another is Odette: the very first thing she said to me when we met was that she had years ago given a promise not to tell what she knew because it involved naming someone within SOE. At first I didn't know what she was talking about; later, as I continued my research, I began to have ideas. As memories, facts and testimonies have continued to emerge, a little here, a little there, given by diverse people to diverse listeners, they have come together to reveal a story which is extraordinarily intricate.

In telling this story I must declare a debt to two books: one, *Double Webs* by Jean Overton Fuller,[1] was published back in the 1950s; the other, *All the King's Men* by Robert Marshall,[2] came out in 1988. I had read *Double Webs* of my own accord, and found it a disturbing, bewildering book. It tried to explore the Déricourt affair, through interviews with German witnesses and with Déricourt himself. It was not conclusive; Déricourt had already admitted in court to a lot of duplicity and lying, yet through the interviews his voice could be heard, strangely convincing, asserting that there was much more to it all than had come out, that there were things he was not free to say. I was inclined to rationalize these as his attempt to fudge the issue, until I met Odette. Then what she said to me struck the same convincing note and set me wondering again. A few months after my first talk with her, she rang me up and said that a new book had just come out called *All the King's Men*, which I should read. She said that if I put together what this book told me with what I had learnt from her, I should be able to arrive at a real understanding of what had happened

---

[1] *Double Webs*, Jean Overton Fuller, Putnam's, 1958
[2] *All the King's Men*, Robert Marshall, William Collins Sons & Co Ltd, 1988

in 1943. So I read the book and found it a fascinating piece of detective work. Robert Marshall, with the resources of the BBC behind him, has been able to investigate the background to Déricourt's SOE work, and look into the exact nature of his dealings both with the British and the German intelligence services. His findings illuminate Déricourt's words in *Double Webs*; they make sense of much else besides.

I believe that the following account of events is the true account. There is not room here for me to explain which sources substantiate the various statements. For information about the records and the process of investigation and corroboration, I recommend Robert Marshall's book, read together with Overton Fuller's. I am concerned to put these findings into the context of the agents' lives and to allow them to illuminate areas which previously were dark; also to make sense of the hints and clues which Odette patiently but enigmatically put before me. . . .

But Odette's involvement comes much later. To trace all the threads in this affair we have to go back to the very beginning. The beginning is earlier than one might think – not the night of 22 January 1943, when Déricourt dropped blind into the French countryside, nor even 1 December 1942 when Déricourt joined F Section. It lies back in 1938 in pre-war Paris when three ambitious men made each other's acquaintance.

They were a German secret service officer Karl Boemelburg, a French pilot Henri Déricourt and a British journalist who wanted to be a spy, Nicolas Bodington.

Meetings before Prosper

Nicolas Bodington, who was to become F Section's deputy head, and Henri Déricourt, who was to become its most notorious agent, first met in Paris in 1937. They came from very different backgrounds – Bodington was ex-public school and Oxford, Déricourt's childhood had been spent in the poverty of a peasant's cottage and his career had begun in the post office – but their characters were alike in many ways. They were both ambitious; they shared a fascination with power and with the idea of an inner circle; they were both assiduous contact makers.

At this point in the pre-war years Bodington was a Reuter's correspondent and Déricourt had become a pilot, flying commercial airmail routes. At twenty-eight, Déricourt's history was already colourful – he had been a trick pilot in a flying circus – and he was by everyone's account a charming, debonair young man. He was also already an inveterate liar, remaking his past whenever it suited him. Meanwhile, Bodington, just thirty, had come into contact with intelligence agents through his journalistic work and had developed a fascination with the world of spies and intelligence. In a way they were both vicarious livers, eager to be around people they considered glamorous or powerful. When they met, introduced by a mutual friend, they got on well.

In 1938 a German intelligence officer named Karl Boemelburg came to Paris under cover of being an Interpol officer. Boemelburg was older than the other two, in his early fifties, a high-ranking officer in the Sicherheitsdienst (SD), the Nazi Party's security organization, and his real mission in Paris was to seek out possible agents to recruit to the Nazi cause. Through his friends in intelligence, Bodington got to know Boemelburg and that summer he introduced Déricourt to him. Bodington and Déricourt were both impressionable young men, attracted to the world of spies and agents; they enjoyed a social friendship with Boemelburg. It did not last long though – in the autumn the French authorities saw through Boemelburg and sent him unceremoniously out of the country.

But Bodington's interest in intelligence was now strong enough for him to want to enter that world directly. In the spring of 1939 he applied to MI6, the British overseas intelligence organization. Bodington was a sociable person who enjoyed spending money and talking – it probably made him amusing company but it did not exactly fit him for MI6: they turned him down.

In September 1939 Britain and Germany went to war, and in 1940 Bodington left France. He returned to London and there got a job in political intelligence. Meanwhile the Germans invaded France and brought Karl Boemelburg back to Paris. He settled himself in to the new SD headquarters and by the end of 1940 Déricourt had run into him again.

For the next two years, the paths of Déricourt and Nicolas Bodington did not cross. Déricourt was dedicated to making a living for himself in occupied France. He was certainly not an early resistant: accounts of his early career showed that he made use of all his contacts, be they black market, Vichy or German, to get by as best he could. Before long he had seen Boemelburg again and reminded him of their old acquaintance. Boemelburg, now much promoted, was not particularly interested in the young pilot – for most of 1941 and 1942 he was too busy stamping out Soviet agents in France – but he did tell him there was work going for pilots on the Vichy government's airline. Déricourt duly began work as a Vichy pilot in 1941, flying government officials between towns in the unoccupied zone and occasionally to North Africa.

Meanwhile, Bodington, the first point of contact between the

German officer and the French pilot, had finally got himself into an inner circle of British intelligence. But it was not MI6 to which he belonged, despite a second attempt to get in: he was now in the new 'amateur' organization concerned with Resistance, SOE. He had gone into SOE's French Section and was directly involved in recruiting and briefing the agents who were sent to France.

The Unlooked-For Enemy: MI6 Against SOE

It is an open secret that there was, as Maurice Buckmaster puts it, 'no love lost' between MI6 and SOE. When in 1940 Churchill created SOE, many people in MI6 saw it as a disastrous incursion of amateurs into the professionals' territory. MI6 had its own networks of intelligence agents operating abroad: the arrival of sabotage and Resistance agents who would inevitably disrupt life and draw attention to themselves, could only appear to be bad news to MI6. What was more, MI6 actually lost some of its own staff to SOE when its sabotage division was co-opted into the new organization.

The chief of MI6, Stuart Menzies, had little option but to agree to Churchill's demands. But his deputy, a man named Claude Dansey, soon emerged as SOE's most hostile critic.

Claude Dansey was a man who excited extreme reactions in people. Books have been written about his deviousness, his exceptional flair for manipulating events and people, his cool professionalism. He was largely responsible for building up MI6 into an intelligence power in the 1920s and 1930s. He has been called everything from 'brilliant', through 'corrupt', to 'truly evil'. He was extremely ambitious and devoted to the ways of intelligence – especially his own ways – and he had no intention of allowing SOE to weaken his influence.

Dansey's contacts were vast: many people who were now involved in clandestine and intelligence work had at one time worked with or for him. It wasn't difficult for him to negotiate channels of communication into SOE, especially as in the early days MI6 was actually asked to make recommendations on certain key SOE appointments. Unsurprisingly, a number of former MI6 people were recommended for positions of power in SOE. One such was Sir Frank Nelson, a former agent in one of Dansey's own MI6 networks, who became director of SOE. Other SOE appointees were also helped on by Dansey but in a less overt way and one of these was almost certainly Nicolas Bodington.

In July 1940 Bodington applied to MI6 for the second time. As he had been the first time, he was rejected. For whatever reason, MI6 recruiting officers (and Claude Dansey took a strong interest in recruitment) did not consider him suitable for their organization. But although MI6 had found him wanting, it nevertheless passed his name on to SOE – specifically to Leslie Humphreys, the newly-appointed head of SOE's French Section. In December 1940, then, Nicolas Bodington joined F Section.

It is established that Bodington's name came to F Section from MI6. This means that at some stage Claude Dansey had seen it, to say the least. It's likely in fact that Dansey was responsible for first investigating and rejecting Bodington and then passing his name on. But why would Claude Dansey want Nicolas Bodington in F Section? Did he honestly believe that, though Bodington was not right for MI6, he could be valuable to F Section? It seems unlikely – whatever made Bodington unfit for MI6 intelligence work would be likely to make him unfit for SOE work too. Besides, no one who worked alongside Dansey in those days would believe for a minute that he wanted to do SOE a good turn. He made no secret of his desire to see SOE wound up.

It is far more likely that Dansey recognized in Bodington a possible tool for his own use. Bodington badly wanted to be in MI6: he had applied twice in six months. Moreover, it would certainly have been reported to Dansey by his agents in France that Bodington had long cultivated intelligence contacts, and he would be aware of the lure which intrigue held for him. Such a susceptible young man would be a useful plant in F Section. Inevitably, as F Section got going Dansey would have to fight harder for control over British intelligence in France: it was only sensible to prop open as many doors as he could.

So as 1941 began, Nicolas Bodington was newly installed in F Section, helping to recruit agents and devise the first missions for SOE in France. 1941 progressed, with the first agents being successfully dropped into France in the spring, more following in summer and by the end of the year Virginia Hall was in place in Lyon and agents were beginning to build up *réseaux* on either side of the demarcation line. F Section's work was underway. Claude Dansey, as he had anticipated, found it harder to exercise his influence over F Section's activities, especially when, in December 1941, there was a change of staff at Baker Street. Maurice Buckmaster took over as F Section head – brought in above Bodington. Nicolas Bodington was now his official deputy.

It was in spring 1942 that MI6 first got on to Déricourt. For the previous few months Déricourt – ever the dabbler in the underworld – had been in touch with some American intelligence officers, to whom he gave snippets of information about the Vichy airfields he used. He had also come up against one or two MI6 agents in Marseille, where he was now living. In the spring he asked an MI6 agent for help to get him out of France: he made up a story that he had been a pilot in Syria and therefore had flying experience he could put at the disposal of the British. He was, by everyone's accounts, a convincing story-teller: eventually, in August, he was put on to the PAT line and in September he arrived in London.

Such records as there are show that Déricourt now passed through MI6 hands. Dansey would naturally have checked Déricourt's story and found out that he had lied about Syria; he would almost certainly have found out about Déricourt's contacts with Boemelburg. In any case, Déricourt declared these contacts himself – when he arrived in Britain he was quick to claim that he had useful contacts with German intelligence in Paris. Dansey kept him for two months in MI6 'on hold' and by the end of November Déricourt's name had been brought to the notice of F Section.

As usual, MI5 was asked to clear Déricourt from a security point of view. When being interviewed by MI5, Déricourt kept quiet about his German contacts. Nor did Dansey tell MI5 what he knew about Déricourt. MI5 was basing its assessment on the belief that Déricourt had indeed been a pilot in Syria and had escaped through France to reach England. Even on this basis, MI5's recommendation was that F Section should reject Déricourt: he had been through occupied France on his way to England and they couldn't rule out the possibility that he had been picked up by the Germans and 'turned' to work for them.

But F Section desperately needed someone like Déricourt to organize a system of clandestine landings and pick-ups in France. The Baker Street staff were always having to balance risk against the need for action and MI5's objections were based on a mere hypo-thesis. And now Bodington stepped in and said that he had known Déricourt in France before the war: he recommended him highly. In December 1942, Henri Déricourt joined F Section and began intensive training as its air movements officer, destined to go back into the field.

What do we make then of the links and manoeuvres so far? We have Dansey, an open opponent of SOE and a man who everyone acknow-ledges to have been absolutely ruthless in pursuing his own ends. We know that Dansey had already passed on to F Section Nicolas Bodington, a would-be MI6 member with connections to the German security forces. We know that Dansey had now also passed on to F Sec-tion Déricourt, an adventurer and an old acquaintance of Bodington's, with the very same links to the German security forces. Dansey almost certainly knew of Déricourt's and Bodington's dealings with the Germans; he did not pass on this knowledge to F Section.

Bodington and Déricourt, now reunited, became good friends. They took a third into their friendship: André Simon, F Section's liaison officer with Air Intelligence. André Simon helped negotiate all the special operations flights and pick-ups to France and so would be closely involved with Déricourt's future work. Simon had also had MI6 contacts in the past.

Nothing but a list of coincidences? But there is evidence that it was more than that: after the war, in 1946 when he was awaiting trial, Déricourt wrote in a sworn statement that when he joined SOE it was controlled by MI6. He also wrote that besides taking his orders from Buckmaster he had 'entered into an additional commitment, through André Simon, about the secrecy of my work.'

What was going on? MI6 did not, of course, control SOE – though it was not only Déricourt who was confused about this. German intelligence also assumed that the two services were one. But this was probably a genuine error on Déricourt's part for a very simple reason: Claude Dansey allowed him to believe it. Déricourt was certainly reporting to Dansey a few months later (in June 1943 an MI6 flight took him from France to London and back without Buckmaster knowing); I believe that it was now, before he went into France on his mission, that the secret relationship with Dansey was established and the mission-within-a-mission agreed.

The mission-within-a-mission was also a mission-against-a-mission. For the 'additional commitment' which Déricourt made to Dansey was to get back in touch with Boemelburg and become an apparent double agent for him, giving him information about the SOE operations he was involved in. At the same time, however, Dansey would be monitoring the progress of this arrangement. It was a classical triple agent device, a subtle manoeuvre of the kind dear to Dansey's heart. It offered him many things: in Déricourt, he would have a direct line into the SD. He could assess from the SD's questions the extent of its knowledge about SOE and – more importantly to him – MI6 operations. If he chose, he would be able to feed them disinformation. Once the SD was receiving information about F Section, he could use F Section agents as a smokescreen for the activities of his own agents. Moreover, the plan had the advantage of dealing a blow to SOE in general and F Section in particular.

Dansey was an inspired improviser. All the pieces he needed had been nudged into position and now he was free to make his move. In cold intelligence terms, it was a justifiable one: he thought SOE a nuisance and a threat to his own very effective organization in France. But he never bothered to hide his antagonism to SOE either, and when the Prosper downfall came he would openly rejoice.

In Déricourt, Dansey had the ideal man for his ends. Everyone who knew Déricourt agrees that his chief loyalty was always to himself, that he was clever and charming and had the soul of an adventurer, always ready to take on something new, especially if it promised excitement, prestige and financial reward. He was not fastidious and did not baulk at dirty jobs. In a tight corner, he extemporized well. But he had his vulnerabilities, which were a useful safeguard against his becoming too clever for Dansey to handle. He had recently married and he loved his wife very much; he would be rejoining her in France and Dansey would be able to play on his fears for her safety should any emotional blackmail be required to keep him in line. Then, Déricourt was impressionable and inexperienced in the world of intelligence and once in the field would be relying on Dansey to cover for him. Also, significantly, he had come from outside MI6 and therefore would not be in a position to sell Dansey or his organization back to the Germans.

And in Bodington, Dansey had the ideal minder for Déricourt. Both Bodington and Déricourt had come first to Dansey before being passed to SOE. Where Déricourt might well have believed that Dansey was in authority over SOE, Bodington knew that this was not strictly true but then Bodington was infatuated with MI6. He still wanted a career in intelligence and Dansey was well known to be the man of the future at MI6. And then Bodington had been passed over for the top job in F Section.

There is, of course, the small matter of loyalty to the agents he was helping to recruit, train and send out. Maurice Buckmaster and Vera Atkins have both spoken over and over again of the bond they felt with agents, the anxiety they suffered for them and the struggle to balance their sense of human responsibility with the demands of war. Nicolas Bodington, when the time came, would rise above such human feelings with apparent ease. During the months that followed he must have felt the conflict, but however he felt about it he did not let it interfere with the fulfilling of Dansey's requirements. When agents were due to be sent to what he knew was a German-controlled reception, Bodington would see to it that they were sent. And when voices of unease were raised from the field, he would soothe them; when Baker Street worried about the safety of sending any more agents by that route, he would assure his fellows at HQ that it was all right. He was to smooth the paths of many agents into German arms.

There may be much more to Bodington than anyone has yet worked out. Vera Atkins says that he was always a slightly mysterious figure: for one thing she had no knowledge of his dealing with Virginia Hall. For another, he never seemed to have any money at all. He was reluctant to part with money socially – it was a joke among his colleagues that here was Nic coming into the bar again, hands in pockets – but more than that, he actually seemed to be permanently short of it. Yet he lived simply enough. Was there some hidden financial drain on him? Had he got himself into something outside his SOE and MI6 connections which meant that he was not a completely free man? Or was he simply a small-time romancer who played out of his league with Dansey?

That he was involved with Dansey at the expense of F Section is certain. What is not clear is exactly when the intrigue began. Did he know of Déricourt's 'commitment' at the time it was made? All things considered, I think not. He was not the most discreet of people and Dansey had no need to take a risk on him yet. Besides, that statement of Déricourt's makes no mention of him. Dansey might well have let Bodington lie for a while longer: it would be soon enough to bring him in when Déricourt had contacted Boemelburg and the information had started to leak in both directions. Then, when the various F Section *réseaux* began to crumble, Bodington would be needed to cover for Déricourt in Baker Street.

And this is exactly what he did.

Déricourt and Prosper

Déricourt was sent into France in January, just when the Prosper *réseau* began to receive arms drops. He went in on a cold moonlit night, travelling with another agent bound for the Prosper territory: this was Jean Worms, mentioned earlier, who was going in with a mission to set up a sub-*réseau* of Prosper, east of Paris. But the two of them did not drop together: Déricourt had asked Baker Street to drop him blind whereas Jean Worms was going to a pre-arranged reception. So Jean Worms jumped out of the plane first and parachuted down to a reception organized by Andrée Borrel and *Prosper*; meanwhile the plane flew Déricourt fifty kilometres further east and disgorged him anonymously into the night to start his mission alone.

There was already a sense of urgency among the agents in France. Baker Street was relieved to be able to send out the news over the illicit airwaves that an agent code-named *Gilbert* was now in the field who could arrange for clandestine flights to ferry agents in and out of the country.

February

The Prosper agents did not make contact with Déricourt at once and he had several weeks on the loose in which to organize his affairs. He wasted no time: first he made contact with Boemelburg at the SD headquarters in Paris. According to various German testimonies, Déricourt presented himself to Boemelburg as a pro-Nazi and offered to provide information on the SOE agents he was now working with. Nothing was settled immediately: Boemelburg wanted time, probably to liaise with Berlin and investigate the possibilities of using Déricourt.

So Déricourt travelled south to Marseille and was reunited with his wife. While there he also recruited a friend and fellow pilot, Rémy Clément, persuading him to come to Paris and work as his assistant and on-the-ground organizer of landings. Clément was Déricourt's friend but he didn't share his adventurer's personality. He had grave doubts about working outside the law. But he was unhappy in his desk job and longed to get back into flying work again and so after a good deal of agonizing he decided to accept. Leaving Clément to give his notice and put his affairs in order, Déricourt returned to Paris with his wife. Here he recruited another friend and in this case ex-lover, a woman in her twenties, Julienne Aisner. He gave her the job of finding safe houses and she began by finding an apartment for him and his wife in the Rue Pergolèse, in the sixteenth arrondissement. Rémy Clément and *his* wife were expected in Paris at the end of the month: the new air movements *réseau* Farrier was taking shape.

During these past weeks, the Prosper agents and their helpers had been busy handling arms drops and dealing with all the extra demands that such operations made on their communications. Now, soon after Déricourt settled into Paris with his wife, Andrée Borrel and Jack Agazarian came to see him. It wasn't a momentous meeting – they introduced themselves and talked about the possibility of working together in future – but it was the first contact. Then Lise de Baissac got in touch – and she brought an urgent request for a pick-up for her brother Claude and some other agents, who needed to get back to London as soon as possible. By now Rémy Clément had just arrived in Paris and Déricourt sent him out to the Vienne to look for suitable landing grounds. He also sent a message to London, through Jack Agazarian's radio, alerting Baker Street to the need for an operation in the next moon period.

While setting up this first operation, Déricourt saw Boemelburg again. Boemelburg had been in touch with Berlin and had received instructions to use Déricourt. The growing Resistance activity north of the demarcation line had not escaped the SD; through its monitoring centre the organization was well aware that clandestine radio broadcasts between France and England were on the increase and rumours had reached the high command in Berlin of a large scale operation involving something or someone called *Prosper*. Boemelburg was told to exploit Déricourt and to find out all he could about *Prosper*.

A deal was duly struck between Déricourt and Boemelburg. The terms were that Déricourt would go ahead with his mission while providing Boemelburg with information on all the SOE agents who came into France by his operations, informing on where they went and what they did. For this he would receive certain payments.

So Déricourt now became a double agent for the Germans. SD records show that he was registered as an agent under Boemelburg's direct control, number BOE/48. The SD now had a direct line into F Section's operations and Déricourt would soon lead them to the *réseau* in which they were so interested, Prosper.

March

During March, *Prosper* and Déricourt met for the first time. It was to be the first of several meetings: Déricourt, with the responsibilities Baker Street had entrusted to him, was an important agent. In his own way he was as important as *Prosper*. The Prosper *réseau* was still growing – and now arming as it grew – and Déricourt's work and *Prosper*'s would inevitably overlap during the coming months. Meanwhile Déricourt continued to use Prosper radios to set up the forthcoming operation.

In mid-March this first Farrier pick-up went off successfully. As has already been told, from the field near Lise de Baissac's base in Poitiers, Claude de Baissac, Antelme, *Gaspard* and one other passenger were picked up by Lysander and flown back to England. Four new arrivals were left in their place: one was a Gaullist agent; the other three were F Section agents who went to the Paris area – including a new Prosper courier, Francine Agazarian.

What exactly did Déricourt tell the Germans about this operation? Both Déricourt's and various German accounts confirm that he had made a deal with the SD in February but there seems to be no clear information – at least none accessible to the public – on what passed between him and Boemelburg on this occasion. Whatever it was, it did not satisfy Boemelburg. It could be that Boemelburg hoped for too much, too soon, from his new agent No 48. March saw a good deal of clandestine activity in northern France, quite apart from Déricourt's first operation. Michael Trotobas in Lille had begun to sabotage railway lines and trucks; the three new agents, Garel, Rousset and Fox, dropped and began organizing the sub-*réseau* Butler in the Sarthe; the organizer of Musician, Biéler, who had hurt himself when he dropped in November, finally arrived in St Quentin and began organizing there. The massive increase in radio traffic would have indicated to the SD that things were on the move; the derailments and explosions up in Lille confirmed it, had confirmation been needed. Perhaps Boemelburg thought Déricourt was holding out on him? At any rate, he was about to put pressure on him to disclose much more.

April

The pressure was on the Prosper agents too, in a different sense. Come April, the pace of their mission quickened noticeably. In the past three months well over 100 containers – each holding multiple guns, grenades, rounds of ammunition and explosives – had been dropped on various grounds in the large Prosper area. Now the rate of drops increased phenomenally – in this one month the region took more than *ten times* the volume of arms it had received in March.

The Prosper agents were all working at full stretch. Andrée Borrel, *Prosper* and Francine Agazarian were constantly moving from one rendezvous to another, often crossing scores of kilometres a day by bicycle or train. *Archambaud* and Jack Agazarian spent hours coding and decoding long radio messages and the transmissions themselves were now much longer and more frequent due to the volume of information flying between France and Baker Street. Moreover, other *réseaux* – like the newly-forming Musician in St Quentin, Trotobas's Farmer and even occasionally Scientist in Bordeaux – were sending messages in to the Prosper operators for transmission. Jack Agazarian in particular transmitted for a number of *réseaux* at one remove from Prosper. And *Archambaud*, besides transmitting, was helping *Prosper* on certain active expeditions. In their territory south of Paris, Yvonne Rudellat and Pierre Culioli were now leading a sub-*réseau* of Prosper which concentrated on sabotage and they were beginning to make small but successful attacks. Meanwhile they continued to receive agents – on the 11th, Ben Cowburn and a radio operator dropped to them, *en route* to set up Tinker in Troyes – and they were also planning a major sabotage attack, to be undertaken with *Prosper* later in the month.

Meanwhile, Déricourt and Boemelburg were meeting regularly in various discreet apartments, many of them in houses which the SD had commandeered in the smart district of Neuilly, on the outskirts of Paris. Boemelburg, only too conscious of the Resistance gaining strength around him, raised the stakes of their game. He demanded that Déricourt not only report back to him on the operations he organized, but that he provide advance warning of landings and pick-ups so that the SD could observe them. Déricourt agreed but made one important condition: the SD must guarantee not to arrest any of the incoming agents. If one of his operations were interrupted or the new agents picked up shortly after arriving, he would inevitably be implicated.

In his turn, Boemelburg agreed. He wasn't after a few easy arrests of new agents who could tell him nothing: as Dansey would have recognized, it was infinitely more valuable to Boemelburg to stay his hand and allow the new agents to establish themselves and build up *réseaux*, all the while under his surveillance. In this way he could gradually penetrate the very foundations of the British-backed resistance and when he chose to pull in his haul it would be a massive one – and one which would almost inevitably include the organization Berlin and the SD now perceived as the greatest threat: Prosper.

So a routine was devised by which all Farrier operations would henceforth be observed. From now on Déricourt would tell the SD where landings and pick-ups would take place and at what time; he would pass on to them how many agents were expected to arrive and how many were due to leave. The SD would then brief a special band of hired observers to watch the incoming agents and trail them to their destinations.

It was the stuff thrillers are made of: the agents would arrive and be received by a fellow agent whom they trusted but who was in fact betraying them. He would lead them through the dark country roads to the station of a nearby small town: when the first train was due they would come out of hiding and, following his instructions, would enter the station, buy tickets and board the train, not showing by their behaviour that they knew him. They would feel the train start up, taking them towards their destination, and they would relax slightly, thinking so far so good. But their welcoming fellow agent sitting some way away from them had already sold them on, and among the other people who had boarded the train were several men who were not the innocent travellers they seemed. They were in reality members of the notorious Bony-Lafont gang, an underworld collection of professional criminals and corrupt ex-policemen who worked as Gestapo informers. And they had been waiting for the agents all night: now they were shadowing them and would do so all the way to their destinations. Before the agents could begin their work, information on their whereabouts, their appearance and their contacts would be in the hands of German intelligence officers.

It sounds melodramatic but it was a perfectly feasible plan and in mid-April came the opportunity to implement it. Déricourt was asked to organize another double Lysander operation to bring in four agents. Baker Street was sending out two pairs – the first comprised agents named Liéwer and Chartrand, who were heading for Rouen; the second consisted of Frager and Dubois, who were going east to the Yonne. (This was the same Frager who had been in Carte and had flown back to England with Peter Churchill: he was now being sent back by Baker Street to start up a new *réseau*, Donkeyman, in the Yonne.)

Déricourt made his usual arrangements with the help of Rémy Clément and the two of them were at the landing ground on the appointed night, with bicycles for the agents. The Lysanders arrived; the reception committee flashed up the morse light and the two craft came to land. Frager, Dubois, Liéwer and Chartrand climbed out and went into a huddle with Déricourt. Déricourt showed them the bicycles and explained that they should cycle to the small town of Amboise nearby and take a train from Amboise station to their destinations. But now Frager upset the plan by deciding that they should give the station a miss and cycle straight to Tours, thirty kilometres away, where Dubois' mother-in-law was head of a school. Frager, as impulsive and obstinate as ever, insisted on setting off at once, throwing Déricourt into a quandary. The Bony-Lafont men were waiting at Amboise station – if he turned up without the agents he would immediately be under suspicion of double crossing the SD. He was very exposed in his position between the agents and the SD; he relied on Boemelburg's protection and could not afford to antagonize him. So Déricourt himself cycled to Tours with the agents and saw them into the school-house; then he returned as fast as he could with the address.

At 7.30 a.m. the next morning there was a knock at the schoolhouse door. The agents just had time to hide before a party of German SD officers came in. They were very polite, explaining to Dubois' mother-in-law that they were simply making a 'library inspection' to check that the text books were ideologically sound. Sure enough they took a cursory look at the books and went away again. No search had been made and the agents were able to slip away later, apparently undetected. But to Frager the timing of the inspection seemed too much of a coincidence to be accepted at face value – for one thing SD officers did not usually concern themselves with such trivia as school books. He had an uncomfortable feeling that there had been a tip-off and he suspected Déricourt. He went off to the Yonne with this suspicion planted in his mind; it was soon to grow stronger.

In Paris Boemelburg was well satisfied. The first observed operation had had its problems but it had been successful: the SD had been able to pick up the trail of the new agents at Tours. This system of surveillance now became the norm for almost all Déricourt's operations. Rémy Clément, who was present at most operations from April onwards, used to recognize the Bony-Lafont men loitering at the country stations. He knew who they were – they were well known in Paris as the Germans' hirelings – but he did not realize that they were there specifically to watch him and his charges. When he described them to me last year he still seemed to think it was coincidence that he had seen them so often:

'They were easy to spot – they were well dressed and to be well dressed in Paris then was to be working for the Germans. I was often followed by them. They were very often waiting at railway stations – I would see them when I was on an operation.'

This system now established between Déricourt and the SD, Déricourt pressed on, apparently whole-heartedly, with his Resistance mission. He arranged a pick-up for Julienne Aisner and she was flown to England for training.

Déricourt saw some more of *Prosper* and made his way deeper into the circle of Prosper agents. He met *Archambaud*, spent some more time with Andrée Borrel and Jack Agazarian and was introduced to the group of resistants in the *Ecole Nationale d'Agriculture* near Versailles, where *Prosper* liked to hold meetings. Several people who met him during this time remarked in some way on his inquisitiveness: he seemed to have an avid appetite for facts about other people's affairs.

There was plenty going on to interest him. But now he was called back to England. It was not Baker Street who recalled him but Captain Hugh Verity, head of the special operations air squadron; all Déricourt's operations so far had been successful but there had been problems with some of the landing grounds and Verity wanted to reprimand him and put him through his paces again. Déricourt went back to England as the sole passenger on a Lysander operation on the night of 22 April; he stayed there several days, during which time he reported to Maurice Buckmaster that all was going well with his mission. Did he see Dansey too? The answer must be, almost certainly, yes. And now Bodington moves from the edge of the intrigue into the centre, for an interesting report arrived on his desk while Déricourt was over in England.

It was an MI5 report, compiled from information supplied by de Gaulle's intelligence people in France. According to this non-F Section, non-MI6 source, Déricourt was known to be mixing with

Germans. Is it possible that Bodington honestly believed this to be
a false accusation – after all he knew of Déricourt and Déricourt's
friendship with Boemelburg? To believe so would have required him to
be either perverse or obtuse and his actions later on show him to have
been neither. Yet he dismissed the allegation. If Bodington's initiation
into Dansey's plan has to be fixed at some point after Déricourt's, then
this is surely the moment. On the other hand, of course, he might have
known about it all along. In either event, his handling of this report was
significant. He dismissed it, noting blithely: 'This sounds like typical
French back-biting.'

His recommendation was accepted and the matter was not pursued.
Déricourt made preparations to go back into France on 6 May. In
France during his absence, the SD noted with anxiety that illicit radio
transmissions were up by 500 per cent on earlier that year. The arms
continued to drop on to lonely fields and to be stashed in barns and
outhouses. Down on the Loire, *Prosper*, *Archambaud* and a group of
resistants from Yvonne Rudellat's and Pierre Culioli's *réseau* attacked
a power station: they managed to cut off the power for eleven hours.
Elsewhere within the Prosper *réseau* the very first arrests were taking
place: Germaine and Madelaine Tambour had been arrested, but not
by the SD. There was another German counter-resistance force out
to get Prosper and it was closing in on the *réseau* from an unexpected
angle – via St Jorioz.

NINE

The Net Closes on St Jorioz

When Peter Churchill and Paul Frager finally climbed into their England-bound aeroplane on the night of 24 March, in a field near Compiègne, Odette was stranded twenty kilometres away, exhausted. She had spent a day and a night travelling from St Jorioz in a bid to catch them before they left, and in the last few hours she had been following their trail from one contact address in the area to another. She had found the hotel where they had been staying and had discovered from the hotel stables that in the afternoon they had taken a pony and trap out to a large estate. She too had hired a pony and trap and gone the same route. Arriving there, she had learned that they had gone back to the town to a certain address, to listen for the *Messages Personnels*. Having let the trap go, she then walked back to the town, hitching a lift on a lorry for part of the way. She reached the contact address to find them already departed for the station, on the first leg of their trip to the pick-up ground. She had run after them to the station but had arrived just too late – their train had already left. The long trip had been for nothing: the new information she had for Peter Churchill, including a report on the recent arms drop to the Glières *maquis*, would be staying behind in France.

It was not a decisive failure. But it marked the beginning of a series of mishaps and mistimings which were to prove disastrous for Odette and Peter Churchill. They had never been exactly lucky and now their luck was about to run out altogether.

It had taken Churchill and Frager over a week to achieve their pick-up. At their first attempt, near Tournus, no aircraft had arrived and since then a courier had been liaising between them and Odette and *Arnaud* in St Jorioz. *Arnaud* had been in contact with London over his radio, and finally the new operation had been organized on a ground miles away, near Compiègne in the north-east. Meanwhile, on the Glières plateau, *Tom* Morel and his *maquis* had received a large drop of arms. Odette had decided to take the news of this, together with some other recently received information, to the new landing ground and intercept Peter and Frager there – and she had failed at the last minute. But as she was contemplating her failure in Compiègne, another member of the *réseau* was surprising Peter Churchill with his appearance at the landing ground.

This was Marsac, who announced that he had come to see the agents off and to meet the new agent, Francis Cammaerts, who was expected to arrive on the same plane. Peter Churchill was more dismayed than delighted to see Marsac and his little coterie of helpers. Surprises like this were a security nightmare, just the sort of thing which had made the Cannes *réseau* so impossible to run. But Cammaerts was an important arrival – Baker Street had plans for Frager to take over a large section of the old Carte territory, up in the Yonne, and to run it as his own *réseau*, and Cammaerts was being sent out to work with him and liaise between him and London. And it was unarguable that the car Marsac had managed to find would get Cammaerts to Paris more swiftly than any other means; moreover Marsac said that he had arranged all the papers they needed for the journey. So when the plane arrived, Peter Churchill and Frager greeted the new agent in passing, climbed aboard in his place and commended him to the care of their comrades.

Francis Cammaerts, code-named *Roger*, was a young Englishman in his twenties, tall and loose-framed and English-looking. Despite his eye-catching physique, however, he was extremely security conscious and was eventually to set up and run a huge, tightly-controlled *réseau*. His reception and the journey down to Paris, with the car crammed full of resistants all apparently impervious to the risks of curfew, bewildered him. He later described to Baker Street how he had comforted himself with the thought that these were people who knew Resistance work and that therefore they must be right when they told him there was no danger. 'If I had known then as much as I know now about clandestine work,' he added, 'my hair would certainly have gone grey during the drive.'[1]

But they arrived in Paris safely and Marsac took Cammaerts to his lodgings. They spent much of the night talking; the following day Cammaerts wandered around Paris trying to acclimatize himself and had lunch with Marsac. They were making plans to go eastwards soon, and when they separated to go their different ways they made

[1] *SOE in France*, M.R.D. Foot, HMSO, 1966

another rendezvous for the next day. But when Cammaerts arrived at the rendezvous, there was no Marsac. He stayed as long as he dared and then during the afternoon he made cautious contact with one of Marsac's comrades. He heard that Marsac, together with his secretary Suzanne, had been arrested.

Cammaerts immediately left Paris and took a train to Annecy, where he made contact with Odette and *Arnaud*. Uneasily, they laid low and awaited developments.

The Abwehr

These developments were now unfolding in Paris. But it was not Boemelburg who held Marsac, nor was it the SD which now began to pursue the St Jorioz agents. It was another organization, the Abwehr, and here another complication enters the tale of the agents of 1942-3.

The St Jorioz agents and the Prosper agents had long had a number of crucial contact points. There was the overlap between Carte and Prosper – the Tambour sisters and Jacques Bureau had all been early Carte recruits before they became founder members of Prosper. So had many of the resistants now handling Prosper drops in country areas. What was more, Peter Churchill and Marsac had both used the Tambours' flat as 'letter boxes', places to leave and pick up messages.

But there was another way in which the fates of the St Jorioz agents and the Prosper agents were linked. In an odd reflection of the MI6 and SOE relationship, there were two rival German intelligence forces. One was the SD, currently casting its net around Prosper and Déricourt's passengers; the other was the German army's intelligence agency, the Abwehr. The rivalry between these two was acute, more thorough-going than that between the British services and more overtly political. The Abwehr was the established military intelligence service; its allegiance was to the army and it contained strong anti-Nazi elements. In fact its head, Canaris, would later be executed for his part in the plot to assassinate Hitler. The SD was the newer organization, grown out of the Nazi Party itself and close to Hitler. The SD had been growing ever stronger over the last few years and now its influence approached the zenith. The Abwehr, however, still had many highly placed friends and it was fighting the SD every inch of the way. The enmity between the two organizations was bitter. In 1943 they were anxious to capture Resistance leaders – and particularly British agents – not only for the sake of crushing Resistance and discovering British strategy, but also to steal a march over one another.

In spring 1943, the prize which both the SD and the Abwehr coveted was Prosper, the large phantom organization in which Hitler and his Berlin colleagues were so interested. The SD had Déricourt, a fact which the Abwehr had recently discovered. But the Abwehr had a trump card too: since November it had been holding the list of Carte names. It is conjecture, but logical conjecture, that the Abwehr might have thought the Carte names were Prosper names. The list clearly outlined an ambitious resistance organization and the names and addresses showed that some of the resistants were in Paris. It looked strongly as if this list would at least give access to the Prosper *réseau* – and in fact before the end of April the Abwehr would manage to pull in two Prosper figures from the list. Was the Abwehr trying all along to get at Prosper? Certainly the agents of St Jorioz now joined the agents of Prosper as pieces on the board to be moved around by men in intelligence – and men in rivalry with one another.

The man who brought the Abwehr into play against the Carte names was a non-commissioned officer, Sergeant Hugo Bleicher. He was a man from a modest background, with a penchant for devious games of impersonization and bluff and a driving ambition, so far unfulfilled, to rise in the Abwehr. He had come across F Section agents before; in late 1941 he had for a while infiltrated his lover (a Belgian woman) into Autogiro and had managed to make some arrests. Now he devised another infiltration plan by which he hoped to work his way towards the main figures in Carte/Prosper. Like Boemelburg and Dansey, he knew that by getting a line into the *réseau* he could reap far greater rewards than by making immediate arrests. He just needed someone with whom to start. Marsac, the original carrier of the incriminating list, was that someone.

'Colonel Henri'

Marsac and his fellow resistants were not the most discreet of people. With the names and addresses of Paris contacts to guide him, Bleicher moved in on Marsac as he sat in a café. Marsac was arrested; so was his secretary Suzanne, and they were taken to Fresnes prison on the southern outskirts of Paris.

Later that day, Marsac was visited in his cell by Bleicher and heard from him a surprising and stirring tale. 'Lieutenant-Colonel Henri', as Bleicher introduced himself, was an old-guard, honourably anti-Nazi German. There were many of them in the Abwehr and the army, he told Marsac, people who were horrified at the pass to which Hitler had brought their country, people who could see all too clearly that Germany would now inevitably lose the war. They wanted to salvage what they could. As their representative he wanted urgently to go to England and meet with the Allied High Command. There he could discuss with them possible ways of ending the war.

It was not a particularly original story but it was one which had a certain compelling plausibility in occupied France. France was a nation divided within itself; resistants knew what it was like to live a lie and to hate and fear their own government. 'Colonel Henri's' story struck a chord in Marsac and stirred his hopes just when he thought everything was over for him. He believed it. Convinced of Bleicher's integrity, he said that his comrades in St Jorioz should be able to organize a pick-up for him. When Bleicher left the prison he carried a letter of recommendation from Marsac and information on where to find Odette and Marsac's second in command, Roger Bardet.

Bleicher, alias 'Colonel Henri', arrived in St Jorioz in April. He went first to Annecy and from there he caught the late morning bus to the village. As it happened, Odette was also on that bus, coming back from a rendezvous in Annecy. Bleicher caught her eye: he was a stranger, not dressed like the people from this part of the world, and there was something about his bearing which rang a warning bell in her mind. He looked around him with rather too much interest, as if he were seeking something in particular.

Odette watched him descend the bus ahead of her, and ask for directions. She hung back and decided to watch him. She was due to have lunch with a friend at the Hôtel de la Poste: instead of going in to the hotel she walked up to the terrace outside the first floor, which gave her a perfect view of the village. She saw the stranger go into 'Les Tilleuls'. All her suspicions roused, Odette walked swiftly down to the street and followed him carefully into the house: she saw the stranger sitting in conversation with one of the local resistants.

Anxious, but feeling that it would be unwise to butt in straight away, Odette went back to the Hôtel de la Poste and ate lunch with her friend. Just as they were finishing the meal, the door opened and a member of the local Resistance group came into the dining-room, with the stranger. The Resistant was talking to the stranger in an over-loud voice; Odette could hear that he was telling him things about their work. She was irritated as well as apprehensive: she called the resistant over and told him to be careful. The stranger watched her from a distance but didn't speak. He just looked at her very hard and smiled. Then the two men left the hotel together.

That afternoon, the stranger seemed to have gone. Odette went to 'Les Tilleuls' to find out what was happening, and what she heard there dismayed her. The resistant who had been with the stranger at lunch time told her, with much excitement, that the stranger was a very senior German officer but not a Nazi. He said that the German, who was called called 'Henri', wished to get in touch with London and needed a radio; moreover 'Henri' had brought a letter from Marsac, which he had here . . . .

There were several members of the group in 'Les Tilleuls' that afternoon, including Roger Bardet. Now Bardet too spoke up for 'Henri'. Bardet had been in 'Les Tilleuls' when the man had arrived earlier that day; he had had a private talk with him and in his opinion 'Henri' was sound. Bardet believed they should give him the *réseau*'s spare radio set. He also told Odette that 'Henri' wanted to get to England to see someone at the War Office. 'Henri' had said that if they could arrange a pick-up to take him to England, he would get Marsac and Suzanne out of Fresnes and take them with him.

Odette listened to all this, read the letter from Marsac, which was recognizably in Marsac's handwriting, and felt the walls of 'Les Tilleuls' moving in around her. She did not like this story; she did not like what she had seen of 'Henri'; she did not like Bardet.

Bardet seems to have been someone who provoked extremes of trust or mistrust: Odette and *Arnaud* had never trusted him. Francis Cammaerts, who had met him during these last few days hiding out in Annecy, likewise suspected him. But Marsac had always thought him an excellent resistant and had made him his assistant; Peter Churchill had seen no reason to question his loyalties and later on Frager would live and work alongside him in utter confidence. It would be misplaced: whether or not he had been working for the Germans when he first came to them, Bardet certainly began to do so now. At this moment, and from now on, he was working with Sergeant Bleicher.

Bardet told Odette that he had seen 'Henri' off on his return journey to Paris. Why didn't he himself now go to Paris and take him an answer about the radio set and the pick-up? He could also check up on Marsac at the same time, to verify 'Henri's' story?

Odette reluctantly agreed to let Bardet go. She disliked him but she could not prove, even to herself, that he was a traitor. So far he had done nothing to harm them and even if he were disposed to betray them, it might be safer to have him hundreds of kilometres away in Paris than here among them. At least it would give her some time to think the situation through.

So she agreed that he could go to Paris, though she refused to let 'Henri' have their spare radio set, or any access to *Arnaud*.

So Bardet left for Paris and Odette went to see *Arnaud* and confide her worries to him. She also gave him a short message for London, saying that an Abwehr officer had arrested Marsac and Suzanne and wanted to bring them to England to discuss ways of ending the war. Perhaps Baker Street would give them some guidance.

But neither Odette nor *Arnaud* were happy with the situation. Both were full of foreboding about what would happen and they decided that it would be best to send Francis Cammaerts away. *Arnaud* had some friends in Cannes at a safe address which both he and Odette knew. He agreed to call on Cammaerts in Annecy as soon as possible and send him south to this address.

Odette spent the next few days anxiously awaiting new developments. The first message which came back over *Arnaud*'s set from London changed nothing: Baker Street told them to go very carefully, because this sounded like an obvious trap. Baker Street also asked them to find a dropping ground for Peter Churchill: he was coming back in.

Meanwhile Roger Bardet came back from Paris with ostensibly reassuring news: Marsac, incarcerated in Fresnes, had confirmed all that 'Colonel Henri' had said. He had voluntarily written that letter; moreover, he too, Bardet, believed that 'Henri' honestly wanted to seek an end to the war. What about the pick-up?

Odette was now playing for time. She told Bardet to go back to Paris and to tell 'Colonel Henri' that she was trying to arrange for a pick-up within the week. She told him that she thought it might not be possible before the night of 18 April.

Bardet argued angrily with Odette, accusing her of dragging her heels and being inefficient. He said he was going to go back to Paris and try to get Marsac out of Fresnes himself. He also demanded to know when Peter was coming back. Odette and *Arnaud* were actually liaising with London to get him brought back as soon as possible, but Odette did not want Bardet to know this. She said that she wasn't sure. Bardet insisted that he had heard Peter was due to come back very soon; hadn't she said something about it earlier?

They parted angrily and Bardet left for Annecy, declaring his intention to go back to Paris. Odette went to see *Arnaud* to tell him what had happened. By now both Odette and *Arnaud* were almost sure that Bardet was going to betray them. *Arnaud*, characteristically, responded with a murderous rage. He always kept a gun at hand and now he swore that he would shoot Bardet. He knew that he could still find him in a rendezvous café in Annecy and he set off to finish him. Odette, fearing that a killing would bring 'Henri' down on them at once, had to jump on her bicycle and pedal after him, arguing and reasoning with him until he finally agreed to wait.

Their position was now extremely dangerous, but Odette believed that she had won them a respite until the 18th. Bardet, she reasoned, would go back to 'Henri' and tell him that there was a possibility of a pick-up on the 18th, and 'Henri' would wait until then, in the hope that he might be able to arrest not only a couple of agents, but three agents, a British plane and a pilot. So until the 18th, they were safe.

And now, on *Arnaud*'s sked, their instructions came through from England. On reflection, Baker Street considered that 'Henri' was highly dangerous and Odette was to cut all contact with him. She was also to cut her contacts with the now compromised St Jorioz and Annecy groups. She was to go into hiding across the lake and *Arnaud* was to leave the Faverges house and hide out in Les Tissots with his set. Meanwhile they were to find a dropping ground urgently for Peter Churchill who would return at the earliest moment.

The moon period was upon them and they had to move swiftly if they were not to miss it. They needed somewhere close by but the plains around the lake were too open and vulnerable. It would have to be a plateau or a hilltop. They thought of the Semnoz, the highest peak on the western shore of Lac Annecy, which rose to over 1,700 metres. When they asked Jean Cottet, he confirmed that it had a flat summit; there was even a disused tourist hotel up there. They sent a message to London that they were exploring its possibilities and the following day, 13 April, they climbed up to look at it.

The first leg of the journey was easily walkable, on a road which ran for about eleven kilometres to the foot of the slope. From there the going was harder, along a mountain path which climbed through woods and over the snow-line. It took them two hours to reach the end of the path and they found themselves on a convex hilltop, with a deserted hotel, a precipice to the west and in between a flattish area on which a parachutist might land. There was loose wood around to fuel a fire and the position of the summit meant that the glow would not be visible from St Jorioz. The drop would have to be an extremely accurate one but they did not have the time to be fussy.

By the time they got back to the lakeshore it was late in the evening. *Arnaud*, obeying the instructions, moved his belongings from Faverges to his hillside den, Les Tissots, and in the early hours of the morning transmitted confirmation of the Semnoz dropping ground. Odette had not had time to organize her move and she decided to give it low priority. She still had to contact the various members of the Annecy group and warn them to lie low. Some of them would have to be paid money owing to them. And in any case, she felt sure that she was safe until 18 April, the date when 'Colonel Henri' expected the aeroplane. So she stayed in the Hôtel de la Poste.

Why was she so sure of this? It looks now like a rash error of judgement. Did she simply believe she had out-manoeuvred 'Colonel Henri', despite Bardet's probable treachery, despite the fact that the

Abwehr knew exactly where she and her comrades were and were almost certainly watching them?

Odette might be holding things together so far, but surely the immediacy of the peril should have been evident?

Odette herself, years and many post-mortems after the event, had a curious light to shine on this discrepancy:

> 'There is a mystery there,' she commented. 'When I sent a message through *Arnaud* to London, I wanted Peter Churchill to depart on the 14th, knowing that until the 18th we would be all right. Now, the funny thing is, it is claimed that it is not so, but I do know that *Arnaud* came to me and said, "I have received a message from London to say keep the game up with the German." That is to keep it going until the 18th. Now the office here claims that message was never sent.'

Could this be true? Were Odette and Peter Churchill deliberately delivered to the Abwehr by someone in Baker Street? Certainly, if she had received such a message Odette would have obeyed it: sustaining combat was more in her character than abandoning it. But I hesitated before writing this into my account; it seemed to me so very much the product of a wounded and bewildered memory. It seemed too much like a retrospective explanation for something Odette herself could no longer understand – why she had felt so sure of the timing of this affair. Yet I felt I couldn't just ignore it.

This mysterious message is not mentioned in either Tickell's *Odette* or in Peter Churchill's memoirs, nor in M.R.D. Foot's official history of F Section. Both Maurice Buckmaster and Vera Atkins declared themselves astonished when I raised the matter with them: they said they had no knowledge of any message being sent and that this was the first time they had ever heard any such suggestion. But then if a message were sent with a sinister motive, it would not be sent with their knowledge, nor would it be carefully preserved in the official files. There is every reason to believe that Buckmaster sent an unequivocal message, telling Odette to cut contact with 'Henri'. But it is conceivable that Bodington, with his MI6 contacts, could have sent a separate, contradictory message, without Buckmaster's knowledge. And there was another piece of knowledge which Odette brought back from the war and which has been kept out of all books and public records ever since. It is a piece which fits into the Déricourt-Dansey-Bodington jigsaw and it is a piece which specifically incriminates Bodington as being involved with the Germans.

The information which Odette brought back to England in 1945 was this: in the summer of 1943, a few months after her arrest, Bleicher came to see her in prison. He told her that Nicolas Bodington had been in Paris that night; that he had stayed in Bleicher's flat and that he had now returned to London to continue his work in F Section HQ.

Thus, too late for her own safety, Odette learned that there was indeed a 'traitor' in Baker Street.

This information has never been made public. When she returned to England in 1945 Odette told the senior staff of F Section what Bleicher had told her. (Again, Buckmaster says he knew nothing of her report.) The initial reaction from SOE was receptive and she was asked for exact details of what Bleicher said. But within a few days, SOE's attitude changed. Odette was told that they didn't wish to pursue the matter officially; they had reason to believe that Bodington had indeed been involved in double-dealing but it would do more harm than good to expose him. The war was over; an exposure would only bring further suffering to the families of the dead agents. They requested an under-taking from her that she would never make public what she knew.

After a lot of thought, Odette made that undertaking and she has never broken it. But when she met me, more than forty years after giving her promise of silence, she was still haunted by her knowledge. She was anxious that I should have some idea that a breach of trust had occurred. She badly wanted me to understand, she said, that there was more to what she would tell me than she could freely say. I was to appreciate the complexity of it; I was to glimpse something of the turmoil. In that first conversation she told me only that she had come back from the war with painful knowledge about someone highly placed in F Section, knowledge that he had betrayed his colleagues. In all the times I spoke to her afterwards she would never name Bodington as that person but she gave me hints and suggestions: if I read this book and put it together with that one; if I thought about what she'd said in this new context, I might begin to understand.

All kinds of evidence now reveal that Bodington played a central role in the Déricourt-Dansey-SD intrigue. By the MI6-sells-SOE theory, he was working ultimately for Dansey rather than for the Germans but the result for many F Section agents was the same: he deliberately allowed them to fall into German hands, consigning them to probable torture and almost certain death.

There *was* after all someone in Baker Street delivering agents to the Germans. And as far as Dansey and Bodington were concerned, there was one clear advantage to be gained from making sure that Bleicher arrested the St Jorioz agents: it would keep Bleicher occupied. Dansey knew of the SD/Abwehr rivalry; he would almost certainly have known, through Déricourt, that Bleicher was ambitious to infiltrate Prosper and that he was becoming a thorn in Boemelburg's side. Feeding the Prosper agents to Boemelburg was one thing; losing them to Bleicher and the Abwehr was another – what would then happen to the carefully engineered relationship between Déricourt and Boemelburg, the line from MI6 into the SD? Assuming that Dansey knew of Bleicher's hunger for Prosper (and his intelligence on such matters was usually good), then what would he be likely to do about it? The answer is, provide a diversion. And the events in St Jorioz would have presented a very good opportunity. So did Dansey, via Bodington, help 'Colonel Henri' along? Was that unclaimed message sent, and was Bodington the person who sent it? It has a certain undeniable logic of its own. And Odette, who suffered the consequences, cannot believe otherwise.

But that night of 13 April, Odette went to sleep in the Hôtel de la Poste with her faith in Baker Street and in herself still intact.

The next day, 14 April, Odette went into Annecy and visited different members of the group, explaining to them that they were all to disperse and go into hiding. She told them that none of them should come to St Jorioz any more. She also met with *Arnaud* and agreed with him that they should each listen to the BBC that evening for the signal announcing Peter Churchill's return. During his sked of the night before, *Arnaud* had been given the message to listen for: '*Le carabe d'or fait sa toilette de printemps*' (The golden beetle decks itself out for spring).

At about 7 p.m. she sat beside her radio set in her hotel room – it was the same portable receiver she had used in Périgueux – and waited for the *Messages Personnels*. If Peter Churchill were to return the operation would have to be tonight or the next night. The *Messages Personnels* began, read out in the announcer's precise, expressionless voice. Straining her ears to hear through the crackles of poor reception and the German jamming waves, she suddenly heard the message that was meant for them: it came through twice: the golden beetle decks itself out for spring.

Arnaud was installed in a back room of the hotel, also listening to a radio. When Odette went down into the bar to meet him, she was taken aback to find him drinking with Jean Cottet and looking very unready for a mountain climb. He said that he had not heard the message. Nor had Jean Cottet, who had been listening to his own clandestine receiver in the basement. But Odette was sure that she had heard it through the interference. So they set off, not just two of them but Jean Cottet and Simone Cottet too, as Jean Cottet offered to drive them to the foot of the Semnoz in his car.

It should have been an easy trip but it was not to turn out so well.

First of all, the car, which was fitted with the obligatory charcoal-gas burner, was difficult to start and it was nearly eight-thirty before it got going. Then, worried about the ability of the engine to cope with the mountain road, they took it on a gentler, longer route. But after a kilometre or so the car broke down, leaving them further away from the Semnoz than before. The four of them had to walk twelve kilometres to the foot of the Semnoz; when they arrived there at around 11 p.m., breathless and behind schedule, they had to press straight on with the steep climb up the rocky path.

It took them two hours to scramble to the summit. They were climbing over boulders and crashing through undergrowth, stopping every so often to listen for the sound of a plane which would mean that they were too late. But it didn't come and they made it to the summit, built and lit the fire and shortly afterwards they heard the distant sound of an aircraft engine.

Peter Churchill dropped alone on to the top of the mountain, where Odette and *Arnaud* – and further back, the Cottets – waited for him. It was an emotional reunion – in Churchill's memoirs it stands as the moment when his and Odette's love came into the open. He describes floating down to the ground in front of her and into her arms. Even Foot's official history, based on a report from *Arnaud*, acknowledges that Odette 'greeted him affectionately'.[1] Churchill, meanwhile, speaks of them embracing each other in the darkness and the snow, 'at this crowning moment of their lives'.[2] Odette herself cannot be drawn on their love and its manifestations: she states simply that it was very great.

Peter Churchill was now back; the three-strong team was reunited and Peter and Odette were openly in love. They spent the next few hours on the mountain top: Odette explained to Peter Churchill exactly what had been happening during the past few weeks; *Arnaud* and Jean Cottet gathered the different containers which had been dropped and together they carried them into the disused hotel and hid them. Finally the small group burned the parachute silks, tried to disguise the evidence of the bonfire and all but *Arnaud* began the long climb downhill. *Arnaud* stayed in the old hotel with the containers; Odette arranged with him that the next morning she would go to *Tom* Morel and tell him about the drop and members of the Glières *maquis* would come to collect it.

It was a difficult walk back down the Semnoz in darkness and at one point Odette slipped and fell heavily down a bank, knocking herself out. The group did not reach the Hôtel de la Poste until 8 a.m.

[1] *SOE in France*, M.R.D. Foot, HMSO, 1966
[2] *Duel of Wits*, Peter Churchill, Hodder & Stoughton, 1953

Peter Churchill had been ordered by Baker Street not to return to the St Jorioz centre. He, like Odette and *Arnaud*, was to go into hiding – moreover he was supposed to stay away from Odette who was compromised by her contact with 'Colonel Henri'. But Odette only had time to change her clothes and wash before she had to go out again, to make the promised visit to *Tom* Morel. She left Peter at the hotel and caught the Annecy bus. All that morning she was busy in Annecy: she made contact with *Tom* and explained about the arms stored up on the Semnoz; she looked up other people too, whom she had not managed to see the previous day, and warned them to lie low. Then she caught a bus back to St Jorioz in time for lunch.

Peter Churchill was troubled by this lingering in St Jorioz. He wanted them to leave the Hôtel de la Poste immediately. But Odette told him that she was sure they were safe until the 18th. It was now the 15th; they had time. Peter had not been in St Jorioz for a month and Odette was much closer to the situation than he was; he agreed that they should return to the Hôtel de la Poste for the night, and move on the following day.

In the afternoon Odette and Peter rowed across the lake to see Madame Frager and give her news of her husband. (In fact at that moment he was just a few hundred kilometres away embarking on his new mission and harbouring grave suspicions about Déricourt.) They also went further from the lake shore and found new rooms for themselves in a quiet hamlet. They then rowed back to the western shore and returned to St Jorioz.

In the evening *Arnaud* appeared at the Hôtel de la Poste. Men from the Glières *maquis* had taken over guarding the arms up on the Semnoz; everything seemed to be under control. The three had dinner together at the hotel and arranged to meet again the following day – not here but on a quiet road. *Arnaud* left on his bicycle for Les Tissots and his radio set. Within a couple of hours he would be in his hillside hideout nearly twenty kilometres away; this time the next day Odette and Peter planned to be on the other side of the lake.

But Bleicher was not in Paris, where Odette supposed him to be; he was much closer. He had no intention of waiting until the 18th; he knew there would be no pick-up and he knew that Peter Churchill had already returned to St Jorioz.

In Roger Bardet, Bleicher had an efficient spy. Bardet was suspected by Odette and *Arnaud* but he was still a member of the group, able to come and go in 'Les Tilleuls' and share all the inside information. It had not been hard for him to find out that Peter was expected back imminently and to pass on that information to Bleicher. And Bleicher had journeyed back east to take advantage of this knowledge: Odette obviously suspected Bardet and intended to out-manoeuvre him and Bleicher. It was time to close the net on her and her comrades.

At about eleven o'clock that night, shortly after Odette and Peter had gone to bed, one of the couriers from Les Tilleuls came in to the hotel. He told Jean and Simone Cottet that he had some urgent news for Odette. Simone went upstairs and fetched Odette from her room; she came down in her dressing-gown. She was not particularly worried – she was used to being summoned at odd hours. But as she reached the hall a familiar figure stepped out in front of her: 'Colonel Henri', holding a gun.

Odette was exhausted from the last few days and was momentarily stupefied by the sight of Bleicher and a party of men standing round her with guns. Bleicher immediately warned her not to call out to Peter Churchill; he told her that there were troops surrounding the hotel and that if Churchill tried to escape he would be shot. He ordered Odette to lead him upstairs to Churchill's room.

Out of the shock, Odette was beginning to formulate a thought. It was a practical thought, which gave her mind something to cling to: she knew that upstairs in Peter's wallet were new instructions and radio codes which he had brought back from England. She began to wonder frantically if she could get hold of the wallet and dispose of it before they were taken away.

She took Bleicher and his men to Peter's room – inside, Peter was asleep in bed. The men went in ahead of her, switched on the light and addressed the befuddled Peter Churchill by his name. They ordered him to get up and dress; as he did so, Odette came into the room and began helping him. She saw his jacket hanging on a chair and, fiddling with the pockets, managed to find the wallet and slip it out. She tucked it into her clothes and went on helping Peter.

Odette was taken to her own room to get dressed. Then she was marched back to Peter and they were taken downstairs. Jean Cottet was standing aghast in the hall – as they passed him, Peter apologized for making him 'unknowingly' involved, hoping the Germans would at least believe the Cottets were in the clear.

Outside the hotel cars were waiting in the night: Odette and Peter were put into one and driven away.

It was the end of the Haute-Savoie *réseau*. As the car drove through St Jorioz, Odette was able to push the wallet behind the car seat, where it was safe at least for the time being. But she and Peter were far from safe, and they were only the first agents to be caught in the big Abwehr/SD swoop of summer 1943.

TEN

The Net Closes on Prosper

At the beginning of May the Prosper agents were working harder than ever, innocent of the fact that, having broken the St Jorioz *réseau*, Sergeant Bleicher had turned his attention to them.

On 22 April, unknown to the agents, the two sisters Germaine and Madelaine Tambour had been arrested. As the original Carte contacts in Paris, their names and addresses were on Marsac's list, and Sergeant Bleicher now pulled them in. For the last seven months the sisters had been in the Prosper inner circle. It had been to them that Andrée Borrel had gone upon arriving in France, before *Prosper* was even in the field. Their apartment in the Avenue de Suffren was often used as a letter-box and place of rendezvous by the Prosper agents. Now that the *réseau* was so busy the agents made contact with the sisters less regularly and for some time they went on with their growing burden of work unaware of their arrest; but the Abwehr had come a step closer to them.

There was unease among the agents, however, albeit vague, and murmurs were beginning to make themselves heard here and there, mainly against Déricourt. Frager had been suspicious of him ever since the Tours incident and now, during Déricourt's absence in England, he contacted *Prosper* and confided his misgivings. *Prosper* listened and added Frager's complaints to those of Andrée Borrel and a few others, who had grown unhappy with Déricourt's incessant questions.

When Déricourt came back into the field in May, the feelings of a number of agents were turning against him.

Had the F Section agents in France known about the MI5 report which Bodington had dismissed, they might have made louder noises against Déricourt and sooner. But they did not know, for Baker Street had decided not to act on it. In Baker Street's view, there had been allegations against agents before which had proved totally unfounded. And Déricourt's record to date was excellent. Without Bodington's inside knowledge, there was too little evidence on which to withdraw such a successful agent. On the contrary, when Déricourt came back into France on 6 May, Baker Street had already planned a greatly intensified programme of operations for him. It was intended that during the next few months he would supervise a steady flow of new agents into the country: through his hands would pass many future *réseaux* chiefs.

But though Déricourt's place in all this has now been shown to be crucial, for the agents out there at the time it was a minor concern, the doubts only small nagging ones. More important and more time consuming was the Resistance work itself, now growing still more intensive. In May the number and volume of drops went on increasing. They doubled on the number taken in April: all over the occupied zone agents and resistants were turning out to receive drops, to drag the arms away, to store and transport them. The activity was almost too intense: it was at the limit of what could be contained by the *réseaux*. The men and women of the *réseaux* were sure that the invasion must be imminent: the agents waited anxiously for the signal.

Boemelburg came to the same conclusion. Unsettled by Déricourt's recent trip to England and convinced that the date of the invasion would soon be passing through the Prosper channels, he tightened the screws on Déricourt. When they next met he demanded that as well as giving him advance warning of all pick-ups, Déricourt passed over for copying all the 'airmail' that was carried out of France on these trips.

This was the step which finally took the SD right into the vulnerable heart of the agents' operations. The use of airmail had been made possible by Déricourt's regular operations. Previously, reports and plans which were too detailed to be transmitted by radio had to be written down and smuggled out of the country by couriers, going to Spain or to Switzerland before being forwarded to Britain. It had meant delays of weeks, more often of months, before Baker Street received the information. Now the growing amount of vital information about agents' whereabouts, operations, needs and forecasts, could be sent to England via Déricourt's Lysander operations. The reports were written down, sometimes in code, sometimes in clear, and smuggled to the landing ground to be sent back to England. The volume of airmail had been growing as all the other activity grew: hard-pressed agents, anxious to get accurate reports back to England so that they might get more badly needed support, had been entrusting them to Déricourt. As the organizer of the flights, he would be brought the mail shortly before the night of the operation; he would take it to the landing ground and hand it into the Lysander as the departing agents climbed aboard.

From now on Déricourt would take each batch of mail to Neuilly, to one of the houses comandeered by the SD. There it was photographed in great detail; by the time the original mail reached Baker Street, its copies were already being studied at SD headquarters.

The effect on the Prosper agents was to be heavy, but it was not immediate. The sense among many of the Prosper *réseau* that it was getting late, that they were being overtaken, was not attributable to the Germans' manoeuvrings. It was due to the fact the arms drops went on relentlessly increasing, so that it seemed impossible that the Resistance groups could handle the receptions, use the supplies for the desired sabotage acts and preserve their own safety. Sabotage excursions were now going on in earnest, especially in the Sarthe, west of Paris, and the Sologne, where Yvonne Rudellat and Pierre Culioli worked as members of a very active sabotage team.

Then in mid-May something happened which increased the pressure still further. A message came over the Prosper radios urgently recalling *Prosper* to England for briefing. Something decisive was surely at hand.

On the night of 13 May, *Prosper* went back to London. The operation was arranged by Déricourt as usual. Two Lysanders came, bringing new agents: Julienne Aisner was back from training to take her place in Farrier; three others, Sidney Jones, Vera Leigh and Marcel Clech, had come to set up a new *réseau*, Inventor. Their arrival took place under the surveillance of the Bony-Lafont gang; as *Prosper* was being carried back through the dark sky to London, the incoming agents were trailed to their destinations in France. Yet more corners of the Resistance were being exposed to German scrutiny, even as they struggled to come into being.

Prosper stayed in England for one month, from the middle of May to the middle of June. While he was gone, the last phase of the Prosper struggle began in France. To the amazement of the agents in the field, the pace of their lives now changed from hectic to frantic. The volume of drops went on rising, so that in June the amount of arms received was – astonishingly – more than twice the amount received in May. In some areas, reception committees were out almost every night. Sabotage teams were at work night after night too, blowing up bits of railways, bringing down power lines. Andrée Borrel travelled ceaselessly from one region to another, helping to arrange for the transport and storage of the dropped supplies. Her sister and brother-in-law, the Arends, acted as go-betweens and stored *Archambaud*'s radio set. Yvonne Rudellat went out on repeated sabotage trips with Pierre Culioli and the local Resistance groups. *Archambaud*, when he was not at his radio, was also working at receptions and *coups de main*; Jack Agazarian transmitted not just for Prosper agents but for many other *réseaux* in touch with them – for Biéler's and Trotobas' *réseaux* in the north-east, for Scientist in Bordeaux, for the new *réseaux* Butler and Juggler which were being set up as Prosper associates west and east of Paris – and Francine Agazarian was on the move doing courier work which she was finding ever more exhausting. Yet *Prosper*, the leader of the *réseau* and the man on whom Baker Street placed so many hopes, was in London. What was going on?

The many-layered intrigue which lay behind the life and death of the Prosper *réseau* was now taking on its final twist.

For years there have been different speculations about what really took place during *Prosper*'s last visit to London. For though it was Maurice Buckmaster who recalled *Prosper*, he did so on the order of a higher authority – Winston Churchill. And when *Prosper* arrived back in London, it was Winston Churchill who he was summoned to see. He did of course see Buckmaster as well, but not at this meeting. The briefing which *Prosper* received from Churchill was strictly confidential. Maurice Buckmaster, though head of F Section and *Prosper*'s commanding officer, wasn't invited to share in the exchange.

This wasn't as peculiar as it sounds today. Churchill liked to meet agents personally and had had interviews with several F Section agents in the past. Moreover, SOE made a point of maintaining secrecy between its sections, giving information only to those whose responsibility it was to know. This summoning of *Prosper* for a confidential meeting with Buckmaster's chiefs was suggestive but not out of order. In fact, if what it suggested were true, the very highest security was vital. . . .

Later on Maurice Buckmaster would write of how, in the late spring of 1943, a top secret message came into F Section advising that D-Day 'might be closer than we thought'.[1] In response to this

---

[1] *Specially Employed*, Maurice Buckmaster, Batchworth Press, 1952

news, F Section went into overdrive. Its priority now was to prepare
for an approaching invasion, working to ensure that within the shortest
possible time the agents in France would be ready.

So it was that while *Prosper* was in London, his colleagues in
France were bombarded with arms, supplies and radio messages.

Meanwhile it seemed certain that this too accounted for *Prosper*'s
summons to Churchill. In the minds of those who knew he was back,
there was little doubt that *Prosper* had been told when to expect the
invasion.

And here lies the final convolution to the Prosper tale. *Prosper*
had indeed been recalled to receive just that information. In his
office, in an atmosphere of stealth and urgency, Churchill had told
him that he and his comrades would not have much longer to wait for
the invasion. It would take place in the first week of September 1943,
in the Pas-de-Calais in the north. *Prosper* was to return to France
and prepare his groups for their supporting role.

But this was a lie.

In fact, *Prosper* and his fellow resistants, together with the staff
of F Section, were now being duped by their own high command.
It was part of a deception plan designed to mislead the Germans.

The F Section staff weren't aware of what was being done;
but Colin Gubbins, overall head of SOE, was. His deputy, Harold
Sporborg, was also in on the plan, and it is largely thanks to his
recent statements that we know what actually took place. Here, in
a nutshell, is the sequence of events and decisions which led to
one part of France being set deliberately and prematurely ablaze.
Not surprisingly, Claude Dansey plays a well-camouflaged part.

SOE was not the only organization Churchill had caused to be
set up to fight in unorthodox ways. Another was the organization
known as London Controlling Section, which was in charge of
devising and implementing deception plans to leak false information
to the Germans. Claude Dansey was not an official member of the
Section but he very often sat in on its meetings. In April 1943,
London Controlling Section had agreed to start a deception plan
to make the Germans think the invasion of France was coming that
year.

Soon afterwards, in May, an interesting piece of information
was passed by MI6 to a few senior figures in SOE and also to
London Controlling Section: MI6 advised these people (but did
not tell F Section) that the important Prosper *réseau* in France was
compromised.

For London Controlling Section it was, if not exactly good news,
certainly well worth knowing. For if a large SOE *réseau* had already

been penetrated by the Germans, then would it not be possible for London Controlling Section to feed false information into this *réseau*, and deceive the Germans? Here was an opportunity to implement a deception plan; in consultation with Dansey and MI6, and with the highest levels of SOE, London Controlling Section set about exploiting the Prosper *réseau*. Churchill, who was enthusiastic about the work of London Controlling Section, agreed to authorize false 'invasion preparations' through the Prosper channels.

Senior SOE figures like Gubbins and Sporborg knew of this; as a matter of deliberate policy, however, F Section was not enlightened. The exploiting of Prosper meant feeding into it false information about the invasion; when the agents were captured – as would inevitably happen sooner or later and probably sooner if arms drops and radio traffic were piled on – this false information would be forced out of the agents. The hope was that the Germans would believe it and would gear all their efforts to fortifying the north of France, taking troops away from the eastern front in order to do so, and thus relieving the now desperately hard-pressed Russian troops. If it worked, the strategic value to the Allies might be considerable, but it involved the deliberate sacrifice of the Prosper agents and hundreds of their helpers. No one was in any doubt that they would face deportation and execution, and that the agents were likely to be horribly tortured. 'Obviously' – as Sporborg has recently put it – 'in a situation like this we would not want Buckmaster to know.'[1]

So instead, Buckmaster was told only that Churchill wished to see *Prosper* in person and as soon as possible. *Prosper* was brought back and interviewed; a buzz went round F Section that *it* was really at hand and suddenly, with aircraft for special night-time drops noticeably easier to come by, the race against the unknown date was on.

While *Prosper* was in England digesting what he had been told, the deception plan was already going full speed ahead, its tokens raining out of the sky into the fields of France, where the agents and the people of the Resistance gathered them hopefully in.

On or around 12 June, *Prosper* was dropped back in to France. He did not fly in to a Déricourt reception; he was now deeply suspicious of Déricourt and did not inform him of his return. Instead, he asked London to get Pierre Culioli and Yvonne Rudellat to arrange his reception. Their Monkeypuzzle *réseau* was well liked by agents and by staff for its reliability and efficiency; in the urgency of the past few weeks Baker Street had been directing an almost continuous series of arms drops there and now they gave *Prosper* a message to take with him: two Canadian agents would be parachuted in

[1] *All The King's Men*, Robert Marshall, Collins, 1988

to one of Monkeypuzzle's grounds in a few nights' time, on 15 June.

Pierre Culioli was at the ground to receive *Prosper*. He was harrassed – a few nights previously there had been a fire at one of the *réseau*'s receptions and the Germans were on the trail of the local resistants. Having *Prosper* dropped to him was risky enough; he was incredulous when he heard that he had to make arrangements for two new agents as well. He warned *Prosper* that the area was dangerous; he did not know how long they could last.

Prosper now went to Paris where he swiftly made contact with his immediate circle – Andrée Borrel, *Archambaud*, the Agazarians and a few others. He found them frantically busy; he also heard some disturbing pieces of news. He learned belatedly of the Tambour sisters' arrest. He also learned of a curious incident during his absence when some Dutch agents had got in touch with the group looking for Déricourt; Jack Agazarian had taken them to a rendezvous where they were arrested, though he escaped. This last was actually an involved and unsuccessful attempt by the Abwehr, posing as Dutch agents, to get their hands on Déricourt. But even without knowing that, *Prosper* was filled with anxiety about the way things were going. He was alarmed by such a near escape; he was also uneasy about Jack Agazarian's wide range of contacts and he sent a message to London requesting that Jack and Francine Agazarian be taken back on the next pick-up, due very soon on 16 June. Francine Agazarian was in any case exhausted to the point of sickness by the workload which had recently been placed on her.

The accounts of the few people who were part of Prosper then and who survived the war suggest strongly that *Prosper* now realized he and his comrades were doomed. Madame Balachowsky, one of the *Ecole Nationale d'Agriculture* group in Versailles, recalled him being withdrawn and anxious. Jacques Bureau, the radio expert, talked to me of the change that he saw in *Prosper* on his return and of what *Prosper* told him:

> 'Before May *Prosper* always had the air of someone who would win the war, who knew that it would be won. But when he came back from London he was overwhelmed. He was intoxicated with the idea of the invasion – London had intoxicated him with it, deliberately. He told me, "The invasion will come in the first week of September." But there was too much going on now; he was overburdened, exhausted.'

Perhaps this was why, along with all his other work of meeting people, devising plans and passing on instructions, *Prosper* became embroiled in a peculiar and very risky attempt to free the Tambour sisters. Through Jacques Weil, a Juggler agent, he heard that the Abwehr was holding the Tambours; this news had come to Weil through business contacts of his who themselves had a line into the SD. *Prosper* asked Weil to set up negotiations with the SD, offering one million francs for the women's release.

Through the trail of contacts, the offer reached the ears of Boemelburg's deputy, Josef Kieffer. He did not actually have the authority to get the women away from the Abwehr but he strung *Prosper* along, arranging to hand over the women and then sending two old prostitutes along to the rendezvous in their place: a little SD joke.

But *Prosper* wouldn't give up: he renewed the approach and now Kieffer saw his chance to close in on him and take the initiative away from the Abwehr. He sent a message back that he could and would release the women this time, but that *Prosper* himself must turn up at a certain restaurant to collect them.

Why did *Prosper* agree? Had he gone so far in this business that he had lost his judgement altogether? Perhaps he thought that if it came to a shoot out he and his fellow resistants could defend themselves and escape. Whatever his reasoning, he did agree and when the time came *Prosper* was sitting outside the restaurant with a number of resistants around him. Suddenly a car drew up immediately opposite him, and men jumped out. They were holding cameras which they pointed at *Prosper* and his companions; before anyone had a chance to take cover they had photographed them all and were back in the car.

For *Prosper*, it was a bitter blow, frightening and mystifying. But it was only one of many things going wrong in this last frantic week of the *réseau*'s life. The two Canadian agents, John Macalister and Frank Pickersgill, had arrived on the night of the 15th, and had been received by Yvonne Rudellat and Pierre Culioli in their now over-active, highly dangerous territory.

On the next night, the 16th, a Déricourt double Lysander operation picked up the Agazarians and three non-F Section agents, and brought in Charles Skepper, *en route* to start a new *réseau* in Marseille, and three women. They were Diana Rowden, an English woman who was going to the Jura as a courier; Cecily Lefort, an Irish woman who had married a French doctor and who was also going east to work as a courier for Francis Cammaerts in the Drôme; and Noor Inayat Khan, a young Indian woman who was going to Paris to be the radio operator for Cinema, one of the Prosper sub-*réseaux*. The arrival of the four new agents was monitored by the Germans' men. Diana Rowden was tailed to her destination and began her mission with no chance of completing it safely. Skepper was tailed to Lyon, where he slipped out from under surveillance. Noor Khan and Cecily Lefort travelled back into Paris by train with Rémy Clément; the SD had agreed to keep clear of Clément and so these two weren't followed. But somehow Noor Khan had been given the address of a Prosper letter-box that was no longer safe, even though *Prosper* had already told Baker Street to eliminate it. When *Prosper* discovered this, and the fact that other agents had probably been using it, he realized that a lot of his other addresses might be compromised. On 19 June he had to cancel all the letter-boxes and passwords he was using.

He also decided to move from his current address. On the 19th or the 20th he left his flat and moved into an hotel in Rue de Mazagran in the St Denis quarter of Paris. He was deeply uneasy and worried; he went down to the *Ecole Nationale d'Agriculture* and talked to Madame Balachowsky. He was, according to her, distressed: he had become convinced that for a long time the Germans had known about him and his colleagues.

He didn't have to wait long for confirmation: the blow was now ready to fall. The explosion of Resistance activity down in the Sologne had decided the SD, and while *Prosper* was moving from his old address they moved into the countryside south of Paris and began their searches. They got a good haul: arms were discovered in barns and farm buildings, in houses and lorries; resistants were being pulled in; by the 21st, road-blocks were being set up to catch more of them.

Yvonne Rudellat and Pierre Culioli were still sheltering the two newly-arrived agents, Macalister and Pickersgill. The new agents' mission was to set up a new sub-*réseau* to the east of Prosper, and they needed to get in touch with *Prosper* himself. With their own *réseau* going up in flames around them, Yvonne Rudellat and Pierre Culioli decided to drive the newcomers to a station and go with them to Paris to help them find *Prosper*.

June 21st was a Sunday; that morning they set off in a car for the nearest station. But they had not realized quite how much German activity was taking place around them. Their quiet region was crawling with Germans – patrols, barriers, checkpoints. Soon they were stopped at a road-block. The night before, the Germans had found arms hidden in a lorry on this route and now SD officers were interrogating everyone who tried to pass. The two Canadians, whose accents were distressingly un-French, kept silent; at the wheel Pierre Culioli bluffed his way through.

They had made it through one obstacle, but there were more to come: further along, a second road-block met them. Two SD officers turned the Canadians out of the car and ordered Culioli to drive to the village *mairie*; the Canadians were made to follow on foot. Yvonne Rudellat and Pierre Culioli, reaching the *mairie* before the Canadians, were taken inside, and there they saw that the round-up was a comprehensive one. Many of the local resistants, with whom they had been working, were lined up for questioning. They were immediately questioned themselves, but once again, their cover held – Pierre Culioli convinced the officers that he was a local forestry official, and they were released and allowed to go back to the car.

They sat there waiting for the Canadians and wondering if their accents could possibly survive the SD's scrutiny. They didn't have to wait long for their answer – suddenly an SD man strode out of the *mairie* and ordered them back inside: in response Pierre Culioli put his foot down on the accelerator and drove off.

The car rattled away from the *mairie* and down the country road but before long two German cars were after it. The German cars were more powerful and though the agents had the advantage of a start, within a couple of miles the Germans had come right up behind them and were shooting at them. Yvonne Rudellat was shot in the head – she fell forward, across Pierre Culioli, and she was unconscious when the car crashed. Pierre Culioli was pulled out, brutally beaten and kicked. The first Prosper agents had been arrested.

The other arrests came swiftly. Andrée Borrel, *Archambaud* and *Prosper* were all in Paris; moreover, through Déricourt, Boemelburg's men knew exactly where to find them. On the evening of Tuesday 23 June, Andrée Borrel and *Archambaud* had dinner with Armel Guerne and his wife in their flat in Montparnasse. At about eleven o'clock the two of them left and made their separate ways to *Archambaud*'s current address, a flat belonging to contacts Madame and Monsieur Laurent. The flat was in the residential sixteenth *arrondissement*, on the corner of the Boulevard Lannes and the Avenue Henri-Martin, and here the two agents met up again and began to work at coding messages for transmission. Soon after midnight they heard a banging at the door and shouts of 'Police!' Madame Laurent, thinking it was a neighbour playing a joke, opened the door and armed German officers burst in. Andrée Borrel and *Archambaud*, Madame and Monsieur Laurent were arrested; the flat was turned over and *Archambaud*'s radio and his key-code were found. The Germans had more than enough to seal the fate of these four people; they took them to Gestapo headquarters in the Avenue Foch for interrogation.

Early the next morning *Prosper* was on his way back to Paris, after
a meeting in Gisors, east Normandy, with one of the Prosper sub-
réseau organizers. He had just heard about the arrest of Pierre
Culioli and Yvonne Rudellat; he was hurrying back to his hotel in
the Rue de Mazagran to prepare for a meeting with Claude de Baissac.
He entered the hotel hall and greeted the *concierge*, went upstairs
to his room and there found Germans waiting for him. It was 9 a.m.
on Wednesday 24 June and every agent of the Prosper inner circle was
in captivity.

Who can imagine what the agents went through in the next few days?
The woman who wound up the affairs of the Prosper *réseau* after the
war said that *Prosper* was interrogated non-stop for three days and
nights; he was made to stand until he collapsed and then forced up
again; he was allowed no food, water or sleep. Information came back
through other sources that he was beaten unconscious and his arm was
broken. There is no record of the treatment the agents received but it
would have been harsh: Culioli, who was the only one to return, had
already been badly injured on arrest; after a few days' respite he was
again 'interrogated' and savagely beaten. *Archambaud* would probably
have received similar treatment to *Prosper*, though perhaps to a lesser
degree. Yvonne Rudellat, with a serious head wound, was alive but
unconscious in a hospital in Blois. Of the details of Andrée Borrel's
treatment we know nothing, but German accounts of her in captivity
disclose a last glimpse of the born resistante: they all agree that she
told them nothing and that she showed a fierce contempt for all their
threats.
    The SD, triumphant in the capture of the key agents, was now
working on them in the hope of scooping the entire Prosper operation. The SD interrogating officers wanted the names of contacts,
the addresses of safe houses, the locations of the arms dumps.
    It was not only physical abuse which was used to weaken the
captive agents. The SD had a store of psychological weapons too.
They had the copies of the Prosper airmail, the contents of vital,
confidential messages to flaunt before the agents. They told them –
as Odette was told – that there was a traitor in Baker Street and that
they were all being manipulated. They displayed devastating glimpses
of their knowledge of F Section operations, which made it clear that
infiltration had taken place at a high level. They had – through the
airmail and through Déricourt – an enormous amount of information
on Prosper contacts and sub-agents: they trailed some of it before the
agents, enough to indicate the extent of their net, and then suggested
that the only way to save the lives of these hundreds and thousands of

people was to co-operate in revealing the whereabouts of the arms.

The pressure was concentrated on *Prosper* and *Archambaud*. For three days and nights they said nothing. Then an agreement was reached: in return for an assurance that all prisoners taken would be treated as prisoners of war, the agents agreed to lead the Germans to the arms.

It's not clear who was the first to agree to this, nor has the exact sequence of events ever been established. Some people argue that it was all *Archambaud*'s doing; others say that *Prosper* wrote and signed a letter to resistants telling them to hand over their arms to the bearers of the letter.

Now why did they – or one of them – do it? Both *Prosper* and *Archambaud* were dedicated to the Resistance; for the past nine months they had been risking their lives and braving all kinds of hardships and fears in order to help organize and arm the French Resistance forces. All their work had been directed to building up arms and supplies for the invasion, and they believed that invasion was only two months away. What lay behind this decision to co-operate?

They were of course weakened by days of physical suffering, suffering that it's impossible for us to imagine. But there was another force at work: the truth which now seemed to face them from all sides, that they had been betrayed. They were told that there was a traitor in Baker Street; perhaps they, like Odette, were given Bodington's name. All the agents had recently been struggling to bear up beneath the extraordinary weight London had placed on them; now so much of the last few months' activity must have appeared suspect. Still out there in the extended Prosper *réseau* were hundreds of people who sincerely believed they were fighting for France yet who were already compromised.

And then there was the matter of *Archambaud*'s radio message. In those first few days the SD radio experts made contact with London on his captured set. They transmitted pretending to be *Archambaud* himself, free and well. They had forced him to give them his security check and he, in line with his security teaching, had given only the first, 'false' check. This should have signalled to the receiving station that the set was being controlled by the enemy. But when the Germans transmitted with this check they were interested to receive in return a quick rebuke for forgetting the true check and a reminder to use it in future. They immediately confronted *Archambaud* with this and, according to one SD officer, it was this which broke his spirit and made him decide to co-operate with them.

An honest mistake? Probably – there were quite a few instances of the receiving station taking deliberate clues for accidental errors. But to a captured agent, debilitated and shocked by evidence of betrayals, it might have seemed more sinister. Did London really think he was free? Or did they know he was captured but were pretending to think him free? Who in all this was telling the truth, who lying, who playing games?

Whichever of *Prosper* and *Archambaud* was the first to agree to the pact, and whoever signed what, by the end of June the Germans were moving in on local groups and arms dumps all over the Prosper region. The Prosper sub-*réseau* in Gisors was raided, so was the Juggler *réseau* around Châlons-sur-Marne. News of the arrests spread. *Réseau* organizers Biéler, Trotobas, Worms – together with sub-agents like Monsieur and Madame Guerne – held an urgent meeting to discuss security measures, but couldn't stem the tide. On 1 July Jean Worms of Juggler and Armel Guerne were arrested; Jacques Weil fled to Switzerland. Jacques Bureau was arrested. The Satirist *réseau* in the Sarthe was smashed. The remaining arms dumps around Blois were seized. *Archambaud* himself took a party of plainclothes Germans to the home of Andrée Borrel's sister and brother-in-law, where he had kept a spare radio set. The set was taken and Andrée Borrel's brother-in-law arrested.

The arrests went inexorably on. Significant members of the organization, when arrested, were quickly faced with other members who knew of the pact. Different organizers, faced with a *fait accompli*, became involved in different degrees: Pierre Culioli, for instance, sincerely believing that the pact would protect resistants already compromised, wrote letters to several of them, explaining the terms of the pact. The clean up had taken on a momentum of its own and wave after wave of arrests washed over the vast Prosper territory. By the end of August 1943, almost all the arms had been taken and hundreds upon hundreds of resistants had been captured. The French estimate that 1,500 people were arrested during these two summer months. The great Propser *réseau* and all its hopes were finished.

ELEVEN

The End of the Intrigue

But that was not the end of the Prosper/Déricourt story, for Déricourt himself was still free and remained so until February 1944. The machinations of Dansey, and Bodington's role in them, remain a murky area but the evidence that exists points to intense double-dealing. There is an account by one of Dansey's colleagues of Dansey laughing and celebrating when news came in of Prosper's downfall. There is a note written by Bodington in Déricourt's file which makes no sense in the official version of events: dated 21 June – the day of Yvonne Rudellat's and Pierre Culioli's arrest – this pencilled note states surprisingly: 'We know he is in contact with the Germans and also how and why.' We? This 'we' certainly did not include Buckmaster. Nor did Buckmaster know anything about a trip Déricourt made to England on 19 July; but we know that Déricourt made the trip for he is recorded as being a passenger on a certain clandestine flight, an MI6 flight. He did not stay long; another MI6 flight returned him to France on 21 July. And now Bodington's part in all this becomes a central one for on the next night he too flew out to occupied France.

It was an extraordinary thing for a member of headquarters staff to do, especially one who ranked high in the F Section hierarchy. Baker Street knew by now that something had gone terribly wrong in Prosper: radio transmissions had been coming in from other agents in northern France, bringing confused accounts of disaster. It was clearly dangerous for anyone to go to Paris now, yet Bodington went: in his official history, M.R.D. Foot refers to his having 'persuaded Buckmaster' to let him go.[1]

[1] *SOE in France*, by M.R.D. Foot, HMSO, 1966

Bodington's official F Section business was to find out the extent of the damage done to Prosper; his real reason was to see how the land now lay for Déricourt. He took with him as a radio operator Jack Agazarian, specially recalled from leave. Now, Jack Agazarian had already spoken against Déricourt in his debriefing report; he had told Baker Street that *Prosper* was worried about Déricourt's security. In the cover-up that Bodington was now orchestrating around Déricourt, Agazarian was therefore a wild card and one which might prove dangerous. It does not require too much ingenuity to imagine what Claude Dansey would have wished to do with him. And sure enough, Jack Agazarian never came back from this last 'short' mission.

According to Bodington, it happened like this. He and Agazarian were landed safely in France, thanks to Déricourt's arrangements. They went to Paris where Déricourt also found them lodgings in Paris. They could find no Prosper contacts still at large and sent messages saying as much to Baker Street, over Agazarian's radio. Within a week Baker Street sent an instruction to Bodington to rendezvous with *Archambaud* at a certain address. Both Agazarian and Bodington had doubts about the security of the address; they therefore tossed a coin to decide who should go and Agazarian lost. On 30 July he went to the address and didn't come back. Bodington surmised that he had been arrested.

There had indeed been a message from Baker Street to go to *Archambaud*'s address; it had been sent in good faith. Baker Street was still in touch with *Archambaud*'s set, now controlled by the Germans, and had received the address from it. At this point, though they were worried about the authenticity of the signal, Buckmaster and his colleagues were still inclined to think that *Archambaud* was genuinely free; Bodington, of course, knew better. But when the coin was tossed -- if indeed it ever was – Bodington kept his knowledge to himself. And so Jack Agazarian, potential trouble-maker for the Déricourt camp, went off to a bogus rendezvous: finally, belatedly, the last member of the Prosper inner circle was captured.

This trip of Bodington's lasted another two weeks, during which he met a number of F Section agents still at large. He spent some time with Julienne Aisner and her fiancé Charles Besnard. Julienne was working for Déricourt and now Bodington laid plans with her and Besnard to expand Farrier's activities. They would take over a small bar in the Rue St-André-des-Arts in St-Germain-des-Prés and use it as a contact point for agents wishing to leave France by Déricourt's operations. The bar would be a useful front and the beginnings of an airborne escape line. After the war, Besnard said that during these meetings Bodington reassured him about Déricourt; Bodington told him London had recommended that Déricourt work with the Germans.

Bodington also met Frager, now working in the Yonne organizing his own *réseau*, Donkeyman. Frager's suspicions of Déricourt had now been confirmed from an unexpected source. For through his trusted lieutenant, Roger Bardet, now once more working with him, Frager had been put in touch with Sergeant Bleicher who was once again posing as anti-Nazi 'Colonel Henri'. Up in the Yonne, the same cat-and-mouse game that had caught Odette was playing itself out again, but more slowly this time.

And now Bleicher's game deliberately interlocked with Boemelburg's. For at this point Bleicher told Frager at one of their meetings that Nicolas Bodington was in Paris. Bleicher said that he had this information from his own sources in the SD and that the SD knew it through Déricourt. Bleicher told Frager that Déricourt was busy reporting all his own and Bodington's movements to the SD. He could even tell Frager the confidential F Section information that Déricourt's code-name had been changed.

This conversation reinforced all Frager's own suspicions of Déricourt. He took himself off to see Bodington at once and angrily confronted him with what Bleicher had said, insisting that Déricourt be withdrawn. But Bodington was reluctant to take him seriously. Frager was beside himself with rage; he threatened to go over Bodington's head and send a report against Déricourt back to London. So Bodington assured him he would act.

What did Bodington do? Well, he certainly didn't tell Buckmaster and the other F Section staff to withdraw Déricourt. On the contrary, he warned not Buckmaster but Déricourt, telling him that Frager was out to discredit him. In turn Déricourt appealed to Boemelburg and Boemelburg, his kudos greatly increased by the Prosper arrests, leaned on Bleicher to stop him interfering. There is an account of this in Roger Bardet's papers; there is even confirmation from the Foreign Office that Bodington warned Déricourt.

This is what the Déricourt/Prosper affair had become, a farrago of lies and betrayals and cover-ups. Bodington worked skilfully in Paris during these weeks, papering over the cracks, deflecting suspicion from Déricourt. German records show that they knew Bodington was there – they had of course observed his arrival – but it was in the SD's interests to leave him free. After all, he seemed to them to be squarely on the side of the person they thought of as 'their' man. And in effect he was: on this visit he set Déricourt fair for another six months of triple agenting. Long after Bodington flew back to England and the dust settled on the Prosper arrests, even into 1944, Déricourt would still be bringing agents in and out of France under the watchful eyes of the Germans and Claude Dansey.

There is one more relationship to be considered in this tangle of illicit relations: that between Bodington and Bleicher. Did Bleicher really have direct contact with Bodington as he claimed to Odette? Did Bodington stay the night in his flat? Or was Bleicher simply making the most of information he had learned from the SD, hoping to demoralize Odette and persuade her into a full confession?

Odette – while naming no names – clearly believes that Bleicher did know Bodington personally and after the war Bleicher himself repeated his claims about Bodington having been in his flat. While Bleicher's word must count for something, it cannot be conclusive given his history of inventive lying. If he was in touch with Bodington, then Bodington seems to have been using him as a second string, saving the strategically valuable Prosper betrayals for the SD. However, Bodington certainly did nothing to stand in Bleicher's way. He did not warn Frager against 'Colonel Henri' despite knowing what had happened to Odette and Peter in April; and then of course there is the message Odette says she received. Was Bodington the sender of that message and if so, was he simply assisting Bleicher in order to get him away from Déricourt, or was there yet another layer to the intrigue? These are questions which must remain open until someone produces more evidence one way or another.

But in any case, Bodington's position was about to change. Baker Street decided it was time he came back to London; the staff also sent instructions to the Scientist radio in Bordeaux that Claude de Baissac and Lise de Baissac should also return from the field. Both Claude and Lise had had contacts with Prosper and were endangered by the recent arrests; Baker Street asked that Déricourt arrange for them to be on the same plane out as Bodington.

Duly, Lise and Claude settled their affairs as best they could and took leave of their comrades. On the night of 15 August, Bodington met them in a haybarn in the country and together they boarded a plane for England. They all arrived back safely (more of Lise and Claude later) and Bodington returned to his post in Baker Street. He reported that Prosper did indeed appear to be smashed but that Déricourt's Farrier team was 'completely sound'.

And then a few weeks later Bodington was moved from SOE. He was sent instead to the Political Warfare Executive, the outfit in charge of black propaganda. Who moved him? And why? Had F Section finally rumbled that its second in command was selling its operations and agents down the river? Surely not, for that must have incriminated

Déricourt and he was left at large to handle many more operations before he was finally recalled. It's more likely that Dansey or Churchill or both of them in the shape of London Controlling Section decided that Bodington had now served his purpose and should be got out of F Section before his position became untenable.

And so Bodington departed and was away from F Section for the next six months. And not until Déricourt's recall in February 1944 would Bodington return to Baker Street. He had done his job of protecting Déricourt – for the time being.

I wish it were possible to leave Déricourt here, along with the whole sordid story of Bodington's split allegiances and Dansey's expert manoeuvrings. While they were machinating in London, people were fighting and dying in France. Many of the Prosper agents were brutally tortured during this summer and almost all of them would eventually die. Whatever strategic justification there might be for sacrificing the agents and their hundreds of Resistance comrades, it is not to be found in the politickings and career moves of Dansey and Bodington.

But before I leave them and return to the agents, I must look ahead to what ultimately happened to Déricourt. He was eventually brought out of France, in early 1944, and his recall was largely thanks to Frager, who finally managed to get home in October 1943 to make his allegations. Buckmaster had heard enough about Déricourt now to make him uneasy, despite Bodington's energetic support of the man and the lack of firm evidence against him. It was difficult to get Déricourt to return, but Baker Street prevailed against his prevarications and in February 1944 he was flown back, with his wife. Nothing could be proved against Déricourt, but at least he was out of the field: and although in its report on him, MI5 said Déricourt had 'no case to answer' as a traitor, it recommended against his return to France. Sporborg, as deputy head of SOE, had known about the use of the compromised Prosper in the invasion deception plan; but he had not known *how* Prosper came to be penetrated in the first place. He now tried to investigate Déricourt's possible dealings with the SD, to see if he had indeed been giving them information. He got nowhere, however; strangely enough (it seemed to him) MI6 was conducting its own investigations and effectively blocked all his attempts to interview Déricourt.

Julienne Aisner and Charles Besnard, by now married, were safely returned to London in April. In October a radio operator, André Watt, had joined Farrier; he came back on the April plane with them. The other member of the team, Rémy Clément, was simply left in Paris and told to lie low. In February 1944 the Farrier route in and out of France would finally be closed for good.

But what, in the summer of 1943, was happening to the imprisoned Prosper agents? They were, endlessly and unbearably it must have seemed to them, under interrogation, and not only for the where-abouts of the arms dumps. Just as London Controlling Section had planned, the SD were on the trail of what they considered the big one: the date of the forthcoming invasion. The agents were kept in cells in Fresnes prison, a huge fortress-like jail near Paris; they were usually taken to the SD headquarters at 84 Avenue Foch for interro-gation. Here they might be – and sometimes were – beaten and tortured. *Prosper*, *Archambaud*, Culioli and Jack Agazarian are known to have been tortured; it's likely that very many of the others were too.

The interrogations were not over once the Prosper agents had signed the pact. The SD wanted from the agents *all* the information they possessed about the Prosper Resistance groups, all their contacts, all their addresses and arms, and not least the date of the invasion. Most of what they wanted, they got. There were various attempts by agents and resistants to mislead them: Jacques Bureau, for instance, was arrested in mid-July. When he was taken for interrogation, the SD wheeled in *Archambaud* to encourage him to speak. Jacques Bureau, one of the holders of that 'precious' piece of information about the date, told me that *Archambaud* managed to slip him a sign of Resistance, while ostensibly co-operating with the Germans. Phrasing his words with a deliberate grammatical error, *Archambaud* told Jacques Bureau to 'give them *some* of the help'. Bureau duly told his interrogators, after much holding out, that the invasion was due in November.

But it was no good. Many of the captured agents probably gave false leads like this, at great personal risk, but they could not stem the tide – the SD got hold of the 'crucial' date. *Prosper* was taken to Berlin for closer questioning; in Paris the interrogations of the other agents continued. The SD continued to pull in agents from Prosper-linked *réseaux* and face them with agents already taken; the SD already knew so much about the *réseaux* and about Baker Street's plans that it was hard for agents to deny their identities or successfully withhold information. An enormous amount of valuable information went to the Germans in these months.

But eventually, by September, the SD had finished much of its interrogation of the inner-circle Prosper agents. Those who were still held in the Avenue Foch were sent on to Fresnes and to a routine of starvation, sickness and often solitary confinement; later they would go off in convoys to the concentration camps in Germany. Andrée

Borrel was held in the women's section of Fresnes prison; she would stay there until May 1944, when she too would set off for Germany. Yvonne Rudellat's record is almost completely dark after her arrest but whether or not she was in Fresnes she was still alive – she was sent on to Ravensbrück concentration camp and finally, at the end of the war, to Belsen.

I write more, later on, of the women's captivity and the conditions in which they existed in these prisons and camps. This chapter now has to let the agents go. What they were enduring and would continue to endure till their deaths was the human cost of the Prosper affair. Was it at least 'worth it', in strategic terms? Could London Controlling Section feel that the elaborate deception plan had been a success?

Well, the officers of the SD were convinced that they had obtained the genuine date of the invasion and, as London Controlling Section had hoped, they passed it on to the German army. But the German army, dealing in vast numbers and battlefields which extended hundreds of miles on the eastern front, was not impressed. It did not consider the threat significant enough to warrant diverting its forces. It continued to send its divisions where they were most pressingly needed – to the eastern front.

As the first week of September approached, the top level of SOE (under the orders of London Controlling Section) ordered the transmission of vast numbers of radio messages to France telling resistants to 'stay their hand'. These were supposed to indicate to the Germans that the invasion was imminent, and indeed did indicate so to the SD. But the Army, thinking on a larger scale than that of the French Resistance, remained unmoved and finally the first week of September 1943 came and went without any major disruption of the German war effort.

So by the autumn of 1943, the importance of the Prosper *réseaux* to the progress of the war was over. And thus the Prosper 'story', or rather the 'plot' finishes. But the people are left – some policy makers, some intriguers, and many hundreds of brave agents and resistants who, mercifully, never knew the full story.

Of the inner-circle Prosper agents taken that summer, only Pierre Culioli survived. *Prosper*, Andrée Borrel, Jack Agazarian and *Archambaud* were executed in concentration camps. The two Canadian agents, Macalister and Pickersgill, were also executed. Jean Worms was executed. Yvonne Rudellat died of sickness in Belsen just after the end of the war.

Hundreds of their associated resistants were sent to concentration

camps. Some – like Jacques Bureau and Robert Arends – survived.
Most did not.

Many agents belonging to Prosper-associated *réseaux* were arrested
later on – most of the Butler agents, for instance, were arrested in
September; Noor Inayat Khan and her chief, Garry, in October;
Trotobas was shot dead on arrest in December; Biéler and his
radio operator were arrested in January 1944; Frager was taken (by
Bleicher) in August 1944. Rousset of Butler managed to escape from
prison in 1944; all the others were executed. Most of the men were
hanged with piano wire to make their deaths as slow and painful as
possible.

The last act in the Déricourt drama was played after the end of the
war when Déricourt, having worked briefly as a pilot for the Free
French, was denounced by a number of people who had lived to return
from the concentration camps. Déricourt was duly arrested and tried
by the French for treason. It was a confusing trial with an immense
amount of circumstantial evidence against him but no definite proof.
Neither Buckmaster nor Vera Atkins attended it but someone from
SOE did: Bodington. Speaking for the defence, Bodington claimed
that he had known all along that Déricourt was working with the
Germans, that he had authorized it and had told him to continue. He
said he trusted Déricourt absolutely and would have no hesitation in
putting his life once more in his hands. Bodington's testimony tipped
the balance and secured Déricourt's acquittal. For almost everyone
else associated with F Section and its agents, dead or alive, it made
a horrible nonsense of the facts. Maurice Buckmaster, Vera Atkins
and all the agents who had survived might have been outraged by what
they heard; the Foreign Office might – and did – disclaim responsibility for Bodington's statement of 'authorization'; but ironically almost all of what Bodington said in this final act of the drama was true.

But by then all SOE's files had been handed to MI6, which arranged
the sorting and editing of them. The files which now lie in the SOE
archives are much depleted: many papers were supposedly destroyed
by an accidental fire; others have vanished. And the MI6 papers which
relate to Déricourt have, of course, always been classified information.
It has taken years, and the efforts of many different researchers,
to reach this point of understanding about the Déricourt/Prosper
affair. The picture as it is given here is not believed by all, but no
one has been able to offer any other convincing explanation of the
kinks, collusions and remarkable coincidences in the chain of events.
Maurice Buckmaster finds it difficult to believe that Dansey would
have plotted the downfall of F Section in such a cold-blooded way,

and is distressed that some people should be trying to get an 'inside story' out of him. 'It's *not* a cover up. At this distance from events it's impossible for French Section people to reconstruct details of events over which they had no direct control or knowledge. These things weren't written down and the things which are picked out now, with hindsight, were tiny details then and not central to our main tasks.' Buckmaster, like everyone else, has to struggle with an incomplete set of facts. However, he has now acknowledged Bodington's involvement in the intrigues: 'I was rather led astray by Bodington who should have known better – I say it now with respect to him because he's dead – he should have known better and he should have warned me more.' Vera Atkins has set aside her reluctance to believe such things; for her, the theory fits the facts. But with all the main players now dead, proof remains locked in MI6 files. Nevertheless, testimonies and clues have been filtering out ever since the war ended; perhaps in the future still more information will come out which will finally provide the proof.

Karl Boemelburg disappeared in 1944 in Holland and is thought to have died in an air crash. His deputy, Josef Kieffer, was hanged by the British after the war for war crimes.

Sergeant Bleicher survived the war but never achieved promotion.

Roger Bardet was convicted of treason by a French court after the war and was condemned to death. He served a prison sentence, then was reprieved and released.

Nicolas Bodington received an OBE and after the war worked for the Foreign Office. He died in 1974.

Claude Dansey continued as deputy head of MI6 until his retirement in 1945. He died in 1947.

None of these people are still living.

Julienne Aisner and Charles Besnard went back to live in Paris after the war; Julienne Aisner died in the 1970s, and Charles Besnard died in 1984.

Rémy Clément continued to live in Paris after Déricourt's departure and, despite the SD knowing his address, he stayed free. His wife died recently; he still lives in their studio in Paris, surrounded by her paintings, and spends the winter in Provence. André Watt returned to France in 1944 on a second mission; he survived and lives in France, keeping in touch with Rémy Clément. Jacques Bureau survived two years in German prisons and camps and lives just outside Paris.

After his acquittal, Henri Déricourt returned to commercial flying. In 1962 he went missing on a flight over south-east Asia. Wreckage of a plane was found in Laos. He is presumed dead.

TWELVE

Missions Under a Shadow

During the summer of 1943, while Prosper and its associated *réseaux* came tumbling down, four women were embarking on new missions in France. They had arrived in the early part of the summer, brought in by Déricourt's Lysander operations: first, on 13 May, Vera Leigh had arrived with her organizer Sidney Jones (*Elie*) and radio operator Marcel Clech (*Bastien*), to start Inventor in Paris. Then on 16 June Cecily Lefort, Noor Inayat Khan and Diana Rowden had come in on the same operation, and gone their separate ways. What was happening to them now?

Vera Leigh was a forty-year-old dress designer whose training reports had recommended her as being very keen and an excellent shot. She had been given a mission as courier, to work with *Elie* and *Bastien* in their small but – Baker Street hoped – soon to be active sabotage *réseau*, Inventor. The courier work would be testing, as Inventor was not to be a self-contained *réseau*: it was to work in close liaison with Frager's new and rapidly growing *réseau* in the Yonne, Donkeyman. Vera would be responsible for travelling between the two and helping co-ordinate their sabotage activities.

From the very beginning, the SD knew about her and her two fellows, for on that very first night Bony-Lafont men successfully trailed them from the landing ground to Paris. Once in Paris, the agents might have had a chance of shaking off surveillance, but whether it was through bad luck or through clever manoeuvring on Déricourt's part, they began to organize their *réseau* right under the eyes of the SD and the Bony-Lafont gang. Vera Leigh set to finding herself and the others rooms: one of her rooms was in a flat in the Rue Lauriston, a few buildings away from the Bony-Lafont headquarters.

Another was in the Rue Marbeau, just round the corner from the Avenue Foch and SD and Gestapo headquarters. This whole area – a section of the 16th and 17th *arrondissements* encompassing the Etoile – was Déricourt's stamping ground and, as the three agents felt their way into the clandestine life of the city, they began to cross over with Déricourt's contacts and addresses. The Café Mas, for instance, on the Place des Ternes, was regularly used by Déricourt and by them as a place of rendezvous.

But they were threatened from another direction too, again from the very beginning. The Donkeyman *réseau* with which they were directed to work was already well infiltrated by the Abwehr, through Roger Bardet. Bardet had rejoined his old friend and comrade Frager almost as soon as Frager had returned to France in April, and they were setting up Donkeyman together. Here in Donkeyman, Bardet was far more powerful than he had ever been in Spindle, for Frager trusted him absolutely and accepted his word and his contacts. Vera Leigh and her comrades in Inventor could hardly have had an unluckier mission; when they were not under the surveillance of the Bony-Lafont men they were carrying out their work in full view of the Abwehr.

Vera Leigh liaised regularly between *Elie* and Frager and yet throughout the summer she and her comrades in Inventor remained safe. The SD, having scooped up their prize Prosper catches, was busy interrogating them and trying to confirm the date of the expected invasion; Boemelburg and Kieffer were happy to leave Déricourt's other passengers in the field for the time being. It was sound counter-resistance tactics to allow them to increase their numbers and build up their strength before arresting them. And Bleicher, through Bardet, was playing the same waiting-game on behalf of the Abwehr.

But by the autumn, Bleicher was restive. He had his main double agent, Bardet, well ensconced in Donkeyman, but he had failed to play off Frager against Déricourt as he had hoped to do. He needed some arrests – the Abwehr needed some arrests to raise its stock in Berlin – and on 30 October as Vera Leigh was sitting in the Café Mas with a resistant called *Jacky*, who worked as *Elie*'s bodyguard, Abwehr men came to arrest them.

Vera, vainly insisting that she was one Suzanne Chavanne, her cover, was taken to Fresnes and locked into cell 410 in the women's section. *Bastien* transmitted news of her arrest to Baker Street a few days later, and then on 20 November *Elie* was picked up too. Finally, in December, *Bastien* also was arrested and Inventor was finished. It had never had a real chance of survival.

Of the three women who arrived together on 16 June, Noor

Inayat Khan was the only one whose mission lay in Paris. Diana Rowden set off for the Jura, and Cecily Lefort was bound for the Drôme as Francis Cammaerts' courier. But Noor went to Paris and into the heart of turmoil and danger, arriving there just a few days before the Prosper arrests began.

Rémy Clément was at the landing ground to receive the two Lysanders that night. He had laid out the lights in the correct pattern and had guided the aircraft in; he saw the three women and the single man climb down on to the grass and sent the five passengers he had waiting with him (two of them were the Agazarians) hurrying across to take their places. In darkness and haste he greeted the new arrivals and ushered them to the edge of the field while the two aircraft made their short runs and took off once more. He guided his new charges along the dark roads to the country station and they waited for the early trains. The man, Charles Skepper, code-named *Bernard*, took a train on his own; so did Diana Rowden. Clément himself took the train to Paris with Noor Inayat and Cecily Lefort. His own tension and anxiety made him acutely aware of theirs and he still remembers the bewilderment of those first few hours for them:

> It was a very difficult thing for them, to come from England, where they were protected, to a foreign country. To come under cover of night to a field in an occupied country. To be met and taken away by a man whose face you hadn't even seen, it was terrible. There were so many things they didn't know about France – the ration cards for food, for clothing, the identity papers that kept changing, the curfew.

Rémy Clément remembers Noor quite vividly, but then she seems to have been someone who made vivid impressions:

'I travelled to Paris in the same compartment as *Madeleine*. She was very uncertain, very worried by finding herself there. She was with another who felt herself more at home.'

It was typical of Noor Inayat Khan, code-named *Madeleine*, that she should appear vulnerable and that next to her other people seemed strong and capable. She was physically fragile and had a shy, polite manner: her trainers – especially those at Beaulieu – had expressed doubts about her suitability for field work. She was born into an affluent family, with an Indian father and American mother, and had lived in both Germany and France. In 1940, she and her family had left France for England and she had joined the RAF as a radio operator. Her radio skills and her knowledge of France made her a possible SOE recruit and she began her training in late 1942.

Noor Inayat (Khan was just a courtesy title, like 'Lady') was twenty-nine, but her reserved, dreamy manner made her seem younger. She was extremely keen to become an agent, and she already had radio expertise, but she did not take easily to the security training and she struck a number of trainers – in their perennial quest for decisive natural leaders – as too emotional and sensitive to survive life in the field. The head of the Beaulieu schools at that point was a man named Colonel Spooner, and he recommended strongly that she should not go to France. Her final report from the Beaulieu schools stated:

'Not overburdened with brains but has worked hard and shows keenness, apart from some dislike of the security side of the course. She has an unstable and temperamental personality and it is very doubtful whether she is really suited to work in the field.'

Maurice Buckmaster, though, believed in her. He detected in her a steady courage and determination which he believed would see her through. F Section accepted her. She was assigned the code-name *Madeleine* and was sent out to join an agent named Henri Garry, who had been recruited in France by Philippe de Vomécourt and who was now running a Prosper-linked *réseau* Phono in the Eure-et-Loire. He was in touch with France Antelme and with *Prosper* and had recruited some resistants of his own south-west of Paris. His mission now was to prepare sabotage attacks on railway and telephone installations in the area. Noor was to be his radio operator.

So Noor arrived in Paris on the morning of 17 June, and parted from Cecily Lefort and Rémy Clément. Thanks to Clément's company in the train, she had not been followed by Bony-Lafont men – Déricourt's agreement with the SD was that Clément was to be left alone. She therefore had a better chance than most of Déricourt's passengers of going safely to ground.

For the first few days, she seemed to do this successfully. She met up with *Prosper*'s contacts, the Balachowskys, in Paris and moved into rooms of her own. She met her organizer Garry, but did not move out to Le Mans, where Baker Street expected her to go. Garry was carrying out much of his work in Paris at that time, where he was also spending time with his fiancée, Mademoiselle Nadaud; they were to be married very soon. So Noor also stayed in Paris and began making contacts. She met France Antelme who helped her on her way and she left messages for other people; it seemed as though her mission were getting off to a smooth start. But in fact, (as has been already mentioned) the letter-boxes Baker Street had given her were '*brulés*' (no longer safe), and had been dropped by the Prosper agents. Two days after her arrival, on 19 June, *Prosper* discovered what she was doing. He sent instructions to her to abandon all the letter-boxes at once; meanwhile he, by now worried to the end of his endurance, set about reorganizing Prosper's other letter-boxes, for fear they too had been compromised.

But it was much too late for *Prosper* to save his *réseau*: within one week of her arrival, before she had managed to begin her work proper, Noor saw the entire Resistance network she had entered disintegrate around her. The arrests began, starting with the Prosper agents and rippling on outwards to bring down resistants, reception committees, and agents in neighbouring *réseaux*. France Antelme left Paris, taking with him the lawyer and resistant Savy, and headed for the countryside. They asked Déricourt to arrange a pick-up for them: they eventually left on a Lysander on 19 July.

At the very end of June, Garry and Mademoiselle Nadaud had a quiet wedding, but there was very little the Phono *réseau* could do in the way of Resistance work or sabotage. Noor and Garry made contact with one of the surviving *réseaux* in the Paris region – Chestnut, just south of Paris – and for a while they laid low there. But at the end of July, the Chestnut agents were also arrested and Noor fled back to Paris.

There, in August, Nicolas Bodington found her. He was in the city on his supposed 'fact-finding' mission; when he made contact with her, Jack Agazarian had already walked into the trap and been arrested. So Bodington was looking for a radio operator. He found Noor and helped her to move to a safer address. He learned from her that Garry was still free and the Phono *réseau* still intact if not exactly operating. In the middle of August he was picked up by a Lysander, along with Lise and Claude de Baissac, leaving Noor in Paris.

Did the SD know where Noor was? It seems not, for resistants belonging to Chestnut – especially the women, with whom Noor spent a good deal of time – were now being interrogated by the SD for her whereabouts. She was safe from betrayal by these sources: even if the captives had their silence broken, they did not know her new address. But Bodington did. Logically, Bodington should have told Déricourt, as he told him so much else. And if Bodington did tell Déricourt, Déricourt would have had no reason not to pass it on to the SD. Yet the SD did not know Noor's address in the late summer and autumn. Had Bodington decided that as Noor was no part of Prosper, she should stay free? Was this where he drew his line of loyalty?

Or perhaps it was simply that after Bodington's visit, Noor moved house yet again. Certainly, in the middle of September when she finally came on the air, she told Baker Street that she now had two transmitting addresses: one on the edge of the Bois de Boulogne (perilously close to the SD houses in Neuilly), and another in Bondy, a district on the eastern edge of Paris. And by the end of October she was using yet another flat in the 16th *arrondissement*.

Now, in the aftermath of the arrests, Noor began transmitting regularly to England. She was the only radio operator left in Paris and as such she was an important figure for Baker Street. What she, Garry and their few remaining contacts could find out about their fellows, she transmitted: melancholy lists of those taken, a resumé of those still free. Baker Street sent her instructions for renewed action; at the end of September she arranged for an arms drop to take place.

Baker Street, worried about her safety, sent her instructions to return to England. She transmitted a message back, asking how they would manage without a radio operator and saying she would stay until they could arrange to send out a replacement. This was the kind of steadfastness Buckmaster had expected of her; Noor was brave and conscientious, as he had sensed, but she also seems to have been naïve. There are many stories about Noor as a slightly exotic, gentle, dreamy woman; there are a number of second-hand tales about peculiar security lapses and gaffes, such as going to call on an old childhood friend, or leaving her code sheet lying around in her lodgings. Most of these stories are beyond checking, but they do tend to be similar in nature, pointing to someone with a blind spot for security; a kind of vague, unquestioning acceptance of anomalies. She did one thing in particular which was to cause a lot of future harm to F Section: instead of destroying her radio messages after transmitting or receiving them, she kept them all carefully written down in an exercise book.

Why? The reason was not perversity or carelessness; on the contrary, she probably thought she was being conscientious. The final mission instructions Baker Street had given her included the specific order: 'You must be extremely careful with the filing of your messages.' This wasn't unique to Noor; Jack Agazarian's instructions and, more recently, *Bastien*'s had used the same phrase. 'Filing' here was almost certainly being used in a journalistic sense: journalists are said to 'file' stories for their newspaper or magazine when they send them in – especially if they are sending them in over the telephone or telegram system, as Bodington would have done from Reuters. Whether or not it was Bodington's choice of words isn't clear, but in any case, though Agazarian and *Bastien* understood it correctly, Noor did not. It is in keeping with the other stories that abound of her trusting nature, and her faithfulness to orders, that she kept a careful record of all the messages which passed through her set – not only in code but also in clear.

The SD had meanwhile been making avid enquiries about a British radio operator. They were monitoring her transmissions through their D/F equipment, and although they could not trace her location, they had ascertained from her 'fist' (the rhythm and volume of her signals) that she was a lone operator handling a good deal of material. The SD let it be known via the Bony-Lafont gang and others that they would pay money to anyone leading them to her. Gestapo records show that the informant – whoever it was – asked for and received 100,000 francs, the equivalent of £500. Had he or she known, the Germans at that time were prepared to pay up to ten times that to get their hands on a 'British agent'. But £500 was all it cost them to get Noor: in the second week of October Noor was walking towards her 16th *arrondissement* flat, when she saw two SD men outside it. Before they could see her, she melted away into the crowds.

But she could not simply abandon her flat – in it were her set and her recorded messages. When enough time had passed for the men to have moved on, she returned. The SD were sure of their information and of their prey: they had posted men to wait for her inside the building. When Noor entered the flat they arrested her, and took her straight to the Avenue Foch. With her they took her set and the incriminating, horribly informative exercise book.

Noor's captivity has made her famous, in much the same way as Violette Szabo's behaviour in captivity has made a legend out of her. Noor was determined, once arrested, to say nothing that would harm her colleagues or help the Germans.

Her first instinct was to escape, and as soon as she was left alone, allowed to go into a bathroom on the fifth floor of the Avenue Foch, she managed to scramble out of the window and on to the roof of the building. But there was no way down from there; she was instantly spotted from the street and guards were sent to bring her back inside.

Her interrogation was formidable. Kieffer questioned her at length and in depth – by this time he had a large amount of information to throw at her, and he was able to show her how very much the SD already knew. But Noor refused to say anything about F Section work. After the war, under interrogation himself from Vera Atkins, Kieffer praised Noor Inayat's bravery and affirmed: 'We got absolutely no new information out of her at all.'

But the capture of Noor's set, along with the records of her messages in codes and clear, gave the SD all they needed to start another radio game. From Noor's exercise book the SD radio experts could work out not only her code but her security checks. Under interrogation she continued to divulge nothing, although she was told that Garry and his wife had now been arrested too. Particularly, she refused to discuss her security checks, which she still believed she might be able to withhold.

She was kept in the Avenue Foch for two months, while an SD operator began to play back her set to Baker Street, pretending to be Noor. The operator had often monitored Noor's transmissions and so could do a fair imitation of her fist; the coding experts, led by a man named Götz, composed messages in her style.

In England, the receiving operators and the staff at Baker Street were perturbed. The messages did not sound quite like Noor Inayat's distinctive voice and Baker Street decided that she too had probably been arrested. The staff continued to send messages to the set, while they devised some personal messages which only she would be able to answer.

Meanwhile, in November, Noor made another attempt at escape. There were other F Section agents being held in the Avenue Foch – one was John Starr, former Acrobat organizer, and another was a French Resistance leader, Faye. The three of them managed to get out of the building, but only into the building next door. They tried to hide from the search that was initiated but after an hour they were caught: all three were told to swear, on pain of being immediately deported, that they would never try another escape. Starr gave his word, but Noor and Faye refused. They were locked into separate rooms and within a few days they were put on to a convoy for the east. Noor travelled with other women into Germany and was put into a prison at Pforzheim.

In December, Baker Street sent its carefully devised messages to Noor's set. For a while no answering transmission came on the air – then suddenly it did, and it not only sounded like Noor but responded to their questions in a way which made them think she must after all be transmitting freely.

But it was not Noor. Somehow – most likely in simple, apparently trivial conversation, for Noor was not good at detecting deviousness – the SD had extracted from her the nuggets of personal history they needed. Now the staff at Baker Street puzzled further over the transmissions, and called in Antelme, as a former comrade of Noor's, to read them and give his opinion. As 1943 ended, Antelme and Baker Street were inclined to believe that Noor was in fact free and the Phono *réseau* still operating. To the SD's pleasure, Baker Street agreed to organize an arms drop for Phono.

But Noor herself was in Pforzheim jail, suffering terrible conditions. The prison authorities had received an order that she was a dangerous prisoner, and she was put into a solitary cell, locked into leg irons and manacles. There, scarcely able to move unless the guards loosened her manacles to let her eat, Noor was to survive ten long months.

The woman who had been Noor's first travelling companion on her mission, Cecily Lefort, spent just three months at liberty before being captured. Cecily Lefort was Irish, about forty, married to a French doctor, and until the war she had lived with him in France. She had returned to England at his insistence but she had been unhappy to go. Her background and knowledge of France got her into F Section; before she even got into France it had also helped DF Section with a new escape line project.

While Cecily was in training, P.J. Harratt, the DF officer in charge of seaborne projects, was trying to prepare a maritime escape line on the Brittany coast. Based in England, he was working on the river Dart with a young recruit called Deman, training Deman to go into France to set up the line. Cecily was a yachtswoman and she and her husband had a villa at St Cast, west of Dinard: she knew the tides and the beaches of the coast. As so often happened in SOE, news reached her through the ether that information was needed about good landing beaches for small craft. She was introduced to Harratt and she recommended to him the little private beach below her villa: it was both sheltered and secluded – ideal. She told Harratt that his agent should go to the villa and speak to the maid looking after it; he should explain that Cecily had given him the use of the beach, and as a token of good faith he should show the maid an old Irish ring which Cecily always wore and which she now took off her finger and gave to Harratt.

Later that summer, while Cecily was working in Jockey in the Drôme, Deman would take that ring to St Cast and gain entry to the beach. By autumn the 'Var' line was set up and through the winter of 1943–4 it carried many agents safely between Falmouth and Brittany.

Cecily's own mission was very different. In the Hautes Alpes of south-east France, Francis Cammaerts was beginning to build a new *réseau*. He was a cautious man and in spite of the Germans' eagerness to track him down he continued to elude them and to form contacts of his own. In May, through *Arnaud* (now on the run southwards) Cammaerts met *Albert*, a radio operator who had been attached to Carte and who was now in hiding in Montélimar. They began to work together and at the end of May *Albert* sent a message to Baker Street from Cammaerts, suggesting that the new *réseau* Jockey

should be completely independent of the other post-Carte *réseau*
Donkeyman, and that it should be based down in the south-east.
Baker Street agreed and looked around for reinforcements to send out.
Buckmaster and his staff decided on a young Frenchman, code-named
Alain, to be a sabotage instructor, and Cecily (now code-named *Alice*)
as Cammaerts' courier. They left almost immediately, but separately:
Cecily boarded the Lysander operation of 16 June, while the following
night, as she was settling herself temporarily in Paris, *Alain* dropped
into the Touraine and was received by Yvonne Rudellat and Pierre
Culioli.

There exists very little information about Cecily's time in France.
It's possible that while she was in Paris she looked up her husband
and his group of friends, but in any case she, like Noor Inayat, had
initially escaped the attentions of the Bony-Lafont men. But in Paris
she met up with another of the Lysander passengers, *Bernard*, and as
he was going down to Marseille they travelled south together. The
SD records show that *Bernard* was trailed for much of the journey
south, until he lost his followers in Lyon. Does this mean that Cecily
too was trailed? And if so, how far – just to Lyon or all the way down
to her destination in Montélimar?

Given what we now know about Déricourt's operations, and the
SD's waiting game, it's certainly conceivable that she was followed
all the way to Jockey territory. The SD might have known for some
time where she was and yet been unable to use that knowledge
to trap Cammaerts – for Cammaerts was rigorously, scrupulously
careful about using cut-outs. He kept his meetings, fraught with
danger, to strictly safe environments: in these months of building
the Jockey *réseau*, of forging links between the Resistance groups of
different communities, Cammaerts never went to a strange address
without checking up on it or being personally introduced into it by
an existing, trusted member of the *réseau*. He instructed all those he
recruited to adopt the same methods. Resistants in Jockey knew him
by sight but only group leaders knew his identity or how to contact
him. He would meet Cecily his courier very often, but the places of
rendezvous were chosen with such care that it would be hard for an
uninitiate to get close.

Whatever the truth of Cecily's legacy from the time of her arrival,
she worked as Jockey courier for three months, throughout the
summer of 1943. In September, on her way to a rendezvous in
Montélimar, she was arrested. She was to meet up with others from
F Section in 1944, in Ravensbrück concentration camp.

When she came into France on the night of 16 June, Diana Rowden's mission was to work in the new Acrobat *réseau* with organizer *Bob* (John Starr) and radio operator *Gabriel* (John Young). These two agents had dropped into the Burgundy region of France in May to set up a new *réseau*; Diana Rowden, as *Paulette*, was to complete the team.

Diana was an English woman in her twenties whose family had spent a good deal of time in France. She was very English-looking in a pale, athletic style, but her physical fitness and a certain natural unobtrusiveness of manner made the Baker Street staff decide to accept her as a courier. Baker Street had high hopes of *Bob*, whose second mission this was, and of the new Acrobat *réseau*. In the aftermath of the Carte débâcle, F Section needed new developments in the east of France; perhaps Acrobat could spearhead them.

But Diana was a marked woman from the moment she stepped down on to the landing ground. She was under the surveillance of the SD then, and the Bony-Lafont 'shadows' followed her throughout her long and careful journey east, until she arrived in her new territory, the Jura mountains.

The Resistance was strong in the Jura villages and, at first, the Acrobat *réseau* seemed to be growing quickly and well. For the last weeks of June and the first weeks of July, Diana worked hard with *Bob*, carrying messages between the thriving local Resistance groups and helping to receive the arms drops which *Gabriel* arranged over his radio. *Gabriel* stayed and transmitted from a château in the village of St Amour, a beautiful hideaway where he was secure from roving D/F vans. Diana stayed in the village of Andelot, with *Bob*, and she worked closely both with him and with a wine merchant from St Amour, Monsieur Clerc, organizing arms drops and putting people in touch with one another. They also had a new agent come to join them; this was *César* (Harry Rée) who had just fled the break up of a *réseau* in the Massif Central. He did not stay with them long: in early June a message came from Baker Street instructing him to move south to Belfort; there he was to start Stockbroker, a *réseau* working in association with Acrobat.

Soon after he had moved on, disaster struck: one of the Acrobat resistants denounced *Bob*, and he was arrested. He tried to escape but was shot and wounded and taken to Dijon prison: Diana and *Gabriel* went temporarily to ground.

Transmitting the news to Baker Street, they received instructions to resume Resistance work, but this time under the leadership of *César* in Stockbroker. Moving east with *Gabriel* to the region round Lons-le-Saunier, Diana began to act as courier again, liaising between the Acrobat resistants and *César*. In August, *César*, working with Monsieur

Clerc and some others, approached the Peugeot family and persuaded them to agree to help with the sabotage of their own car factory at Sochaux, which had been requisitioned by the Germans to make tank and aircraft parts. It was a new development in sabotage and a great victory for the Resistance when, in the middle of August, a serious explosion rocked the factory and put it out of action.

It began to look as though the new *réseau* of the Jura would survive the arrest of *Bob*; Acrobat was gone but Stockbroker was already getting results, without putting its members in too much danger.

But they were already in danger from the SD. The SD knew that Diana Rowden had gone to the Jura; with the arrival of autumn and the non-event of the 'invasion', the SD began closing in on all the agents whom they had seen come in but so far left alone. With the move to Stockbroker, Diana Rowden had given them the slip, but another Déricourt operation in November, a Hudson landing and pick-up, gave the SD the chance to find her. Five agents came in on this operation; three of them were trailed to Paris where SD officers immediately arrested them. One of them was on his way to join Diana and *Gabriel* and was carrying a letter to *Gabriel* from his wife. The SD got the agents' destination out of him, and the address of the farmhouse at which he was to seek his new comrades. Then they sent an agent along in his place.

Diana and *Gabriel* were alone in the farmhouse, a safe spot in the village of Clairvaux. They were expecting a new agent to arrive and when a man came to the door asking for them, and produced a letter written by *Gabriel*'s wife, they welcomed him as a new member of the group. He left again after a while, saying that he had business to do, and shortly afterwards a group of men came to the house and pushed their way in, seizing Diana and *Gabriel*.

The SD had caught up with Diana at last. But in the months that they had been free, she, Noor Inayat, Vera Leigh and Cecily Lefort had helped push the Resistance effort a little further along.

THIRTEEN

Developments South of the Line

By the summer of 1943 Jacqueline Nearne had been working in the 'unoccupied' zone for six months. Few of her fellow agents knew she existed, for she was extremely security-conscious and so was her chief, Maurice Southgate. But they were engaged in building one of the most important *réseau* in France.

Stationer was assiduously linking groups across the Massif Central, the large high plateau in the heart of France. It was also active two hundred kilometres further south, down in the foothills of the Pyrénées. During this summer, while the Prosper *réseaux* collapsed and the whole future of Resistance in northern France came under the shadow, F Section's hopes rested on the new *réseaux* emerging in the south. In the far south-east, in the hill country of the Drôme and the Hautes Alpes, Francis Cammaerts was building Jockey. In Marseille, the small *réseau* Monk still held steady under Skepper, Steele and Eliane Plewman. The *réseau* Pimento, established by Tony Brooks in 1942, survived. And in the south-west, although Scientist was beginning to fall apart, two new *réseaux* were spreading across the country further inland. These were Wheelwright, in the Dordogne and the Gers – of which more next chapter – and Stationer. Both were characterized by heavy security; both had at their centres an exceptionally strong working relationship between a male organizer and a female fellow agent. In Wheelwright the woman was a radio operator, Yvonne Cormeau, and the next chapter tells her story. In Stationer it was a courier, Jacqueline Nearne.

Jacqueline Nearne was born the second of four children in her family: there were two boys and two girls and when the children were young the whole family moved to France. Jacqueline and her sister Didi were brought up as French girls, going to French schools and speaking French much more fluently than English. When France fell to the Germans in 1940 they managed to get out of the country and to Gibraltar, and from there, with the usual interminable delays, they finally made it to Britain. They arrived in London in the middle of 1942 and began trying to get war work.

The Ministry of Labour, instructed to pass on details of applicants with foreign languages, sent the sisters' papers to the FANY offices and from there they reached F Section. Didi was not yet twenty-one and was considered too young for clandestine work, but Jacqueline was twenty-six. She was requested to go to Whitehall for an interview and was sounded out about returning to France. She agreed to do the training. Meanwhile Didi was asked to train as a home-based signals operator, receiving messages from people overseas. Jacqueline did not tell Didi that her own training was for something more dangerous: she gave her the FANY cover story, that she was driving officers' cars and generally providing support services. Didi was unconvinced, but that's another story.

Jacqueline was in the second batch of women to train for F Section – she trained in mid-1942 with Lise de Baissac, Mary Herbert and Odette. Though there was a ten-year age difference, Jacqueline and Lise had a deep natural sympathy: they were both quiet, discreet and independent. Each disliked and mistrusted flamboyance. They became very good friends during training and would remain close until Jacqueline's death.

But Jacqueline's training was not a great success. She took easily to the practical activities – she was toughened and made fit by the physical training; she could handle arms and shoot well – but she could not cope with the theoretical side of it. At Beaulieu she floundered. Her training officer reported to Maurice Buckmaster that he was not happy with her progress – she could do all the practical exercises with arms and explosives and the security manoeuvres but she could not give an intelligible account of what she was doing or why. When Buckmaster went down to Beaulieu he found Jacqueline aware of her difficulties and anxious about whether she should continue her training. She had already made an excellent impression on him and he encouraged her to go on. She would not after all be required to write a text book on her activities in the field, only to be careful, brave and steady, which he was convinced she was.

When her final report came from Beaulieu it was bad. The extracts available from it are quite damning: 'Mentally slow and not very intelligent . . .' they read; '. . . has a certain amount of determination but is inclined to waver in the face of problems . . . a reserved personality and somewhat shy.' The comments remain brusque, almost dismissive, even when making allowances for her: '. . . lacking in self-confidence, which might be entirely due to inexperience' the report observes and it finishes off decisively: 'she might very well develop after long and careful training but at present she could not be recommended.'

With hindsight, it's interesting to see how many of the successful agents did not pass muster with the training officers. These officers seemed blind to certain of the quieter, subtler qualities. There was a tendency to look for strong, evident organizational and leadership skills – not Jacqueline's forte. But Baker Street kept the prerogative to act on its own instincts and, as it had done with Francis Cammaerts and Odette, it now overrode the school's negative report on Jacqueline. 'I think her one of the best we have had,' wrote Buckmaster on the report and accepted her.

Maurice Southgate, the man who was to be Jacqueline's partner and 'chef', was an Englishman of thirty who had been brought up in France. His parents had gone to France for their honeymoon and decided that there was no reason to return, and Maurice had been brought up and educated in Paris. Once war had come he had left France and his French wife and joined the British forces; he had survived the sinking of the troop ship *Lancastria* in 1940 and had later joined the RAF. He had chafed under the lack of action (he was considered too old to fly) and longed to do something positive and direct for the war. When he heard about the possibility of going back into France he jumped at it.

In *Specially Employed*, Buckmaster writes with real admiration and affection of Maurice Southgate: '*Hector* is a man of intense devotion to a cause. His discipline and his creative imagination united to make of him a very intelligent and gifted leader. As far as he himself is concerned, his personal comfort counts for nothing.'[1] Vera Atkins said of him: 'He was one of the greats.'

He needed to be. The mission he was given was a broad one: with his courier Jacqueline, he was to organize a new *réseau* across hundreds of kilometres of virgin territory in central and southern France. Baker Street knew of two Resistance groups which existed at either extreme of this region: Ben Cowburn had brought back from his 1942 mission the names of Octave Chantraine, a French farmer who had a group near Châteauroux, and Charles Rechenmann, who had about one hundred helpers much further south, near Tarbes in the Pyrénées foothills. These names and their addresses were given

[1] *Specially Employed*, Maurice Buckmaster, Batchworth Press, 1952

to *Hector*, apart from that he would have to shift for himself.

Jacqueline in her turn was given a contact name and address in the city of Clermont-Ferrand. This, it was recommended, was to be her first port of call when they arrived in France.

Armed with these three pieces of information, and with maps, compasses and hand guns, Jacqueline (she was to be known by her own forename in the field) and *Hector* were driven out to Tempsford airfield on the night of 25 January 1943.

They were dropped blind into the countryside of the Auvergne, an arrival clothed in the obscurity of a particularly dark night. As the plane flew over the dropping ground, Jacqueline chose to go first. She dropped safely down and landed, watching the plane fly away. But she could not see where *Hector* had come down: the moon was not so bright at ground level and there were shadows cast by trees and bushes which fell across the ground and confused her vision. She had just begun to fold up her parachute when she froze: a few yards away there were three shadowy figures and one of them was pointing a gun at her.

Jacqueline thought that she was about to be taken. She felt fury that she should be caught before she had even begun and in a desperate attempt to gain time she pretended to notice nothing and began walking up and down, trying to assess her chances, wondering whether she should reach for her gun and fire first. Then she heard her name being whispered and one of the men moved out of the shadow to become *Hector*. He too had been confused by the shadows and then he had seen her moving and thought at first that she must be a German. Now that they moved cautiously over to investigate the other two shadows, they discovered that they were trees. It wasn't a comforting start: they were both shaken to realize how easily they might have shot one another.

Being alone, without a reception committee or any protection, they decided they could not take the risk of carrying with them weapons and maps. They hid them and their parachutes and set off, taking bearings with their compass (also illegal but more easily concealed) in an attempt to get to the nearest station. They were heading for a small town named Brioude, which was 'miles and miles away'; from there they would take the train to Clermont-Ferrand, where Jacqueline had been given a contact name and address. *Hector* did not share this contact: for security's sake it was Jacqueline's alone.

They walked a long way and for a long time, unsure if they were going in the right direction. Eventually, through the darkness of the early winter morning they saw a woman cycling towards them along the road, by her clothes a local farmer. They agreed to ask her if they were on the right road for Brioude.

But their arrival into the wilds and the long trek in the darkness had disoriented *Hector*. When they came face to face with the woman he opened his mouth and asked her the way to Brioude in English. The woman looked bewildered; even in the bad light *Hector* saw Jacqueline turn pale. Jacqueline realized that *Hector* didn't even know what he'd done; he was repeating the question, again in English, and she managed to stammer out under her breath 'Speak French!' before she took over speaking to the woman: '*Pardon Madame, sommes-nous dans la bonne direction pour Brioude?*' *Hector*, stricken, fell silent. The farmer, however, smiled a rather ghastly comprehending smile and assured them yes, they were on the right road for Brioude. She pointed them along their way and they took it hurriedly; it was then that it occurred to them with a mixture of relief and horror that the woman had been terrified of them, not because she knew them for *parachutistes* but because she had taken them for Germans.

It was their second close escape and the day had hardly begun. They were both now tense and unnerved. But nothing more happened to alarm them until they reached Brioude and the station, where they had to go through the first dangerous identity check. They were asked for their identity cards, and duly handed over their fakes, freshly made in England, and untested. But this time there were no mistakes or misfortunes: the cards passed the scrutiny and Jacqueline and *Hector* got safely into the station.

The train arrived and took them to Clermont-Ferrand without mishap. Once there, Jacqueline went on ahead to find the address she had been given and to make the contact. If it turned out to be no good, *Hector* had a contact address in Tarbes – the home of a Spanish woman called Pilar, Charles Rechenmann's fiancée. Jacqueline did not know this address, just as he did not know the Clermont-Ferrand one: this was good security, for it meant that if one of them were taken at this early stage the other would still have an uncompromised address to go to. Both Jacqueline and *Hector* had an instinctive appreciation of cut-outs; it was one of the reasons Baker Street felt they would make a good team.

Leaving *Hector* in a café, Jacqueline explained that her contacts lived close by and that she would be back to fetch him shortly. She went to the address she had been given – it had come from a radio operator who had worked in the area before, and who had been brought back to England: 37 Rue Blattin. There she found the family she was looking for – the Nérauds, a father, mother and a daughter of about twenty. After the alarms of the night and morning, she was almost overwhelmed with relief at her welcome. The Nérauds immediately offered both her and *Hector* shelter, for as long as they wanted it. She explained that they would be moving around a good deal and could not predict when they would be passing through Clermont-Ferrand - neither the dates nor the time when they might turn up needing shelter. That didn't matter, said the Nérauds; she and *Hector* could come and go as they needed; they could count on always being taken in. Meanwhile, she could go and fetch *Hector* at once and bring him to the apartment.

For Jacqueline, the time in the Rue Blattin had passed swiftly. For *Hector*, sitting exhausted and disoriented in the café, drinking beers and acorn coffees and wondering how long to give her, the wait seemed interminable. But eventually her composed, typically French figure reappeared at his side and the two new agents were on their way to their first base.

Hector described Jacqueline as 'a girl who could go anywhere. She could go into a ballroom; she could go into a post office; she could walk up to a German sentry and ask her way, with a smile – she'd get the information.' She was physically slight and delicate; her social manner was polite but reserved. She had that quality which attracts people but keeps them at arm's length. Even *Hector*, after all their work together, found her elusive: 'I was fascinated by that girl.' Her cover, as sales representative for a pharmaceuticals firm, suited her perfectly; looking at her, no German soldier or Vichy policeman was likely to suspect her of being a resistante, let alone a British agent.

This natural camouflage was extremely useful, because Jacqueline's mission was to involve an enormous amount of travelling and keeping of rendezvous.

During the early months of 1943, Jacqueline and *Hector* slowly built up Stationer. *Hector* made contact successfully with Chantraine near Châteauroux and with Rechenmann near Tarbes; they and their helpers were recruited to Stationer and Jacqueline then became the main point of contact between these two far-flung groups and *Hector* himself. This means that she had to travel almost continually on the train between Châteauroux in the north, Tarbes in the south and Clermont-Ferrand, carrying messages, instructions, requests, taking back the replies. In Clermont-Ferrand at least, she had something like a base: she usually stayed at 37 Rue Blattin and *Hector* would rendezvous with her there. But in other towns different safe houses had to be used: Jacqueline had to think ahead to where she was going to stay and let *Hector* know where he could find her. Security dictated that, as *réseau* organizer, *Hector* could not have a fixed address – indeed, he moved on constantly, keeping his whereabouts a secret from the growing number of groups he recruited. So he had to know where Jacqueline could be reached while on her travels.

For the first few weeks of her mission, Jacqueline stayed in hotels when she was away from Clermont-Ferrand. Initially she was lucky and had no difficulties but then, on a visit to Châteauroux to liaise with Chantraine's group, it was brought home to her just how risky these places were.

She was spending several days in Châteauroux, making contact with members of the local Resistance group there. She checked in to the local Hôtel des PTT (the post office hotel, found in many big towns and rather like a British railway station hotel) and from there travelled to different quarters of the town and its outlying villages to keep her rendezvous. She gave the name of the hotel as the place where she could be found if necessary. One morning, as she was in her room washing her underwear, there was a knock on the door. It was almost certain to be a Resistance contact and she could not leave him or her outside, so she hurried to open the door, apologizing for her disarray and feeling herself becoming red and flustered with embarrassment. Outside was a young man she had never seen before. She waited for the password but it didn't come; instead the young man asked for her identity papers. It was a police check.

Jacqueline had just picked up a new identity card the evening before, made illicitly by contacts of one of the groups. She handed it to the policeman, dreading that its obvious newness would make him ask questions or that some detail on it would be wrong. But the policeman was very young and rather shy and he was even more embarrassed than Jacqueline at discovering her half-undressed and washing her linen. He looked at the card, gave it back to her and moved on, covered in confusion.

The next morning, at six o'clock, there was another alarm – Jacqueline was awoken by a banging on the door and noises in the corridor: it was a police raid. The guests had to show their papers, answer questions: the police were looking for resistants, black marketeers, British agents. Once again Jacqueline showed her papers; once again they were accepted as genuine. But it was clear that hotels were too dangerous for people with something to hide: she left the hotel that day and set about asking Resistance contacts for safe houses. From then on wherever she went she would stay in the apartments or outbuildings of Resistance contacts. It was safer.

The southern half of France was a traumatized place in 1943. Until the Germans had marched over the demarcation line the previous November, the people of the unoccupied zone had had at least the illusion of self-government. Pétainists believed – or tried to believe – in that illusion. It was sustained by the influx of people who fled from the north to settle in the relative freedom south of the line. For those who were opposed to the Vichy government from the start, Resistance seemed more feasible than it did in the north. The official penalties for Resistance were less severe: minor acts were punishable (in theory at least) by a prison sentence rather than deportation to a concentration camp or execution. Counter-resistance was carried out by French police and Vichy officials rather than by German troops and Gestapo, and the Mediterranean coast and the Pyrénées offered clandestine routes in and out of the country for fugitives, resistants and agents.

But since the Germans' arrival in November 1942, all that had changed. There was the physical presence of German troops, in the towns and cities, on the trains. There had been mass arrests of resistants and black marketeers and the controls on civilians' movements were growing ever stricter. The Mediterranean coast was guarded and in January the evacuation of old Marseille and the deportation of its inhabitants to the concentration camps had served as a warning of how the Germans meant to control the population.

The 'unoccupied' zone, still called such by the now desperately appeasing Vichy government, had also borne the worst of the STO evacuations. Large estates and small-holdings alike lacked able-bodied men to work on the land. Food and cloth were being requisitioned by the Germans, which meant even less for the indigenous people, who were inadequately clothed and hungry. 1943 was the hardest year of the war for France: in the south the physical hardships were exacerbated by the blows to morale. At the end of January, at the order of the Germans, the Vichy government had created the *milice*, a force of volunteers who were to uphold the laws and keep order in the 'unoccupied' zone. The *milice* propaganda identified it as a morally healthy defence against the threat of bolshevism – that useful old bogey – but its real function was to suppress the black market. The shortage of food was so acute that the Germans feared it would cause subversion and unrest. The cutting edge of the *milice* was a uniformed, hierarchical unit of eighteen- to forty-five-year-old men, known as the Franc-Garde; they were to perform the glory stuff – physical evictions of black market restaurants and the redistribution of food in poorer quarters.

The *milice* was in existence by March and grew rapidly. It drew its members from all sections of society and had a place for women too (they were supposed to help establish community restaurants for the redistribution of confiscated food). People joined it from many different motives – it offered a kind of status and power; it had a gloss of moral rectitude; it was a chance to strike a blow against suspected 'bolsheviks'. Vigilante movements have always had a powerful appeal.

The main activities of the *milice* in the first half of 1943 were spying on their neighbours, raiding the homes of people suspected of black market activity and harassing communists, Gaullists and Jews. *Miliciens* intervened to stop Gaullists getting public office; they arrested Jews in synagogues on suspicion of crimes; they brought off a particular coup in the Rhône valley in April when they rounded up two Resistance groups with communist links.

These activities brought about bitter divisions among the population of the 'unoccupied' zone. Gradually people were becoming forced to take sides. As the *milice* grew, so did the number of people willing to resist. And so did the German counter-resistance measures. Checks and controls were intensifying; and mistrust pervaded the communities. But the will to resist was rising.

In the early months of 1943 *Hector* was building on this will, working tirelessly as he used his contacts to recruit across a huge stretch of central France. And at different times and on different trains from him, Jacqueline too travelled to make contact with representatives of the groups, to liaise with them and find out their needs, to bring them instructions from *Hector* and take him back news. She did not always see the same people *Hector* saw; on the contrary, the system of cut-outs they practised meant that they had few common contacts. Sometimes, as in that hotel in Châteauroux, Jacqueline would not know whom she was to meet; she would identify the person at the time only on hearing the password.

At the same time as working within Stationer, Jacqueline also liaised with a neighbouring *réseau*, Headmaster, which had been operating around Clermont-Ferrand, in the Puy de Dôme, since the previous winter.

Headmaster was a small *réseau*, organized by Brian Rafferty. He was a young undergraduate, adventurous and outgoing, and known as *Dominique*. Headmaster's radio operator, a man named Jones, had originally liaised with Baker Street over possible reception arrangements for Jacqueline's and *Hector*'s arrival.

Jacqueline was in regular touch with members of Headmaster, keeping rendezvous – often in Clermont-Ferrand – so that the two *réseaux* could be aware (within reason) of one another's activities. She sometimes passed on messages from herself and *Hector* for Jones to transmit to Baker Street.

Jacqueline spent a lot of her time that spring on trains and railway stations. She had contacts in Toulouse and would regularly travel down overnight. It took fifteen hours for the train to cover the 250 odd kilometres – it would leave Clermont-Ferrand at 7 p.m. and arrive in Toulouse at 10 a.m. the next morning – but Jacqueline used the time to sleep. She did not have enough safe houses for her needs and she did not dare to use hotels: she felt safer sleeping on the train than anywhere else.

Often, having made her contact in Toulouse, she would then embark on another leg of the journey, down to Tarbes. The best train for this was a morning train – the Toulouse-Pau express which left Toulouse at 10.20 a.m. and reached Tarbes at 12.30 p.m., *en route* to Pau. The repeated journeys were tedious and tiring; more seriously, they were becoming increasingly dangerous as the months passed. In the earlier part of the year she had rarely come across controls or spot checks on the trains themselves: by spring she had to be ready with her identity card and cover story because controls had begun to be instituted, particularly on the fast trains.

In April, *Hector* and Jacqueline received a message from Baker Street that a radio operator would be joining them. They organized a reception on a dropping ground near Tarbes and on the night of 14 April a Frenchman, Amédée Maingard, dropped to them. He also brought with him a travelling companion, Harry Rée, who seemed to be intended as an addition to Stationer or Headmaster. *Hector*, striving to keep a tight control over his burgeoning *réseau*, was dubious about adding a fourth agent; moreover Harry Rée's French was conspicuously accented. Soon Harry Rée moved on to Headmaster. (Eventually he would arrive in the Jura, and work with Diana Rowden and *Gabriel*.)

Meanwhile Amédée Maingard, code-named *Samuel*, settled in Châteauroux, where Jacqueline helped to find him safe addresses where he could stay and from which he could transmit. Now Stationer had its own radio operator – 'our first and best' as *Hector* later said.

Liaising with *Samuel* now became a large part of Jacqueline's life. She would go to Châteauroux to see him about three times a week, taking him messages from *Hector* and from other contacts, picking up messages which had come in from England. Some messages could be carried verbally but others had to be recorded: they were written in tiny script on small, thin slips of paper and Jacqueline travelled with them always within easy reach, so that if the need arose she could throw them away or swallow them.

Sometimes she had to carry larger and more incriminating objects – longer documents for *Samuel*, parts for his radio, supplies for one or other of the Resistance groups within the *réseau* – and these she put in her 'rep's' briefcase. The most dangerous part of transporting these was usually leaving the station, where there might be a control of papers and luggage. Often, if she feared a control at the exit, Jacqueline called a porter and had her briefcase taken to left luggage. She would then leave the station empty-handed and return later when the coast was clear to collect her case. She approached warily on these occasions, looking for signs of a police or German presence which might indicate that something incriminating had been discovered – she was always prepared to disappear if things looked bad.

Her precautions paid off, helped by her demure appearance. Sometimes German soldiers would help her down from the train and gallantly carry her case for her – one of the best ways of getting it through any control.

Throughout her heavy schedule of travelling and liaising between different parts of the *réseau*, Jacqueline kept in close touch with *Hector*. She met him two or three times most weeks to discuss the needs of the different groups and to plan the next stage of their work. They worked, as *Hector* said, 'hand in hand', serving the growing *réseau*.

Through the spring and summer months of 1943, Stationer spread over hundreds of kilometres and nurtured many groups of resistants. Some of these were existing groups whom *Hector* found through a cautious process of recommendation, a resistant in one village telling him of a group he knew twenty kilometres away. These groups usually existed more in spirit than in any other sense – they were generally unarmed and unorganized, a source of potential strength but in need of training and supplies. But this was not Stationer's only source of recruits. Alongside these Resistance-minded civilians another anti-German phenomenon was emerging: already forming here and there in the first half of 1943, and becoming more numerous as the year went on, were the *maquis*.

The story of Stationer and of the other countryside *réseaux* which grew with it through 1943, is also the story of the *maquis*. *Maquis* is the Corsican word for the dense bushes and grasses which cover the hills of the island, and of Provence. Towards the end of 1942, when STO had begun, some Frenchmen had gone into hiding rather than answer the German call-up. They had left their homes and villages and gone to live rough in the countryside. They lived in disused farmhouses and barns, sometimes in makeshift shelters in the open; their families brought food to them when they could and at other times they poached and raided. They could not take part in community life; they could not let themselves be seen by the Germans or by the Vichy police. They had become outlaws.

At the end of 1942 these bands of men were few and small in size – half a dozen here and there. But in 1943 the scope of STO widened and more and more men from all over the country received their instructions to report to the local railway station. Rural districts were ordered to sacrifice their male farmers, crop tenders, teachers and administrators. In towns professionals, civil servants and workers alike were served with their STO papers. The number of *réfractaires* (as STO evaders were known) mounted; some laid low in their own communities; others, in growing numbers, took to the open country. By spring there were many bands of *réfractaires* living rough, territorializing their parts of the French countryside, and turning their thoughts to Resistance. Random attacks on the German forces took place. The outlaw *réfractaires* had become bandit resistance fighters, their name that of their habitat, the *maquis*.

Liaisons began to form between *maquis* and their local organized Resistance groups – often these were the Communist FTP groups, who were active sooner than most of the others, but there were many areas where the *maquis* made contact with F Section *réseaux* – just as the Plateau de Glières *maquis* had managed to contact Odette and Peter Churchill and *Arnaud* in St Jorioz. Some arms drops were made specially to such *maquis*; arms and supplies from others began to find their way to them. By the summer of 1943 the *maquis* formed a vital part of the Allied plan for an organized uprising in France. Young *réseaux* like Stationer and Wheelwright searched out local *maquis* and recruited them. In many people's eyes they were criminals and thugs; to the F Section agents they were comrades.

In the summer of 1943, this comradeship was still maintained at arm's length. While the *maquis* grew in numbers in the hills, the agents masqueraded as law-abiding French civilians. Contacts between agents and *maquis* were carried out secretly and cautiously, using cut-outs. But the partnership was being established, all outward signs of it held firmly in check.

Réseaux like Stationer, Wheelwright and Jockey represented a new generation. North of the line Prosper was start to implode under a barrage of arms drops; west of the line along the Bordeaux coastal strip Claude de Baissac's Scientist was doing likewise. Up in the north-eastern region of France the *réseaux* Farmer, Musician and Tinker were launched on their own fierce sabotage campaigns.

There was activity and fury and they were bringing with them all their attendant dangers – for it would soon become evident that the fuse had been lit too early.

By contrast, the younger southern *réseaux* were growing quietly. They eschewed cities and rooted – buried – themselves in the countryside. Their aim was to survive intact and prepared, for as long as it took until that desired, elusive invasion. In *Hector*'s words: 'Security. Always security.'

So even when, in spring, the arms drops began, only a little sabotage was undertaken. And while the *maquis* and the other groups within the *réseaux* were armed and trained in weaponry, the agents restrained them from beginning guerrilla warfare.

There were, however, controlled sabotage operations within the different *réseaux* as they cautiously flexed their muscles. Stationer had its share of these. Early in the summer Charles Rechenmann's group in the south tried to blow up the arsenal in Tarbes. They succeeded in destroying the arsenal's chief electrical switchboard – but like the first Prosper sabotage attempts, it was a symbolic success rather than a major tactical gain, for the switchboard was repaired within a day or two. More sabotage expeditions followed, in the south and up around Châteauroux; but this was by no means the kind of sabotage offensive which had occurred in parts of Prosper and the other northern *réseaux*.

Disaster brushed the Stationer *réseau* for the first time in June, when on his way to a drop near Clermont-Ferrand, Headmaster chief *Dominique* was arrested. His radio operator Jones was also taken but later the Stationer agents heard he had managed to escape; he made his way back to England. *Dominique* himself was interrogated endlessly by the Germans but gave nothing away, either about his own helpers or about Stationer. *Hector*, Jacqueline and *Samuel* waited anxiously but as the weeks passed they remained free; still, they could not afford to relax their vigilance. It was yet another warning to observe all security precautions and to avoid premature attacks.

So, as the summer of 1943 set parts of northern France alight with sabotage attacks and claimed numerous Resistance victims from Prosper, what were F Section's agents doing in the south? There were the three large, growing *réseaux* – Stationer, Wheelwright, Jockey, each doing a little sabotage but mainly training and gathering strength. There was Pimento, started by the young Tony Brooks north of Toulouse the previous autumn, and this was the most active *réseau* sabotage-wise. Like Stationer it was in two parts and its eastern part, over in the Rhône valley, repeatedly sabotaged railway communications with Italy in July and October. This was done on

London's orders, to impede the movement of German troops and supplies.

A number of other *réseaux* – like Peter's and Odette's – had been blown or had dispersed in the face of danger earlier that year. Spruce, Henri Le Chêne's propaganda *réseau* north of Lyon, was in the final stage of dissolution. Henri had fled over the Pyrénées some months before and now in August Marie-Thérèse was picked up by a Hudson aeroplane and flown back to England. The *réseau* Monk, in which Eliane Plewman was courier, was establishing itself in Marseille and preparing to undertake some communications sabotage.

In the summer, then, new foundations were rising south of the demarcation line. They rose in deliberate obscurity, and they were stronger for it.

Autumn came and the invasion did not. Baker Street, struggling to react to the blows which had crushed Prosper and destroyed the infrastructure of *réseaux* in the north, began reviewing and planning.

One day Jacqueline took *Hector* a radio message from London: he was personally to organize and attend a reception for an agent's parachute drop. He didn't normally go to all the drops and was mystified at the request, but he complied and was there on the ground near Châteauroux when the plane flew overhead. He and his helpers watched containers float down under mini-parachutes and saw the figure of the agent dropping beneath a larger canopy. The agent landed some distance away and then seemed to disappear into the darkness. Octave Chantraine said he thought the agent had landed on the other side of a pond so *Hector* and the others walked round the pond and peered into the shadows and eventually they saw a figure crouching down behind a tree. The agent, they realized, was having a discreet pee. They gave the newcomer time to finish and then approached and *Hector* found himself looking at Pearl Witherington, an old schoolfriend.

Pearl, code-named *Marie*, had been sent to join Stationer. In her twenties and engaged to a Frenchman who was also training to be an agent, she was strong, resourceful and brave. She was to be a fellow courier to Jacqueline, to help with the running of the ever-growing *réseau*. But by the nature of their missions and the rules of security, they would do little work together.

Pearl's arrival was timely because *Hector* was now recalled to London to report back. He went back on the night of 16 October, being picked up by Lysander from a field near Amboise. It was one of Déricourt's operations – stepping down from the plane were Rémy Clément back from a training stint, and André Watt, arriving to be Déricourt's radio operator. *Hector* got safely back to England; meanwhile Jacqueline and *Samuel* took over the running of the *réseaux*.

This meant even more travelling for Jacqueline; it also required *Samuel* to move around too. Sometimes they travelled together – in November, for instance, they went down to Tarbes together. Charles Rechenmann was picked up and taken back to England for training – Jacqueline and *Samuel* were down there tying up the loose ends.

Hector's absence lasted all through the autumn and into the new year. There was little sabotage during those months but even without it, and even with Pearl Witherington in the *réseau* shouldering much of the courier work, Jacqueline's burden was exhausting. She was not particularly strong and now she was covering a wider area than ever with her travels, co-ordinating communications between all the different parts of the *réseau* and having to report directly back to London. There were also the usual unlooked for demands of Resistance life – an air pilot to help on to an escape chain, an arms drop to attend.

Back in England *Hector* was putting in an enthusiastic report on her. Fiercely security-conscious himself, he recognized the skill and the sheer dedication with which she kept herself and her comrades safe, while coping with her workload. 'I could not have done half what I have without her,' he said.

So Jacqueline's 1943 came to an end. It had been a year of clandestinity and strain; a year spent among a divided people. But whereas at the start of the year the Germans' grip on France had seemed unchallengeable, now the French people were beginning to talk of revolt and uprising. The news from abroad was good: in January the German armies had surrendered at Stalingrad. Then this defeat had been followed by the end of the North Africa campaign, with the Allies victorious. Most importantly for French morale, in July the Allies had landed in Sicily, and in September Italy had surrendered. The Italian troops had withdrawn from the south-east of France, leaving the Germans more to do alone. The first cracks had appeared in the German rule of Western Europe.

1944 began in France with the stirrings of Resistance up and down the country. After *Hector* returned at the end of January, Jacqueline would be busier than ever.

FOURTEEN

The South-West, 1943–4

Yvonne Cormeau, known in the field as *Annette*, was the second woman radio operator to be sent to France. Her predecessor was Noor Inayat Khan, but whereas Noor was sent to northern France and became embroiled with the ruins of the Prosper *réseau*, Yvonne was dropped far to the south-west of her, in the Gironde. By mid-October 1943 Noor's mission was over and her long harsh imprisonment was beginning. Yvonne on the other hand, arriving in August 1943, was to stay in the field for thirteen months, surviving all the attempts of the Germans and the *milice* to capture her. She was a phenomenally successful radio operator. She worked with George Starr in Wheelwright and by the end of her mission she had sent 400 radio messages, some of them put on to the air under frantic pressure from attics, café back rooms, even from fields.

But all this was still in front of her when she dropped to a reception outside the village of St Antoine de Queyret, in the Gironde, on the night of 22 August 1943. She was a lonely figure in many ways: in her early thirties, the war had already cost her a lot. Her husband, a second generation Frenchman born in England, had been killed in action early on. His death had left her with their young daughter to care for. Yvonne had felt a strong need to contribute to the war against Germany and she had joined the WAAF: her c.v. detailing her language skills and knowledge of France was swiftly passed to SOE and in the summer of 1942 she was called to the dingy War Office room for an interview.

The proposition that she train to return to France plunged her into a whirl of conflicting reactions. This was evidently the way she could best help Britain and France; and the most direct way of honouring her husband's death. On the other hand, if she were to go to France and be killed, her daughter would be an orphan – and in what sort of a world? It took her a long time to make up her mind. Finally, she decided to say yes: she was prompted by her religious faith, which made her believe that she should fight for what she believed to be right. She comforted herself with the thought that in the long run she was doing more for her daughter in this way than by giving her a normal mother's care. She entrusted her daughter to a convent boarding school in Oxfordshire and in March 1943 she began her training.

She did her initial training with a number of other women and men, including Yolande Beekman, Cecily Lefort and Noor Inayat Khan. Then she, Yolande Beekman and Noor Inayat went on to radio training. Noor already had radio experience from her WAAF days so she was taken through her paces faster; Yvonne and Yolande went through their longer, extremely thorough training together.

Yvonne seems to have baffled some of the training establishments. From the beginning she earned praise for her abilities in such practical skills as fieldcraft, weaponry, explosives, signalling and map-reading, but her character evidently bemused and provoked certain instructors. One commented early on in the course that she had 'very little personality or aggressiveness', and therefore 'may be all right as a WT operator'. It's already been mentioned how another instructor, looking on at the relationships which developed within the group, noted rather plaintively: '[She] is the only member of the party who seemed to have sex-appeal for the male members but it was exerted in a very quiet way.'

By June yet another observer had found the elusive 'personality' in her: 'There seems to be plenty of strength of character in this student . . .' while in July her report from the radio course had her down as 'intelligent and quick-witted without being intellectual,' a conscientious worker with a lot of common sense who, however, 'seems to live on her nerves and might become rattled in a difficult situation.'

Evidently convinced of her technical prowess but bemused by her character, Yvonne Cormeau's instructors recommended her for a mission in the field. After the usual preliminaries – the visit to the dentist, the latest tips about life in occupied France, the clothes fittings – she was given her mission. She was to be radio operator to a man known as *Hilaire*, organizer of a large, promising *réseau* in the south-west of France. She was given photographs of *Hilaire*'s wife and two children to take out to him and, looking at them, she recognized them. Before the war, when she and her husband had lived in Brussels, he used to play cricket with a man named George Starr. These were his wife and children.

Agents who worked together in the field were supposed to be strangers in their 'real lives'. But Yvonne did not tell Maurice Buckmaster and Vera Atkins that she recognized her new '*chef*'; she did not want her mission to be cancelled and besides she had had a good impression of George Starr the once or twice they had met. So she kept quiet. She was given her false papers; she was also given her code-name, *Annette*.

Some former agents seem to identify especially deeply with their code-names, and Yvonne Cormeau is one of them. She used the name *Annette* in the field, both with other agents and with members of the Resistance. Ever since the war her old comrades have continued to call her that whenever she goes back to visit them or when they write to her; even within SOE (perhaps because another Yvonne joined in 1944) she is widely known as *Annette*; Maurice Buckmaster certainly still speaks of her by that name. From the time that she jumped out of the aeroplane on 22 August 1943, she was *Annette*.

Annette had hoped to be met by *Hilaire* but when she landed on the field and focused on the people who came to greet her, he was not among them. Instead there were five local resistants and, she saw to her dismay, a general air of confusion. The leader of the reception committee introduced himself to her and led her into the farmhouse attached to the land. Entering the kitchen, she was horrified to see it crammed full of people. As they were introduced to her as members of the local Resistance, she counted thirty-two of them. They were dressed in the makeshift finery typical of 1943 social occasions – they had, it transpired, all come on from a dance to see her.

On hearing that some containers (13 containers and 4 packages) had been dropped with *Annette*, the whole company went out into the fields to help bring them in. They were gathered up and brought back into the kitchen, together with their parachutes. It was the first drop the area had ever received; the massive reception committee was uncertain what to do with the arms but very excited.

'There was a great relief that at last things were coming in. They were very – "Oh, we've got weapons! We've got ammunition – it's quite true, they *are* doing things for us!" '

Worried by the chaos she was leaving behind her, *Annette* was glad to get away from the farmhouse at St Antoine. There was a bicycle ready for her and a guide and they cycled the twenty-five kilometres to the town of Pujols. Here, the cousin of the farmer at St Antoine had a house at her disposal. She was given a room on the first floor.

Annette had arrived at a very bad time. Three days earlier, arrests had begun taking place among the Pujols resistance and *Hilaire* had gone into hiding. She stayed in the Pujols house for two days, with everyone unsure what to do next; then the son of the house cycled fifty kilometres to take a message about her to *Hilaire*. Another two days passed and then a liaison person arrived in Pujols; *Annette* left with him and together they travelled down to the Pyrénées, where *Hilaire* was hiding.

Hilaire already had suspicions that he was not going to receive the radio operator he had asked for. He had requested a man over thirty-five, because it was increasingly difficult in the south-west for men under thirty-five to move around. They were likely to be picked up in a *rafle* and sent to the labour camps; even if they escaped this, they attracted unwelcome attention simply because they were an unusual sight. He looked forward to getting an older man sent in. But the BBC message which had been broadcast to announce the radio operator's drop was 'Jacqueline has got a red and green dress.' It sounded as though they were sending him a woman. *Hilaire* was a quiet, tough, unobtrusive man who had a gift for leadership. He was, in Maurice Buckmaster's words: 'What the French call a *"numéro"*.'[1] He attracted followers in a quiet sort of way and was able to control them. But he didn't want to rock the French Resistance boat: he wasn't sure how they would take the arrival of a woman.

When *Annette* arrived in his Pyrénéan hide-out, he recognized her.

'As I got out of the train itself with the courier who had brought me, and walked through the little station – the ticket office was no bigger than a shed really – and the courier was going "This is Madame . . .", he stopped him. "*Je connais Madame.*" '

Annette and *Hilaire*, who before the war had used to meet by cricket greens with their families around them, now met once again. It was the beginning of a long and close partnership.

Annette's most pressing task was to establish radio contact between their *réseau*, Wheelwright, and London. For six months *Hilaire* had been building his *réseau* so that now it covered great tracts of land from the valleys of the Gironde and the Lot-et-Garonne in the north of the *réseau*, down across the Tarn-et-Garonne in the centre and extending southward across the rolling green country of the Haute-Garonne and the Gers and the western hills of the Basses Pyrénées. Already there were tiers of authority, organized by *Hilaire* on a cell basis to run the

[1] *Specially Employed*, Maurice Buckmaster, Batchworth Press, 1952

réseau. He was in overall command but two resistants, *Philibert* and *Albert*, had charge of the southern and northern sections respectively: he directly ran the middle section. Moreover, there were sub-sections within the sections of the *réseau*: the structure was intricate and designed to be secure; a courier called *Félix* carried out most of the liaison between *Hilaire* and the other section leaders.

With this structure already in place and with night-time drops beginning to provide arms for the groups, Wheelwright was in acute need of regular communications with London. *Annette*'s first priority was to begin transmissions; *Hilaire*'s was to find her safe places from which to do so.

He went into action immediately, finding her houses. Both he and she had strong ideas about the importance of security for radio operators. They both knew from Beaulieu training that it was important for the operator to move on every few days. The advantage of having such a wide territory was that the safe houses could be scattered – this would mean that the different houses might fall under different German direction finding teams, making it harder for them to trace the signals. But the neighbours had to be considered too – through a contact in the Feldgendarmerie, *Hilaire* learned that direction finding – or D/F'ing as it was known – was plagued with technical difficulties and that the Germans actually relied more on denunciations to expose the radio operators. So the safe houses had to be in areas friendly to the Resistance.

Through his own efforts, and the help of his couriers, *Hilaire* began to find them. One of the earliest houses *Annette* used was an isolated house down in the Pyrénées, set behind a long garden. Many neighbours came and went, giving cover to *Annette*'s own arrivals and departures. And the long approach to the house gave extra security to *Annette* – were anyone unusual to be seen approaching the house she would have time to hide her set. The house was old and its comforts were very basic: there was no bath, but it had something she would learn to do without in many of her places – an outside lavatory.

Then there were farm houses – sometimes the main dwelling of a farm, sometimes the cramped homes of tenant farmers. As far as possible, *Hilaire* tried to find houses isolated but not too far from a railway station. But there were some unorthodox premises too – in Agen, there was a café whose back rooms were at *Annette*'s disposal. Elsewhere a car repair shop opened its doors to her. These were the places in which *Annette* would spend much of the next thirteen months.

The life of a radio operator was not like that of a courier or an organizer. It had at its heart a strict routine and the sustaining

Lyon, resistance centre and home of Virginia Hall from autumn 1941 to November 1942 (Popperfoto)

Parisians build a barricade during the battle for Paris, 19-25 August 1944 (© Deux Guerres Mondiales)

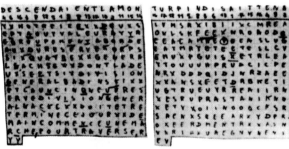

A radio transceiver, type 3 Mark II, as used by Annette and other agents, with an example of coding using the Double Transposition code (courtesy of the Imperial War Museum, Pierre Lorain and BBC Books)

Sergeant Hugo Bleicher (standing, right), alias 'Colonel Henri' (courtesy of Weidenfeld and Nicholson Archives)

Vera Atkins (courtesy of Vera Atkins and the Special Forces Club)

Francine Agazarian (courtesy of Francine Agazarian and the Special Forces Club)

Maurice Buckmaster (courtesy of Maurice Buckmaster and the Special Forces Club)

Jacqueline Nearne (courtesy of the Special Forces Club)

Violette Szabo (courtesy of the Special Forces Club)

Jack Agazarian (courtesy of the Special Forces Club)

Nancy Wake (courtesy of the Special Forces Club)

Adam Rabinovitz, Arnaud (courtesy of the Special Forces Club)

Pearl Witherington (courtesy of Pearl Cornioley and the Special Forces Club)

Francis Cammaerts (courtesy of Francis Cammaerts and the Special Forces Club)

Henri Déricourt (courtesy of Weidenfeld and Nicolson Archives)

False identity card belonging to Harry Rée (courtesy of Weidenfeld and Nicolson Archives)

Collection of forged stamps and 'official' documents (courtesy of Weidenfeld and Nicolson Archives)

Sten gun, of the type used by maquis and agents (courtesy of the Imperial War Museum)

Lac Annecy, looking from Talloires south-west across the lake. St Jorioz, where Odette stayed, lies on the western shore on the extreme right-hand edge of the picture. The mountains behind rise to the Semnoz summit, where Peter Churchill was dropped by parachute (Popperfoto)

The mountainous country of Haute-Savoie, where Odette worked (J. Allan Cash Ltd)

Odette Hallowes *(courtesy of Odette Hallowes and the Special Forces Club)*

Andrée Borrel *(courtesy of the Special Forces Club)*

Yvonne Cormeau, Annette *(courtesy of Yvonne Farrow)*

Didi Nearne *(courtesy of the Special Forces Club)*

Noor Inayat Khan *(courtesy of the Special Forces Club)*

of this, day after day and week after week, in careful solitude, was the 'radio's' *raison d'être*. The radio operator was bound to her set: where it was taken, she too must go; if she moved on, the set must follow, and these manoeuvres must be timed so that at a certain hour she would be in a place where she could safely assemble the set, hitch up the aerial and meet her sked.

It was a rhythm from which the radio operator never escaped. Even if she were involved in other activities for the *réseau* – as *Annette* was – the responsibility to her set and her skeds came first.

Annette's radio traffic was heavy from the start. *Hilaire* had long been waiting for regular contact with Baker Street and there was a large amount of information and requests to be sent. Her skeds were several times a week, usually during the Monday to Friday period, and she would normally transmit from one house during each week and then use the weekend to move on. She and *Hilaire* agreed that she should try not to transmit more than three times in a row from the same address; it was excellent security but it imposed a wearisome burden of travel upon her, especially as the safe houses were approximately eighty kilometres apart. She travelled by train, coach or bicycle, setless; that was carried separately, often by *Félix*. Sometimes, though, *Annette* and *Hilaire* travelled together by bicycle and then they would carry the set between them, the various compartments wrapped in clothes to protect them and hidden in the saddle bags, under their food or personal belongings. Travelling, like Andrée and *Prosper* before them, as sister and brother, they were unlikely to attract attention, but in any case *Hilaire* was well versed in the art of moving about this part of the country and he knew that road controls were rare.

When *Annette* arrived at her next safe house, she would usually hide the set in an outbuilding. The occupants of the houses knew what she was doing there: she had insisted on that, feeling that they must know the risk they were taking in harbouring her. But the neighbours, of course, did not. Once she had arrived in this week's house, she tried to lie as low as possible and not attract outside attention. She would receive the messages for her next sked, either from *Hilaire* or brought by a courier (usually *Félix*) and shortly before the sked she would code them for transmission. Then, as the time for her sked approached, she would fetch and assemble the set.

Annette's set was a model 'B. Mk II', which came in four compartments. One she attached to a car battery, for power; then she set up one for reception, set another smaller one for transmission and kept the fourth, a back-up compartment, to one side. She erected the indoor aerial, hooking it over a clothes-hanger or whatever else could be improvised.

She tried to have a look-out posted during her skeds, watching the approach roads to the house. It was not always possible to find a resistant who could be spared from other work; but the people of the household were often eager to help. They, after all, were as much at risk as she. If no one could be found, she would station herself and her set at a window, behind a curtain, so that she could keep watch herself.

With everything prepared, she would twist the dial, tuning in. The wavelengths London assigned her varied and it was sometimes hard to find the right one. When she found it, with greater or less interference, she would begin sending her signal. It was not always immediately that the response came back. On the contrary, there was often a tense wait, as nothing but crackles or silence came over the receiver. Eventually though, the signal would come back that the operator at the other end was ready to receive, and *Annette* would begin the swift tapping of the key which sent streams of morse letters across the ether.

Sitting in her room, concentrating on keying in the right letters, her ears full of the crackles and bleeps of the transmission, the radio operator was very vulnerable. She could hear little of what was happening outside her room; she had to rely on her look-outs, or her own eyes, to alert her to danger. From the beginning of her mission, *Annette* handled a large volume of radio traffic. Transmitting and receiving on the same sked, it required all her skill to keep the skeds down to the safe 20–30 minutes. Speed was vital but her keying had to be clear and accurate as well as fast; interference could easily distort signals and if operator error were added to this, the receiving operator in England might be taking down gibberish.

Annette, fiercely conscientious, was always aware of this danger. She had no way of knowing how each transmission was reaching England; she could only continue to send them. But she need not have worried – from the start her messages had been getting through clearly and intelligibly. 'From the moment she started work in the field,' her final report stated, 'it was evident that she was one of the most technically efficient wireless operators we had ever sent out.'

At the end of each sked, *Annette*'s first task was to dismantle and hide the set; her second to decode the signals which she had received and noted down. Coding and decoding was not difficult for operators who had learnt the system but it was detailed work and very tiring. Working from her key code, *Annette* transcribed the newly received messages into clear language and then immediately memorized them. Then she burned the incriminating papers. Sometimes figures, for instance the co-ordinates of a landing ground to be used for a drop, needed to be on record for slightly longer. In these cases she used a form of shorthand for extra security, but at the longest, she would usually keep a written record for just three or four hours.

As the *réseau*'s only radio operator, *Annette* quickly came to play a central, if very low profile, role. She and *Hilaire* were often on the move together in the autumn of 1943, partly because *Hilaire* liked to be near *Annette* to cut out the delay in sending and receiving radio messages. But also she was doing other work for him, using the time she was not on the air to liaise between him and the leaders of local groups. There were receptions to organize for drops; groups had to be trained in the use of weapons and explosives; there were communications to be maintained within the *réseau* so that the different sections were working in synchronization. *Annette* worked closely with *Hilaire* to co-ordinate the groups; at first she was afraid they would object to taking instructions from a woman, but to her relief there was no trouble. The resistants accepted her and seemed to have confidence in her.

The sheer size of the *réseau* made a heavy burden both of internal communications and of security. Wheelwright could already count on thousands of people to resist when the call came, and the number was rising to tens of thousands. Thanks to a strict cellular structure and the fact that *Hilaire* and his lieutenants allowed no premature action, it was very secure. But both the police and the Gestapo were active in the area and there was always the danger of penetration.

The great asset of the Wheelwright *réseau* was the local people. The region had a long history of Resistance to central government and many of its inhabitants, individually, as families and communities, even as institutions, were prepared to put their weight behind these Allied agents – and to do so silently. The local gendarmerie was working with Wheelwright and had been from the start; twice *Hilaire* took refuge from other pursuers by hiding in a police station. But the local gendarmerie only really covered the villages and rural areas – above them were the Police d'Etat and they were mostly Vichy recruits; so were the police in the towns. They were identified by the Vichy insignia they wore on their caps and they were hostile to the Resistance.

Worse than the Vichy police, however – and worse than the Germans – were the *milice*. Even this region of France was not united in its support of the Resistance and a sizeable number had joined the *milice*. The resistants had quickly found that *miliciens* were the most dangerous adversaries. Just as zealous as the Germans in hunting the Resistance, they were local people who understood the ways of the

communities and who were able to pick up information on the grapevine. Some of them had scores to settle. All over southern France the
enmity between the *milice* and the Resistance was growing deeper and
more bitter; by early winter resistants were carrying out anonymous
attacks and assassinations on *miliciens* and the *milice* was retaliating,
with growing force. The worst of the violence – which was brutal on
both sides – was in the east, around Grenoble, but it was mounting
in the west too.

There were denunciations of resistants to the *milice* – some
from political conviction, many for money, some for more obscure
personal motives. *Hilaire* used his far-reaching web of contacts to
keep himself informed: it was possible for resistants to infiltrate even
the *milice* and *Hilaire* knew three supposed *miliciens* who warned him
of developments.

There were Germans in the area too, bearing down on Resistance
activity. They were not concerned in everyday policing; this was left
to the gendarmerie in country areas (which was why *Hilaire* favoured
a rural existence) and the Vichy police and the *milice* in towns. But the
Gestapo had offices in towns like Agen and Condom from which they
co-ordinated counter-resistance campaigns and they were called in to
other areas if anything significant was happening. *Hilaire*'s contacts
were especially good in this area of the Tarn-et-Garonne over which
he had direct control, and he had two valuable contacts among the
Agen Gestapo office staff, a man and a woman, who were able to
give him limited information about Gestapo affairs. The man could
warn of *rafles* about to be done and both could supply retrospective
information about what had been done and why and sometimes –
crucially – who had been involved. This proved very useful as the
agents could learn the identities of Gestapo informers who might be
pretending friendship to the Resistance.

One such leakage of information shed light on certain events which
had been happening up in the Pujols area, where *Annette* had spent her
first few days. Soon after she had joined *Hilaire* down in the south of
the *réseau*'s territory, it had become clear that she had been lucky to get
out of Pujols so quickly. Shortly after her departure almost everyone
in the Pujols group was rounded up and arrested – the owner of the
farm to which she had dropped, the cousin in whose house she had
then stayed and his family, and many other people – about fifteen in
all, including not only the men who were active at the reception but
women, children and even the grandparents of some resistants. The
places where the arms had been stored were also given away and the
arms were seized. It was clear that someone had told the Gestapo
everything.

It was a tragedy for the Pujols families, many of whom were sent to the camps in Germany. It was also a bad shock for Wheelwright. The damage seemed for a while to be contained, but in fact, while Wheelwright's other groups were safe thanks to the *réseau*'s cell structure, *Hilaire* and *Annette* themselves were in danger. For the person who had been responsible for giving the Gestapo the information had been at *Annette*'s reception and had met *Hilaire*; he had given the Gestapo a full description of both of them.

At first they did not know this but, as it seemed certain that someone had betrayed all he or she knew, *Hilaire* asked his contacts in the Agen office to find out all they could. Eventually a woman contact in the office smuggled out valuable information – copies of the actual statements made by the resistant who had talked. It was bad news, but now that they knew it they were in a better position to take the necessary precautions.

Controls – always a point of danger and becoming more frequent than before – would now have to be avoided even more assiduously. But it was impossible for either of them to lie low completely. Not only did *Hilaire* have to organize the *réseau* and *Annette* to move from one safe house to another, but even more pressure was put on them in late autumn when *Albert* of the southern sector and *Félix* the courier were given away and had to flee to England. *Albert* had at least left an assistant, *Roland*, who could take over his sector but there was a lot of work to be done ensuring the safety of the other resistants and *Annette* had to take over a large part of *Félix*'s courier and liaison work.

She travelled by bicycle, or sometimes by train or coach, carrying messages, almost always memorized without being committed to paper. The distances she covered often made it impossible for her to return to her previous safe house to meet her sked, so arrangements were continually being made to have her set transported separately to another safe house in the region of her destination. New safe houses now had to be found to cope with the extra travelling. The knowledge that the Germans were circulating descriptions of her put an extra strain on her.

Annette spoke French like a native and, small-boned and correct in manner, looked the part. But as Odette pointed out, even this was not the same as being French, with the instinctive ease which true belonging confers. *Annette* found that London's tips on the manners and customs of the French were incomplete: for instance, here in the Gascogne, women always wore jewellery – even women in the remotest areas wore a necklace, bracelet or ornament of some kind. *Annette*, who had arrived with no jewellery, was aware that she looked different. She bought jewellery; she also learned to correct her table manners when she found herself the only person at the table drinking soup from the side of her spoon. Even her walk marked her out: *Hilaire* pointed out to her that she took longer strides than a Frenchwoman would and she had to practise walking with smaller steps.

There were problems, too, with the documents and clothes London had sent her. She had been told before leaving that she would work mainly in towns and so her clothes were town clothes, quite unsuitable for the country. Her official cover story was that she was a refugee from northern France but her identity card had no stamp on it to show that she had crossed the demarcation line. She had to have this rectified locally.

Moreover, she had to give up smoking when she found that rationing meant scarcely any Frenchwomen could smoke and certainly not in public. Cigarettes were usually only available on the black market and to be seen with them would attract unwanted attention.

Annette paid endless attention to details like these so that she might pass unnoticed in the local population. She eschewed unnecessary contacts or public exposure: she kept away from cafés, the traditional places of rendezvous, and did not even frequent them to get food or drink – when she was travelling she would carry a package of food, not an unusual sight in those austere days. She was careful not to go into districts where she had heard of recent German activity.

All the same, it was impossible even with these precautions to avoid controls altogether. On one journey between safe houses, *Annette* had just boarded the coach and sat down, with a German soldier next to her, when she noticed that outside there were other Germans gathered round the vehicle in front, doing some sort of inspection.

She didn't have her set with her, naturally, but she carried a little attaché case in which she had put her wash things and a change of clothing. It also held her current cipher key, slipped in behind a false lining. She was gripped with fear. At any second the inspection might move into this coach: there was a description out on her; she was obviously going somewhere for the night; if her case were searched and the cipher found it would be desperately incriminating.

The German soldier next to her had placed his haversack next to her case. 'And I got up and said to this soldier – "Get up! *A la porte!*" I was going to the loo, sort of thing. I left my case and the coach and went into the station. I looked back and through the glass window I was able to see these two Germans, one getting on at the front of the coach and one at the back – they were going up and down on opposite sides.'

The inspection reached her empty seat and passed it; she watched the soldiers get off the bus empty-handed. Now she had to get back on the bus without attracting attention. She waited until she saw a new passenger approach and start talking to the driver; then she walked out of the station and boarded the bus with him, excusing herself and going back to her seat. Her little case was still there, next to the soldier's haversack. She thanked him politely and sat down as the bus was starting up. 'I sat down very quietly. I felt washed through.'

The strain of combining courier work and radio work was beginning to tell and *Hilaire* had urgently requested reinforcements from Baker Street. Meanwhile he and *Annette* had become a very close team. He trusted her and relied on her; he sent back a report saying, 'She is always ready for anything and follows instructions to the letter.' She in turn trusted and respected him and knew that he went out of his way to secure her safety. Maurice Buckmaster later wrote: 'Only *Annette* was entirely in his confidence.' In fact *Annette* did not know all *Hilaire* did, nor did she expect to; but he shared more with her than with the others and theirs was a strong partnership.

It was not the fierce camaraderie of Andrée Borrel and *Prosper*. It was not the cool, unspoken faith Jacqueline and *Hector* had for one another. It was a friendship, strong but decorous. *Annette* had in another life been the wife of *Hilaire*'s friend; their Resistance partnership was flavoured by that.

One night at the beginning of December, when *Annette* was staying in a safe house not far from *Hilaire*, he came to see her:

> It must have been about ten o'clock at night and I was already in my room. The lady of the house asked me if he could come up, he wanted to speak to me. So I said all right, wait a minute. I had to put my dress on again and I got ready and I took a book and sat in the chair – a real picture! – and she said, yes, it's OK. She brought him up and left us very discreetly – all became very discreet – and he said 'I don't know, shall we go back to England for Christmas?'
>
> And I said, 'Oh I don't know.' Because you see, I knew it meant an eighteen-hour walk up the mountains in the snow. I'd recently had to take some Poles, who were trying to escape, to the Pyrénées to find a guide. The guide had explained to me how you went. You couldn't go by road because the Germans were up and down the road. You couldn't go over the mountains by the pass because they used dogs there to track you. So you had to go through the snow on a snowy night so that your traces were quickly

covered, and you had to go from bush to bush. It was an eighteen-hour journey and you didn't have many stops. You were told to try and bring a hot drink and some food. I knew that and I told him. He wasn't a terrific walker; he hadn't done any mountain climbing or things like that. I was better trained than he was, from holidays.

Then he said, 'Well, I'll think about it and you think about it but I'd like you to come with me if I go back.'

For the next few days, she thought about it. The idea that she could voluntarily leave this life of strain and clandestinity and return to England, see her daughter again, spend something like a family Christmas with her, was a disorienting one. Now that the suggestion had been made, she longed to do it

But at their next meeting, *Hilaire* said he had decided against it. He had told one of his fellow resistants that he intended to go to England for a while and a fight had immediately started within the organization over who should take over from him in his absence. It had been at best a quixotic suggestion – uncharacteristic for *Hilaire* – and now it was dropped. *Annette*, naturally, decided that she would not go either. It was the sensible decision and probably the kindest for her daughter. To be with her daughter for a day or so, perhaps just for a few hours, and to leave her again would not be fair on the child. So the option which had opened up before *Annette* closed again; and neither she nor *Hilaire* spent the Christmas of 1943 with their families but pushed on with their Resistance work in the villages and towns of the Gascogne, hoping to evade attention.

As soon as 1944 arrived, things changed for *Annette*. On the night of 4 January, two new agents were dropped to the *réseau* – one was a young woman, Anne-Marie Walters, code-named *Colette*, and the other was a young man, Claude Arnault. The young man was to be *Hilaire's* assistant; *Colette* was his new courier.

Drawing an accurate picture of *Colette* is difficult. From other people's comments and from the voice which sounds in her book of memoirs, written shortly after the war, she was evidently an independent, high-spirited person. She records that she quarrelled regularly with Claude Arnault but that they were close despite it; she describes her first impression of *Hilaire* as an alarming, almost sinister tough. *Annette* is not mentioned.

For her part, *Annette* has little that is complimentary to say about *Colette*. It is evident that the two were incompatible (Vera Atkins said rather slyly, 'I don't imagine Yvonne Cormeau had anything good to say about her,' and refused to enlarge). But in *Colette*'s favour, she worked in Wheelwright until 1944 and saw D-Day and its aftermath. At any event, from January she formed part of the Wheelwright team and *Annette* now found herself free to concentrate on her radio work.

This was heavily on the increase. For during the next two months Baker Street repeatedly tried to arrange for arms drops to be made to Wheelwright; but the Gascogne, like all of France, was suffering a stormy winter and repeatedly the operations were set up only to be called off nearer the time. Head winds, cloud and snow made it difficult for the pilots to navigate with accuracy, and even if the craft made it to the agreed dropping ground, the pilots might not be able to see the vital signal from the ground. Throughout January and February as the frustration continued, *Annette*'s radio transmitted and received ever more frequently. Her skeds were changed and increased until she had them every day.

It was more important than ever, with this heavy traffic through her set, that she keep moving around between different areas. She now began moving on every few days, almost always by bicycle. The sheer physical demands of it told on her: at the beginning of March she strained a muscle cycling. She was taken to hospital for treatment and for a time she could do no more travelling.

Her recuperation period coincided with the coming of the fine weather. The promised arms drops were beginning and there was no respite from her skeds. She solved the problem by taking a calculated risk: at the beginning of May she went to ground in the house *Hilaire* was staying in. The dangers this incurred are obvious, but they were counterbalanced by advantages. The house was in a very small village without electricity, so it was the last place the Germans would think of searching for a radio operator. *Annette*, however, always used car batteries to power her radio, rather than mains electricity (using the mains carried a risk – the Germans would sometimes switch off the electric currents in certain areas, to see if it caused a break in transmissions. If it did they would know where to concentrate their D/F efforts). So lack of electricity was no hindrance to her skeds. Moreover, the villagers knew *Annette*, were already aware that she was a 'refugee' from the north, and also knew that she had been ill recently and had spent some time in hospital. It seemed quite natural to the village, therefore, that she should rest there and recuperate.

And so she did, without interference. Her rest, though, was disturbed by the rearrangement of her skeds. As an extra security precaution, London was now splitting agents' transmissions and receiving activities into two separate sessions. *Annette* transmitted to them during the day and, not having to wait for their messages, was able to get off the air quickly. But they then broadcast to her at night. Sometimes they transmitted at 11 p.m., which still allowed her to get a normal night's sleep; but at other times she had to wake to receive them at 1 a.m. or 3 a.m.

> 'That was a nuisance because it put me into a bad habit of having to wake up. Well, with the three o'clock one I didn't go to bed again. In the country the cocks crow at dawn and they all get up early and I would have to get up like the others. Also, I didn't want to keep a light burning too long at night, so I would wait until daylight came and decipher the messages then. I would learn them while I was having my so-called coffee for breakfast.'

And so another day would begin. Hidden in *Hilaire*'s house, tied day and night to the rhythms of her skeds, *Annette* regained her strength and kept the communications flowing between Gascogne and England. Here, as all over France, the build-up to D-Day was beginning.

FIFTEEN

Early 1944:
Eliane, Yolande, Elizabeth

1943 had been a bitter year for France. Food shortages, forced labour, the birth of the *milice* and the *maquis*, had combined to score deep wounds through the already divided nation. True, by the end of the year German defeats abroad had kindled a tentative hope among the French for their future and the spirit of Resistance was beginning to draw people together – but this was no self-assured, triumphal movement. On the contrary, three and a half years of German occupation had splintered the French Resistance so that now different groups worked independently of one another and would-be new resistants faced problems in deciding whom to join.

The three largest co-ordinated Resistance movements remained *Combat* (politically centre right), *Libération* (largely socialist and trade unionist) and *Francs-Tireurs et Partisans (FTP)* (communist). There were many other movements, however, and there were many issues on which certain of them co-operated while others followed their own lines. The FTP and other communist Resistance groups stood out from the rest as being active in sabotage and guerilla attacks; most of the others followed de Gaulle's official *'attentiste'* line, preparing and training for action but not launching it.

Besides these groups there was now the burgeoning *maquis*. In some areas the *maquis* had political affiliations but mostly they had come together for survival rather than ideology.

Then, trying to weld these groups together and to recruit their own, there were the agents who had come in from abroad – F Section agents reporting to Baker Street and RF agents reporting to de Gaulle; DF agents who ran escape lines. Quite apart from these SOE agents there were agents of neighbouring occupied nations – Polish agents,

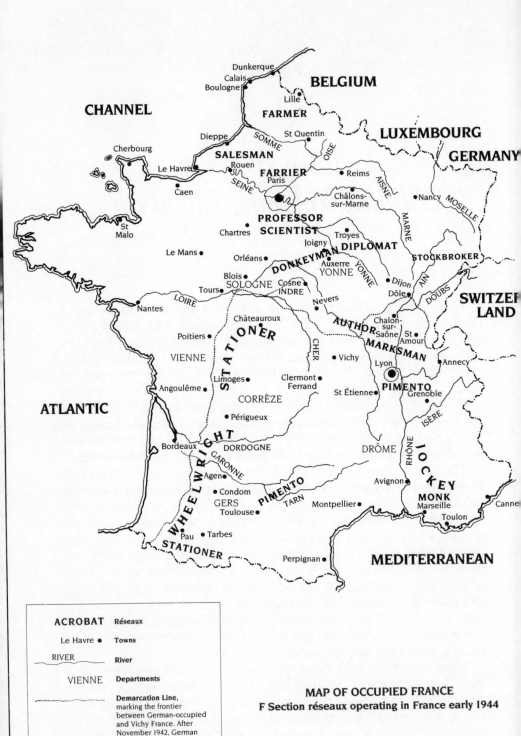

CHANNEL

BELGIUM

LUXEMBOURG

GERMANY

SWITZER-
LAND

ATLANTIC

MEDITERRANEAN

Dunkerque
Calais
Boulogne
Lille
FARMER
St Quentin
Dieppe
SOMME
SALESMAN
Cherbourg
Le Havre
Rouen
FARRIER
Paris
Reims
Nancy
MOSELLE
Caen
SEINE
Châlons-
sur-Marne
AISNE
MARNE
St
Malo
Chartres
PROFESSOR
SCIENTIST
Troyes
Le Mans
Orléans
DONKEYMAN
Joigny
DIPLOMAT
STOCKBROKER
Auxerre
YONNE
YONNE
Blois
Cosne
Dijon
AIN
Tours
SOLOGNE
INDRE
Dôle
DOUBS
Nantes
LOIRE
Nevers
Châteauroux
AUTHOR
Chalon-
sur-Saône
St
Amour
Poitiers
STATIONER
MARKSMAN
Annecy
VIENNE
CHER
Vichy
Lyon
Limoges
Clermont
Ferrand
St Étienne
PIMENTO
Grenoble
Angoulême
CORRÈZE
Périgueux
ISÈRE
WHEELWRIGHT
Bordeaux
DORDOGNE
DRÔME
JOCKEY
RHÔNE
GARONNE
Agen
Avignon
Condom
PIMENTO
MONK
GERS
TARN
Montpellier
Marseille
Canne
Toulouse
Toulon
Pau
Tarbes
STATIONER
Perpignan

Legend:

ACROBAT   Réseaux

Le Havre ●   Towns

RIVER   River

VIENNE   Departments

··········   **Demarcation Line,**
marking the frontier
between German-occupied
and Vichy France. After
November 1942, German
troops occupied all of
France but the
demarcation line stayed
officially in place, though
restrictions on crossing it
were eased

MAP OF OCCUPIED FRANCE
F Section réseaux operating in France early 1944

WOMEN IN THE RÉSEAUX

ACROBAT
Diana Rowden, June 1943. When ACROBAT'S organizer was arrested in July, she moved to STOCKBROKER.

ARTIST
Lise de Baissac, Sept 1942-Aug 1943. ARTIST was F Section's official name for her operation in Poitiers.

CLERGYMAN
Denise Bloch, March-June 1944. After setting up the réseau in Nantes, she and her organizer also worked near Rambouillet.

DONKEYMAN
Peggy Knight, May 1944-Liberation DONKEYMAN refers to an offshoot of the réseau in Normandy.

FARRIER
Julienne Aisner, Mar 1943-Apr 1944. She was based in Paris.

FIREMAN
Paddy O'Sullivan, Mar 1944-Liberation.

FREELANCE
Nancy Wake, In the fighting after D-Day, the FREELANCE agents and their associated *maquis* moved north, following the German troops into the Allier.

HEADMASTER
Sonia Butt, May 1944-Liberation.

HECKLER
Virginia Hall, Mar 1944-Liberation. After D-Day she joined a Free French force and followed German troops to the Jura.

HISTORIAN
Lilian Rolfe, Apr-July 1944.

INVENTOR
Vera Leigh, May-Oct 1943. She was based in Paris and liaised with DONKEYMAN in the Yonne.

JOCKEY
Cecily Lefort, Jun-Sept 1943. Krystyna de Gyzicka (Christine Granville), July 1944-Liberation

MARKSMAN
Elizabeth Devereux-Rochester, Oct 1943-Apr 1944.

MINISTER
Yvonne Fontaine, March 1944-Liberation. She had been a local recruit to TINKER in 1943.

MONK
Eliane Plewman, Aug 1943-Mar 1944.

MONKEYPUZZLE
Yvonne Rudellat, Jul 1942-Jul 1943.

MUSICIAN
Yolande Beekman, Sept 1943-Jan 1944.

PHONO
Noor Inayat Khan, Jun-Oct 1943.

PIMENTO
Lise de Baissac, Apr-May 1944. PIMENTO marks the main body of the réseau. Lise worked in an offshoot.

PLANE
Marie-Thérèse Le Chêne, Oct 1942-Aug 1943.

PROSPER
Francine Agazarian, Mar-Jun 1943. Andrée Borrel, Sept 1942-Jul 1943. They were based in Paris and liaised with resistants throughout the PROSPER region. The PROSPER réseau shown here includes the territories of PROSPER sub-réseaux like BUTLER and SATIRIST

SALESMAN
Violette Szabo, Apr-May 1944. She and her organizer dropped back into France the day after D-Day, in the Limoges area. She was captured three days later.

SCHOLAR
Yvonne Baseden, Mar-Jul 1944.

SCIENTIST (1)
Mary Herbert, Oct 1942-Dec 1943. She was based in Bordeaux and liaised with resistants throughout SCIENTIST (1) territory. SCIENTIST (1) denotes the réseau as it existed in 1942 and 1943.

SCIENTIST (2)
Lise de Baissac, May 1944-Liberation. Phyllis Latour, May 1944-Liberation. SCIENTIST (2) denotes the réseau as recreated in 1944.

SILVERSMITH
Madeleine Lavigne, May 1944-Liberation.

SPINDLE (1)
Odette Hallowes, Oct 1942-Feb 1943.

SPINDLE (2)
Odette Hallowes, Feb-Apr 1943.

SPIRITUALIST
Didi Nearne, Mar-Jul 1944. She had arrived to work in a new réseau WIZARD, but when circumstances stopped it developing, she switched to SPIRITUALIST. She was based in Paris.

STATIONER
Jacqueline Nearne, Jan 1942-Apr 1944. She travelled widely over STATIONER territory, and frequently made trips between the main body of the réseau in central France and the offshoot in Tarbes. NB: STATIONER originally covered an enormous area. As its recruits multiplied, new réseaux like FIREMAN and VENTRILOQUIST 2 formed within the same area. Odette Wilen, Apr-Aug 1944. Pearl Witherington, Sept 1943-May 1944. When STATIONER's organizer was arrested in May 1944 she took over the northern half of the remaining réseau, renamed WRESTLER.

TINKER
Yvonne Fontaine was recruited from the local resistance to TINKER in 1943.

VENTRILOQUIST (2)
Muriel Byck, Apr-May 1944. (VENTRILOQUIST 1 was a much larger réseau operating from 1941 to 1943.)

WHEELWRIGHT
Yvonne Cormeau, Aug 1943-Liberation. Anne-Marie Walters, Jan-Aug 1944.

LYON
Virginia Hall, Oct 1941-Nov 1942. She worked in Lyon as a contact for agents and resistants. Blanche Charlet, Sept-Oct 1942. She worked as a courier with radio operator Brian Stonehouse till their arrest in Oct 1942.

MD
Madeleine Damerment, Feb 1944. She was dropped near here with her organizer and radio operator to start a new réseau. They were arrested at the dropping ground.

for instance, had their own small *réseaux*-in-exile in France.

There were already tens of thousands of resistants in France but at the start of 1944 they were uncoordinated and largely unarmed. It was this lack of arms which was beginning to turn them in the same direction: towards SOE.

SOE in London, acutely aware from its agents of the need for arms, was starting to campaign for more aircraft to be made available for drops. It was also anxiously trying to strengthen its existing *réseaux* and to build new ones. As 1943 became 1944 the tide of the war might be turning, but both F Section and RF were behindhand with their plans.

The Prosper/Déricourt affair, coming to a head in June 1943, had devastated F Section *réseaux* north of the line. A similar blow had fallen on RF *réseaux* in the very same week when Germans had captured a whole group of RF Resistance leaders at a meeting near Lyon. (Jean Moulin was one of those arrested; he had died under torture ten days later.) At the end of 1943 F and RF Sections had a number of *réseaux* in place and active but they were still struggling to establish an overall presence in France.

(The map on pages 194-5 shows F Section *réseaux* in France at the start of 1944. The areas in which women agents worked are marked out.) ie F Section had several large country-based *réseaux* south of the line: going from west to east were Wheelwright, Stationer, a *réseau* called Author started in the autumn in the Corrèze, and Jockey. North of Jockey, spreading across the Ain and into Haute-Savoie, was another *réseau* which had been founded in the autumn, Marksman.

Then there was Pimento, still going strong around Toulouse, and several small *réseaux*, including one called Monk which operated around Marseille.

Above the line F Section's activity looked more ragged: a couple of small *réseaux* were still trying to pick up the pieces around Paris. A large *réseau*, Salesman, was active in Normandy but a number of other *réseaux* further west had recently been blown or else had had to go temporarily out of operation. Of the north-eastern *réseaux*, Farmer and Stockbroker were still active but had lost their original organizers. Tinker, round Troyes, had had to disband and a new *réseau*, Diplomat, was being cautiously started in its place. The Musician *réseau* around St Quentin was in its last month of survival.

In the Yonne, Paul Frager led Donkeyman, together with his trusted friend and lieutenant the double agent Roger Bardet. Meanwhile, based in Paris, Déricourt still ran Farrier, threatening the safety of every agent he met.

There were three other women agents at work in France during that winter of 1943–4. They were far from the south-western Wheelwright and Stationer territory; all were on the eastern side of France. They were Eliane Plewman, Yolande Beekman and Elizabeth Devereux-Rochester.

Eliane Plewman was in the volatile city of Marseille, working as a courier for the small *réseau* Monk. She was twenty-five, Anglo-Spanish by nationality and only recently married to an Englishman, Tom Plewman. Her family name was Browne-Bartroli; she had lived a cosmopolitan life before the war and had come into SOE through personal contacts. Her brother, Albert Browne-Bartroli, was an F Section agent too: he had followed her into France in October 1943 and was working in the upper Rhône.

Eliane was, by the accounts of her which survive, a vivid personality. Robert Maloubier, a Frenchman who trained as an agent with Eliane and who later on worked with another, more famous woman agent, Violette Szabo, said that the two were alike. They shared high spirits and a readiness for action. They also shared good looks; Eliane was striking, with dark hair and fair skin.

But however vibrant her looks and her civilian way of life, Eliane was to be called upon to bring steadiness and cool judgement to her mission. Not only was she sent to work in Marseille, always a dangerous place for agents, but as soon as she arrived in France a number of problems waylaid her.

She was dropped alone on the night of 14 August, supposedly to a reception near Lons le Saunier in the Jura mountains. Her instructions were to go to Marseille and to contact the agent *Bernard* who was in charge of the Monk *réseau*. *Bernard* had been in France since June, along with a radio operator *Laurent*; Eliane was to join them (under the code-name *Gaby*) and to act as courier. Even as she jumped from the plane she was performing her first task as the *réseau*'s courier: alongside her was dropped a briefcase, fastened to its own mini-parachute and packed with one million francs. It was her job to carry this briefcase safely down to Marseille and her new comrades.

But as Eliane descended she could see no lights and no reception committee – nor even anything which resembled a likely dropping ground beneath her. On the contrary, she seemed to be coming down over a farmhouse. She drifted over its yards and then over its roofs; somewhere beneath her a farm dog, outraged at her intrusion, began to bark. She was over the house and into the fields beyond. Praying that no one had looked out of the windows and seen her, she landed heavily.

The dog continued to bark and a bad pain was throbbing in her ankle where she had twisted it under her. She struggled out of her parachute and hid it; searching warily across the dark ground, she found the briefcase. She didn't know where she had landed, except that it was obviously not in the right place, and she decided that it would be too great a risk to keep the briefcase with her now. She took her bearings carefully and then hid the case in a thick bush; if all went well she could return to this area and collect it later. She set off to put a safe distance between herself and the farmhouse. When daylight came and she could show herself openly on the roads she would make for the town where lived her Baker Street-supplied contacts.

In the event, it took Eliane nearly two months to get to Marseille. The Jura region was not a safe one for Resistance in the late summer of 1943 and she had to go very carefully. The first people she tried to contact had vanished; their neighbours told her that they had been arrested by the Germans. She was able to make contact with other resistants soon after that and gradually began to make her way to the south. She did not manage to recover the one million francs though: when a courier was sent to search for the case it was found in the bush – but empty.

Eliane had to travel along a chain of contacts in order to reach her comrades in Monk. This chain linked her, albeit tenuously, to some of the agents who were caught up in the Prosper/Déricourt affair. The agent *Elie* of Inventor, with whom Vera Leigh was now working in Paris, had first started Inventor as a *réseau* in Marseille in 1942. He therefore had a number of contacts among the Marseillais resistants and now some of these were working in Monk. There was another, more direct link with the unlucky Prosper/Déricourt agents: *Bernard* himself had been one of Déricourt's arrivals and had been followed by the Bony-Lafont 'tails' until he managed to lose them in Lyon.

The shadow of the SD and Déricourt was reaching out to Eliane and the other members of Monk but it fell just short of them.

When Eliane arrived in Marseille that autumn, she called at the apartment of a Frenchwoman, Madame Chaix-Bryon. Eliane's story is full of cross-references and connections: this woman was later on to marry her brother and fellow agent. But at this point she was simply the last, welcome stage in Eliane's journey to her *réseau*. Madame Chaix-Bryon gave Eliane *Bernard*'s address: 8 Rue Mérentié.

The Rue Mérentié was a side-street, one of many in a modest, residential quarter of the city, near the top of a hill. Here *Bernard*, a careful, middle-aged man, was based. One hundred kilometres to the east, in a villa perched on the coastal hills of the Var, *Laurent* the radio operator was hidden away. From now on Eliane was plunged into a demanding schedule of courier work which took her repeatedly from one to another of these places.

The journey from Marseille to Roquebrune-sur-Argens, the nearest village to *Laurent*'s safe house, was made by train or – if Eliane were lucky – by an old Ford truck. The *réseau* had this truck for transporting arms and equipment; two charcoal burners had been added to it in compliance with the law but for urgent jobs the resistants ran the engine on precious black market petrol. On these trips red battery lights were arranged in the burners to simulate the glow of burning charcoal. '*Le gazo de roi*', as the truck was known within the *réseau*, was driven by its owner and *réseau* member, Jean Hellet; sometimes Eliane travelled beside him, helping with the distribution of whatever the illicit load was *en route* to the villa *La Cavalière* and *Laurent*.

Laurent was a young man – at about twenty, younger than Eliane. It was hard for him to stay permanently hidden at the hillside villa, despite the company and care of the villa's owner, Madame Régis. Eliane's routine, by contrast, alternated between the travels, rendezvous and liaisons of Marseille and the tense calm of the days she spent with *Laurent* in *La Cavalière*. Because of the distance she had to cover with each trip, she usually stayed at least a few hours at the villa – if she needed a response to a message for Baker Street she might stay a day or two, waiting for it.

Madame Régis was a quick-witted and reliable host. One day she was standing at a window, keeping watch for *Laurent* as he transmitted, when she saw a German on the terrace outside. Warning *Laurent* to get off the air and hide his set, she went out to greet the German. He was carrying out a routine check; Madame Régis invited him into the house and proceeded to give him a drink of her dubious home-made schnapps and to introduce to him the delicate-looking *Laurent* as her son, home from college to recover from illness. The German was very taken with Madame Régis and came back several times to repeat the visits; it required strong nerves to make him welcome each time but Madame Régis did it and later on she was to see it pay off. When a D/F van picked up transmission signals in the area and the Germans began searching houses, *La Cavalière*, known as a place friendly to the occupiers, was left alone.

But there were plenty of dangers and near-misses for the agents to worry about, all the same. And Madame Régis worried too: her house was a refuge but it was not inviolable. Winter heralded some bitter *maquis* attacks and fierce German/*milice* reprisals up in

Haute-Savoie; the effects were felt further south in intensified German counter-resistance. This, together with the fact that the *réseau's* activity was on the increase, put agents and resistants under severe strain.

Eliane spent Christmas at *La Cavalière* with *Laurent* and Madame Régis' family. It was a celebration edged round with fear. She travelled to Roquebrune on Christmas Eve on a train packed with German soldiers; unnerved, that evening she and *Laurent* took his set out on to the hillside and erected it in one of the old Roman aqueducts, preferring to transmit away from the house full of guests. Eliane checked that no one was around and went back to the house; the hours then passed agonizingly by without any sign of *Laurent*. He turned up at 10 p.m., dishevelled. Away from the other guests, he explained that he had had to lie low when he had seen dogs out on the hills, and then he had been forced to take a long circuitous route back to avoid them. That night he got drunk; Eliane and Madame Régis watched him and one another anxiously. The Christmas holiday seemed to be bringing them only menace.

In the New Year, the Monk agents became increasingly concerned with active sabotage. A Frenchman, Julien Villevieille, was the co-ordinator of sabotage activities among the local groups, and Eliane undertook a good deal of liaison work between him and *Bernard*. She continued to go back and forth between Roquebrune and Marseille; now she also accompanied Villevieille and fellow resistants on certain sorties, to collect and transport arms, to lay explosives against a target. The Monk group of agents and resistants was a small one and there was much shared labour: Eliane was deeply involved in almost all that happened.

Their sabotage attacks were aimed at the rail communications in the area. The Germans were moving troops, munitions and supplies along these routes; whenever the invasion came they would rely on them more than ever. The Monk agents and resistants set about blocking them. They laid charges against tracks and in tunnels: they would lay them at night and then retire; when the next train went over the charge, it would activate it, and the line would explode. In the first two weeks of January the Monk resistants damaged thirty trains. Their most successful operation was the sabotage of a train as it passed through a tunnel east of Marseille; with the explosion, the train went off the rails; the resistants then laid another charge so that the first salvage train which arrived to clear the wreckage was also ruined. The operation blocked the main line to Toulon for four days.

This intensive activity meant that Eliane and the others were working at full stretch. They were exposed and under strain; Eliane, who as a young woman had more freedom of movement than the men, had to do a lot of independent work, carrying explosive charges to the targets and setting them up. Visiting her when he was passing through Marseille, Eliane's brother was horrified to find her carrying plastic explosive on a tram, *en route* to sabotage a railway line single-handed. Angry at the danger this placed her in, he went with her and helped her lay the charge.

The *réseau* held, however, and after the first few weeks of the year the group paced its sabotage attacks more slowly. But by this time Eliane felt that they were in danger from a different source.

Madame Chaix-Bryon, fellow resistant and Eliane's future sister-in-law, saw Eliane's sense of foreboding grow. After the war she described how, when she took messages to Eliane during these last two months of her freedom, she found her. 'She was not foolhardy. She was worried about what was happening in the group; she felt fear.'

She had reason to, for the Monk *réseau* was no longer secure. One of the group's members, a woman, was living with an agent for the Gestapo. Through her, he infiltrated the group and in March, while the group was engaged in another heavy spate of sabotage attacks, he began to prepare his move.

The last time Madame Chaix-Bryon saw Eliane was a few days before the arrests. She had taken a message to her and Eliane was clearly worried. Madame Chaix-Bryon suggested that she leave Marseille for a while but Eliane refused; she said she had too many things to do. But she seemed haunted by a premonition of disaster. When Madame Chaix-Bryon took her leave, saying '*au revoir*', Eliane followed her on to the stairs, saying, 'No, not *au revoir* – *adieu*.'

On 23 March, *Bernard* and Julien Villevieille were arrested in *Bernard*'s apartment at 8 Rue Mérentié. They fought but could not escape. The next day, Eliane, *Laurent* and a French resistant called at the apartment and were taken as well. Other arrests of *réseau* members followed: within a few days there were about twelve of them in the Gestapo headquarters at 425 Rue Paradis.

The usual darkness and confusion reigns over the history of these prisoners. The word-of-mouth evidence is that they were almost all interrogated with torture: specifically that they were beaten about the face and given electric shocks. Someone who claims to have seen them a few days after their capture says that their faces were swollen and almost unrecognizable. There is also a local story among Marseille resistants that during these days Eliane sang from her cell, encouraging herself and the others not to give in. Eliane pretended that she was simply *Bernard*'s lover and had nothing to tell. None of the captured agents and resistants talked.

Eventually they were taken from Gestapo headquarters to Les Baumettes prison; from there they were sent on to Fresnes. In a few months' time Eliane would join the six other SOE women aboard the train for Ravensbrück concentration camp. She would not come back.

*

She was a very careful girl in every way; I liked her. She married Bateman – he was a corporal of signals, a Dutchman, and was involved in our training. I don't know exactly what his role was in the training school but she met him there and she fell for him. He was tall, dark; she was plump and fair – they sort of went together, you see. She came back all sparkling eyes one evening and she said that he'd proposed.

And then we did an exercise together up in Scotland. I heard all the story all the time and they were getting married by special licence as soon as the mission in Scotland was done. So that all happened and they got married. I think Bateman had hoped that if he married her, she wouldn't go after all.

Then a little later, two women came up to me in Regent Street. They were post office operators and had been at the radio training school at Thame to show us what to do. They asked me if Yolande was pregnant – they'd heard a rumour. I said, 'Well, *surely* they won't send her out now.'

We never knew if Yolande was pregnant or not but she went out in September.

That was Yvonne Cormeau talking about Yolande Beekman, her fellow student and friend through SOE training. Yolande was thirty-one when she was recruited from the WAAF into SOE; she came from an Anglo-Swiss family and spoke French perfectly. She had a slight Swiss accent but as Maurice Buckmaster pointed out, this was a positive advantage: 'It diverted attention from her rather typically English appearance.'[1]

She went through her training in a party of men and women which included Yvonne Cormeau, Cecily Lefort and Noor Inayat Khan. She was, as Yvonne Cormeau remembers, a careful person and seemed

[1] *Specially Employed*, Maurice Buckmaster, Batchworth Press, 1952

obviously suitable for training as a radio operator. Like Yvonne she
had no experience of radio work; the two of them learned together.
It was a long process, for the training procedures were rigorous and
the women had to learn not only to handle codes and ciphers and
to transmit in morse code but also to maintain and repair their sets.
During this training she met Corporal Bateman and so, when she
went out to France in September 1943, she was newly married.

She travelled by Lysander with three male agents and was put down
on the same landing ground near Angers that had received Cecily
Lefort, Diana Rowden and Noor Inayat in June. It was a Déricourt
operation, with all the dangers that involved, but Yolande seems to
have escaped being followed, or else to have successfully thrown off
her trailers. Perhaps the sheer length of her journey saved her: from
this landing ground south-west of Paris in the Maine-et-Loire, she
managed to get herself and her set safely across 350 kilometres to
St Quentin in the north-east.

Yolande's mission was to be radio operator to *Guy* (Gustave
Biéler), organizer of Musician. The region in which they worked was
becoming a dangerous one for Resistance; for the last six months the
industrial north-east had been jumping with sabotage attacks and the
Germans were determined to put a stop to it. Much of the sabotage
was being done by the groups working with Farmer, further to the
north around Lille. *Guy* himself was a cautious man and he limited
Musician resistants to just a few, specific attacks, but all the same the
St Quentin area too was heating up. The Prosper collapse had hit
the Musician *réseau* hard, for *Guy* had been using the Prosper radios
right up until the end and since June he had not only to worry about
the security threat from the captured Prosper sets, but to find other
radio operators to take his messages. Added to that was the fact that
Musician now had enough arms and explosives dumps, well enough
distributed, to be intensifying sabotage coups. The rail link between
St Quentin and Lille was one which the Germans liked to use and
which the Allies were anxious to impede: when Yolande Beekman
arrived in the area, Musician sabotage groups were already laying
charges against the line every few weeks.

Yolande, (code-named *Yvonne*) settled in a village named Fonsommes, outside the town of St Quentin. She worked closely with
Guy and with a Frenchman named Cordelette who organized one of
Musician's sub-*réseaux* and who also lived in Fonsommes. Yolande
had qualities of care and steadfastness; she needed to draw on them
during this troubled autumn and winter. Safe houses were hard to find
around St Quentin and for much of her time there she transmitted
from one house in Fonsommes. She had an attic room and in this

she would wait for hours before each sked. Her landlady remembered her sitting quietly in the room, reading, waiting for the agreed time to arrive.

Guy was already a local hero in the area. Buckmaster called him 'one of the toughest-looking men I have ever met' and had reasoned that his appearance and his manner would make him fit well with the rough-and-ready groups of resistants growing up in the north-east. He was continually proving his physical courage: the injury he had done to his spine on arrival had never fully healed and he was in pain, and unable to walk without a limp, all through his mission.

Yolande's quiet efficiency complemented *Guy*'s stoic courage. They worked together for nearly four months. Her first priority was to her skeds but she also helped *Guy* with local liaison work, trying to keep to a minimum the need for his painful travels. In the face of increasing counter-resistance activity *Guy* tried to ensure the safety of the *réseau* and for Yolande that meant much tedious lying low, day after day passed in her attic room. Meanwhile, through her skeds she organized arms drops and sent the news of sabotage strikes to London.

These were now coming more frequently, within the Musician area and further north, in Farmer's area. The Farmer organizer, Michel Trotobas, had been shot dead by Germans at the end of November and about twenty Farmer resistants had been arrested, but the *réseau* had survived the blows. There were many resistants still left around Lille and they contacted the Musician resistants to reassure them that they were still there and ready to continue the underground war. Yolande transmitted the message to London, while to the north of her the Farmer resistants blew up a dozen railway engines and a repair shop, and *Guy* and her other comrades in Musician planned an attack on the St Quentin canal lock.

The canal was used by Germans to transport submarine parts from the requisitioned factories of the north which produced them, down to the Mediterranean and to Bordeaux. Baker Street hoped that the sabotage of the St Quentin lock would hold up the transport of these parts and would launch a new phase of activity for Musician. On the night of 10 January a new agent *Théodore* dropped to join the *réseau* and to help carry out the sabotage attack.

But the mounting activity in the region had focused German attention on to it. The Germans were aware that they were probably dealing with organized, British-backed Resistance and they put teams of men and D/F vans into St Quentin and the outlying villages. *Théodore* was taken; without him, *Guy* and a few resistants went to the locks one night and laid charges against lock gates and barges. It was a successful operation: when the gates next opened the charges detonated and the lock was jammed with broken gates and barges for weeks. But the *réseau* had run out of time.

Transmitting regularly from the same attic room, Yolande was unprotected against the D/F vans. In the middle of January, they pin-pointed her house as the source of transmissions, and observed it. The next day, when Yolande met *Guy* in a café in St Quentin, Gestapo officers rushed in and arrested them.

Yolande and *Guy* were taken to Gestapo headquarters in St Quentin; there they were interrogated and tortured by beatings. Neither of them spoke. Many of their fellow resistants were also taken, including Cordelette – he too was tortured. As usual, it is impossible to know what the different people suffered. But although the main figures in the *réseau* were in captivity, it didn't entirely collapse. Its teams of railway workers, in particular, stayed together and in the months ahead they would be able to help the resistants and agents who took the place of the originals.

As for Yolande herself, her history over those months is lost. We know that she was transferred, like so many others, to Fresnes. But the next glimpse of her is in July when, handcuffed to Odette, in the group that also included Eliane, she was to travel to Ravensbrück.

Elizabeth, La Grande

The last woman to go out in 1943 was a striking figure, Elizabeth Devereux-Rochester. Born of an English mother and American father, she had been educated at Roedean school in Sussex and in the 1930s had settled in Paris with her mother, moving in a privileged circle and spending much of her time on sport. When the Germans invaded she got out of the country over the Pyrénées, like so many other SOE recruits, and in 1943 she was training to return as an agent.

She went out by Hudson on the night of 18 October, with three other agents: her organizer *Xavier* (an Englishman Richard Heslop), a male radio operator, and an RF agent who was to work alongside *Xavier* organizing the Free French recruits. They were going to the mountains of the Jura and Haute-Savoie to start the Marksman *réseau*.

From the beginning, Marksman was a *maquis*-based *réseau*. *Xavier* and his RF comrade had already spent three weeks in the rugged countryside, meeting some *maquis* and local Resistance leaders and sizing up the possibilities of the region. They had found it promising; like Odette and Peter Churchill before them, they liked the small mountain communities and the tough, down-to-earth nature of the resistants. In the six months since Odette's and Peter's arrest, however, the *maquis* had really taken hold in the hills of the Ain, the

Jura and Haute-Savoie. The Marksman group of agents spent the next six months arming and co-ordinating them.

Elizabeth (code-named also *Elizabeth*) was the Marksman courier. Her duties of liaison between *Xavier*, local resistants and the *maquis* took her on gruelling walks over hills to isolated farmhouses, and on train journeys to the eastern towns of Lyon and Grenoble. In the towns she was badly exposed, for her physical appearance marked her out: she was tall and athletically built, with red-gold hair and a pale complexion. She looked much more English than French. Back in the country areas among resistance friends she was known as '*La Grande*'.

In the winter months of 1943–4, the Marksman region was the most violent in all France. The earlier autumn clashes in the east between *maquis* and *milice* continued to escalate. As arms were dropped and distributed to the *maquis*, they used them, and reprisals and counter-attacks now came in force from the Germans. Hundreds of farms were burnt down by the Germans that winter and hundreds of resistants were arrested.

But the *maquis* were now well dug in to their hostile territory and they continued to grow. Through this winter, Elizabeth carried out her courier work with – in the words of *Xavier* – 'guts and imagination'. She had a memory which could hold long verbatim messages; she also had physical strength and courage. She was, however, extremely noticeable. The impression she made on George Millar, a young man escaping from France with the help of Marksman contacts, is recorded in his memoirs. He was hiding out in a farmhouse far from anywhere, waiting for the courier to come and take him on the next leg of his journey, when she strode in:

> She was genially commanding. They called her *La Grande*. She demanded a drink and the location of *les waters*. Her appearance was intriguing. Mannishly impeccable. A superb tweed costume with a divided skirt, perfect shoes and stockings, expensive luggage including a dressing-case with gold-topped bottles and jars. Her hair was reddish and her skin pale but healthy.[1]

She wasn't the sort of person who lent herself physically or temperamentally to camouflage.

Elizabeth was recalled in spring 1944, principally because she was simply too conspicuous to leave in the field. She left Marksman

---

[1] *Maquis*, George Millar, William Heinemann Ltd, 1945

when she was ordered to but she did not go home; instead she went to Paris, where she had heard that a good friend of hers had been arrested and was being held in prison. Characteristically, Elizabeth was hoping to organize her friend's escape. She went to her mother's house but her mother was under supervision and Elizabeth was arrested herself. She had a good chance of survival: her cover story held under interrogation and she had no compromising material on her to identify her as a British agent. But as the Marksman *réseau* went from strength to strength, with arms dropping to it in ever growing quantities, Elizabeth was in a French prison.

Besides these three relative newcomers, the beginning of 1944 saw two women agents from earlier missions lying low. They were Blanche Charlet and Mary Herbert. Blanche had been in Castres prison since November 1942, but in September 1943 some fellow prisoners had found a sympathetic warder and got hold of pistols and spare keys. A group of about fifty prisoners escaped in a mass break-out, among them Blanche and her cell-mate, a young resistante called Suzanne Charisse. The two women reached the open country and, after asking help of a priest and a farmer, they eventually took refuge in the grounds of a monastery. They were sheltered in a guest house there for two months, and then the monks managed to get them on to an escape line to the Pyrénées.

They reached the Pyrénées safely but it was mid-winter and heavy snow made it impossible for them to get across to Spain. They made the long journey back to the monastery and in the early months of 1944 they began to do courier work for the escape line. In April, Baker Street got a message to them via their French contacts, telling them to return. A sea pick-up was organized from the coast of Brittany and after all these months of imprisonments and fugitive living, Blanche and Suzanne were sailed back across the Channel, under fire from German boats.

During this same winter of 1943, Mary Herbert's mission was coming to an unexpected end. Mary Herbert – 'Mariel' as she was called by many of her friends – had been in the field well over a year, working for Claude de Baissac in Scientist.

Mary was English, and in her early twenties. Despite Peter Churchill's first impression of her as someone too fragile for the rigours of Resistance life, she stood up to a heavy burden of courier work in the growing *réseau*. She was based in Bordeaux with Claude, but she travelled widely, by bicycle and by train, liaising with different groups in Scientist territory and occasionally with contacts in other *réseaux*. She visited Poitiers several times, exchanging information with Lise de Baissac and bringing messages which had come for her over the Scientist radio. She and Lise liked and trusted one another and Lise introduced her to a few of the Poitiers resistants, including the Gateau family, and two old sisters who did what they could to help the Resistance.

But most of Mary's work was in the Bordeaux region. The Scientist *réseau* had two kinds of group within it – sabotage groups based at Bordeaux docks and led by Claude, and the more usual groups of resistants in surrounding towns, villages and countryside. These were organized by Claude together with an F Section assistant and a number of local Resistance leaders. In 1943 the agents were kept very busy ordering and receiving arms drops, and distributing them among the groups: Mary covered hundreds of kilometres every week on her bicycle.

Claude de Baissac was not an easy man to work with. He was proud and determined; his own capacity for hard work and leadership made him demanding on others. Maurice Buckmaster called him 'the most difficult of all my officers without any exception.' But he was an irresistible force: he succeeded in recruiting tens of thousands of people to Scientist, and although the stringent German security at Bordeaux docks made it hard for his group to do much sabotage, he and his comrades kept London supplied with a lot of vital information about German naval movements.

Mary and Claude, working closely together in the hectic town of Bordeaux, had a love affair. In the late spring of 1942, Mary realized that she was pregnant. She made the discovery just as the Prosper arrests began and the shock waves travelled down to Bordeaux. Through his links with *Prosper*, Claude was endangered; so was Lise, up in Poitiers. To add to that, there was trouble within Scientist: one of the main French leaders with whom the agents worked, a man very right wing in his politics, was now persuaded by a German officer that only by working with the Third Reich could France keep out the bolsheviks. The former resistant, repenting his work for Scientist, told the Germans where to find many of the arms dumps, and a series of arrests began.

Messages came over the radio from Baker Street that Claude and Lise were both to return by Lysander, and in August they went. Mary continued to work in Bordeaux for the next few months, still cycling until she grew too big, after which she travelled more on trains and coaches. The Scientist *réseau* was breaking up, however, and it was soon politic as well as physically necessary for her to lie low.

At the very end of 1943, Mary gave birth to a girl. She was

staying with friends in Bordeaux, the child just a few weeks old, when news came that she and other resistants were being hunted in the city. She left and went to Poitiers, taking refuge in Lise's old flat.

Here she found shelter only briefly: in February the Gestapo raided the flat, in search of Lise. The Gestapo also arrested other Poitiers resistants, including Madame and Monsieur Gateau. The timing of the arrests is suggestive: they happened at the same time as Déricourt's final return to London, when the SD would no longer have anything to gain from leaving Lise and her helpers free. Was Lise due to be one of the very last agents captured through Déricourt? Very likely, but it was not Lise whom the Gestapo caught – it was a young woman they had not expected to see, nursing a tiny baby.

Mary was separated from her baby and put into prison. Her baby, she was told, had been put into a children's home. Desperate to get out and find her daughter, Mary declared her innocence over and over again. She knew nothing of the woman who had had the flat before her, she said. She had been staying there only a few weeks with her baby. It was a terrible mistake.

Poitiers was a long way from Bordeaux, and there was no reason for the Gestapo to suspect Mary of not being the young French woman she said she was. It hardly seemed likely that a woman who had just given birth could be a British agent, and they did not connect her with events in Bordeaux. Mary was released: she went straight to the children's home and by arguing vociferously that she had been wrongly arrested, she managed to get her baby back.

Now she was at a loss for what to do. She could not risk trying to contact an agent with a radio – besides, she had no idea where to find one. The Gateaux had been arrested. She went to the two old sisters whom she had met through Lise: they had escaped arrest, and she asked them for help. They found her a family, living in a house in the countryside near Poitiers, who agreed to take her in as a lodger. In early spring 1944, she took shelter there with her baby, no longer an agent of the Resistance but a lost, anonymous young mother in an occupied country.

Mary Herbert was out of the fight now, and Elizabeth 'La Grande', Eliane Plewman and Yolande Beekman were in captivity. But their efforts, and those of their comrades, were now bearing fruit. Across the country, the Resistance movement was gathering momentum: the French people were mobilizing at last.

SIXTEEN

France Mobilizes

It was the French spring, 1944, and the people of France were turning in their masses to Resistance. The long hardship and privations of the previous year, the creation of the *milice* and the birth of the *maquis* had brought the country to a crossroads. Since January the *milice* had spread into the north of France too, as the Germans strove to tighten their grip on the occupied land. But they formed too late to check the growing will to resist among the French, and too late to uproot the groups of resistants and *maquis* and the burgeoning SOE *réseaux* which offered encouragement and protection and the promise of arms. Francis Cammaerts, who had already been in the field for a year, was in no doubt that he was seeing a genuine national uprising. 'What happened in France in 1944 was a revolution. A lot of people today won't believe it was that, but it was.'

For the SOE *réseaux*, recruitment now became mainly a screening process. Whole extended families, entire communities began to involve themselves in Resistance and the group organizers and the agents had to select their new contacts carefully, and try to ensure that they understood the need for security.

The characters of the Resistance communities were different, one from another. In the fertile Gascogne, *Annette* and *Hilaire* and the other Wheelwright agents nurtured security by maintaining cut-outs, as they found that security training often induced confusion among the region's resistants. Many of the people who made up the local Resistance were related to one another, living in expatriate communities of Spanish and Italian – predominantly communist – families. They had endured and escaped oppression before and had their own ways

of acting in solidarity, which often involved a free passage of information between themselves. The SOE agents had no God-given right to
impose their own rules: instead they adapted their methods, to limit
the extent to which the activities and knowledge of one community
seeped into another.

On the other hand, Francis Cammaerts, working a lonely and
gruelling routine in the south-eastern uplands of the Drôme, found
that security was often already built into the self-contained communities there. In one small town which he visited regularly, the head
of the Resistance group was one half of the local refrigerator makers',
together with a fellow resistant, the town carpenter. The carpenter
made the refrigerator boxes and the group leader put in the lead
lining. The group leader and his wife lived in a two bedroom flat and
put up *Roger* (as they knew Cammaerts) in the second bedroom when
he visited. Just across the road lived a garage manager – the group's
number two – with his wife and two children. An older man living
down the road was another group member, and so were a handful of
others – about seven households in that town worked together in the
Resistance, helping and protecting each other and laying on a special
welcome for *Roger* behind closed doors whenever he appeared.

It was the participation not just of individuals but of entire
households – husbands and wives, children, even grandparents –
which characterized the French Resistance. In the society of France
in the 1940s, where three generations often lived in the one home
and all worked together, it could not be otherwise. It was the men
who went out to receive the arms drops and to lay the sabotage
charges but it was the women who ran the houses in which explosives
or radio sets or agents were hidden; who had full knowledge of the
men's activities and who covered for them, who organized their own
children to further the Resistance, whether it be by taking messages
or acting as pathfinder or providing natural camouflage.

The French Resistance had grown out of French homes and
families. Since the very earliest days of the occupation it had been
so and now that confidence and the will to resist were spreading, the
four walls and the kitchen tables of French homes were more than ever
their crucible. The *maquis* were sustained by the willingness of their
families to let them go, and by the protection they offered: the families
of *maquis* members were the first line of defence – they brought the
maquis groups warnings of German searches in the district; sometimes
they were also able to pass on to them much-needed gifts of food and
clothing.

In 1944 the women of France had not yet been given the vote.
In the country districts, households still existed where the women

did not sit down to eat with the men but stood behind their chairs, waiting on them. The divisions between men's and women's spheres of activity were deep and wide – but the need to resist was closing them. Younger, single women were acting as couriers, carrying explosives on trains and in their bicycle saddlebags, bluffing their way through German and *milice* controls. These were still a small minority, but the traditional work of the majority of women – giving protection, nourishment, shelter and love – had taken on a new meaning.

Now women would cycle ten or twenty kilometres every day to find food and the basic supplies of life: wool, cotton, soap, fuel. Their families relied on their travels and their physical labour – they made soap from animal fat and coffee from acorns, shoes from wood and cardboard – to survive. The women were also able to feed their communities with something else – information. They brought back from their foraging trips news of sabotage attacks in neighbouring regions, of Resistance developments and counter-Resistance measures; often they also brought secret messages from the Resistance grapevine.

The groups of resistants who gathered to learn the use of arms and explosives were almost all men but there was no longer any doubt that their work was made possible by the women. While the men were out planning and enacting Resistance strikes, the women fought to preserve them. In areas where the Resistance was known to be active, the women faced repeated raids on their homes, underwent repeated interrogations and threats. Francis Cammaerts can give any number of examples from his mission in the Drôme – such as the day when he was out on a sabotage job with a petit bourgeois French resistant, and a message reached them that it was not safe for the resistant to go home. The message came from the man's wife: in his absence Germans had come to the house, looking for him and *Roger*. They had seized his wife and the three children, aged twelve, ten and seven, and taken them to the nearby administration centre. There they had stripped them all and demanded to know where the men were. They threatened that if they did not get the information they would start shooting the children one by one, first in the knees, then in the stomach, then in the head; they would save the mother till the end.

The woman had not given in: she had stuck to her story that her husband was off drinking and womanizing with a dreadful friend of his. She just kept on repeating it, saying that she was entirely in the dark, her husband's behaviour was disgraceful; she didn't know where he and his reprobate friend were nor when they would come home. Finally the Germans decided to believe her. They allowed her and the children to get dressed and go home; from there the woman managed to send a message out to her husband, warning him to be careful how he returned. It was a horrible incident but it was not an unusual one: families connected with Resistance lived under continuous threat and the women were the first in line.

Jacqueline and *Hector* passing in and out of the Néraud household; *Annette* hiding in her farms, *Roger* moving from one set of French 'parents', as he called them, to another: they all saw and understood the courage required of these women. Yet it was not all grim; the family nature of the Resistance also kept alive its sense of humour. There was a zest in surviving a close call or outwitting a party of Germans; a brother whose clumsiness nearly overturned a vanload of hidden arms was still a clumsy brother to be teased and laughed at. Quarrels and jokes and relieved laughter kept the resistants sane.

Women and men, children and grandparents, brothers, sisters and neighbours were knitting together the fabric of Resistance so that soon it would stretch over the whole country. But soon was not yet; and in the early spring of 1944 the French people still lacked organization and, most of all, arms.

For the staff at Baker Street, monitoring reports from their agents in France, the first two months of the year had been a time of anxiety and frustration, mixed with hope. Everyone now expected an Allied invasion of France during the next six months; the Resistance groups in France had a firm foothold and F Section had dozens of agents trained and waiting to join them.

But the Resistance, and SOE's role in nurturing it, were hampered by the lack of aircraft for drops and pick-ups. There was bitter rivalry over the use of aircraft – at the end of 1943, after three years of clandestine activity in occupied Europe, the Allied forces were still providing only twenty-three Halifaxes for special operations over the whole of north and north-west Europe. These planes were shared not only among countries but among the various Resistance and intelligence organizations. The Resistance was growing, but it was obvious that in France it would soon be choked off unless more aircraft were available to serve it. SOE senior staff were repeatedly lobbying Churchill for more planes; they were opposed by Bomber Command, determined to keep as many planes as possible for the bombing of Germany, and by intelligence organizations, including MI6, who claimed that the supply of arms to resistants would bring German reprisals against their own agents.

Despite this opposition, however, opinion was shifting in SOE's favour. At the end of January Churchill officially put his weight behind SOE. The arming of the French Resistance became a priority.

SOE now had the promise of more night-time flights for its drops and pick-ups. It was not a *carte blanche* by any means: arms drops and other 'special operations' still took second place to the demands of strategic bombing – German cities were currently being flattened, and in France there was regular bombing of industrial targets considered useful to the Germans. Bombing continued to come first, but the arming of the *maquis* was about to become a reality.

Poised for action, with agents on stand-by ready to go out and containers packed with guns and explosives and medical supplies ready to be dropped, and the planes ready to make the journeys, SOE now came up against the weather. The moon periods were marred by storms and thick cloud; one operation after another was cancelled. Desperate to get supplies out to the *maquis*, Baker Street tried some risky manoeuvres. In February, planes dropped 220 containers of arms through a layer of cloud: they were aiming for a region of Haute-Savoie controlled by the Marksman *réseau*. Beneath the cloud, some of the containers found their way to receptions but many went astray and were picked up by Germans. It was good and bad news for the *maquis* – the arrival of any supplies strengthened their position immeasurably, but the loss of the rest had alerted the Germans to their drops. This method of arming the *maquis* gave too much to the enemy:

> [Extract from a memo sent from Headquarters, Bomber Command to the Special Operations squadrons, dated 20/3/44]
>
> ### Marksman Operations
> The following message from the field should be of interest to all pilots who took part in the blind drops. 'Due to blind drops and scatter during February moon 45 containers dropped near Châtillon, Germans got all. 15 containers dropped near Virieu and the Germans got 8. 15 containers dropped near Abergement de Varey, the Germans got all. 15 containers dropped near Aranc and we got all. One parachute did not open and the rifles were broken.

Throughout the month of February, the French Resistance waited to welcome the new tide of support from England. But it was damned by the weather, and for all the willingness of the Special Operations

squadrons and the newly-trained agents, help arrived only spasmodi-
cally, in spurts and trickles.

As always, the future of the new *réseaux* in France grew out of
the events of the past: in February a number of agents slipped
through winter storms and clouds into France, only to find that the
disasters of 1943 were still waiting to pull them down. Almost all of
these agents were being sent on missions north of the demarcation
line, to fill the gaps left by the Prosper collapse. But although they
no longer had to contend with Déricourt himself – he had gone
back to England permanently at the beginning of the month – the
arrests of the previous summer and autumn had left plenty of booby
traps behind. So during the early spring of 1944, a stream of agents
went pouring in to northern France, on missions that were never to
be realized.

One grave danger for new agents was the fact that, four months
after Noor Inayat's arrest, Baker Street still believed the Phono *réseau*
to be secure. Buckmaster and his staff had certainly had their doubts
about the transmissions they were getting from Noor's set, but now
they had decided that she was probably free after all. They therefore
sent out some arms drops in response to radio requests, and arranged
for some agents to go to Phono receptions.

But of course, Noor was not free and Phono no longer existed,
except as a German radio game. The arms and supplies that dropped were gathered in by the Gestapo with great satisfaction, and the
advent of the new agents was eagerly awaited. So on the night of
7 February (coincidentally, the same night that Déricourt and his wife
were leaving from a different ground), four agents, all young men with
missions in the area between Poitiers and Paris, were dropped to a
Phono reception near Poitiers. The reception consisted of the Gestapo
and they were immediately arrested, with their radio set. Soon, this
set in its turn went on the air, transmitting to London apparently free,
but really under SD control. It was not such a convincing play-back
as the Phono transmissions, however – the operator's special security
messages were missing and Baker Street guessed that something had
gone wrong, and that the set was in German hands.

This cast further suspicion on Phono, but not quite enough. The
agent France Antelme had seen the messages coming from Noor's
set and was convinced that they were genuine and that she was free.
He had recognized *Archambaud*'s messages as German-controlled the
summer before and had helped convince Baker Street that the Prosper agents must be in captivity, and so his opinion was respected.
Furthermore, he was soon to go back to France himself, with a radio

operator and courier, and as he had no reliable contacts of his own left in France, the team would need a reception committee. He was a cautious man; he specifically asked the Baker Street staff to arrange a reception for him and his two new comrades. They arranged a Phono reception, through Noor's set.

On the night of 28 February the next moon period began and at the airfield, the newly formed team of three waited to leave: they were Antelme, the radio operator Lionel Lee, and a young Frenchwoman called Madeleine Damerment. Like Andrée Borrel, Madeleine was a native Frenchwoman who had been living in France when the Germans invaded and who had become involved with the Resistance at the very beginning. She too had worked on the PAT escape line until she had had to flee herself. Arriving in England, she had been recruited by F Section and trained as a courier. Her reports from the schools were good: she was quiet and unobtrusive; her courage was proven, and she had seemed a good choice to accompany Antelme and Lee on what would inevitably be a dangerous mission.

It would be dangerous because the agents were being sent into an area known to be insecure, to investigate what was happening and to establish a new *réseau*. They were dropping to a Phono reception near Chartres, south-west of Paris, but their first priority was to go further west to Brittany and to see what remained of the Parson *réseau*, which F Section knew to be broken up. Then they were to arrange a double Lysander operation near Le Mans – this, in the circumstances of Déricourt's withdrawal under suspicion, carried obvious perils. F Section had only just begun to suspect that the Butler *réseau* in the Sarthe might be unsound – in fact the agents had been in captivity since the summer before and their radio set was German controlled. Antelme and his comrades had instructions to investigate this *réseau* too, before finding a congenial place south of Paris to establish a new *réseau* of their own, to be named Bricklayer.

Baker Street knew that these were tall orders; they were given to Antelme because Baker Street's regard for him was high, and his past work marked him out as tough enough and clever enough to have a chance. He was assigned a radio operator and a courier who had both been in the field before (Lee had been in Corsica) and who were similarly highly thought of. Madeleine Damerment would need all her skill and courage and her ability to pass unnoticed to carry out the work ahead.

But as the newly formed team climbed aboard the bomber on the British airfield, German soldiers and Gestapo officers were already gathering at the dropping ground in France, ready to receive them. The plane left English soil, climbed through the sky as the south of

England passed beneath it and began the bumpy, juddering passage over the Channel and northern France, flying without lights through the unwelcoming darkness. Madeleine sat in the hold along with her two fellow agents, her ears like theirs filled with the roar of the engines; waiting to hear that they were nearing the ground. Then they were near it; the pilot reported the lights in place, the reception ready for them; the hatch was opened and in quick succession they jumped.

They landed, each safely, and from the shadows the German reception team rushed out to seize them. Antelme, a physically big man, put up a fierce struggle but was overpowered. They had no chance at all – the Gestapo had been able to prepare everything perfectly – and they were handcuffed and driven straight back to Paris, to Gestapo headquarters on the Avenue Foch.

It was Antelme who bore the brunt of interrogation. The Gestapo were able to identify him from his Prosper links in 1943 and knew that he was an important agent – they interrogated him repeatedly about F Section and about plans for the invasion. He refused to say anything, maintaining that he had been supposed to take orders from Garry and so had nothing of his own to tell. The Gestapo didn't believe him but could never persuade or beat anything more out of him – no information useful for their own ends, nor anything which they could feed back to Baker Street over the captured set to give the impression that the agents were still free.

They therefore devised a stratagem to account for his silence. At the end of March, Buckmaster and his staff at Baker Street received their first messages from the Bricklayer set. The decoded messages were all marked 'Special Check Present' but they gave unexpectedly bad news: Antelme had apparently hurt his head badly when dropping and was now unconscious and seriously ill. More messages followed, reporting his continual deterioration. The radio operator Lee had been briefed before he left by Gerry Morel and Morel was unhappy about the wording of these messages – they did not sound to him as if they genuinely came from Lee himself. He asked the signals people to go over the transmissions again, and now that they did so, they found that the special checks they had recognized were not correct – Lee, who had been forced to 'co-operate' with the SD, had deliberately fed them misinformation about his security checks, in the hope that London would spot the errors. With this discovery to confirm Morel's suspicions, Baker Street realized that Antelme, Madeleine and Lee had been captured. When, at the end of April, the message came through the Bricklayer set that Antelme had died, the staff at Baker Street recognized it for a lie.

But this, of course, did not help the captured agents. Antelme undoubtedly suffered under interrogation; Lee must have been put under duress. There is little information about Madeleine's treatment. Perhaps with the SD concentrating their efforts on Antelme, she was spared the worst of their interrogation techniques. She still had to face the solitude of imprisonment and the bitterness of finding herself part of a deception game. She was sent to Fresnes, the first stage of a journey which would end in the concentration camps.

By the end of April, Baker Street knew finally that the Phono agents must also be in captivity and the set under SD control. At last the exchanges with the Phono set were stopped; so were the arms drops to the supposed Phono region. But it was not the end of F Section's 'radio game' problems, nor the end of the Prosper fall-out. Madeleine was the only woman agent to be sent straight into the hands of the Gestapo, but before she had finished her first month of imprisonment another ten male agents would have travelled the same route.

Four agents were sent out to supposed Butler receptions at the very end of February and the beginning of March. Two had missions to start railway line sabotage in Britanny; two were instructed to rebuild Satirist north of Paris: all four were arrested on arrival by the Gestapo.

The other six agents were all sent out to a *réseau* which was not only in German hands now, but which had never actually existed as anything but a radio game. The *réseau* was called Archdeacon and it had grown out of the ashes of the Prosper arrests the summer before. At the time of its birth the SD was still successfully playing *Archambaud*'s set back to London; it was not long before Baker Street saw through that pretence but as the bogus *Archambaud* went off the air, the bogus Archdeacon had been coming on. It was to do much greater damage.

To set up Archdeacon had been the mission of the two Canadian-born agents Macalister and Pickersgill, who had been dropped into the Sologne in June 1943. Chapter 10 tells how they had been received by Yvonne Rudellat and Pierre Culioli and a few days later had been arrested with them, in the small village of Dhuizon. The party had been carrying with it Macalister's set and his codes, ready for use: these were seized by the SD and used to transmit to London as if nothing had happened.

It was a gift for the Germans: the radio was still unused so there was no likelihood of the signals staff recognizing a strange 'fist'. Macalister's codes were pristine; from scraps of information they were extracting from various prisoners, the Germans discovered that the new *réseau* was intended for the north-east, the region of the Ardennes. This information, together with the correct security checks (they seemed to have these early on – had they been written down with the codes?) was enough for the SD to perpetrate a long and successful hoax on Baker Street.

Under an officer called Joseph Placke, SD men played the Archdeacon set back to Baker Street as if Macalister and Pickersgill were still free. They pretended to be sending messages from their new region, reporting on the progress of their *réseau*, and the staff at Baker Street had no suspicions. Meanwhile, the deadly serious hoax actually extended to the real Ardennes, because Placke himself, who spoke French well, travelled there posing as Pickersgill. He recruited among the local resistants and established reception committees for arms drops. The resistants believed he was Pickersgill; Baker Street believed his messages came from Pickersgill; all through the remainder of 1943 the incubus was allowed to flourish and by early 1944 a number of large arms drops had been made to receptions organized by Placke. The containers were stored in the houses and barns of local resistants initially, then they were loaded on to trucks provided by Placke and driven away to a German depot near Versailles.

Baker Street was heartened by the smooth running of the Archdeacon *réseau*. There had been one mishap – an agent sent out in autumn 1943, to act as sabotage instructor to Archdeacon recruits, had apparently disappeared. But there were many dangers waylaying agents and resistants in 1943, and as Macalister's set continued to transmit encouraging news the Baker Street staff were not alarmed. On the contrary, Archdeacon seemed a good *réseau* to entrust with receptions for new agents. Baker Street alerted Placke to prepare receptions for incoming 'bodies' and as soon as the bad weather let up, the infiltrations began. At the end of February an agent was sent out by sea: his mission was to start a *réseau* near Verdun. He went to his contact address in Paris where he was to meet his assistant, another incoming agent. The contact address had been given by Placke and he was arrested there.

On 2 March four agents due to start a *réseau* round Valenciennes (including a radio operator), dropped to an Archdeacon reception and were instantly arrested.

In a different part of the supposed Archdeacon territory, another two agents were dropping to the ground. One was the assistant and radio operator for the Verdun *réseau*, the other was someone who has already appeared in these pages – *Arnaud*, former colleague of Odette. *Arnaud* had managed to elude the Gestapo after Odette's and Peter's arrests and had closed down the *réseau* around Annecy. He had revisited St Jorioz a few weeks after the arrests and salvaged from the Hôtel de la Poste a suitcase of Peter's which Jean Cottet had kept hidden from the Gestapo and which contained money, radio messages, a gun and parachuting equipment. He had gone back down to the south coast and helped tie up the Carte/Spindle contacts there, and then had got away with a fellow resistant over the Pyrénées. He seemed to have nine lives: while he was working his way to the mountains, Odette was in Paris, being tortured for information about his addresses. Her silence helped his trail go cold; his own fierce dedication kept him safely on course.

Once back in England, he had been eager to return to France. Now he had instructions to go back in and start a new *réseau* in the hills around Nancy, 500 kilometres due east of Paris and near the German border. He and his travelling companion landed and were already out of their parachute gear before the Germans approached them, then as the figures drew near they heard them speaking in German. In a bid to escape, they got away into the trees fringing the field and fired at the 'reception committee'; the committee and its reinforcements fired back. The battle killed two Germans and injured both agents; they were taken prisoner.

During the next couple of months, as Baker Street realized that the Bricklayer team had been taken and discovered the Phono radio game, the staff also began to suspect that something had gone wrong with the recent arrivals. The two radio operators eventually came on the air but never transmitted their pre-arranged messages, which would show that they were safe. By May, Baker Street was suspicious of the Archdeacon *réseau* and Gerry Morel arranged to be flown over one of Archdeacon's grounds to have a personal talk with Pickersgill over the S-Phone. Pickersgill was brought back from a concentration camp and told that he would have to go to the ground to talk, but he refused to co-operate. In the Avenue Foch he physically attacked his guards and jumped out of a window trying to escape before he was shot down and recaptured. John Starr, who was still in the Avenue Foch giving limited information to the Germans, was then drafted in to take his place, but when he reached the ground he too refused to talk. A German officer impersonated Pickersgill but Gerry Morel, listening overhead in the aeroplane, realized that the voice crackling through the S-Phone was a German one.

The false Archdeacon *réseau* was at last uncovered. Baker Street kept up radio contact for a while, to try to mislead the SD into thinking itself undetected, but all arms drops and agent drops to the *réseau* stopped at once.

The Phono, Butler and Archdeacon radio games were at last at an end, but they had cost F Section dear. In late spring 1944, there were large areas of northern France with no F Section *réseaux* or agents. And any new teams of agents who went in would face extreme danger, because German surveillance already covered many of the indigenous Resistance groups, and most or all of the arms delivered to these groups were in German hands. The invasion could take place at any day; how were they to build and arm new *réseaux* in these areas in time?

It was yet another after-effect of the Déricourt/Prosper affair. The betrayals of 1943 were still costing new lives in the spring of 1944, even as France was rising in revolt.

But France *was* rising and many more agents were coming in, by parachute and boat and aeroplane, to add to the Resistance already there. In February, two agents had arrived and founded Spiritualist in the north-east, to replace Musician. They also started a new *réseau* in Paris. At the end of the month, Frager came back to Donkeyman, which now had two parts, in the Yonne and in Normandy. In March, agents were coming in and new *réseaux* were being founded all over France: one began around Marseille to replace Monk, just destroyed; another was formed in the Upper Loire valley; Charles Rechenmann – one of *Hector*'s lieutenants from Stationer – returned from training in Britain and gathered his groups in Tarbes into a new *réseau*, Rover. New teams of agents also came into the Jura, the Puy de Dôme, the Haute Creuse, Paris, Seine-et-Marne, and the Atlantique, and each of these included a woman.

Denise Bloch arrived on 2 March. She came by Lysander with her organizer Robert Benoist, on a mission to set up a *réseau*, Clergyman, around the city of Nantes, in the Atlantique. Benoist had been in France before – he had been in Chestnut, Prosper's smaller neighbour, in 1943 until it had collapsed; he had escaped from German arrest and got back to England on a Déricourt pick-up. Then he had returned to France in October to set up Clergyman, but the country around Nantes had been crowded and unpropitious for arms drops, his radio operator had been arrested and without the explosives he needed for his sabotage work, he had cut his losses and gone back to England – again on a Déricourt operation. Now he was coming back in once more, to make a second attempt at establishing Clergyman. Once established, the *réseau*'s main task would be sabotage strikes against communications to Brittany. Denise was coming in as his radio operator, on what was bound to be a difficult mission.

Denise was French; she was also Jewish and so ran a double

risk in returning to France. She had been involved in the Resistance before she was forced to flee to England; now, after SOE training, she was going back under the code-name *Ambroise*. The aim of her and Benoist's mission was to effect immediate sabotage around Nantes and to prepare for more come D-Day. Nantes was a port and a crucial point of supply for Brittany; the *réseau*'s first job was to bring down high pylons over the Loire, so cutting the electricity supply into Brittany and disrupting German manufacture there. At the same time the agents were to prepare for sabotage on the railway lines and the telephone lines running through Nantes, so that when the invasion took place, German troop movements and communications would be seriously impeded.

There was an urgency to the Clergyman mission, born of the growing certainty that D-Day was imminent and sharpened by the failure of the *réseau* to get off the ground the previous year. Benoist had reported to Baker Street that sabotage teams were being organized on the railways when he left, but they had no arms and no training. The instructions Baker Street gave him before he and Denise left bristled with a sense of hurry:

(a) You will return to the Field by Lysander accompanied by your W/T operator during the March moon.

(b) You have been given particulars of a ground where you can receive the materials necessary to carry out your mission, and you will organize a reception on this ground as soon as possible.

(c) You will thereupon organize:

    1. An immediate attack on the high pylons crossing the river Loire at *Ile Héron*.

    2. The formation, training, and supplying of teams to cut, on receipt of orders on D-Day, the railway lines converging on Nantes. It is at this stage important for us to know exactly where these cuts will take place and we require therefore for you to report back to us where action may be expected, and for this purpose if your cut is proposed 15 km. from the line Nantes-Clisson you will report this to us as: '*Nantes Clisson Quinze Rotten*', 'Rotten' being the code-word indicating that the target is prepared and ready for action, and 15 km. being the distance from Nantes on the line Nantes-Clisson where the cut will take place.

    3. The formation, training, and supplying of teams to cut the civil telephone lines converging on Nantes. We do

not advocate attacks on telephone exchanges since these are heavily guarded and require a larger personnel, but rather a series of cuts on the lines themselves which will have the same effect. A map of these lines has been shown to you and you have been given a micro photograph of it.

(d) We emphasize that apart from the destruction of pylons already mentioned the main importance of your mission is to ensure that we have in the Nantes area an organization capable of interference on an effective scale with German communications on D-Day.

We have not therefore given you any further targets for immediate action in order that you may concentrate on the formation and the security of the groups necessary for carrying out your tasks for D-Day. . . .[1]

The instructions also included the messages which would be broadcast on the BBC *Messages Personnels* to send the sabotage teams into action. When the agents heard these they would know that D-Day was here, and it was time to strike.

We have explained to you our system of BBC messages for transmission of orders for target activity on D-Day.

The following are the messages for your circuit:

1. For railway targets:
    A. *C'était le sergeant qui fumait sa pipe en pleine campagne.*
    B. *Il avait mal au coeur mais il continuait tout de même.*
2. For telephone targets:
    A. *La Corse ressemble à une poire.*
    B. *L'Italie est une botte.*

The pylons of course require no BBC message since they are for action at the earliest opportunity.[2]

Conscious of having no time to waste, Denise and Robert Benoist stepped down from the Lysander in the late hours of 2 March and set off for Nantes.

That same night also brought Didi Nearne into the field. She too was a radio operator; she too was travelling with her organizer, a Frenchman named Savy, none other than Lise de Baissac's old friend and first recruit. But their mission was very different from that of the Clergyman agents. They were to set up a small *réseau* called Wizard in

[1] *SOE in France*, MRD Foot, H.M.S.O., 1966
[2] *Ibid.*

Paris, not to carry out sabotage but to organize channels of finance and supply for the arrival of the Allied troops. It was an extension of the work Antelme had tried to do in 1943: indeed it was Antelme who had brought Savy back to England the previous summer for SOE training. Antelme, of course, had come back into France a few days earlier; ignorant of his arrest, the instructions for Wizard's new mission anticipated that Savy could make use of his and Antelme's mutual contacts.

Didi's role would be to maintain communications between Savy and London: her set would also be used to offer verification to French backers that the SOE cause was genuine. The radio method of authenticating the agents' claims had already been used with success, and it promised to be especially useful in reassuring people about financial transactions. In theory, Savy would ask potential supporters to choose any messages or phrase they wished to hear broadcast on the BBC. Didi would then transmit the request to Baker Street on her set and within the next few days it would take its place among the other *Messages Personnels*.

But the Wizard mission was not to go as planned and Didi Nearne and Savy would not be together for long.

Two women dropped by parachute that month: one was bound for the Jura in the east, the other for the Haute Creuse in the geographical heart of France.

Yvonne Baseden, a twenty-one-year-old radio operator, dropped with her organizer *en route* to the Jura. She had a French mother and a lifetime's association with France, and had been recruited into SOE from the WAAF. She had been teamed with a Frenchman, *Lucien*, and their mission was to reinforce the Director *réseau*, adjacent to Marksman, and to start their own *réseau* if necessary.

Although their destination was the eastern border of France, on 18 March Yvonne and *Lucien* were dropped in the south-west, to a Wheelwright reception. *Hilaire* was on the reception committee to supervise their arrival and to take over the mail they had brought; then *Lucien* went off to make some contacts and Yvonne cycled with *Hilaire* to his house nearby. There she met *Annette*, still more or less immobilized with her muscle strain, and Anne-Marie Walters.

She lay low for a day or so and set off on the long trip east. She and *Lucien* travelled by train, separating to minimize the effect of possible capture. Yvonne was carrying her radio set and the journey was agonizingly slow; the train was held up repeatedly by sabotage attacks on the line and by German controls. It took four days to reach Dôle, a town on the north-west fringes of the Jura, four days of travelling alongside German soldiers and security officers, of proffering false papers, of sleeping in the crowded carriage and praying that she would not speak in her sleep.

But she reached Dôle safely and rendezvoused with *Lucien*. They immediately set about making contacts. The organizer of Director had in fact been arrested in January; their mission, as they soon discovered, was to take over the remnants of his organization and build a new one of their own.

The other woman *parachutiste* was Patricia (Paddy) O'Sullivan. She was Irish but had been educated in French convents and was bilingual. SOE had recruited her from the WAAF; like almost all the women who went out in March, she had a radio operator's mission. Amid the rumours and indications that D-Day was imminent, F Section was struggling to send out more radio operators as soon as possible. Radio operators were vital for the arranging of arms drops and arms drops, many many of them, were what the French Resistance needed desperately. There was no longer time for perfect preparations: Paddy's training had been shortened to get her into the field quickly.

She dropped on 22 March to join the Fireman *réseau* which was just setting up in the northern part of the Haute Creuse. Two Mauritian brothers, E.P. and P.E. Mayer, had dropped two weeks earlier and were organizing Resistance groups around Limoges. She came down to a Stationer reception, arranged by one of *Hector*'s teams. Stationer by now commanded groups over a consolidated sweep of territory (from Périgueux, up north to Châteauroux and the demarcation line, and east to the town of Moulins) and many of the new agents were being sent out to its receptions – Paddy's new colleagues, the Mayer brothers, had come to Stationer and over a dozen more agents would come through the same channels in the next two months.

Paddy dropped into a field full of cows that night and was hidden away in a safe house by the Stationer resistants. The following day she left by bicycle for a farm in the neighbouring Haute Creuse, where she would start transmitting for Farmer.

On nights without a moon, there was another way into France. In the third week of March, two motorboats cut their engines and drifted towards the coast of northern France. Each brought a woman agent back into the field.

The first sea-borne woman to arrive that March had already played a major part in F Section's work, though it had been back in the early days of the occupation and in a region far distant from the north Brittany coast where now she came ashore. A tall figure, she carried a radio set and limped. Eighteen months after she had fled

Lyon, Virginia Hall was returning to France for the final uprising.

It had not been easy to get back. She had had to argue against Buckmaster and the Baker Street staff who felt, understandably, that she was too well known by the Gestapo. Not only had she been declared a prime wanted person by them, but she had no chance of disguising herself – her height, her red hair and her limp identified her clearly.

She had been kept busy since her arrival back in England in January 1943. In May she had been officially transferred to DF Section and sent to Spain with the cover of being a correspondent for the *Chicago Times*. She had worked for the agent in charge of SOE's Spanish Section, principally trying to improve DF escape routes between France and Spain. But the work had been slow and unsatisfying and in September a reunion with two men who had been fellow resistants in France spurred her to write to Buckmaster:

> I have had the luck to find two of my very own boys here and send them on to you. They want me to go back with them because we worked together before and our team work is good. . . . I suggest that I go back as their radio, or else as aider and abetter, as before. I can learn the radio quickly enough in spite of scepticism in some quarters . . . after all, my neck is my own, and if I am willing to get a crick in it because there is a war on, I do think . . . well, anyhow, I put it to you.

That letter had got her brought back to Baker Street in November to take a 'briefing officer' post. But she had gone on arguing and by January she had won admittance to the SOE radio training school, and two months later she was here in Brittany officially registered as an OSS agent working with SOE and setting out on her second French mission.

This mission was a solitary one. She was to make her way to central France and there, as 'organizer cum W/T operator with roving mission', she was to locate and arm *maquis* groups. She would have to work independently of existing F Section *réseaux*, with or around other Resistance organizations. Resistance groups were proliferating; *réseaux* were in flux and radio operators' skeds were increasingly taken up with requests and instructions for arms drops, not reports. Baker Street could only give its new agents a limited idea of which *réseaux* operated where. Virginia Hall, like other organizers, had to find her own way and provide her own induction.

She went about it with the same independence and strength which had kept her safe in Lyon and carried her across the Pyrénées, artificial leg and all. Two weeks after her arrival on the north coast of Brittany she reached the Haute-Loire in central France and came on the air. From there she began working her way north along the Loire valley, carrying her radio set with her, following up contacts in the search of safe houses and *maquis*, and looking for the right territory to start *réseau* Heckler.

The last woman agent to arrive in March, Yvonne Fontaine, was also making her return to the Resistance. This was her first mission as an SOE agent – indeed, Vera Atkins claims that she never officially joined SOE – but she had already proved herself in one of France's most turbulent areas. Yvonne Fontaine – now code-named *Mimi* - was a Frenchwoman who had begun working as a member of Ben Cowburn's Tinker *réseau* around Troyes in 1943. She had worked as a courier in the *réseau*, and had become part of its nucleus along with Cowburn, his radio operator Barrett, and Cowburn's lieutenant, another local recruit named Pierre Mulsant. When, in September 1943, the railway sabotage around Troyes had brought the Gestapo on to his trail, Cowburn had gone back to England and left the *réseau* under Mulsant's control. But the Gestapo continued to close in and in November Mulsant, Yvonne and Barrett were all taken back to England on a Déricourt pick-up.

In England, Yvonne and Mulsant had undergone SOE training. Now they, together again with Barrett as radio operator, were launching a new *réseau*, Minister. They were to build it in the Seine-et-Marne, just south-east of Paris, a region where organized Resistance had been repeatedly broken. Through the Seine-et-Marne ran many important railway lines to the industrial north-east, ripe for sabotage. Mulsant and Barrett had been dropped into France at the beginning of March; as Yvonne Fontaine came ashore on the north coast, on the night of the 25th, they were already reconnoitring their targets.

These women came into a France very different from that of the year before. As they travelled to their new bases and settled in, the Resistance was springing into life all around them. Railway lines were being blown up; German soldiers were being shot; news came from country districts of *maquis* ambushes. At the end of February teams of RF agents had carried out a campaign of assassinations against senior Gestapo officers around Lyon. And in answer the German reprisals were fierce. French 'hostages' were rounded up from villages where attacks had taken place and shot – several Frenchmen being summarily killed for every German death. Teams of Germans roved the countryside looking for arms dumps and trying to intercept drops. The D/F vans were out in force; houses and farms were burnt in areas where the Resistance was active; there were raids in towns and shooting in the streets.

On the Plateau de Glières, the *maquis* led by *Tom* Morel had been making repeated strikes against Germans and *milice*. When heavily armed German troops attacked them on the plateau, they decided not to disperse but to stand and fight. The battle was fierce but the *maquis* were outnumbered and out-gunned. Hundreds of *maquis* died and the Germans took the Plateau; *Tom* Morel was killed by *miliciens* reinforcing the Germans as he tried to lead a party of men to safety.

Once the Germans had the plateau they freed the *miliciens* whom the *maquis* had taken prisoner and took them round the villages in the neighbourhood asking them to identify resistants; those identified were then killed.

There was terror but there was also pride at the *maquis*' actions, and growing defiance in the face of reprisals. Acts of courage inspired hope and confidence. And now resistants all over the country were receiving arms drops and being trained in the use of guns and explosives.

[Extract from memo to Bomber Command Headquarters, 20/3/44]:

Drops to the Maquis

A report has come through that on 14 March the *maquis* were fighting an engagement with the *milice* near Laroche-sur-Foron. The *maquis*, who had just received deliveries of stores, inflicted heavy losses. It is wished to point out that the Marksman deliveries were, therefore, opportune.

And sometimes the Resistance strikes brought entirely unexpected rewards, like the attempt of one of the Stationer groups to derail a train carrying munitions for the Germans. The saboteurs had laid their charge against the railway line and retired, waiting eagerly to hear reports of the train's demise. Sure enough, the train had arrived and had triggered the explosion, being violently derailed. But the timetable had been changed and this was not the munitions train: it was a cargo train loaded with wine, which was now running in pools and rivers alongside the tracks. By the time *Hector* arrived on the scene, everyone from the nearby village was already there.

Wielding basins and barrels and pans and any other remotely suitable vessel, they scooped up the gallons of spilled wine. The party went on all day.

Didi Nearne: a life in the shadow

I had met my chief in the office and we were going out together on a night of the new moon. He said, 'Are you quite sure you want to go?' and I said, 'Yes, I do.' So we left and went to Tempsford where the planes were.

So we were at the aerodrome and I remember how dark it was and we saw the pilot but he was very much in the shadow . . . .

. . . It was bitter cold that night and it was cloudy. Then after a while we saw the lights of the committee of reception . . . .

Didi Nearne's story, as she tells it today, is a sequence of vivid scenes, rushes of action, and gaps. After all that happened to her in the field and later in the prisons and concentration camps, some memories shine clearly for her while others have vanished altogether. Pivotal moments in her mission – the journey out, her first contact, her first transmission – live with her still. In between them are stretches of vaguer recollections, and it is hard to supplement these from the SOE archives. Factual information on Didi's mission is scanty: she sent 105 messages in under five months, but no indication of their contents has survived. Yet through her memories and such facts as are available, a compelling picture appears. Didi was, even when she climbed aboard the Lysander, an unusually solitary, dedicated character and her mission would develop in the same way.

Didi, five years younger than her sister Jacqueline, had been training as a FANY radio operator when Jacqueline left for France in 1943. Didi was not destined for France: at twenty she was considered very young and Jacqueline was not eager to have her exposed to the risks of an agent's life. Instead, Didi began working in summer 1943 at the SOE Base Signals Station in England.

Her job was as a radio operator, receiving transmissions from agents in France. But as soon as she realized the nature of the agents' work, and the qualifications they needed to do it, she decided to apply to go into the field. She did not find her application readily accepted: her youth was against her and her reserved personality and her unworldly air made SOE hesitate. The staff contacted Jacqueline (as the only available next-of-kin) and asked if she would consent to Didi working in the field. She refused and to Didi's chagrin maintained this refusal for several months. Eventually, however, she changed her mind (why remains undocumented) and Didi was called up for training.

In training, Didi's radio experience made her an obvious candidate for a radio operator's post. She trained with Yvonne Baseden at Wanborough and then went on the practical course in Scotland. There, the mountains interfered badly with radio transmissions, giving the operators a trial run in the very worst conditions.

'It was terrible interference, awful. I could never get the messages and I was very worried about it. But that was done a bit on purpose to see how you coped with the pressure.'

Coping under pressure: that was the essence of the training and for the different agents, different aspects of the training acted as catalysts or points of recognition about themselves. For Didi, the lessons in interrogation technique revealed a source of strength in her own character.

As the SOE instructors carried out their mock-interrogations of her, trying to break down her cover stories, watching to see how well she lied, Didi found that she was able to resist them. The more they questioned her, even pushing her and threatening her physically, the more she stuck to her story, engaging with their questioning but never shifting her ground. She saw other people breaking down beneath the onslaught and realized that she wasn't like them. She had always been secretive by nature and extremely determined (her sister Jacqueline was later to speak of her as having always been different, the odd one out among her siblings), and now she drew strength from her inclinations.

'You had to be a bit tougher you see, a bit hard on yourself. You had to live in the shadow.'

The perception of a life 'in the shadow', as it developed from her training, held a powerful attraction for her.

And her steadiness under interrogation clinched her place in F Section.

'When Maurice Buckmaster was testing my cover story, he said, "No reaction." There was no reaction when I lied. They thought I would be all right because I lied so well. Also I could be a bit hard and secret. I could be lonely. I could be independent.'

So Didi, code-named *Rose*, was teamed with another recent graduate of the SOE schools: Lise de Baissac's old friend, Savy. They were briefed to go to France as soon as possible.

The Lysander flight on 2 March was Didi's and Savy's third attempt to get into occupied France. They had prepared to leave twice before, at the end of February, but on both nights bad weather had kept them in England. This time, despite the cloud, they had reached their destination and below them they saw the lights of the reception near Châteauroux.

When they got down from the Lysander, two young men came forward to meet them.

'One said, "Oh, a young girl! Ah, go back, it's so dangerous." But I said no.'

Didi and Savy watched two other, anonymous agents take their places in the Lysander. The plane made its short run and took off again and they followed their reception committee across the fields and into a stable, their bed for the rest of the night.

Early the next morning, at around 5 a.m., Didi set off with the two young men for Orléans, about ninety kilometres away. Savy was not coming with her: he was going independently in search of Antelme and some former contacts. So Didi and her escorts took the train to Orléans, where a safe house awaited her. Didi had not been in France since the Germans' arrival and was unprepared for the sight of German soldiers which greeted her at Orléans station.

'It was full up with Germans and I turned to look at them. The people with me said, "Don't do that! Oh my God, never do a thing like that." ' Jolted by her own instinctive reaction, Didi walked cautiously through the streets, trying to look as though she wasn't noticing the occupying forces. They reached the safe house and she took refuge there until the next day.

The following day, Didi arrived in Paris on her own. She had instructions to meet a contact there, a young woman called Louise. It was snowing in Paris: as Didi walked across the Pont-Neuf, the statue of King Henri IV in the middle of the bridge was being speckled white. People were walking quickly past the statue, huddled into their coats against the cold. But as Didi reached the figure she paused and looked carefully at the other people in the little clearing. A woman of about her own age met her eye: it was Louise. She had made her first contact.

For Didi as for most people, the early days were taken up with finding shelter and acclimatizing herself to her surroundings. On that first day in Paris, Louise took her to her home on Boulevard St-Michel where she lived with her mother and sister. This would be where Didi would come in future to leave or collect messages for the group; but she herself could not stay there. Her most pressing needs, therefore, were a room for herself and a safe place from which she could transmit.

This was not easy. The Paris of 1944 was a crowded city; accommodation was in short supply and as Gestapo officers and police were continually closing in on suspect addresses, the resistants were often out in the cold. In January, through the arrests and confessions of some SOE escape line workers, the Germans had exposed the organization's Paris safe houses. The line itself survived but new houses had to be found. Resistants and agents were now competing with one another for the available Resistance-friendly shelter, as well as trying to elude the Gestapo. Didi, posing as an innocent young girl from the south of France, come to Paris to look for work, was able to find an apartment for herself in Porte Champerret in the north-west of Paris. But finding a place from which to transmit, with complaisant neighbours or none at all, was much more difficult.

While she tried, through her Boulevard St-Michel contacts, to arrange safe houses for her set, Savy – who had also arrived in Paris – was discovering that their original mission could not be pursued. He failed, of course, to get in touch with Antelme, as Antelme had been arrested on dropping. While following up former contacts of his and Antelme's from 1943, he discovered information completely outside the remit of his Wizard *réseau*: in some stone quarries near Senlis, north of Paris, the Germans had hidden 2,000 V1 rockets. They were ready for firing on London. Savy could not risk sending the intelligence by radio; by the end of March he had decided that he must return to England to report on this. This would leave Didi in Paris alone.

By now a house had been found for Didi's skeds, in Bourg-la-Reine, a suburb to the south of Paris. 116 Rue de Bagneux was empty, the owners having left the country, and Didi was to take her set there and make her first transmission.

Didi was relieved to have a place at last but before she could make the much longed-for contact she had to carry her radio all the way across the city and into the new house.

Didi looked much younger than her age and while her air of innocence made her an unlikely Resistance suspect, it also made her vulnerable to other attentions. She got as far as boarding the train for Bourg-la-Reine, carrying her heavy case, and then the problems began.

> I saw an empty compartment and I thought, 'Ah, there's no one here,' but then it filled up with soldiers – not officers – and there I was with my suitcase. And there was this German soldier who kept looking at me and smiling, so I smiled back. Then I was looking through the window and

he said, '*Cigarette, Mademoiselle?*' and I said, 'No, thank you,
I don't smoke.' And my hands you see, were stained with
nicotine. You could make mistakes like that.

He was looking at me and he said, 'What is in your
suitcase?' So I said, '*Oh – c'est un phonographe, savez, de
la musique,*' and he said, '*Oh, oui*' and he was looking at
me and I thought Oh la la, I must get out quickly, but I
thought I'd better not get out the next station. I waited –
I could see them looking at me in the window. Then I got
out at the station after. They were still looking and speaking
together – de de de de de de de de de! – and I went off with
my case and walked away. My heart was beating!

It was such a tiny slip, but she felt it had put her in danger. Didi
was a perfectionist and she found it hard to forgive herself mistakes.
'I left the train about four stations before I was due. I walked the rest
of the way. I couldn't have accepted a cigarette but it would have been
better – you had to be a bit like that. It was impulsive to say no, with
my hands stained for him to see.'

She reached the house in Rue de Bagneux, shaken by the encounter.
Once safely inside, she was faced with a new anxiety – would she
be able to get through to Home Station? She remembered only too
clearly the interference on her training exercises. But she hooked up
her aerial and prepared her set and to her relief when she turned to
her frequency the sound came over loud and clear. 'It was so loud!
It was blazing in that room! So I sent my message, which was "Met
Louise, my contact." '

Her first transmission successfully made, Didi hid the set and
returned to Paris. That evening she went to Louise's house to listen
to the *Messages Personnels* on the wireless. Among the other messages
was one she recognized: 'Happy to know that the duck has had a good
trip.' Baker Street was acknowledging her first transmission.

Didi's life now began taking on the rhythm of her skeds. She
travelled between Porte Champerret and Bourg-la-Reine, sometimes
taking the train; often walking to avoid any risk of controls. From
Bourg-la-Reine she came on the air twice a day, sending messages
on one sked and receiving them on another. In these early weeks she
met Savy almost every day to exchange information. He would not be
with her much longer: through her set, arrangements were now being
made to return Savy to England and reassign her to another *réseau*.

This did not mean that she had to leave Paris: events were moving
fast in the capital city and from certain of the resistance groups, a

new *réseau* was beginning to form. It was being drawn together by a Frenchman, *Armand*, who had been dropped in February as an organizer of Spiritualist. The first priority of Spiritualist had been to knit up the loose ends of Farmer and Musician; now this had been achieved, drops received outside Paris were being sent on to arm the north-eastern resistants, and *Armand* was concentrating on Paris.

Since autumn 1943, Paris had been almost a no-go area for F Section. The Phono radio game had duped Baker Street into thinking there was still an organization in the city and only now was the truth beginning to dawn. Meanwhile, there were many Resistance groups springing up of their own accord but they were fragmented and most of them were barely equipped. Outside the city, in the industrial suburbs, the communist *Francs-Tireurs et Partisans* (FTP) groups were thriving – they had long been receiving arms from Allied drops and had developed good organization and support structures – but in Paris itself the various groups of resistants were divided, sometimes by politics, sometimes simply by lack of communication.

Armand began a campaign of vetting and recruitment among Paris resistants. Many different groups joined Spiritualist, swearing absolute loyalty to the Allied armies as they did so and promising to put the interests of the invasion above any political or personal ones.

Among the Spiritualist contacts were Louise and other resistants who used the Boulevard St-Michel house. F Section saw that with Savy's return, Didi would be free to work for this new, promising *réseau*.

So at the beginning of April, arrangements were made to take Savy back to London and to send out another radio operator to work alongside Didi. On 6 April, the radio operator *Arnaud* (no connection with the St Jorioz agent) dropped into France. Three nights later Savy was picked up by Lysander and flown out.

By an odd coincidence, the small aeroplane which carried Savy through the night skies also carried another connection of Didi's: her sister, Jacqueline. At last, after fifteen long months, Jacqueline was leaving the field. Despite her own protests, Buckmaster, worried about her health, had ordered her home. Neither she nor Savy knew the other's identity; they were flown back to England with their anonymity intact, while Didi, disguised as a country girl come to town, stayed on in Paris with her radio set.

April and May were frantic months for the Resistance, the exhilarating, nerve-wracking crescendo of underground preparations. So much still had to be done: *maquis* were still unarmed, Resistance groups were still in disarray; more and more of the French population now wanted to do something positive to strike against the Germans and Resistance groups were swelling, sabotage attacks and ambushes igniting hitherto quiet areas. In the countryside arms drops fell night after night to hastily convened receptions; towns, cities and ports were reeling under another form of anti-German warfare: Allied bombs. Throughout the war there had been raids on selected targets such as German-used factories and airfields, and on certain towns considered strategically placed for a German advance on Britain – towns in Normandy, Brittany and the Pas-de-Calais had been bombed repeatedly from 1940 onwards. Industrial towns and ports had recently been attracting a growing number of raids – in September 1943 Nantes had been severely bombed, killing 1,400 and injuring 2,300; in December Marseille had been bombed; now the raids were increased, and in towns like Rouen massive efforts had to be made to rehouse, feed and clothe the thousands of people made homeless by the bombs.

Few bombs fell on Paris; there the violence and the danger were of a different kind. The Gestapo and informers and D/F vans worked ceaselessly to uncover and break Resistance groups. There were daily arrests and the only way to stay free was to be constantly alert and wary. For Didi, life was now reduced to a strict discipline of meeting her skeds, processing and passing on her radio messages – once or twice a day she met her new 'chief', a Frenchman, to exchange messages – and keeping herself away from all other kinds of human contact.

I used to go out a lot and have my meals in restaurants, alone. Sometimes I would meet my contact Louise but all we would do was to pass a note. It was very solitary.

I wasn't nervous. In my mind I was never going to be arrested. But of course I was very careful. There were police and Gestapo in plain clothes everywhere. Whenever I was in the streets I was always looking in the shops, in the windows, to see if I was followed. One day I went into the *métro* and on the train I saw a man. He was very nervous and he was reading a newspaper but at the same time he was looking at me, my shoes, my clothes. This made me suspicious so I got off the train suddenly, about two stations before the one I wanted, and then I looked to see if I was being followed. But there was no one there.

Didi sunk herself into this life of wary solitude. It suited her, and for most of the time she was calm. She was also fulfilled: she respected the Frenchman with whom she met regularly to exchange messages, and despite the danger, the actual process of transmitting to England gave her a deep satisfaction.

> I liked it – I liked to get in contact. When I used to put my hand on the keynote, it was England, and there came the feeling of patriotism. I was pleased that I was doing something. I was perhaps a little emotional.

The messages which Didi transmitted daily were important ones, for they not only served the needs of Spiritualist, which was rapidly receiving arms for its members, but also gave Baker Street valuable intelligence about German activities, gleaned from the many different Spiritualist contacts. Baker Street was now varying the times of operators' skeds for safety's sake so Didi transmitted at a different time each day. But the Germans had become very efficient at monitoring illicit radio traffic and very often towards the end of a sked Didi would hear the ba-ba-ba-ba-ba of a D/F van picking up her transmissions and trying to locate them.

Obviously, it was dangerous to transmit repeatedly from the same house but there was little choice. She had to keep up radio contact.

On many evenings, Didi went to the house on Boulevard St-Michel to pick up messages for transmission and to listen to the *Messages Personnels*. She liked to be briefly with other people, in the atmosphere of secrecy and shared trust. Even when she was just walking past the house it pleased her to look at the white curtains with the light burning behind them: from the outside the house looked peaceful and anonymous but for Didi it was a sign that she was not alone.

Didi did not seek out other people to assuage the solitude of her life; she did not feel it as loneliness. For her it was 'the life in the shadow', one which she enjoyed and in which she felt useful. She went working on in her quiet, rigorous, utterly committed way as the last weeks passed before the invasion.

SEVENTEEN

Lighting the Fuse

During these last two months before D-Day, small groups of agents all over France were pursuing their separate missions. There were scores of agents at work in France by June 1944, among them nineteen women, and for each woman – as for each male agent – the reality of life was different. A radio operator in Paris did not live as a radio operator in the Gascogne. And while a courier in the Corrèze might have the same tasks to perform as a courier in the Yonne, and across similarly rural territory, local conditions would inevitably govern each group of agents and their work, making them subtly different from one another.

I am not going to try to follow each one of these nineteen women into her *réseau*. There are too many of them: the only way of telling all their stories would be by reducing them to a list of dates, names and facts. Instead, I prefer to approach D-Day through the eyes of a small number of the women. Their stories are theirs and no one else's, but in the things they share and the gaps in between them, we can also glimpse the stories of those other women who are mentioned here only briefly.

For in France now, the fuse was lit for a national uprising. Thousands of French people turned from their private, law-abiding lives and began to ask how they could help; and the women going out to France in these months found things very different from their predecessors of even a few months earlier.

One of these women had already been in France on a mission. She had spent nearly a year in Poitiers from autumn 1942 to late summer 1943, and then she had led a life of rigorous clandestinity and solitude.

The France she entered in April 1944 was a much more turbulent place and the work which awaited her there was entirely different from that which she had grown used to on her first mission. Lise de Baissac had to call on new talents in 1944.

For Lise, the last seven months had been a welcome respite. The year in Poitiers, and the break up of Prosper had taken their toll. On that final August night in 1943, she had lain in a haybarn with Rémy Clément, Claude and Bodington, waiting for the Lysander to arrive, and she had felt herself strung tight with the accumulated tension of the last eleven months. Climbing aboard the Lysander after all that time had seemed like a dream.

Back in London there had been formalities to go through: she had reported to the staff at Baker Street and been debriefed. She had been given instructions about security, which still applied strictly now that she was back in Britain. Then, the procedures over, she had been allowed to go away and rest.

Meanwhile, the staff at Baker Street had added their own assessment of her, based on reports of agents who had known her in the field. This report sits in her file still, a characteristic Baker Street observation, at once official and highly personal:

> One of our most successful girls. A good organizer and administrator. Was popular with her contacts and much loved in the region. She perhaps suffered from the family faults (excess of personal ambition and touchiness), but she is always ready to see reason and invariably put her work first.
>
> Is 'difficult' but devoted and has made a very large contribution to the success of F Section.

It wasn't surprising, in the light of this, that F Section had more plans for her. The staff asked Lise if she would continue to work with F Section; in the months immediately ahead she could be useful as a conducting officer working with recruits in training. And would she also consider the possibility of returning to France at some stage?

As on the first occasion when she had been asked to go into France, Lise replied yes, of course. She was now more qualified than ever; there was no reason why she should not return.

And so, after several months of 'resting' and helping with training, Lise was alerted to stand by for another mission.

The original plan was that she would drop back into France in early spring 1944, but this was made impossible by an accident. It took place while she was doing a stint as 'conducting officer' to a batch of new recruits, who included two women, Yvonne Baseden and Violette Szabo. The women were due to make their practice parachute jumps and Lise, who had enjoyed parachuting, was asked to go up with them 'to give them encouragement and moral support'. So the experienced agent went up with the tyros to show them how to do it and all the new trainees completed their jumps well; it was Lise who landed badly and broke her leg.

The injury meant that she could not go back into the field for at least a few months. So the early spring came and her brother Claude was dropped on a new mission to south Normandy, and many other agents including Yvonne Baseden went out, but Lise remained behind while her leg mended slowly.

It was the beginning of April before she was fit enough to go and then she was still limping slightly. Because her leg was weak she could not be dropped, so instead on 9 April she climbed aboard a Lysander with two other agents (one was Philippe de Vomécourt) and was flown over to France.

She was going to Lyon to work in a branch of the flourishing Pimento *réseau*. Started around Toulouse in 1942 by the young agent Tony Brooks, Pimento was still going strong and had split into a western section, round Toulouse, and an eastern section in the upper Rhône valley between the cities of Lyon and Grenoble. It was to this eastern section that Lise was going, to work as a courier.

The plane made for the centre of France and landed to a Stationer reception. *Hector* was at the landing ground to receive the new agents and to say goodbye to one of those taking their place on the plane – by one of those odd crossings of invisible threads, this was the same flight which took Jacqueline Nearne and Savy back to England. Lise and Jacqueline, who had been such friends in training, passed one another on the dark turf as they headed for their very different destinations.

Lise was once more on French soil, once more a part of that shadow life of the Resistance. She had never been present at any of the landings she had helped arrange; it was curious to be an incoming agent, in the hands of someone else. She followed *Hector* and the others on the reception committee as they led the three newcomers to a stack of bicycles hidden for them. There was a roar of engines and then a lessening buzz as the Lysander took off into the sky, and then the party mounted their machines and took to the roads. *Hector* told the new agents to stick close behind the reception committee – there were about half a dozen of them and it did not seem a difficult instruction to follow. But as they all began to cycle down the country roads, Lise found that she couldn't help falling behind. The others were all men, pedalling powerfully; she was a slight woman and more-over her injured leg was painful. She was soon tired and the distance between her and the others widened. She didn't dare call out to them for fear of drawing attention to them, and they got farther and farther ahead of her until they turned a corner and vanished.

Lise cycled as fast as she could to the corner, but when she reached it she saw that the road forked and she had no idea which direction to take. There were houses at the junction, a small village, and so she couldn't possibly shout to the others. She had a moment of pure panic and then she forced herself to make a decision: she turned right and cycled painfully on. She followed the road for some distance, calming herself with the thought that they would soon notice her absence and come back to look for her – but then what if they had gone in the other direction? Should she return to the junction and hide? She was just beginning to think she must stop and go back when she turned another corner on to a straight stretch of road and saw the group up ahead. They hadn't even noticed she was gone. She put on a last spurt and closed the gap; they were going more slowly now and she managed to stay with them until they reached their safe house. But it had been a worrying start.

After passing her first night in a Stationer refuge, Lise set off for Lyon where her new mission lay. The journey there was uneventful, though Lise noticed how many more German controls were now in operation on roads and in stations. She reached the city and made her way to the address she had been given, where she was to meet her contacts. And as soon as she met them, she realized that she was going to find this mission very difficult.

This part of Pimento, which operated over the countryside between Lyon and Grenoble, was run by a group of committed socialists. They were men who moved in predominantly male, left-wing circles and from the beginning Lise and her principal contacts struck sparks from one another.

She settled into a safe address and tried to take her place as a member of the group, but there was no escaping the fact that she simply did not fit in. Lise's political sympathies lay to the right, which was one insurmountable problem in this politically bonded group. There were ideological arguments; moreover, Lise did not relish group living or working as her new comrades did.

She was supposed to work as the courier for a resistant named *Julien*; he was an intelligent, independent-minded man and Lise hoped at first that they would find a way of working together without acrimony. But she found his attitude towards her insulting: he gave her only unimportant, message-carrying work and joined in with the others in making what she considered to be snide remarks against her. When Tony Brooks (*Alphonse*) visited the group, Lise heard the other resistants saying to him, 'What can you expect? She's not one of us,' or 'Maybe if she was twenty we could do something with her, but a grown woman with these set ideas is past help.'

It was all the more infuriating for Lise because she could see that the group was effective in co-ordinating strikes against the Germans. This region had for many months been a violent one, with clashes between *maquis*, Germans and *milice*. The group was well organized in supplying the *maquis* with weapons and had many useful contacts among railway and industrial workers, which allowed them to mount sabotage operations with success. Yet in these circles, Lise could not easily come and go unnoticed. She recognized that she did not look at home among groups of trade unionists or even alone, in the parts of town where she often had to go to take messages. She felt that she could not in conscience ask for more work as she might compromise the security of the group.

It was a galling and frustrating position to be in. Lise could see from everything that was happening that France was poised for revolt. Arms drops were being made regularly in the country; and the resistants of the region were taking the containers of guns, ammunition and explosives and using them in sabotage attacks and ambushes on the German and Vichy authorities – but Lise could not play her part in it as she wished. After Poitiers, it left her feeling unused and wasted.

'I was just taking messages,' she explained. 'And I didn't have the heart to do that, to be a message courier, after having done something with a bit of responsibility. It involved very little – carrying a letter or a verbal message and nothing more.'

Spoken forty-four years later, that comment is mild enough. But Lise's remarks nearer the time – just after her return to London – show a much sharper anger:

> If I had known all this [the group's politics] before going out, I should have realized at once that I was not the person they needed. I'm not at all surprised that they didn't want me, but what does revolt me whenever I think of it is the disloyal manner in which *Julien* behaved towards me, who arrived in his organization with the best intentions. I think his behaviour has been unworthy of his intelligence, which I know to be great.

As Baker Street had already noted, Lise knew her own abilities and could be 'difficult' if they were ignored. She was certainly not going to appease the Pimento resistants and she saw no reason why she should stay where she was not wanted and where she could not be used. Within a few weeks she made a strong appeal to Baker Street for a transfer. She knew that Claude had restarted Scientist in Normandy. She asked if she could join him.

Baker Street said yes. Lise had no special briefing for this new mission but she was confident that she could work well alongside her equally 'difficult' brother. She took curt leave of *Julien* and Pimento and travelled north-west to Normandy.

Claude's new Scientist *réseau*, meanwhile, was piecing itself together across great sweeps of northern France, from Cherbourg on the Manche peninsula, through Calvados and the Orne, right down to the Mayenne and the Eure-et-Loir, south-west of Paris. It was large and it was disorganized: there were thousands of resistants to arm and to train – some were *maquis*, living wild; many more were undercover resistants, still living in their communities and anxious to rise against the Germans. Everyone now knew that the invasion must come soon and along with the eagerness to strike, disorder and confusion prevailed.

Lise arrived at Claude's base in the Mayenne and, welcomed rather than rebuffed this time, she plunged into the turmoil. She found Claude coming and going from a near-empty house in a small village; there also was his radio operator, *Paulette*. This was Phyllis Latour, a young woman in her early twenties, only just arrived and disoriented by the furious pace of activity. Lise joined them in the house and proceeded to work under Claude's orders as he battled against time, distance and the Germans to organize and arm the newly forming Resistance groups. He worked with a number of dedicated helpers, including his lieutenant, Jean Renaud Dandicole, and his original radio operator, Maurice Larcher, in Lise's words 'both very fine and gallant young men.'

The main activity of all the *réseaux* in this late spring, the run-up to D-Day, was the arming and training of resistants. Recruitment was largely looking after itself – the care it demanded was control rather than encouragement, to ensure that the groups did not expand indiscriminately or dangerously. Agents' work mainly took the form of imposing cell structures on new groups where possible, and supplying them with arms.

On many nights when the moon was bright enough, groups of resistants formed reception committees in fields and meadows and watched as bombers flew overhead and let fall not bombs but dozens, scores of torpedo-shaped containers, each one flowering into a mini-parachute and floating down to the earth. The resistants ran forward to heave up the heavy containers between them and take them to carts and lorries, or else straight to barns and outhouses where they would be stored. In most regions now there were these drops, greeted with jubilation, and there was endless enthusiasm but the agents were put at full stretch to distribute the weapons, to train the resistants in the handling of them, and to liaise between the groups and *maquis* so that if they used the arms, they did so in a planned, controlled way.

Lise now found that she had action enough to keep her busy every day and many of the nights. She and Claude kept to their rule that they trained and delegated rather than went on operations themselves, and this set them an exhausting task of liaising and explaining and taking messages.

'We had to receive a lot of drops, we had to go round giving orders. We had groups of *maquis* in the woods – I went from one to the other, bringing them orders my brother had given me.'

Paulette's radio sent repeated requests for drops; over the household wirelesses the nonsensical phrases came back, signalling that this drop or that had been agreed and was on for tonight. The size of the drops themselves were now bigger, so large reception teams had to be organized – thirty or fifty people would have to be found and organized. There were many women on these teams now – they were no longer kept for communications work but turned out at night with the men to carry and store the precious containers.

Then transport had to be arranged – in farm vehicles and disguised in vans and gazogenes, the weapons and explosives would be taken on roundabout routes to the *maquis* or the undercover groups. Once the weapons were in the hands of the resistants, Lise often went to the groups to help teach them handling skills.

And throughout all this the Germans were out in force, patrolling main roads, keeping curfew, arresting suspects. They knew that Allied agents were in the region; both Claude and Lise were known to the Gestapo by reputation.

Lise frequently cycled sixty kilometres a day, carrying Claude's instructions, making contacts and liaisons. When he couldn't visit a group, she took his place. The *maquis* groups were small – ten men here, thirty there – but the undercover groups were much larger, often involving the people of several villages. The groups were working diligently, if confusedly, to be ready for the invasion; Claude deliberately restrained them from carrying out sabotage attacks yet and instead concentrated on receiving and distributing arms, reconnoitring targets for D-Day and finding landing grounds for Allied paratroops.

Lise never carried weapons on her during the day – it was too risky if she were stopped by a German patrol. But she sometimes carried *Paulette*'s radio set or crystals and she worked a lot with *Paulette*, who was inexperienced and grateful for the support, not only helping her transport her set but sometimes lending a hand with her coding.

There was always too much to do in too short a time. Claude and Lise discussed the possibility of getting experienced resistants from another region to help them; Claude had heard of some people in Paris who might help and once Lise cycled there, a trip of several days there and back, finding and bringing back with her Claude's contact in the hope that he might help them organize the *maquis*. When they arrived back in the Mayenne, Lise took him off to one of the larger *maquis* – but the anticipated solution was not to be. Shortly, finding the *maquis* totally disorganized, the man left again.

'We were not designed or organized, we had to make do with whatever we had.'

Lise, Claude and *Paulette* were staying together now, living rough in the house a local farmer and resistant had found for them. They had the first floor of it, above an old woman who was infirm and who hardly ever went out, and here they lived in the most rudimentary way. On their first floor there were simply three bedrooms – no kitchen, no bathroom and no water. They had no furniture aside from one table and two benches which they borrowed. They put straw on the floors and that served as beds. For cooking they borrowed a small wood-burning stove; for food to cook on it they had to go to farms in the neighbourhood, foraging for what they could buy. They were living almost like *maquis* themselves. It was a far cry from Lise's previous way of life in Poitiers, but these were changed times. All anyone cared about now was the invasion.

All over France it was the same. The country was rising at last and the invasion was expected daily. In many areas, sabotage was already rife – in central France, for instance, Pearl Witherington was regularly cycling out to meet small teams of saboteurs, bringing them explosives for the night's work. Even before her departure in mid-April, Jacqueline had grown used to being held up in her travels by derailments and power failures – sometimes brought off by the very groups she was on her way to see.

Some attacks were ordered by Baker Street; more were inspired by local groups. These now came in all kinds of formations and spanned every ideological tendency. Internal politics and personality clashes often drove them to pursue different routes, but they were all driving *on*: the momentum had become unstoppable. For the agents themselves, the urgent priority was to arm and train as many of these people as possible, and the drops fell, the containers were gathered and their contents distributed, and still more containers fell, and with them came more agents, landing night after night on secret grounds scattered throughout France.

Almost all the new agents came in to country *réseaux* – the towns and cities had been the centres of early resistance but once D-Day arrived, the fighting would be in the country, for the possession of roads and rivers and railways.

In April, Lilian Rolfe arrived and joined the new *réseau* Historian around Orléans, working as radio operator.

Muriel Byck, in her early twenties and, like Denise Bloch, Jewish, dropped on 8 April with her radio set. She was joined a few days later by her organizer, Philippe de Vomécourt, and they threw themselves into the task of recreating a smaller version of his old Ventriloquist *réseau* in the Limoges region.

Odette Wilen, whose training had been cut short, was dropped to one of *Hector*'s Stationer receptions. Her mission was to be a support radio operator but *Hector*, the stickler for order and accuracy, was unhappy with the idea of a half-trained agent. He sent her on to a new *réseau* which had just started up in the Touraine and Paris, but as she arrived there, the three agents who ran it were arrested. Through contacts, she managed to get in touch with Virginia Hall, who had travelled north to the environs of Cosne, not far away. As ever, Virginia Hall had spun around herself a web of contacts and influences and she and Odette began trying to organize the rescue of the agents from prison.

Of all the women who came out in these last few months, only Violette Szabo went into a city.

Violette is a familiar name to many people – after the war, a book and a film, both called *Carve Her Name With Pride*,[1] told her story. They gave a romanticized version, but then Violette Szabo inspired romance. Her background was unexotic – born Violette Bushell, the daughter of an Englishman and a Frenchwoman (a First World War marriage), she had spent her early childhood in Paris and then moved with the family back to England. They settled in Brixton, then a suburb of London, and when Violette left school she became a hairdresser's assistant and then a sales assistant in the local department store, Bon Marché.

In 1941, at a parade of the Free French Army in London, she met an officer of the French Foreign Legion, Etienne Szabo.

---

[1] *Carve Her Name With Pride*, R.J. Minney, Newnes, 1956

They married – she was just twenty – and were almost immediately separated: he sailed for North Africa. Etienne came back to England once, for a week's leave, but in autumn 1942, a few months after Violette had given birth to their daughter, he was killed at El Alamein.

Violette was desolated by his death. When, a year later, the SOE recruitment officers got hold of her and interviewed her, she immediately declared herself willing to go to France.

Violette was beautiful; almost everyone who met her remarks on it. Maurice Buckmaster described her as 'really beautiful, dark-haired and olive-skinned, with that kind of porcelain clarity of face and purity of bone that one finds occasionally in the women of the south-west of France.' It's a lyrical tribute but it's not untypical. Violette evoked these reactions in people; she had not just beauty but spirit, and she moved the people who came into contact with her. Men seem to have been unashamedly dazzled by her, but women too speak of her as someone special.

Her immediate declaration that she wanted to go to France perturbed F Section and they sent her away to give themselves time to reflect. They did not wish to send out someone made unstable by grief, who might be reckless and endanger everyone. But they decided that she was probably sound and she was called in for training. In April 1944 she was teamed with Philippe Liéwer – code-named *Clément* – who had established the Salesman *réseau* round Rouen in 1943 and fled the Gestapo on one of Déricourt's last operations in February. They were to go back to Salesman and increase the pace of preparations for D-Day, Violette working as Liéwer's courier.

But just before they were to leave, Baker Street received this radio message, sent from a *réseau* far south of Salesman, in the Corrèze:

73 SEVEN THREE STOP
FOLLOWING NEWS FROM ROUEN STOP
XLAUDEMALRAUX DISAPPEARED BELGIVED
ARRESTED BY GESTAPO STOP RADIO OPERATOR
PIERRE ARRESTES STOP IF CLETENT STILL WITH
YOU DO NOT SEND HEM STOP DOFTOR
ARRESTES STOP EIGHTEEN TONS ARMS
REMOVED BS POLIFE STOP BELIEVE THIS DUE
ARRESTATION OF A SEFTION FHEIF WHO GAVE
ASRESSES ADIEU

Despite the errors made in hasty transmission and reception, the message was clear: there had been a major disaster in Salesman and it was not safe for *Clément* to go back to Rouen. This threw Baker Street's plans into disarray. The Rouen area was too important to be abandoned and there was no time for slow, discreet reappraisals. Baker Street could get no detailed information on what had taken place, so the extent of the damage was unknown. Did anything remain of Salesman and the Rouen Resistance? Was it enough to be rebuilt in time for D-Day? Someone had to go and investigate, and Liéwer and Violette went out by Lysander on 6 April.

They landed near Paris and were taken to a safe house in Paris. Liéwer was to stay there – he was too well known as *Clément* to return to the Rouen area, where the Gestapo would almost certainly be looking for him. Violette stayed with him for a couple of days and then, briefed with the names and addresses of some of his most trustworthy contacts, she took a train to Rouen.

She arrived in the bombed city and found it swarming with German soldiers. The *réseau* had indeed been smashed: some of the addresses she tried were deserted; from those people she found at home she heard stories of arrests and hurried flights. No one was exactly sure how many people were in captivity; the resistants still free were trying to find out, but it was dangerous, difficult work.

Violette stayed in Rouen for two weeks, trying to follow the trails of the vanished agents and resistants. She visited contacts still at liberty and gathered what information was coming in. It was bad news. Many resistants had gone and many arms dumps had been seized. Moreover, someone was talking: there were posters up in the streets carrying a description of Liéwer and offering a reward for his capture. Violette waited until there were no Germans or police nearby and tore one of the posters off the wall. She folded it quickly into her pocket and walked back to her rooms – it would be useful for Baker Street to see it and assess from it how much the Germans now knew.

Rouen was smouldering, from RAF raids and German arrests. The invasion was in the air and the Germans knew it as well as the French: they were arresting people continually on suspicion of Resistance activities. Violette was pulled in one day by a suspicious officer and held in a police station for a few hours. But they had nothing on which to convict her and a few hours later she was free again – until the next time.

But the city was an unhealthy place to be and in the last week of April Violette left it. She travelled back to Paris on the train and rendezvoused with Liéwer in the safe house. They arranged through the local resistants to get a message through to England requesting a pick up. Characteristically, on the last day of their mission, Violette

went shopping on the Champs Elysées. That night she carried back
to England with her on the Lysander presents for her daughter, for
Vera Atkins and for friends, together with the carefully folded poster
from the Rouen wall – small trophies from her private war.

In France, now that the fuse was lit there was no going back.
But that did not mean it had become safer for French people to
resist. On the contrary, there were more arrests now than ever. Acts
of sabotage were bringing German reprisals; in areas where drops
took place teams of German soldiers went to farms and villages
and searched for arms dumps. Now that so many more people were
involved in Resistance, the arrest of one person could lead to raids on
numerous families. And arrests were frequent. Even the most careful
resistants had to run risks now, under pressure of time. In the Drôme,
Francis Cammaerts was driving in a gazogene with a French resistant,
explosives hidden in the boot, when they were stopped by SS troops on
patrol. The soldiers ordered the two men out of the car and searched
the interior, cutting the seats to see if anything was hidden inside.

'We knew if they opened the boot we'd be shot. My French friend
spoke German and while they were cutting the seat he said to them,
"You won't find an American pilot under the seat cover. You won't
even find one in the boot." They laughed and let us pass.'

Cammaerts drove on with his friend, one simple act away from
discovery and death; his mouth was as dry as sand and he felt
exhausted.

Near Limoges, Muriel Byck spent hours in a shed behind a garage,
keeping her skeds. The roads were busy with German patrols: as she
waited for her skeds she saw German trucks and cars arrive at the
garage for repairs.

In Gascogne *Annette* recommenced her travels, often moving with
Hilaire, and transmitting from an attic or a field when her house was
unsafe. A new radio operator *Pierrot* had just arrived from England to
take some of the load from *Annette*; she gave him orders and delegated
some of her work to him. The agents were on the move now, keeping
several journeys ahead of the Gestapo who were looking for them.

The dangers were real and sharp. They bred fear among many
of the resistants, who were not sure whom they could trust.

Pearl Witherington, working with her *maquis* contacts and with *Hector*
and the Stationer resistants, cycled north to the Creuse on a special
task – to collect some money brought in to France by newly arrived
agents and left at a safe house. She reached the agreed place – an
isolated café in the country – and introduced herself to the people
there, but her passwords seemed to mean nothing to them and they

were suspicious and hostile. As she offered more messages and field
names to a stony reception, and could not answer any of the questions
put to her, she felt herself to be in danger. It took a long time before
she could establish her bona fides with these strangers; finally they
believed her, but they told her that she had been extremely lucky –
they had been just about to shoot her when at last she had mentioned
a name they knew. They had taken her for a spy. She left the café
feeling shaken and more ill at ease than she had been for months.

There were many incidents like this as throughout France, groups
were having to come out of their carefully maintained isolation and
join forces. Within SOE, F Section and de Gaulle's RF Section had
agreed to work together, so agents in the field were now liaising
and trying to put together their resources. Quite apart from SOE,
but inevitably overlapping with its work in the field, the indigenous
French resistants now found themselves called upon to lay aside their
political differences and unite within one army – de Gaulle's new *Forces
Françaises de l'Intérieur*, the FFI.

The FFI had been created in March by de Gaulle. In April,
the French general Koenig was appointed its head. RF agents and
other of de Gaulle's liaison people spread the news among the French
Resistance groups: from now on de Gaulle expected resistants to join
his army, the FFI. They would take ranks according to the ranking
system of the French army and would receive orders, arms and support
from General Pierre Koenig. The advantages for the Resistance
groups were obvious: they would become part of a co-ordinated
national uprising and their chances of survival and victory would be
much increased.

The advantage for de Gaulle and his government in exile was
also plain: the FFI would give them control over the armed Resistance
movement. Once the invasion had taken place and – please God – the
Germans had retreated, the Resistance would remain a powerful force
in France. Whoever was in control of it would be likely to control the
post-war nation: de Gaulle intended that person to be himself.

Almost all the Resistance movements agreed to unite within the
FFI. The communist FTP was the only large group which refused,
seeing all too clearly the political implications, but even it did not put
up active opposition. Hands were now being extended in all directions, as F Section *réseaux* worked with RF *réseaux* and as different
Resistance groups tried to overcome their ideological differences and
work together. It was often extremely difficult, generating acrimony
and resentments and confusion, but it was happening.

*

By the beginning of May, Virginia Hall had found a large Resistance group near Cosne in the Nièvre, and had been authorized by Baker Street to work with them. She worked with a French resistant named Vessereau and organized arms drops for a group of about 100 resistants and *maquis*. She also met Colomb, the FFI chief for the area, and began co-operating closely with him in arming and training the forces.

At about the same time – the very end of April – another Anglo-French mission, Freelance, began. Nancy Wake and John Farmer dropped into central France to offer arms and training to a string of *maquis* groups known to be operating in the Auvergne under the leadership of a Frenchman, *Gaspard*.

Nancy Wake is one of the better known characters of SOE – her story has been put into books, both by her and by other writers, and it was recently retold in a television mini-series. Nancy Wake is an Australian, now once again living in Australia, but at the outbreak of the war she was living in Marseille and working as a journalist. Early on in the war she had married a rich French businessman, Henri Fiocca, and together they had become involved in work for the PAT escape line (run by Albert Guérisse, code-named *Pat*). When *Pat* himself was captured, Nancy had to flee across the Pyrénées. She got back to England after a long delay in the summer of 1943, not knowing that her husband had been captured soon after her flight, and shot.

In London she was officially recruited by SOE and trained as a courier. Nancy Wake was – is – a flamboyant woman. She was also stunning in a style quite different from Violette Szabo: she was strapping, voluptuous and she radiated sexuality. It's hard to see it in the few blurred photographs of her which were taken about that time, but men as hard-headed as Francis Cammaerts and Maurice Southgate still speak of her with awe.

'Nancy Wake, the sexiest woman it has ever been my privilege and pleasure to know,' Cammaerts said.

Maurice Southgate, in the field as *Hector*, met Nancy Wake in all her glory the morning after she had arrived. She and John Farmer had been dropped to a Stationer reception; *Hector* had not been there but the committee was headed by the very person the new agents had come to help – *Gaspard*. *Gaspard* took them to a farm where they stayed the night and then, learning that they had important messages from London for *Hector*, he went to seek him out the following morning.

Hector had long been working at full stretch. He had 22,000 men in his territory as potential fighters; 22,000 people who looked to him to help them with arms and supplies. When *Gaspard* came to fetch him, he thought he was past surprising.

He said, 'You must come, because these two bodies
need you. They have messages for you from London.' I
said, 'Well, I guessed that old boy, but I couldn't be there last
night.' I was exhausted, tired – and I didn't have time! It
was six weeks before D-Day and I was perhaps one of the
few well-organized sections in France on whom Buckmaster
could rely.

Anyway, I went out to see these two bodies, Nancy
Fiocca and John Farmer, who'd been put up for the night
in a farm. And who did I see but Nancy Fiocca – that I
didn't know before – she was the most beautiful girl that
I think I've ever seen. With a dozen men around her.

She was washing her feet in a small little white, enamelled
basin, with a blue border round it. She could only wash
about two toes at a time, the basin was so small! There
she was with this little basin and water on a half-cut tree;
she was bare from the head to the waist. Titties all over
the place – but by God they were beautiful, they held! –
but what was amazing was that by the side of her she had
a sten gun, ready to shoot.

This was Nancy's style: she was direct, brave and she enjoyed life. She
and John Farmer had a tough mission – although *Gaspard* was willing
to accept their arms, he proved elusive when they tried to arrange for
proper co-operation between them. He wished to continue running
his *maquis* as he had done before; what was more, shortly after their
arrival another team of agents dropped into the area from RF Section
and also approached *Gaspard* with offers of help. In the third week of
May, Farmer met the RF agents and they agreed to work together to
supply *Gaspard*'s men; two teams of agents with two radios were useful
for the arming of more than 5,000 *maquis*, but the *maquis* themselves
weren't easily impressed. The first *maquis* group which Nancy and
Farmer approached was hostile; the men didn't trust the newcomers
and they were inclined to take their money and kill them. The agents
had to argue and negotiate for their lives.

It wasn't until they were joined, a few days later, by a radio
operator that the agents were safe from *maquis* violence. The operator
was an experienced one, used to hardships and danger: Denis Rake
– who had been present on some of Nancy's training courses – had
returned to the field. Now the radio was in place, the agents began
organizing arms drops and – in the eyes of the *maquis* – earning their
keep. Nancy cycled round the hills of the Auvergne finding dropping
grounds and organizing reception committees; she and John Farmer

helped train the *maquis* in arms and explosives. The Freelance team and the RF team shared out the area between them and worked in tandem to supply all the potential fighters. Nancy went from one group to another, taking orders for supplies and assessing the size of the groups. They were growing continually as more men left their families to join the outlaw forces, and now Baker Street was dropping money to help feed and clothe the men and keep their families in their absence. Nancy would take it on her rounds and distribute it.

Nancy and the other Freelance agents lived among the *maquis* they served. Their headquarters was a deserted farm which they shared with a group of about twenty men. They were out much of the time and very many of their nights involved journeys to dropping zones to receive arms. They slept and ate with the others, when they could.

Further north in the Yonne another woman found herself plunged into the middle of a Resistance and *maquis* dispute. She was Peggy Knight, a twenty-four-year-old Englishwoman who had been recruited into SOE only the previous month. Before joining SOE she had been a typist and she had led a fairly sheltered life. She was sent out after less than a month's training into a perilous, treacherous scenario: she went as radio operator to Donkeyman, which had long since been under the direct control of the double agent, Roger Bardet.

Peggy – Marguerite, to give her her proper name – Knight had little in common with Nancy Wake. She had lived a sheltered rather than an adventurous life: born and brought up in Paris by a British father and Polish mother, she had moved back to England with her family at the age of sixteen. She had worked as a shorthand typist in London and when the war came she had joined the WAAF. A bout of pneumonia had got her discharged as medically unfit and she was once again working as a typist in the City when in early spring 1944 a chance encounter brought her into SOE. It began when someone dropped a book near her in a pub and she handed it back to him. It was a French book and she ended up talking to the man who had dropped it about France and her knowledge of it. The man was connected with F Section. . . .

Peggy Knight was recruited into F Section at the beginning of April and rushed through training. She was one of those agents who made very different impressions on different people: she was nervous about her own abilities but deadly serious about the work, and her instructors read her in varying ways. Some found her 'mentally slow', some 'well above average in intelligence'. All agreed that she was a hard worker with a keen and active temperament, probably too active to be a good radio operator but very promising for a courier.

Doubts about her readiness were cut short by the urgent need for fresh agents. She was given brief parachute training – just one jump – and on the night of 5 May she was put into an aeroplane with a male radio operator, *Noel*, and flown over France. They dropped together on to a landing ground in the Côte d'Or, just east of their ultimate destination. They were going out to join Frager and Roger Bardet, organizers of the well-established Donkeyman in the Yonne.

At least, in theory, Donkeyman was well established. It had been founded back in 1943, when Frager had returned from London just after the St Jorioz swoop. Completely unaware of the part Roger Bardet had played in that débâcle, Frager had made contact with him and installed him in the new *réseau* as his trusted lieutenant and partner. Bardet promptly introduced Frager to his important new contact in the German Abwehr – 'Colonel Henri' Bleicher, who was secretly opposed to Nazi policies and desired to help the Allies. And so once more the trap had been laid: this time built in to the very foundations of the new *réseau*.

For the last year Frager had divided his time between the Yonne and Paris. Together with Bardet he had recruited resistants in the Yonne and forged links between a series of groups. He had also pursued his contacts in Paris, trying to start up satellite *réseaux* in other regions. When he was in Paris he sometimes met up with 'Colonel Henri', to see what he could find out.

Frager had long had suspicions of treachery, but they had not been directed against his close colleagues. Instead they had fallen, with good reason, on Déricourt. Ever since the curious events surrounding his reception in the spring of 1943, Frager had been uneasy about Déricourt. Bleicher, in his 'Colonel Henri' guise, had fed his suspicions, hoping to spoil things for Déricourt and the SD, and his hints had also served the purpose of focusing Frager's gaze outside his own *réseau*. When, in August, Bleicher had told him that Bodington was in Paris and that Déricourt was an SD informer, Frager's suspicions about the Farrier chief had become convictions. Faced with Bodington's blocking techniques, Frager had found it difficult to make his case to London, but finally he had got back to Baker Street at the very end of the year.

When he had returned to France this February, he had felt much safer. Bodington was no longer at F Section; Déricourt had been withdrawn from the field. Frager did not dream that he was harbouring another traitor at the heart of his own operations.

Yet, in his absence, Bardet had sown more holes into the fabric of Donkeyman. He had recruited a Frenchman and turned him into a fellow double agent. They had worked together in the Yonne; more recently, when it was decided to spread the *réseau* into Normandy, Bardet sent him into the new area. So the Normandy part of Donkeyman was well penetrated; Roger Bardet himself was presiding over the major part of the *réseau* in the Yonne and Frager in Paris continued his alliance with 'Colonel Henri', encouraged in this partnership by Bardet.

Meanwhile, down on the territory which was Peggy Knight's and *Noel*'s destination, the resistants were in a state of disarray. As the agents landed, they got their first taste of local organization.

There was a sizeable group there to receive them. One of the men came forward and introduced himself as *Casse-cou* (Break-neck), the leader. Introductions then followed all round and as the agents stood in the darkness, struggling out of their parachute harnesses, the men watched with interest, firing questions at them – where had they come from? how long had the flight lasted? where were they going next? what had they brought with them? Baker Street had kitted out the agents with the small change of Resistance – the minor luxuries of cigarettes, chocolates and chewing gum; *Casse-cou* and his men investigated these and took as many of them as they could get hold of. They took *Noel*'s precious radio sets; they even bundled up the two parachutes and bore them away. Eventually, as they were still standing in the open, Peggy reminded *Casse-cou* that the Germans might be around. He considered the matter and told them both to follow him; he led them, disheartened and bewildered, through the lanes to the nearby village of Marcenay, where they were shown into their first safe house.

There they stayed for two days, over the weekend. They hoped to lie low until someone came to get them but it was not to be. The reception committee had lost no time in spreading the news of their arrival and, as Peggy later described: 'We stayed there two days, indoors, hoping to see nobody, instead of which the whole village came in to see us, to wish us the best of luck and ask us how pleasant it was to be parachuted.'

On the Monday Peggy decided they had to leave. She asked *Casse-cou* to find them an isolated farm immediately, to tell no one where they had gone and in the meantime to contact his chief in the area and arrange for them to be guided into the Yonne. After a fashion, she got her wish: *Casse-cou* found a shed into which she and *Noel* moved. They spent an uncomfortable few days there, waiting, and then a car turned up for them. In it were two new comrades from the Yonne: men named Michel and Roger Bardet. Peggy was perturbed to discover that the car displayed no permit. *Noel* was perturbed to discover that his radio sets were to remain behind for a while. Their objections were overruled and after a tense journey they arrived at their new base and the headquarters of Donkeyman's Yonne operation: a house in the village of Aillant-sur-Tholon.

Roger Bardet appeared to be the senior of the two men; he certainly had the greater sense of urgency about their work. He told Peggy and *Noel* that *Jean-Marie* (as they knew Frager) was in Paris; he thought he should take them both to meet him as soon as possible. But there were difficulties with transport and after much discussion with Michel, it was arranged that Roger Bardet should take *Noel* at once and Peggy should stay with Michel.

Peggy was now left with Michel, in the middle of unfamiliar countryside. She was very unhappy with her situation: Michel struck her as unreliable and she did not relish the idea of being what he obviously had in mind, a kind of personal assistant to him. During the following week there were several arms drops in different parts of the *réseau* and under Michel's orders Peggy helped with them. In the daytime she made inventories of the newly arrived arms and took messages for Michel. It was Resistance work, but she felt cut off from the mainstream of activity.

Having proved herself as competent in the first week, Peggy was then allowed to meet various Donkeyman contacts in the district. The development should have pleased her but instead it increased her anxiety, for Michel introduced her to whole groups of people, explaining that she was a *parachutiste*. She became a local celebrity: she would take a message for Michel to a group twenty kilometres away, only to find that her contact had invited round half the village to meet her. Moreover, Michel sometimes used her as a go-between in arguments, putting her in awkward positions. After several days of this, another new resistant turned up in the area: known as *Landsell* and based at Cézy, near Aillant, he also seemed to find Michel difficult. Frustrated by his behaviour, he suggested to Peggy one day that their colleague was slightly mad.

Peggy was relieved when, after she had been in the district two weeks, Frager arrived in Aillant. He stayed two days, making a quick tour to see how the organization was progressing and gave orders to the various groups. To Peggy he said that she should stay with Michel another ten days and then go to join him in Paris.

Peggy's mission had already been dogged by confusion and mis-organization. For the next few weeks it was to be even worse.

Frager's visit seemed to have upset Michel and he now began to act more rashly than ever: for instance, when *Noel* returned from Paris, Michel announced that four of them – himself, *Landsell*, *Noel* and Peggy – should drive over to Marcenay and pick up the radio sets. At the same time they could collect some arms stored there. Peggy pointed out that it was risky for several of them to travel together, especially as the car had no permit and they would be transporting highly incriminating material, but Michel insisted that they all go. The party set off and reached Marcenay safely. But while they were staying overnight there, they heard that just two kilometres away the Germans were raiding a village: it was what the French called a '*coup dur*', complete with armed soldiers and dogs. They had to scramble to get away at once, packing the radio sets and arms into the car and lurching off down back lanes. As they bumped over rough tracks, hoping to avoid German controls, it occurred to Peggy that Michel and *Landsell* were now getting on very well; somewhere along the line they appeared to have become great friends.

Safely back in Aillant (against the odds), Peggy decided she had to get to Paris immediately. But each time she tried to arrange her train, Michel produced an objection and gradually she realized that he did not like the idea of her going. Luckily the stalemate was broken when a resistant arrived from Paris to work with Michel and *Landsell*, and brought news of a rendezvous to Peggy: she was to meet Frager at the Gare de Lyon in Paris, at 11 a.m. on Monday morning. Michel 'raised the roof'. He said that would mean Peggy catching the 7 a.m. train from Laroche, twenty kilometres away, and he had no petrol to drive her there. They had a row which ended with Peggy in defeat: eventually she had to catch the local slow train and did not get to Paris until 5 p.m. that afternoon.

Once she was in Paris she managed to find shelter, at an address she had been given in Neuilly, and after several hitches she managed to meet Frager. In fact, she met him several times and described her concern about the Yonne organization. She suggested that it needed reorganization and discipline; Frager said that he agreed. Meanwhile, a courier brought curious news that the resistant who had recently gone to Aillant had been accidentally wounded in the knee by Michel and *Landsell*.

Frager asked Peggy to go to the Yonne, collect a radio set for the Normandy operation and bring it and *Noel*'s messages back to Paris – by the following day if possible. She got to Cézy at 1 p.m. that afternoon and had to wait hours for Michel. Eventually he and *Landsell* arrived together, both drunk. Peggy's final report still carries a note of mixed confusion and anger at her reception:

Michel was very rude, refused to give me the wireless set, said *Noel* was miles away and he could not be bothered to fetch the messages. He *asked* me to go to a parachutage that night – the tone of his voice was such that I thought I had better go. We did not return from the parachutage until eight o'clock the next morning – again I had missed my train.

Matters in the Yonne had come to a crisis. That evening Roger Bardet arrived from Paris: he had come as Frager's envoy and now accusations and recriminations began to fly.

What was going on? From Peggy's point of view, it seemed that Roger Bardet was a serious, hard-working resistant and that he might indeed be able to put the *réseau* on the right lines. She respected him and she appealed to him for help; he told her to wait, saying that things would be changing very soon. As the evening wore on, she noticed that Michel and *Landsell* appeared to be on very bad terms with Bardet. They spent a lot of time talking to one another in low voices; if anyone else entered the room they would immediately shut up and look ill at ease. It began to look as if Bardet had come to be their nemesis.

And indeed he had. For the next day a large meeting of resistants took place in a farm in the country. Peggy drove there with Michel, *Landsell* and another man; awaiting them when they arrived were Frager, Bardet and several others whom Peggy did not know. The men stood in the farmyard, took out maps and compasses and began a general discussion; they talked across Peggy and made it clear she was not wanted, so she went inside the house and waited. She heard shots and went to the window: there was Michel running towards the house, pursued by the others. She did not at first understand what was happening – even when, going outside, she met Frager and he told her that a very painful job had to be done, she guessed only that a traitor had been found, not the traitor's identity. It was only when it was all over that she realized; Michel and *Landsell* had been shot as traitors. The group went back to Aillant, leaving the bodies to be buried by the farmer's sons.

Were they traitors? Or was Bardet using them as scapegoats, to cover up for his own activities? Or had they perhaps been recruits of his initially, whom he now wished to silence? For Roger Bardet, both intelligent and opportunistic, could see clearly which way the war was going. If and when the Allies won, he would almost certainly be denounced, either by Bleicher or by the victims of the St Jorioz swoop, if they survived. In which case, after the war he would be in danger of execution as a traitor.

On the other hand, he had a long record of Resistance work and now he was in a key position to develop the Donkeyman *réseau* into a powerful force. If he became a genuine Resistance leader it would be harder to make the other charges stick. He had changed sides once, to save his skin; he could do so again. Besides, France was his country; it was the right side for him to be on as well as the expedient one.

At this late stage in the war, Roger Bardet was changing back to his native horse. His new patriotism did not extend to warning Frager about Bleicher; it did not extend to anything which might incriminate him. But he was beginning to think of cleaning up his patch in the Yonne. Michel and *Landsell* might have been independently motivated traitors; they might have been Bardet's own men; they might have been guilty only of bungling their affairs. In each case, Bardet had a strong interest in getting rid of them.

Peggy, though she did not know it, was witnessing the turning round of an entire *réseau*. For another twenty-four hours, suspicion – by association with Michel – hung over her. Frager was inclined to have her sent to Switzerland and interned. But the other resistants who had worked with her in the Yonne confirmed that she had disliked Michel and had tried often to get to Frager in Paris. Was Bardet one of those who spoke up for her? He knew now, from her appeal to him the night before, that she had no suspicions of him. And she was a good courier: if he was to revitalize the *réseau*, he would need her.

And so the second phase of Peggy's mission and Donkeyman's life began. It was now the very end of May and there was scarcely any time left before D-Day. Frager and Roger Bardet both settled in the Yonne, based with Peggy at Aillant, and set about reorganizing the groups. Through her earlier work, Peggy had many contacts which they did not, and now she used her discretion to seek out the more promising of them. The agents imposed security procedures and organized more drops. Bardet, as Peggy was later to report, worked tirelessly. . . .

The fuse had burned almost all the way down. The agents and their *réseaux* were in various states of readiness and still the late reinforcements came in.

On 23 May Madeleine Lavigne dropped to a new *réseau*, Silversmith, in the lower Saône valley. Her organizer was Henri Borosh, who had already worked as a radio operator for VIC; she too had worked on the line. Now they arrived to work alongside the Acolyte *réseau*, on the north-south communication lines which would become vital to the Germans after D-Day.

On 28 May Sonia Butt dropped to Headmaster in south Normandy. This *réseau*, like Scientist, was undergoing intensive arms dropping operations, striving to equip the countryside for its forthcoming battles.

Near Limoges, one agent fell casualty not to war but to illness: Muriel Byck became sick with meningitis. Philippe de Vomécourt drove her to a hospital and authorized operations to be done, but in the last week of May she died. She was buried under a false name as all around her resistants, agents and civilians waited to hear news of the invasion.

And in the large Stationer territory there was a hurried re-organization. Just a few days after he had met Nancy Wake and John Farmer, *Hector* had been arrested. Now Pearl Witherington and Amédée Mainguard (*Samuel*) took over the running of the *réseau* between them. With *Hector* gone, the *réseau* was split into two parts: Amédée took the southern part of it across the Haute Creuse – renamed Shipwright by Baker Street – and Pearl took over the network of large *maquis* and Resistance groups north of that in the Indre. Her part was renamed Wrestler and now, more than ever before, she was playing an active, soldier's role. She worked with a colonel of the FFI, distributing arms to the groups and giving them weaponry training; she reconnoitred sabotage targets and planned attacks. On many nights she went out in a small group of men, carrying plastic explosives and fuses, and laid the charges against railway lines and bridges.

She was already a soldier – but she and others of the women would see yet more action very shortly.

EIGHTEEN

Fighting into the Open –
D-Day and After

During the last days of May, the BBC *Messages Personnels* lasted longer than usual. Almost every household in France was now in the habit of listening to these messages; SOE agents and the resistants who worked with them listened especially carefully. From the long string of bizarre sentences, they listened for those which meant something to their own groups – the signal that a drop was on for that night, or that a certain sabotage operation had been agreed. And now they listened for other messages too – for sentences or phrases they had long been waiting to hear, and which might come now at any time.

They were waiting to hear the D-Day messages. D-Day was when F Section agents and the members of their *réseaux* would finally break cover and launch a co-ordinated series of sabotage raids on railways, roads, telecommunications and power supplies throughout France. The object was to disrupt the occupying Germans just as the Allied troops were landing on the beaches of Normandy, and to continue the disruption so that the Germans found the greatest difficulty in sending reinforcements up to the front line. No one knew how the battles between Allies and Germans would go, nor how long they would last. The Resistance had to be prepared for sustained guerrilla action, systematically attacking the lines of communication and the inevitable movements of German troops.

The agents in different *réseaux* each had their particular targets. Benoist, Denise Bloch and the Clergyman resistants had communications into Brittany; the Wheelwright *réseau* had communications out of Toulouse, including petrol stores in the city and railway lines out of it; the Donkeyman *réseau* had a section of the Marseille-Paris railway lines; Scientist had the roads and railways running through Normandy itself, which would be feeding reinforcements directly into the German front line.

D-Day would mean every *réseau* sending its sabotage teams into action on their targets. A two-stage system of messages had already been agreed with the agents: every *réseau* had been given a 'stand-by' message and an 'action' message for each main target, and it was the stand-by messages which they now awaited.

On 1 June, they came. Agents and resistants scattered around the country heard messages which signalled to them to make their final preparations for action – the invasion was at hand.

The next few days were full of frantic activity within the *réseaux*, as ammunition and explosives were made ready, sabotage targets were once more reconnoitred, resistants went on desperate searches for supplies. Then four days later, at 9.15 p.m. on 5 June, hundreds of agents, sub-agents and sabotage team leaders heard the 'action' messages. The invasion would take place within hours. The shadow army was to rise and strike at its targets now.

When the messages went out, many agents were far from their bases and their close comrades. They were not even necessarily in their own *réseaux*. Lise de Baissac was in Paris, on a second trip to find someone who might come back with her and support the disorganized Scientist groups. Like everyone else, she was listening regularly, avidly, to the *Messages Personnels*, and that night she heard and recognized the action messages.

They had waited so long for this moment, but now there was no time to feel relief, nor even excitement. Everything was subsumed into the urgent need to get back to the Mayenne and to the *réseau*, which would soon be overrun with German troops moving up to the coast. It was vital that Lise get back, but the curfew meant she had to stay hidden till the morning. As soon as day broke, she got on her bicycle and pedalled out of the city.

The bicycle journey from Paris to the Mayenne was gruelling at any time, but the previous night's *Messages Personnels* had brought people other than Lise on to the roads. The saboteurs had been out, laying charges on railway lines and power supplies; early that morning, as news of the landings in the north reached the Germans in Paris, the charges began to explode and German patrols were thick on the roads.

Once Lise had left Paris behind, she was forced off the main roads on to byways, and as she cycled through the country villages, she heard the roar of RAF and USAAF planes and saw fires where bombs had fallen. Up on the Normandy beaches the Allies were invading and these planes were bombing the bridges over rivers, to slow down German reinforcements.

'I was terribly worried because I knew there were German troop movements going on and I thought they might block the roads for me, that I might not be able to get through.'

Going from one village to another, Lise heard excited news of German troop movements on the nearby roads and railways. Sometimes she could see the convoys of trucks moving along distant roads. Every so often she had to take shelter from bombs and fires. She dared not risk a meeting with German troops so she kept to the small roads and it took her three days to cover the distance. She made slow progress, keeping away from the patrols, sleeping in ditches and on waysides while on the larger roads German troops and tanks advanced likewise towards Normandy.

In the Yonne, Peggy Knight and her fellows were on the run when the D-Day action messages came through. On the morning of the 5th, she, Frager, Bardet and some others were gathered in a resistant's house in Aillant, looking over maps and making notes about the *réseau*'s stores and sabotage targets. Suddenly, the boy who had been posted as look-out ran into the house shouting, 'Alert – Germans are outside!' They collected their papers and belongings and rushed out of the back door, hearing the Germans approaching from the front. They ran through the field behind the house and waded across the waist-deep river; scrambling out on the other bank they had to walk through a wide stretch of nettles which stung painfully at their legs and arms.

They had lost the Germans, however, and they made it safely to another friendly house two kilometres away. They waited there, wet and uncomfortable, carrying their belongings, and some hours later a car appeared, driven by other *réseau* members. They could not go back to the house at Aillant, as the Germans were there waiting for them, but they kept their heads down and were driven back through the village to a safe house on its other edge. They had lunch there and discussed their next move: there was a house they could use at the village of Villiers, four kilometres away, and that afternoon they drove on there and spent the rest of the day establishing a new base.

That evening, when they were dog-tired, they heard the action messages for their *réseau*. The invasion would take place in a few hours; they were to attack their sabotage targets at once. The group's main sabotage priority was the railway line at Cézy – the trouble was, it was thirty kilometres away from their new base. And after the German raid at Aillant, there would almost certainly be patrols on the roads tonight. So they walked, carrying explosives and keeping to the lanes, as Lise de Baissac was doing on her journey to Normandy.

Revitalized by the urgency of the task, they reached Cézy in fairly good time. They got to the line unharassed and set the charges carefully; they reached Villiers again at dawn and went gratefully into their safe houses to get some sleep.

For us now, looking back on D-Day, it is seen as a definitive success for the Allies – the beginning of the end of the war. And it is easy to see how the sabotage raids and guerrilla attacks of the organized Resistance were part of a co-ordinated campaign, reinforcing the Allied invasion and hampering the German defences. But at the time it did not seem so simple to the people of the Resistance. The Allied high command might feel in touch with the Resistance, but different groups were still acting very much alone.

For Peggy, as for the other agents and resistants, D-Day was only one stage in the clandestine war. It was the cue for a certain kind of action but it certainly wasn't the end of their underground existence, or even the beginning of the end. Their struggle took on a different momentum, but they remained as they had been before – in the thick of it.

The next day, waking up tired, Peggy was besieged with instructions. She was to cycle into Cézy, taking messages to resistants there. She made the trip, returned to Villiers, and was asked to go straight back to Cézy. In her absence, Frager had received news that resistants were coming from Nancy to fetch arms from the Donkeyman store: they were waiting in Cézy. So Peggy cycled once more into Cézy and went to the address Frager had given her. There, sure enough, were some people from Nancy; there also was a British officer on the run from a German prisoner-of-war camp, Captain Thomson. Peggy took them all back to Villiers, where Frager waited at the new base. From there she went on with them to the arms depot and supervised the distribution of arms.

The Yonne was already full of German activity. During these next few days German reinforcements began travelling along the Marseille-Paris line, reaching the stretch which passed through the Yonne. The charges placed by Peggy and the others exploded along the lines, cutting them, blocking them, derailing locomotives. German soldiers were out in force to protect and repair the lines; sabotage teams crept out again under cover of night and placed new charges wherever they could find the line unguarded. The charges exploded again; the process of repairing them and guarding the line went on. German soldiers and heavy weapons also appeared on the roads, moving in heavily guarded formation up to Normandy.

German soldiers were also turned to the task of routing the Resistance groups – and quickly, before they could seriously hamper German movements. Searches were taking place in many of the villages and it was clearly not safe for Peggy and the others to stay in their Villiers base: on 7 June, the day after D-Day, they moved to an empty farm between the villages of Sommecaisse and Perreux and started a *maquis*.

Because of the problems in Donkeyman in May, and the reorganization that had to follow the shooting of Michel and *Landsell*, the *réseau* had no links already established with *maquis*. At this stage Frager had to start from scratch again, making contacts among local resistants, finding groups of *réfractaires* and *maquis* already living rough, and sharing out the arms among them. Members of the group brought in food from local farms and villages; they visited neighbouring *maquis* and took them arms and training in how to use them. They began to make new sabotage expeditions against railway and road convoys. *Noel*, the radio operator, lived in the farm with the others and every day he was escorted by armed *maquis* to a lonely spot ten kilometres from the farm, where he transmitted and received messages in the open air. Courier work no longer existed in the same way as it had done before, and Peggy did whatever was required of her around the *maquis* camp, cleaning arms, peeling potatoes, doing sentry duty, taking part in armed escorts when sabotage operations were mounted.

Cut off from news of other *réseaux*, cut off from reliable news of the fighting in Normandy, the newly formed *maquis* was engaged in a struggle for survival, not knowing when a German offensive against it might come, nor how effective were its own attacks against the Germans in the region.

And that is what D-Day, and the days after it, were like for most agents and resistants. It was a confusing time: a time of action after long waiting, but of action largely in isolation. The agents carried out the orders which came over the radio sets, and resistants fought to keep themselves alive and to stop the German advance to Normandy, but they could all only hope that their efforts were working in concert, and to a real effect.

On the night of 5 June alone, between the broadcast of the action messages and the Allied troops landing in Normandy, 960 sabotage strikes were made against railway lines across France. For most *réseaux*, the weeks that followed D-Day were a time of repeating these strikes and making frantic attempts to defend themselves against German searches and *rafles*. In many parts of France the Germans had reacted as they had in the Yonne – they had launched determined counter-resistance drives, hoping to clear the routes to the north for their reinforcement troops.

They didn't succeed: the people of the resistance continued to lay sabotage charges and to mount guerrilla attacks, but at a cost. In the *réseaux* of the central and south-west, for instance, resistants and agents were working to stop the Panzer SS '*Das Reich*' division moving up from its base in Toulouse to Normandy. Pimento explosions cut the Toulouse-Montauban railway line; Pearl Witherington's Wrestler and Amédée Mainguard's Shipwright (the old Stationer *réseau*) cut the Toulouse-Paris line where it ran through the Indre, Pearl herself going out with the sabotage teams to lay the charges against the tracks. Wheelwright resistants blew up the petrol stores in Toulouse itself, to prevent the Germans sending out lorry convoys. The SS division, deprived of rail transport, took the only option left and began to march northwards: their route led through – among others – Wheelwright, Shipwright, Wrestler, Ventriloquist and Headmaster territory, and now *maquis* and resistants came out of hiding to attack and ambush them while they were on the roads. The fighting was fierce: the German convoys were well defended by heavy weapons, but the resistants had the advantage of surprise and mobility. There were bad injuries and deaths on both sides; the resistants were successfully holding up the Germans, and the convoys were further damaged by Allied planes which bombed and fired on them from above.

But the cost to themselves and to the local populations was great. The German reprisals on local communities were harsh: after a Resistance attack, the nearest village might be searched and men taken to the village square and shot. It was in the department of the Haute Creuse, territory of a *réseau* called Fireman, that the massacre of Oradour took place. During one attack on the Germans as they passed the village of Oradour, a German officer was killed, and when they heard about it other officers in the convoy decided on an exemplary retaliation. They went to the village of Oradour, surrounded it, took all the men into the square and shot them. Then they rounded up the women and children – about 700 of them – into the church and set it on fire. Almost all of them were burned to death. It was one of the worst atrocities of the war in France, and in an ironic twist this Oradour was not even the 'right' one: the attack had taken place near Oradour-sur-Vayres, just south of Limoges; this was Oradour-sur-Glane, just north of the town. But in this scale of terror, such things hardly mattered: they certainly seemed to make no sense.

The sacrifices forced from people like the inhabitants of Oradour were terrible. Yet as a strategy, this Resistance harrying of the German troops was working: it took the 'Das Reich' division two weeks to reach south Normandy and here, in Scientist territory, it was held up another three days by mines exploding on the roads and by more guerilla attacks. It finally reached the German front after seventeen days – this had given a valuable breathing space to the Allied troops, who had been struggling against the unexpectedly fierce defensive fighting of the Germans already in Normandy and Brittany and the Pas-de-Calais.

It looked as though the Resistance, and the beleaguered French people, were going to have to hold out much longer still. In the last week of June the (mainly British) troops were no further inland than Caen, and most of the British heavy artillery was gathered around the town. Further west, in Brittany, the mainly American troops were being held likewise. Reinforcements were coming for the Germans, albeit slowly. D-Day had established Allied troops on French soil and had called the Resistance 'armies' into open fighting, but the liberation was obviously not going to be achieved by a steady sweep of Allied forces down through France. On the contrary, the Allied forces were pinned down in the north and meanwhile in each region local Resistance battled to shake the occupying Germans from their place, hurling the full force of their secret stores and training and organization into the fight and encountering the full weight of German reprisals.

All the Resistance groups, and all the F and RF *réseaux* connected with them, had sprung into open action. But it was an uncoordinated uprising, with each region having to fight its own fight. There was little scope for the resistants of one region to go to the aid of their neighbours. One group might be able to beg extra supplies or weapons from another, but the only true reinforcements they could expect would come from the air. And though arms drops were going on – sometimes on an ambitious scale – the organizing and receiving of them was even more risky than before.

At least the Resistance was generating its own human reinforcements – daily more and more people were ready to declare themselves for the Resistance, so that outside the ranks of the *milice* almost every French citizen was willing to help the Resistance. But while this helped to confound German counter-resistance moves and to swell the *maquis* population, the resistants still had to make do with only a limited amount of weapons and experience in the fight with their better-armed, better-trained, better-disciplined occupiers.

All over France, Resistance groups were engaged in spasms of open fighting. F Section *réseaux* worked to supply and help many of them.

They operated however they could, according to conditions in their region and the groups at work there. Some, like the Donkeyman agents and the Freelance agents (Nancy Wake, John Farmer and Denis Rake) lived together with the *maquis*, as outlaws; others continued to live in the community, carrying out their Resistance work clandestinely. But clandestinity did not mean the same as it had for the last three years: there was no time now for acting out cover stories and maintaining aliases – survival was down to your ability to slip through road-blocks, to carry weapons and ammunition without being caught.

In the second half of June, with the Allied troops unable to break through at Caen, Lise de Baissac found herself doing extremely dangerous work in the area immediately south of there. The Scientist *maquis* and Resistance groups had to defend the routes which led to the British artillery, and they were continually on excursions to mine the roads and cut the railways and telephone lines.

Lise did not go on these excursions herself, but she cycled on endless trips between the groups, taking them weapons and explosives, relaying instructions, giving precise details about targets and timings. She was in continual danger of discovery: the roads were peppered with German patrols, trying to stop the traffic in arms which they knew to be going on among the *maquis*. It was a soldier's life that she and the others were leading now. Scientist was in a crucial position from the Allies' point of view, and besides sabotage and guerrilla attacks, the *réseau* took on some intelligence work. Two agents, Jean Renaud Dandicole and Maurice Larcher, now concentrated on gathering information about German positions and taking it through the lines to the Americans.

There were frequent German attacks on Scientist bases: in the first week of July Dandicole and Larcher were in a farmhouse, transmitting messages to England, when they were surrounded by German soldiers. They defended themselves with guns; in the gun-battle that followed they and the farmer who owned the house were killed and the house was burnt.

In July, the Jedburghs came into France: they were uniformed teams of officers who dropped – usually in threes, one French, one American and one British – to do much the same kind of rallying, organizing and arming of resistance as the F and RF agents had been doing. They were dropped behind the lines, and one night Lise received six of them. They dropped with a supply of arms containers, new blood and new equipment for the battered French resistants. Their leader, a young man named Captain Blackman, was aghast to see Lise on the dark field.

'He was very afraid: he asked me how could a woman be doing

this? He didn't understand how I came to be there. At first he didn't dare speak to me.'

The arrival of the Jedburghs was heartening for the *maquis* and Resistance, who had now been engaged in fighting the Germans for over a month. The Jedburghs brought new arms and ammunition and the promise of more arms drops; their uniforms gave the Resistance a much-needed psychological boost. But it made more work for Lise who had to organize farms for them to stay in during the day, and to introduce them to the groups of *maquis* which were scattered over the region.

Up in the north, just behind German lines, life was dangerous and violent. But so it was in other parts of France too, and in the south, far removed from the action of the front lines, the Resistance was beginning to suffer very badly from dwindling supplies.

In the Gascogne, *Annette*'s life had undergone a marked change since D-Day. The action messages of the 5th had been the signal for a series of sabotage strikes – including that on the Toulouse petrol stores. Once these had been done, *Hilaire* had taken his central group of agents and resistants and moved to the little village of Castelnau-sur-l'Auvignon, where he made his *maquis* headquarters. Swiftly, other resistants came to join them, including most of the local gendarmes and from now on the *réseau* worked as a *maquis*, with agents and resistants making sorties to renew attacks on railway lines, roads and the German troop movements. Only a few members of the *réseau* still lived in the communities, using their peaceable covers to get urgent medical supplies for the *maquis*; *Colette* also ventured out in the guise of a disinterested civilian to take some messages through to contacts in the Pyrénées.

For *Annette*, daily life now became inextricably linked to *Hilaire*, who insisted that when he moved, she moved with him. She was transmitting frequently and at length still, receiving further sabotage instructions from London and passing on what information they had in the south-west.

The group based at Castelnau-sur-l'Auvignon was growing, and included about ten Catalan men. *Hilaire* had faith in the Catalans as good fighters and the *réseau* needed fighters, for the Germans were determined to hold on to the Gascogne and the Gironde and were trying to purge the area of Resistance. There were regular skirmishes and where the Germans could find *maquis* bases, they attacked them. As the German troops were trying to move north, and being attacked and ambushed along the way, reprisals were falling heavy on the local populations.

Even after the reinforcement troops had got clear of the area, the German troops still stationed there kept up their attacks on resistance. In one skirmish, *Hilaire*'s *maquis* lost several people, and soon afterwards, towards the end of June, a German surveillance plane was seen circling above Castelnau. The entire camp had to go on the run: they gathered up their possessions and *Annette*, carrying her radio set and a case with her codes and crystals in, set off to get herself and the set through the advancing German troops. She left the village with another member of the *réseau*, a doctor: he took her set in one hand and carried his own first aid kit in another; she carried her briefcase with the codes and crystals. Hoping that they would pass as a country doctor and his assistant, they left the village and took to the fields and paths. As they went they could hear gunfire as the troops moved in on the *maquis*; they also heard a series of huge explosions – *Hilaire* and the others were blowing up the ammunition dumps before the Germans could get them.

Annette and the doctor evaded the troops and got away; the *maquis* fought a rearguard action against the Germans, abandoning the base. On the road to Condom, where they were due to meet up with *Hilaire* again, *Annette* and her companion reached a house where the doctor knew people. They went inside and she managed to put up her set and transmit the urgent message of the evacuation to England.

They moved on, eventually reaching Condom itself and finding *Hilaire* and the others, regrouped. They had managed to find cars, vans and lorries for the next stage of their journey: they packed themselves into them and moved on again. They had lost the Germans by now, but they also knew how vulnerable they were.

They settled in a new *maquis* base, in another camp of disused and semi-inhabited houses. They had lost most of their arms and drops were hard to come by now, as they were being concentrated in the regions of the north closer to the German lines. Here in the south-west there was limited ammunition for the arms they did have and basic supplies, clothes and food, were running short. There was probably more safety in numbers, and during the next few weeks they joined together with other *maquis* groups. Although many of these were as poorly-equipped or worse than themselves, their joint strength was now 3,000. They were all waiting for the expected second invasion – the one which should be coming now, on the south coast, to drive the Germans north. But at the end of June they still had some time to wait.

Many of the women were now involved in fierce outbreaks of fighting. In the Indre, Pearl Witherington was now leader of nearly 2,000 *maquis*. Realizing the importance of this region to the Germans – it was their gateway from Bordeaux to Paris – the Allies sent in aircraft to drop arms and supplies to the *réseaux* there. The *maquis* linked to Wrestler grew, as did the *maquis* linked to Amédée Mainguard's Shipwright, and to Digger in the Corrèze – all over these departments of central France the *maquis* were swelling. And the Germans were making concentrated assaults on them.

In Pearl's region, the Germans were sending in thousands of troops to flush out the *maquis*. They also put her on the top of their wanted list, offering a large reward for her capture. Pearl had always been, in Maurice Southgate's words, 'a soldier', handling explosives and arms with the men. Now she led other unofficial soldiers in repeated skirmishes and battles. For diplomacy's sake she worked in partnership with a respected male resistant, a colonel in the French army, but she was giving most of the orders. And she was fighting with the others: one battle lasted fourteen hours, from early in the morning until well into the evening, the *maquis* facing 2,500 German soldiers. Pearl got cut off from the main body of *maquis* and had to crawl into a field of corn to take cover; the Germans lost sight of her but had an idea that she was still somewhere in the sea of yellow grain. Some troops stationed themselves around the field and fired at intervals through the corn. Hours crept by; Pearl lay on her stomach, dizzy and sweating in the sun, waiting until the corn was stirred by a breeze and then under cover of the movement creeping, a little at a time, away from the Germans and towards the far side of the field. She was still in the corn when the sun set and the Germans finally gave up their vigil and went away.

Due east of her, in the Cher, Virginia Hall was moving on from her work with the Cosne-based *maquis*. The *maquis* was in good shape, well armed and trained and in touch with the regional FFI chief, Colomb. Virginia handed over to a new organizer and moved down to the Haute-Loire in July. She set about liaising between the Resistance groups and *maquis* there, and organizing arms drops over her radio set. They were needed, for the Haute-Loire *maquis* were coming under siege from the Germans.

Below Virginia Hall, in the southern part of the Haute-Loire, Nancy Wake, John Farmer and Denis Rake were living from one *maquis* action to another. Nancy went on sabotage sorties and took part in attacks on German troops; with the *maquis* she also fought against repeated German assaults. In late June, a fierce German attack came against the *maquis* of the Corrèze and the Haute-Loire; the Germans mustered 22,000 troops, backed with heavy artillery and planes. The battle lasted all day over a wide area of the Corrèze, and Nancy drove back and forth across the battlefield in a van, carrying ammunition and weapons to the different *maquis*. That night, the *maquis* escaped into the hills to regroup and count their dead; the Germans, with over 1,000 dead, retreated.

But Nancy could not rest: Denis Rake's radio codes had been destroyed in the battle and he could not get in touch with Baker Street to request new supplies and instructions. To lose radio contact with London at this point would be fatal for the *maquis*, so Nancy set off on a gruelling, epic bicycle ride over the hills to where she believed the nearest working radio to be. The trip there took her thirty-six hours and several times she had to hide from German convoys and road blocks. When she finally arrived at the group, and passed on her messages and requests for new codes to the operator, she didn't dare delay her return to her own *maquis*. Another thirty-six hours later she arrived back, sick, feverish and bleeding.

In the *maquis* camp in the hills she slept for three days. When she was fit to work again, she found parachute drops taking place and ambitious strikes against factories and Gestapo headquarters being planned. She went straight back into combat: with fourteen others she drove to the town of Montluçon, where the Germans had a garrison, and raided the Gestapo HQ. It was done in swift, guerrilla style: they drove up to the building, leapt from their cars and ran in through different entrances, pulling open doors and throwing hand grenades. As soon as they had thrown the grenades they ran back to the cars and drove off, the explosions sounding behind them.

Attack and reprisal, attack and reprisal . . . and for some *maquis*, the outcome was to retreat and lie low. In the Yonne, for instance, the Donkeyman *maquis* base came under German attack at the end of June. At 5 a.m., while Peggy was on sentry duty with Captain Thomson, they heard a shot. The *maquis* took position and a resistant went out on reconnaissance – he came back two hours later to say that more than 700 German soldiers filled the woods around the farmhouse, surrounding it. The small *maquis* could not hope to win a battle; instead they dispersed. Peggy and a small group of men ran with as many weapons as they could carry past the German positions and gained the heart of the woods. Shots were fired after them, and some of the resistants dropped their weapons and fled. Peggy was now alone with one other man, *Robert*, and they hurriedly pushed the weapons under brambles and leaves and took cover themselves in the undergrowth. They lay there until early evening, hearing the Germans searching other parts of the wood but not coming near them; then as the light dimmed they crept out of the woods, avoiding the parties of Germans, and walked the twenty-two kilometres back to Aillant, the village where their previous base had been. They arrived at the very end of the Germans' search efforts – lorries were parked outside the village, but after half an hour of hiding in a field they saw them leave. Peggy and *Robert* went cautiously into the village and reached one of the safe houses.

They stayed there for two days, during which news filtered in that all the people from the *maquis* camp were safe. They held a meeting in the village, but it was clear to them all that the area was too dangerous for them now: they dispersed to different villages for a week and laid low, while Frager and Roger Bardet went to Paris. It was the breakup of their *maquis*; the following week Bardet came back to Aillant alone and gave everyone new instructions: from now on they would have a small, mobile base consisting of Bardet, Peggy, *Noel* the radio operator, and three other members of the former HQ. They would move around, contacting other Resistance groups and organizing a new *maquis* camp in the countryside. Frager was to stay in Paris, as it was too dangerous for him to come back to the Yonne.

So for most of July, into August, the Donkeyman *réseau* was rebuilding itself. Frager was in Paris, keeping in regular contact with Bleicher whom he still believed to be the anti-Nazi 'Colonel Henri'. For Roger Bardet, now anxious to disentangle himself from the Germans, it was a convenient development: leaving Frager and Bleicher to one another's devices, he put distance between himself and both of them and turned his best efforts to a last push on behalf of the Resistance. He travelled energetically round the Resistance groups of the Yonne and the neighbouring Côte d'Or, making contacts and organizing arms drops and training sessions. As his courier, Peggy stayed in a house in the village of Senan and bicycled round and round the same route, doing all the liaison work that was needed to set up these operations. Meanwhile, other members of the old Donkeyman *maquis* set up a small camp in the woods; they received some of the arms which began to be dropped in late July and, at Bardet's instructions, carried out sabotage strikes against railway lines and bridges. This small camp grew and linked up with another *maquis* nearby – but two months after D-Day the *maquis* in this area were still fragmented and vulnerable.

In the south-east, by contrast, the Vercors plateau, between Grenoble and Valence in the north of the Drôme, had become a *maquis* stronghold. At the end of June there were already over 2,000 *maquis* there, camping on the heights, and a special team of Allied officers – code-name Eucalyptus – was dropped to the plateau to arm and train them. There was widespread enthusiasm now among the *maquis* and the communities of the Vercors for an offensive against the Germans. Francis Cammaerts, whose Jockey *réseau* covered this territory, had severe doubts about the *maquis'* ability to repulse the German troops: the *maquis* still had not received the heavy arms he had requested on their behalf in the spring. But the Eucalyptus officers established themselves on the Vercors and the *maquis* and the resistants of the Vercors villages were jubilant at their arrival, and eager to prove their strength and liberate themselves. They launched a series of attacks on the Germans on the plateau and quickly drove them off.

By mid-July the number of armed, active *maquis* on the Vercors had reached 3,200; under the Eucalyptus mission, drops were received of more light arms and the *maquis* were trained in the use of them. German reconnaissance planes were monitoring all their movements, and the *maquis* did their training under occasional shelling.

Cammaerts continued to work on the Vercors as well as elsewhere in the region; he had just been joined by a woman called Christine Granville. Her original name was Krystyna de Gyzicka; she was Polish and had come into F Section after being involved in the Polish Resistance. She was dropped to Cammaerts on 7 July and immediately began work as his courier, work which took her inevitably to the Vercors, where preparations for battle continued in an atmosphere of tense anticipation.

On 18 July the counter-attack came, and it was on a far greater scale than the *maquis* had expected. German troops mounted a massive assault on the Vercors: 10,000 troops climbed the slopes of the plateau, while German aircraft fired on the *maquis* from above. It was a fierce and sustained attack, but for three days the *maquis* held the Germans to the edges of the plateau. Then on the 21st, the Germans landed gliders on the plateau, carrying over 200 SS troops. The fighting now became desperate; the *maquis* were seriously out-gunned and the rain poured down, but the battle continued for two days until finally on the 23rd the *maquis* gave way and fled. The German troops took possession of the plateau and as they did so they avenged themselves on the inhabitants: the torture and the killing were appalling. Francis Cammaerts and Christine were both among those who escaped, but as they went they saw terrible things, which they were powerless to stop. At one stage of his escape, as he lay hiding, Cammaerts saw about ninety people, from babies of six months to old men and women of eighty, hung up alive with meat-hooks through their throats and left to die. It was a massacre which, for those who witnessed it, remains indescribable.

*

The Vercors, along with the Oradour massacre, was one of the most terrible Resistance tragedies of the war. But there were others, defeats and deaths which were smaller in number, and less horrible in the execution, but which were still defeats and deaths. There were deaths in *maquis* battles and deaths in the homes of villagers and citizens, as the Germans forced their way into them searching for resistants. Losses everywhere were bitter and deaths everywhere were absolute, and these weeks after D-Day brought many of them to the people of France.

Victories and defeats overlapped: in the Jura mountains, the agents and resistants of Scholar triumphantly received a huge daylight drop of arms, made from thirty-six American planes. Yvonne Baseden, as radio operator, had spent days sending messages to London to arrange the details of the operation, and she had been at the dropping zone as the planes came over, talking directly to the commander of the operation over an S-Phone to give the OK for the drop. It took all afternoon, the evening and most of the next day for the resistants to share out the 500 containers of arms among the *maquis*. Finally finished, the F agents and a group of close colleagues gathered in their headquarters – a house near Dôle, used to store cheese – for a celebration lunch. But while they were there, German soldiers were on the roads stopping and questioning people, and in a young man's cart of logs they discovered Yvonne's radio set. They beat out of him the address of the headquarters and raided it: the resistants hid but in the violent search that followed, the soldiers killed *Lucien* the organizer and captured everyone else except for Monsieur Mayer, the house's caretaker, who escaped. The agents and resistants were taken to prison and badly beaten for information about weapons, and the *réseau*. They had little hope of getting out alive – but the *maquis* and the *réseau*'s sabotage teams now had arms they badly needed.

There were other casualties too among the women agents. Denise Bloch, Clergyman radio operator, had been caught in a Gestapo raid on 18 June, the day after her organizer had been arrested in a similar trap.

On 10 June, Violette Szabo had been captured after a shoot-out, just three days after she had dropped to begin a new mission near Limoges. She had come in once again with Liéwer, to organize sabotage strikes against rail and road and to work with the *maquis*. They arrived while the German reinforcements were still approaching Limoges, and Violette immediately went off on a mission with a *maquis* leader, *Anastasie*, to alert all the other *maquis* in the area. They drove into an advance party of SS troops and were fired on. While they ran for safety, Violette twisted her ankle and fell; she told *Anastasie* to go on without her while she gave him covering fire. She turned and fired at the Germans until her ammunition ran out; then she was wounded and caught. She went biting and kicking into captivity; *Anastasie* escaped.

Lilian Rolfe, radio operator for Historian around Orléans, had been working more or less alone since the end of June, when her organizer had been arrested. At the end of July the safe house she was using was raided and she too was caught.

In Paris Didi Nearne was still working steadily and alone. She transmitted for several Resistance groups, and now her messages included valuable intelligence about German positions. Far removed from the action of *maquis* life, she listened eagerly to news of the Allied forces and waited to hear of a breakthrough, of a movement towards Paris. But she would not see the end of July in freedom.

NINETEEN

Arrested in Paris

In Paris, the Germans were redoubling their counter-resistance efforts. With the Allies in the north, it was vital for them to keep control of the capital. They instituted regular patrols on the *métro*, checking people's papers and searching their bags; they raided hotels and empty houses, looking for resistants. D/F vans were roaming the streets to catch radio operators at work.

Didi Nearne was being especially careful these days. She hardly ever took the *métro* between her flat and her transmission base any more: instead she walked or cycled the twelve kilometres between Porte Champerret and Bourg-la-Reine, watching her reflection in the shop windows to see if she was being followed. She had been using the same house in Bourg-la-Reine for three months now, which was worrying, but at last the situation was about to change. Her contacts from the Boulevard St-Michel had found another house suitable for transmitting from: it was in Le Vésinet, a pleasant residential suburb to the west of Paris. The radio operator, *Arnaud*, who had earlier stayed with Didi, had already been transmitting from there; now Didi was due to start using the house too.

On 21 July, when Didi was all set to move her transmissions to Le Vésinet, she went to the house on Boulevard St-Michel and was given a very urgent message to send to London. She was in a quandary: she could go to Le Vésinet and transmit from there as planned, but *Arnaud* had been having problems with his transmissions recently and she was worried that she might run into difficulties too. She had never used the house before – it might take her some time to establish her signal, whereas she had always done well in the house at Bourg-la-Reine. Didi decided that, despite her chief's orders, she would take the urgent message back to Bourg-la-Reine for one last transmission.

She walked there, arriving in the early evening, and waited until the hour for her night-time sked. But as it approached, all the lights in the house went off – there was a power cut. The electricity stayed off all through the night, making her miss her sked, and did not come on again until the morning.

It was a fine, hot day. Didi was anxious to get the message through, and did not want to wait until the following night, when there might be another power cut. She connected up the pieces of her radio and erected her aerial. She had already coded her messages: she spread them out beside her and began to send out her signal.

She had just finished her transmission when there was an explosion of noise outside – men were shouting and banging at the doors of the next-door house. It was the moment Didi had always dreaded: she wondered desperately if she could escape but she knew that she would have no chance against armed men. She had only seconds in which to hide the evidence: she ran into the kitchen with the messages and burnt them, hiding the ashes under the oven where they would not be immediately noticeable. She dismantled her set as fast as she could and hid it in a little box-room. Meanwhile, she was furiously thinking what to do: escape was impossible so the only alternative was to bluff. She had got rid of the messages; there was no one else there to incriminate her; no matter what happened next she would protest her innocence. Colonel Buckmaster had said she was a good liar: now everything depended on it.

By this time hands were banging at her own door. She opened the door and saw a Gestapo officer pointing a gun at her. 'This is a house search!' he announced. Didi looked astonished. 'What's going on?' she asked, as the man walked in. He looked around and then went back to the door; for a moment she thought he was going to leave, but he called to some other officers, now leaving the house next door, and came back in to begin his search.

He went from room to room and Didi waited in a horrible anticipation. She hoped against all the odds that he might miss the box-room but he went in and then events began to cascade down on her: three more officers burst into the house, wielding guns. They found not only the radio but her codes and her gun. She was handcuffed, dragged downstairs and into a car, and driven off towards Paris. Didi sat in the car in a welter of shock and confusion. She had thought she would never be caught: now that it had happened she did not know how to react – she could only feel her heart thudding sickeningly inside her.

From here on, Didi's memories of her interrogation are vivid but jumbled. The Gestapo drove her into Paris, across the Seine and up through the wealthy eighth *arrondissement*. At the Champs Elysées the car stopped to pick up a German officer – 'He had a black coat and hat – he was a terrible man – and I was in chains and he turned and tried to hit me! And I thought, Oh, if I am interrogated by that man!'

But the appearance of this man had got Didi's mind working again. She realized that she would shortly be arriving at Gestapo headquarters in the Rue des Saussaies and that interrogation lay immediately ahead. She had not given up yet: she was sticking to her plan to bluff her way through. The chances of success were too slight to encourage any logical person but Didi was not logical; she was utterly single-minded. In the car, she prepared herself to 'lie like a tiger'.

Didi's telling of this story is not easy to follow: she leaps from one event to another and back to the theme which means most to her, so I don't have a nice full, rounded version of her encounter with the Gestapo. But I do have a very fresh one, full of gaps probably but also full of urgency and with a kind of thrill that has stayed alive down the years. This is how she set about lying her way past the Gestapo:

In the Rue des Saussaies, in an interrogation room, a short, sallow man began questioning her. What nationality was she? Who else was working with her? Whose was the gun they had found in the house?

Didi said she was French. No one was working with her. There had been a gardener who used to work at the house; the gun had been left by him some time ago.

She was a British agent, wasn't she? She was a spy, sending information to England and ordering weapons for the Resistance.

Didi said she was French; her name was Jacqueline du Tertre. No, she wasn't a spy. She was working for a businessman on his commercial affairs. She didn't know what they were exactly; she couldn't understand the messages she sent. She just did her work and got paid.

At first, naturally enough, her interrogator didn't believe her. But having lived in France since she was two, Didi felt and behaved like a native Frenchwoman. Moreover, she was very young: she was actually twenty-one but she looked seventeen. Her face had a direct, innocent look; her manner of talking was intense and unsophisticated and these things began to work on the interrogating officer; as she persisted in saying she was French he started to have doubts.

So he said, 'How did you happen to do this work?'

And I said this: 'You see, I'm a governess. I came from the south of France into Paris where I wanted to find a job. I couldn't find one. So I was often sitting in a café reading the papers to find employment. I couldn't find any and I went there many times. And one day there was a man there, sitting and looking at me all the time.

(I have heard this story from Didi twice and each time, at this point in the narration I begin to feel something odd happening. Didi is leaning forward and looking earnestly into my eyes and quite without meaning to, I find that I can see the café and the strange man, and I can quite easily imagine what it felt like to be a young girl miles from home and short of money and wondering what on earth to do. It's a very strange sensation, rather like being hypnotized. What's more, when I try to look analytically at Didi to see why she is so persuasive, all I can see are the memories of that day in the bar unfolding themselves in her face: Mademoiselle du Tertre playing back this unexpected encounter for both our benefits. It is all so odd that for a vertiginous moment I even think I am sharing something with the Gestapo officer.)

I was sitting in the café and there was that man looking at me and I was about to go when he approached me and said, 'Can I buy you a drink?' Well, I was going to say no, but I was so upset and so much short of money that I thought it would be nice to talk to somebody.

He said, 'You look concerned.' So I said, 'I am. I came from the south of France, I thought I was going to find a job you see and I can't find anything and I'm getting short of money.'

'Oh,' he said, 'perhaps I can help you. I'm a businessman but of course you mustn't talk about my business. I don't like people to talk about my business but one day you'll know, I will tell you. For the time being, don't talk.' He said, 'I'll give you some money,' and he gave me quite a lot of money! And he said, 'I won't be there tomorrow but a friend of mine will be there and you'll meet other people. Now I'm going on a journey.' So I thought, Oh well, my God, this is getting me out of the trouble I'm in.

(The first time I heard this, I could quite see it: it even flitted across my mind that it was no wonder terrorists and spies flourished when people like Didi were ready to take jobs from them in cafés. And yet I knew this for a lie.)

The Gestapo man was half-hooked by the bait: he asked Didi what this businessman looked like.

'Oh,' she said, 'he had a moustache, glasses—'

Didi went on, describing *Jacqueline*'s employer to the Gestapo. By now she was feeling her own strength; she was almost enjoying it.

> All sorts of things I pulled from my head. And the more I was lying, the more I wanted to and the more it was easy coming to me.
>
> In the training course they were quite right – they could judge. They said I would be a good liar and I would come out of it and I did.

Whenever Didi Nearne tells this story, she radiates a quiet but intense satisfaction. The war made strange demands and called on unexpected talents from the agents; at that point in her war she discovered her own genius for dissembling. It eventually saved her own life; by diverting the Germans' attention away from her it may well have saved others too. But it was not only on these practical counts that she felt she was achieving something; it was a personal victory: she had been caught but she was not beaten. By dissembling, lying, throwing her interrogators off the track, she was carrying the Resistance war with her even into the prisons.

The officer now congratulated *Jacqueline du Tertre* on her operating ability, which he said they had been monitoring for some time over the D/F equipment. How had she learnt to operate a radio?

> I said, 'Well, I was a radio operator when I was very young. I was working in the post office and there we had to—' He said, 'It doesn't exist!' I said, 'It does! We had to learn morse and from there I learned further.'

The Gestapo were half convinced – but not fully. They presented Didi with the codes they had found in the house and demanded that she explain them. Didi said that she had been given most of her messages already encoded; when they threatened her, she gave them a false key, which she claimed she had used in some messages, and struggled to apply it to the message before her.

I said, I don't understand. It's not working. I can't understand this.

When I said that he turned on me – that was their way – and said, 'Liar! Spy!' and came to hit me on the face. So I turned round and he hit me here, quite strongly. And he said, 'We have ways of making people who don't want to talk, talk. Come with us.'

Didi was taken out of the interrogation room and along the corridors to one of the torture rooms, in which there was a bath full of cold water. Incongruously, there was also a man in the room stripped down to his underpants: this was so that he wouldn't soak his clothes when he held her beneath the water. She was pushed, in her blue summer dress, into the bath and held under the surface of the water until she choked; then they pulled her head out and asked her questions. Who was the man she worked for? What was his address? Who were her colleagues? Then they pushed her under again and held her down until she nearly blacked out. Then up for more questions; then down again underwater . . . it was a form of torture the Gestapo often used and they were expert at it, leaving prisoners to suffocate to the limit of consciousness before pulling them out again. The lack of oxygen brought not only acute physical pain but nausea, panic and disorientation. 'I said, I can't talk, you're choking me.'

Eventually they took her out of the bath.

I said, 'I shall complain to the *mairie* of the district; I don't know what you want, what you are doing. What's happening anyway?'

So when I came back to the other room I was full of water. The officer said, 'Did you have a good bath?' I said, 'Excellent.' I was getting rude you see. I said, 'I'll complain about this treatment.'

The next event was the arrival of a German officer, an impressive figure, very tall and wearing a highly decorated uniform. He asked Didi if she spoke German; she said, no, she didn't understand. You're French? he asked her. But yes! she answered.

So he said, 'Didn't you know there are British agents who are parachuted into France?'

I said 'What do you mean, British agents parachuted into France? But where?'

'At night, in the countryside. Didn't you know about the Resistance?'

'But who could tell me a thing like that? It's fantastic.'

He said to me: 'This man who approached you in the café, he was a British agent.'

Jacqueline du Tertre (and now Didi switches unconsciously into French to relive the conversation) was astounded.

'A British agent! But look – ah, I understand now; I understand.' 'Yes,' he said to me, 'If you work for us you'll be well treated.' 'Now I understand.'

It was beginning to look as though she was achieving the impossible.

So they got into their heads that I was French and that there was a British agent looking to recruit girls like me in the café.

'You have been used,' he said.

'Ah!' I said. 'That man should be here, not me!'

The Gestapo officer then asked Didi when and where she was next due to meet her employer.

'I have a rendezvous at three o'clock,' I told him. 'At a café opposite St Lazare station.'

It was a false café, of course. I thought by taking them to this café I could gain time. I might be able to escape through the toilets.

He said to me, 'If you try to warn your chief—' I said, 'Chief? What does that mean?' – 'You will both be shot. The café will be ambushed; you won't have a chance.' But Didi continued to act confusion and misunderstanding.

So men from the Gestapo took her, still dripping wet, to the café opposite St Lazare railway station. They took her to a table at one end of the café and made her sit there. 'I said, "I've got no money; I must have something or it will look strange." And I was all full of water and they gave me some money to buy myself a drink.' The men took a table at the other end of the café, near the door, and sat down to watch.

Didi was not sure what to do now: she wondered how long she could spin out her drink and her waiting, and what would happen when no one turned up to meet her. Then she had a stroke of luck: the air raid siren went off. Hoping to escape in the confusion, she said she wanted to go to the toilet; she was allowed to go, but one of her escort followed her to the door. The ladies' toilet was on one side, the men's on the other and there were quite a lot of people around them. She went into a cubicle and sure enough there was a window, slightly open – but it was not large enough for her to get through. She stayed in the cubicle as long as she dared, searching for a possible way out, but it was no good. However, the siren had at least given cover to her story.

> When I went back to the table, they came up to me and said, 'He didn't come.' I said, 'Of course he didn't come, there was the hooter; he must have been caught in the underground.'
> The man said, 'Give me my money back!'

They were disappointed and angry – especially the officer who had given her money for her drink. She was taken back to the Rue des Saussaies and put into a room guarded by a young man with a gun.

> I said, 'Are you French?' He said, 'Keep quiet or I'll gun you down. Don't be strong-headed with me. You gave false addresses for your employers, didn't you?'
> 'I gave the addresses they gave me,' I said. 'But of course they were false. If they were agents, they would give false addresses, wouldn't they?'

Didi was being fuelled partly by exhilaration, partly by fury: she could see that this young man was French, and a member of the *milice*.

She was taken out of that room and on to another, at the very top of the building. She was locked in with two British RAF officers and instantly she began looking for ways of escape. There was a small window high up in the wall; Didi asked the men to lift her up to it, so that she could climb out on to the roof. But it was no good: the two men had already tried it and there was nothing to hold on to outside and nowhere to go. She was forced to stay in the room, waiting for the next round of interrogation.

But there was no next round. When the Gestapo came for her again, it was with paper and pen for her to make a statement. Didi had done and said enough: they thought she was stupid and tiresome and they believed her. She made her statement and signed it and was sent on to Fresnes, not as a British agent – 'They hated so much the English and feared them so much more' – but as Mademoiselle Jacqueline du Tertre, insignificant French girl who knew nothing of value about the Resistance.

TWENTY

Liberation

Up in the northern departments something was happening which gave new heart to people all over France. At the end of July, Allied forces broke through the German lines in Brittany and all over the peninsula tens of thousands of resistants and *maquis*, who had been rallying behind Brittany's FFI leader, rose to fight alongside them. The Allies and the resistants pushed the German line back, south and east, and as the Allied columns marched after them, the resistants ambushed the retreating Germans, hurrying them out of their positions and preventing them from blowing up the bridges and roads behind them. Harassing the Germans, finding and attacking their outposts, the resistants kept open the Allied lines of communication and kept a conduit of intelligence flowing about German movements.

As the German line broke in Brittany, it also gave in Normandy. Here too, the Germans began to retreat and here too resistants rose in a fury of ambushes to unsettle them whenever they tried to take a new position. Wherever the Germans arrived, the *maquis* were ready for them, forcing them further east and south: the Liberation of France had begun.

The procession of retreating German troops brought a fierce joy to each village and hamlet, but it also brought violence and danger. The Germans were not surrendering; they were armed and ready to fight, albeit in retreat. The resistants of the area could not afford to relax: on the contrary they had to keep attacking the Germans in order to keep them moving on and to prevent them taking up new defensive positions against the Allies. And by the same token, the Germans now had more incentive than ever to beat down the

Resistance which pushed them back, and which kept the roads open
for the Allies to pursue them. The passage of German troops through
a village brought fear and the danger of reprisals. There would be no
more Oradours or Vercors, and the *maquis* now had safety in numbers
and reinforcements, but a group of resistants or agents discovered at
work by the retreating Germans could expect no indulgence.

When the German retreat passed through the Scientist heartland, it
was in Lise de Baissac's words, 'very much war'. The Germans were
defending themselves against *maquis* attacks and German sentries and
patrols were active on the quietest roads. As ever, Lise's instructions
were to co-ordinate the *maquis* groups and help *Paulette*, the Scientist
radio operator, who was transmitting vital information on the German
movements back to London.

Lise knew that she must try at all costs to keep herself and *Paulette*
and the radio set safe. But the set had broken down, now when it was
most urgently needed to relay intelligence to Baker Street and receive
instructions for the resistants' next actions against the Germans. There
was another set in a different village, so Lise and *Paulette* took bicycles
and set off for it, Lise carrying the crystals *Paulette* needed, and her
operating codes, in a belt around her waist. On the road outside the
village they were stopped by a German soldier, doing spot checks
for resistants. He asked to see their papers, examined them, asked
where they were going, heard that they were going to try and buy
food, and then, explaining that there were terrorists around who had
to be caught, he frisked Lise for a gun or explosives. He felt around
her arms, her hips, her waist, and she tried to control her fear while
she gave him her straight, slightly disdainful look. What he thought he
was feeling around her waist, she never knew, but he didn't question
it. He stepped back and told them they could go.

The base the agents and resistants now used for their rendezvous
was a schoolhouse, which they shared with the schoolmistress. They
used the kitchen for their work, co-ordinating their attacks and
exchanging information. One day Lise turned up to find that a party
of Germans had requisitioned the rest of the building for their own
use while their troops passed through the village. The Germans were
in the classrooms and the refectory, organizing the details of their
march; from the kitchen and the back door the agents continued
to come and go discreetly on Resistance business, pretending to be
a desultory flow of villagers making regular calls. The Germans let
them go about their affairs, showing no interest in them – there was
even a note of comedy:

We had the schoolmistress there who was a very simple

person; a housekeeper who liked to make sure that things were done properly. The Germans had asked her permission to cook some eggs – some omelettes, I think – in the kitchen. They weren't unpleasant you know, the Germans, in general they were well-mannered enough. They were so bad at cooking that this good woman took over and cooked for them, saying, 'You don't do it like that.' And my brother said, 'What do you think you're doing, cooking eggs for the Germans?' It was very funny.

It was less funny for Lise when Germans came to requisition the house the agents actually lived in. At the time she was there alone; she was told that she had to leave, but that she might collect her things first. Going into her bare little room, she found that her new 'sleeping bag', made from the silk of a parachute, had already been opened up by the German soldiers, and they were sitting on it. They didn't seem to recognize what it was, but a young officer in the room was watching her suspiciously. Lise gathered up her few possessions – a dress, a bag, her wash things, and left the room. Going into the room they used as a kitchen, she realized that in the small cupboard, along with the three plates were bags of English sweets which had come from parachute drops. She entered the room praying that the Germans had not already looked inside the cupboard. 'Luckily the officer who had told me to leave was there and he said, "I've shut your cupboard door," – he'd done it without looking inside – and he handed me the key.' She thanked him and left, staying away for two days and nights until the troops had moved on.

They moved on swiftly now, the news of their retreat going before them and the *maquis* coming down from their camps to attack them and prevent them from mining the roads and bridges after they had passed. So the Resistance helped to drive the Germans on and to keep the way open for the Allied armies close behind. Across from west to east, the north of France was being liberated. And as the Germans were pushed back towards Paris, another, support invasion, took place in the south.

This had been long planned by the Allies but much delayed. During the last two months, the Allied effort had been concentrated in the north, and while arms drops and Jedburgh missions were sent in there, the Resistance of the south had been running badly short of arms and supplies. Large numbers of German troops had remained in the south, attacking the Resistance groups and trying to dislodge them, and the population had continued to suffer reprisals. Recently the arms drops had begun again, but at the beginning of August the people of the south were longing for the rumoured invasion to materialize on their shores.

Finally, it came. On 15 August Allied troops, Free French and (mainly) American, landed on the Rivièra. The *réseaux* of the south received their radio instructions to strike once more, and resistants and *maquis* leapt into action rising against the German occupiers, sabotaging German lines of communication, and forcing German defences off the main route from Cannes to the north.

The German troops in the south began to retreat within days. They headed north and east, and the job of resistants, re-armed by the continuing spate of British and American drops, was to speed them on their way. The *maquis* groups, banded together into large forces, attacked and ambushed them; in the cities resistants broke out into fierce fighting and as the German troops moved out they pursued them and proclaimed the cities liberated.

Annette continued to transmit messages day and night, going wherever *Hilaire* went. The original Wheelwright *maquis* had joined forces now with others in the area; two Jedburgh officers (both radio operators) were with them as well and *Hilaire* had agreed that a French officer, Lieutenant Parisot, should lead them into action. They were now, at last, on the offensive, chasing the retreating German troops, and there were many battles and skirmishes. *Annette* transmitted under machine-gun fire and strafing from the air.

The great symbolic triumph for the Wheelwright agents was the liberation of Toulouse. *Maquis* converged on the city as the German troops prepared to withdraw, and as the Germans left the region's Resistance marched in to retake the city. They arrived in a long, shabby convoy of trucks and cars, some of them military vehicles stolen from the Germans, others farm vehicles, almost all in poor condition. *Hilaire* and *Annette* were in a car some way down the parade, winding through the outer streets of Toulouse, when Parisot came up to them; he told them that they were considered leaders of the Resistance and should be heading up the procession into the heart of the town. So they led the parade towards the town's main square – and just as they were entering it their car burst a tyre. After a few moments of disarray, a crowd of celebrating resistants gathered round the car, heaved it up and carried it on into the square. Toulouse was liberated, *maquis*-style.

And so the German retreat continued and *réseaux* across the southern half of France rose to the last challenge of liberating their regions. The Allied forces which had landed on the Rivièra were advancing north, cutting off the south-eastern corner of France as an escape route for the Germans. Cammaerts' Jockey resistants worked with other groups to hold the south-north route open for the Allies, fighting off German attempts to blow bridges and communications. Christine Granville infiltrated divisions of the German army which consisted of conscripted foreigners – such as Poles, Italians – and helped to persuade groups of them to give themselves up to the Resistance. In the Ain and Savoie the Marksman *réseau* and other Resistance forces attacked and unsettled the occupying Germans there.

Hoping to outflank the Allied forces in the south-east, the German troops moved north. Nancy Wake in Freelance, Virginia Hall in her new Heckler *réseau*, Pearl Witherington in Shipwright, now saw their Resistance attacks actually unseating the German troops, chasing them across their territories. Village after village, department after department saw spates of fighting which ended in the Germans leaving.

The same process was happening in other parts of France too, as the Allied troops moved from west to east across what had once been the 'occupied zone'. In the Yonne, the Donkeyman *maquis* had linked up with several other groups and now, hearing that the Americans were approaching, they all went to the village of Sommecaisse and occupied it. There were no Germans there but there were German troops scattered around the countryside, and Bardet decided that the Resistance must occupy more villages, distribute arms and begin making ambushes to clear the area for the Americans. During the next few days the *maquis*, which now numbered several hundred men, occupied five villages, and Peggy was cycling between them with messages. Two American officers had been dropped to the region by parachute and she was also liaising with them. As the American troops arrived, Peggy liaised between the resistants in the occupied villages and the troops, often making dangerous trips across German lines. Groups of resistants fought German soldiers in the countryside and Americans and Resistance forces co-operated on some operations. Peggy now spent most of her time going on reconnaissance trips and bringing back information. As Auxerre was liberated, she, Bardet, and the *maquis* moved down to the Loire, to push the retreating Germans out of there.

And now the work of SOE's F *réseaux* was coming to an end. It is impossible to put a date on this end: the *réseaux* were ending their work in the same ragged way that they had begun it, interrupted it, continued it and restarted it over the last four years. In their different regions, many agents were now celebrating the departure of the Germans; others were putting in the last blows against them. Resistance was no longer the activity of organized groups, working together. It had spilled over into a general reclaiming of France.

Everywhere now the French were rising. In what had once been the occupied zone, Paris was liberating itself. Passive resistance, in the form of strikes, had been going on since early August; on the 19th, while the Allied troops were still some way from the city, resistants put up barricades in the streets and began open fighting. Street battles raged across Paris for five days: on 24 August Free French troops reached the city. On the 25th, the Germans surrendered Paris, and on the 26th Allied troops marched through the city, led by de Gaulle on foot, and the people of Paris filled the streets with celebrations.

Elsewhere in the country, a series of German surrenders had begun.

By September, most of France was liberated. There were Germans still in some of the important Atlantic ports, and in the north-east, but in truth the occupation was over. The liberation had not been easy. In every town and village and stretch of country where battles were fought, people were wounded and killed. They died until the last moment of occupation. And now that the liberation had come, most communities were left with a legacy of joy and bitterness. Neighbours had been divided during the occupation; they were so still. As the Germans withdrew, most of the Vichy authorities left behind were deposed and jailed. Recriminations began. Now everyone was a resistant, anxious to prove Resistance credentials. But there was a lot to condemn and a lot to forgive.

For the women agents of F Section, though, the war was ended. *Colette* had escaped over the Pyrénées in August; all the others who were in their *réseaux* at the end of July survived the liberation uncaught.

They celebrated the liberation in their various ways: Peggy Knight moved with Bardet and the Donkeyman *maquis* along the Loire valley, as they reconnoitred the area and chased the last of the German troops out.

Virginia Hall, indefatigable as ever, left the Haute-Loire when it was liberated and accompanied a Free French force to the Jura, to take part in that liberation too.

Nancy Wake marched with *maquis* and fellow agents through Vichy when the Germans left and then went quietly back to Marseille to seek news of her husband.

Annette stayed in Toulouse with *Hilaire* and her other comrades, celebrating its freedom and drinking in 'the great sense of relief' before she turned her thoughts to home.

Lise de Baissac, having seen the Americans pass through the Mayenne and liaised with them, stayed a while to gather information about the people who had worked in the Scientist *réseau*.

For these women, and for all their fellow women agents in other *réseaux*, it was time to take stock of their work, their achievements and their losses. The happiness of the liberation was shot through with grief: each woman knew someone who had died, someone who was missing.

Many of the women would make a trip such as Lise now made, in memory of a fellow resistant.

Towards the end of the summer, Lise left her village and drove northwards through the lanes of the Mayenne. She headed for the countryside south of Caen and the hamlet where Claude's assistant Dandicole, and the radio operator Larcher had died. No one knew much of how this had happened; it had been during the frantic days after the invasion, and they knew only that there had been a German attack, and that the two agents and the farmer who lived in the house had been killed.

When she reached the hamlet and the farmhouse, she found only a blackened oblong of earth and some charred stones. The house had been burned; there was nothing left. She called on the people who lived nearby but found that they could tell her little of what had happened. German soldiers had come; they had surrounded the house and attacked it and then they had set fire to it. Everyone in it had died.

It was a beautiful day, still with the peace of late summer.

'I looked at this house which was destroyed. And the country around it was ravishing, a field all green, covered with pink mushrooms which you could eat. And it was sad because it was death on one side, life on the other. . . .'

TWENTY-ONE

On the Other Side of the Wall

The occupation of France was over; for those resistants who had remained free the national uprising had achieved its aim, and they could now look to the future. It was a future saddened by loss and made complicated by the divisions and conflicts of the last four years, but it was a future for the French to make their own.

Yet there were other casualties of the occupation besides the dead and the bereaved. Since 1940 thousands of people had been arrested in France for Resistance or other activities considered harmful to the Third Reich (black marketeering, for instance, or *rassenschande* – the crime of having sexual relations with a German and thus polluting the master race). Some of these prisoners were in prisons and camps in France; for them, the liberation at last brought relief. But many others had been sent out of the country, to Germany, and there, while France celebrated its freedom, they remained in captivity.

They were held in prisons and in concentration camps. There were many camps, places where captives were herded together in filthy and brutal conditions, and made to work – on armaments or doing other labour for the German nation – until disease or weakness brought them down. The concentration camps were encircled with electrified fences and patrolled by armed sentries; rules were rigid and infringement was punished savagely – beatings, solitary confinement, punitive exercises and starvation were the currency of discipline. The camps had their own crematoria and carried out their own executions.

Hundreds of thousands of people were sent from France to these camps. By the time Germany surrendered in spring 1945, 200,000 of them would have died, and nearly half of these were resistants.

Among them were approximately 200 SOE agents. About 100 F agents were captured; so were about 100 RF and DF agents. They were sent to different camps, including those at Dachau, Buchenwald, Natzweiler, Belsen, Flossenburg and, for the women, the female camp at Ravensbrück.

In the summer of 1944, fifteen of the women agents in this book were in captivity in Germany. Each one had her own story behind her; each one had undergone a separate ordeal of interrogation, in some cases physical torture. As agents in the field they had all lived with the daily possibility of being taken, of vanishing behind the wall which would cut them off from their comrades still at liberty, from Baker Street and the eyes and ears of the world. Now they were there, on the other side of that wall, fighting a different fight: not to inflict damage on the enemy but simply to survive.

Of the fifteen women agents who made this journey into captivity, only three survived. They were Odette Sansom, Yvonne Baseden and Didi Nearne. The experience of each one was different, even though for many months they were in the same camp, Ravensbrück, together. Yvonne Baseden declines to talk about what happened to her, saying it is a subject 'no longer open to discussion'. Both Odette and Didi Nearne do talk about their captivity, quite avidly and yet, after all these years, with a scarcely diminished pain and a note of bewildered questing, as if still trying to tame the experience and make it bearable.

Their memories are not complete; there are blank areas, and jumbles of time; there are doubts about the order in which events occurred. For Didi, whose story is until now unrecorded, it is important to pin events down to the correct date. For Odette, her story well documented and on the way to being mythologized, dates and names matter less than the progress of her inner struggles against despair.

The stories of Odette and Didi, as they now remember them and seek to live with them, are very different. And if it were possible to tell the stories of all the women, each would be unique. Odette and Didi can no more speak for those who died than they could pretend to represent one another, or the silent Yvonne Baseden. But in their differences, as well as in what they share, they at least stand as a reminder. These stories of Odette and Didi take us some way behind the wall of lost memories.

Early in the morning of 16 April 1943, in the chill darkness around Lake Annecy, Odette was escorted into captivity. 'Colonel Henri' and four Gestapo officers marched her and Peter Churchill out of the Hôtel de la Poste, through a ring of Italian soldiers and into a car.

Sitting on either side of a Gestapo officer, they were driven away from St Jorioz and towards prison.

The events of the last half-hour stuck in her mind, impossible to assimilate. They had gathered her up in their momentum and carried her forwards, were still carrying her forwards, to something she realized she had always expected. As they had come out of the hotel, 'Colonel Henri' had asked Peter, with sardonic courtesy, whether he would rather go into the custody of the Germans or the Italians. Peter had replied bitterly that he knew it would make no difference in the long run, but since he asked, they would go to the Italians. Henri had looked angry but had not refused: what would happen now? But before she could think of that, there was something she still had to do. Inside the leg of her underpants, Peter Churchill's wallet was digging into her. She leaned forward and began fussing with her skirt, pretending – with an expression of frosty dignity – to adjust her suspenders. The Gestapo officer next to her looked politely away, and she slid out the wallet and pushed it behind the car seat. Well, she thought, as she smoothed her skirt, they'll find it one day but maybe by then it will be no use to them.

So the car drove on through the night, with the wallet hidden beneath the seat, and drew up finally outside Annecy prison. It was the beginning of a captivity which for Odette consisted almost entirely of solitary confinement and which was to last more than two years.

These first few weeks of captivity were in fact like a ghastly farce. Because Peter had asked that they go to the Italians, the Germans now had to go through a long and convoluted 'hand-over' procedure, first to put them into the Italians' custody and then to retake them for the German authorities. Representations had to be made to the resident authorities at all sorts of different places, and so Odette and Peter were dragged round from one prison to another.

That first night in Annecy, Odette was shut into a cell and left to get through the rest of the night alone. So far neither she nor Peter had been mistreated – on the contrary, 'Colonel Henri' seemed determined to do things by the book. She began to wonder if it were possible to outwit the Gestapo, at least to protect Peter and herself from the worst reprisals. They had gained a little time by coming to Annecy first instead of going straight to a Gestapo headquarters. Perhaps they could make the most of it. Odette felt that she would be able to bear the imprisonment and interrogations ahead, but she was worried about Peter.

The next day the interrogations began. Odette was interrogated by members of the Italian secret police; so, she gathered, was Peter. She answered the more innocuous of the questions, pleaded ignorance to those which might be dangerous. The interrogators were persistent though not brutal – but they told her something which she had dreaded hearing. Already, Peter had tried to escape and he had been badly beaten. Odette had known that Peter would not find captivity easy to bear; the week she spent in Annecy jail, punctuated by hours of questioning, dragged by in an agony of anxiety about him.

After one week, the Italian police announced to Odette that she and Peter were moving on. She was taken out of her cell and into the prison yard, where a lorry stood waiting. As Odette climbed into the lorry, she saw Peter sitting in it. His face was bruised and swollen; Odette, horrified, sat next to him and tried to comfort him. But as the lorry began its journey and they were able to talk, she realized the extent of his despair.

'He said he would have preferred to be dead. He would have preferred to be killed. That made me absolutely furious: I told him as long as there is life there is hope. He thought it was absolutely ridiculous for me to have any!'

The lorry drove the pair from Annecy to Grenoble, and there once more they were separated. They were held in Grenoble for ten days and the interrogations, still under the Italians, resumed. Odette feared for Peter's resilience: she had fallen in love with him for his romantic, active spirit, but it was a spirit which needed action to thrive. Being helpless in prison would sap him of his strength. Odette, on the other hand, was finding new resources in herself; she took comfort from thinking furiously around their predicament, trying to find room to manoeuvre.

Under interrogation in Grenoble, Odette took a decision to link her fate inextricably with Peter's, and to try to draw some of the fire from him on to herself. She felt responsible for Peter; she did not yet understand what had gone wrong with her plan to outwit 'Colonel Henri', but it was possible that, had they left St Jorioz earlier, they might have evaded capture. Now that they were both caught, she felt that she was the stronger. What was more, Odette needed to be active: by nature she could not bear to give in. Her 'managing personality' asserted itself again; it stopped her brain whirling, and brought her some peace, now that she felt she might still have some influence on their fate.

So she claimed that she was Peter's wife and began portraying herself as the leader of the two. Bit by bit, in answer to their questions, she gave her interrogators a picture of herself as a dedicated resistante, who had been determined to come back to France to fight and who had persuaded a more cautious husband to come too. She also undertook a daring, and dangerous, gamble: when the inevitable question arose, were they related to Winston Churchill, she said that yes, Peter was a distant relation of Winston's.

She hoped that the name might afford them some protection. Perhaps they would be considered valuable hostages and kept alive; at least there was the chance that the Germans, with their respect for officialdom, would hesitate before killing relatives of the British Prime Minister. It might gain them time if nothing else. As they were moved on again, to Turin for a day and a night, and from there back to Nice, Odette and Peter were occasionally able to snatch a few words together. On the way to Nice, travelling in next-door train compartments, Odette persuaded the guards to let them lean out of the windows and have a brief marital conversation together. Over the noise of the train wheels, she told Peter what she had said, and he agreed to go along with it. They hurriedly swapped a few details about their pasts and families and invented some about their married life; from now on, they would stick with this story all the way.

They were taken to a villa in the hills behind Nice, and held there for another week. The interrogations continued, the two of them being questioned separately and now with more evidence of menace and threats. In the securely guarded villa, down in their old territory of the Côte d'Azur, both Odette and Peter felt their spirits falter. The endless moving round, necessary to fulfil the extraordinary formalities of German and Italian joint occupation, was disorienting them, as well as prolonging the suspense. For they both knew that they would end up in German custody, at the mercy of the SD interrogators.

Sure enough, from Nice they were taken to Marseille and then to Toulon. And at Toulon they were officially handed over to the Gestapo. It was the first week of May, and now they were heading north, to Fresnes.

Just to the south of Paris, Fresnes was a huge prison built before the war. Since the occupation the SS had comandeered it and now as well as ordinary criminals it held anyone the Nazis considered troublesome: Resistance workers, political activists, people with unsound beliefs were all herded into Fresnes. Odette and Peter Churchill arrived there on 8 May 1943 and they were greeted by a familiar face: 'Colonel Henri' – Sergeant Bleicher – was there to escort them in. They were taken to the main hall where there were lines of wooden cells, the size of cupboards. They were shut into cells next to one another: standing in the cramped dark, Odette talked to Peter through the partition and strained to hear his replies. They called to one another for several minutes and then they heard shouts and blows on the cell doors, ordering them to shut up; shortly afterwards, Odette's door was opened and she was taken away from the hall and Peter, to the women's section. Now the real separation, and the real imprisonment, was beginning.

Odette entered cell No 108 in the women's section. It was a small, bare cell, measuring twelve feet by eight feet and containing a bed and a chair. Set high in the outside wall was a small window, fitted with frosted glass and hermetically sealed. A prison official followed Odette into the cell, made her strip and examined her. Then Odette was handed a blanket and a sheet for her bed and told to get dressed again. She was led from cell No 108 and taken to an interview room, where once again she saw Sergeant Bleicher.

Bleicher told her briefly that he and the SD knew all about her: they knew her real identity; they knew she was an agent for 'The Organization' in London. From now on it would be useless for her to lie. He dismissed her and she went back to her cell. So they knew her real identity: as Odette Sansom, she wondered, or as Odette Churchill, wife of Peter and relative to Winston? She would have plenty of time to ponder that in the weeks ahead.

Locked into her cell, denied exercise, books or any privileges at all, Odette struggled to cope with isolation and fear. A few days went by with a terrible sameness: hours stretching out with no interruption and nothing to look forward to, so that Odette could hear the blood rushing in her head as she tried to live through this minute, then the next, then the next. From the passage outside and from unseen cells came a continual background noise of moans, footsteps and cries; sometimes a prisoner would begin screaming and battering at her door, on and on until other prisoners screamed for her to shut up and the warders came, when the sounds of blows and shouts would rise over the screams. A few times a day she would hear the clanking of the food trolley as it came along the passage, and the hatch in her cell door would be opened, her dish taken out and then replaced: in the morning there was acorn coffee; later came soup or bread, with sometimes a little gristly meat. The food was bad and meagre: already Odette was weak with hunger.

On her second day, she had heard knockings in the pipes and had found that if she dragged her chair to a certain point and stood on it, she could hear the voice of her downstairs neighbour coming through the air vent. Occasionally she and the woman, Michele, could talk to one another through the vent, but they could not risk it often, nor for long.

On the fourth day there, 11 May, Odette was again taken to an interview with Bleicher. He offered her freedom in exchange for her co-operation; she refused. Again she was shut into her cell, and more days went by, and more, and more. And all the time she knew that one day the door would open and she would be taken not to Bleicher but to the SD, and that there her serious interrogation would begin.

Odette had already lost track of time when, on 25 May, the warder banged on her door and told her to get ready for an interview at the Avenue Foch. She tried to prepare herself as she was marched out of her cell, to the yard and into a police van. She was driven through streets she couldn't see to No 84 Avenue Foch, the SD headquarters. She entered and was locked into a small room. Time passed, and to her astonishment she was brought a big plate of meat and potatoes. She ate some of it; soon afterwards she was taken to see an officer. Sleepy from the food, she gathered her wits about her, but the interrogation was not particularly tough. It lasted two hours, she repeated the story she had prepared; at the end of two hours she was shown out and taken back to Fresnes.

But it was only a softening-up tactic. The next day, the warder again shouted to her to get ready for a trip to Avenue Foch, and again she made the blind journey through Paris, locked into the van. This time when she went into the building there was scarcely any delay: she was led straight up to the third floor and the interrogation rooms. She was shown into a room where yesterday's officer awaited her, and without ceremony the questions began.

The SD knew that Odette could lead them to *Arnaud* and to *Roger* (Cammaerts); they also knew that just before her arrest she had received the plan of Marseille Vieux Port. The officer began putting three questions to her over and over again: 'Where is *Arnaud*?', 'Where is *Roger*?', 'Where is the plan of the port?'

Odette knew that she must decide on her answer at once, and that she must stick to it. She must not be drawn in to discussing their questions. To each one, she said flatly: 'I have nothing to say.'

In the long weeks of solitary confinement, she had had plenty of time to dwell on this moment. She knew that she was likely to be tortured; nevertheless she had decided not to speak. It was not a matter open to question: she didn't hope that she would not speak; she *knew* she would not. But that certainty was a bleak one, for she had no way of knowing how to help herself when the time came, and she could not prepare herself for what she knew would be terrible pain.

'I knew I would not speak. Therefore I had no choice. I knew if they wanted to, the only thing was to kill me because I knew I wasn't going to speak. No, I didn't have confidence that I would survive it. I didn't have confidence in anything at all. I only had hope.'

When the officer realized that she would not be broken down verbally, he called in a good-looking young man of about thirty. This young man, he told her, would burn her back with a red hot iron to persuade her to speak. He asked her the questions once more, giving her a chance to answer, and when she didn't, the young man pulled back her blouse and pressed the hot iron against the top of her spine. It burned into her flesh, leaving her faint with pain.

When the young man stepped back, the officer offered her a cigarette and invited her to speak. She refused. He had obviously been prepared for this, for he told her to take off her shoes and stockings. The young man knelt down beside her and began, with a pair of pliers, to pull out her toe-nails one by one.

> You have to find a way. You have to learn. No. I went from one moment to the other. I thought well, there must be a physical point when the body must give up and so it's not in my hands. I will support as much as I can and perhaps they will win and that will be the end of my physical life but they will not – they will not win the rest. So it was a question of battling to have the strength to accept death.

After each toe-nail came out, the officer repeated the same three questions about *Arnaud*, *Roger* and the Vieux Port. But Odette also repeated the same answer, 'I have nothing to say, I have nothing to say.' She looked down at the young man operating on her feet; she registered that he was poised and educated, and she heard herself say to him: 'Do you like what you are doing? You are not doing it for any other reason.'

When they had finished torturing her feet and she still had not spoken, Odette felt a rush of euphoria. She had resisted, and she had survived. She was sick and dizzy with pain but she had come through. She fought the feeling down, knowing how dangerous it was; at any moment they might begin again.

But they didn't: the young man gathered his tools and left and the officer told her that she was going back to Fresnes. She could not walk save on her heels; carrying her shoes she staggered the distance to the van and back into her cell.

Alone again in her cell, the horror of what had happened permeated through her. She tore up a prison rag and bound her swollen, bleeding feet; then she lay on her bed, struggling not to sink under fear and all the conflicting emotions of rage and bitterness and grief.

> A person is made of so many facets, you don't even

know yourself. You discover yourself as you go along. You go through so many emotions. First you have anger of course – how can people do that to you? Then you want revenge – you'd like to do it to them. Then you go through all that and you realize there is *no* point in feeling that way. You have to find a way of living with yourself. And the only way to live with yourself is to have some kind of inner peace about it.

But Odette's quest for inner peace was hampered by a continuing fear: for that was not the last of her trips to the Avenue Foch. About one week later, she was taken there again. Weakened by torture, still in severe pain and unable to walk properly, she dreaded having to withstand another physical attack. But this was a different occasion: she was shown into a room full of German officers in impressive uniforms. They spoke to one another in German for a while and then one of them turned to her and addressed her solemnly: he told her that she was being condemned to death. In fact, she was being condemned to death twice: once for being a British agent, and once for being a French resistante.

At that moment, she suddenly wanted to laugh. It seemed so grotesquely absurd, all these men in uniforms telling her that she was to die twice. But she noticed something else: she was being condemned to death as Mrs Churchill. Whatever happened to her, they had evidently believed her and Peter's story. When she got back to Fresnes, her cell had a cross painted on the door.

Condemned to death and continually in expectation of more torture, Odette had to live on as best she could. She remained in her single cell for weeks which turned into months; every so often in the early weeks she was called out and taken to the Avenue Foch for more interrogations. The calls could come at any hour of the day or night, and each time she left her cell she did not know what would happen or if she would ever return. Each time an interrogation passed without physical torture it was a relief, but she never knew if this time she might not be facing it once more – or perhaps not going to interrogation at all but to her execution.

It was a long waiting of not knowing when they were going to do it again. And you don't get used to the fact that the door is going to open any time of day or night and you may be going through it again. So you learn to prepare yourself for the ordeal; that is, you don't sleep at night. Because what they used to do, they used to wake you up in the middle of the night just like that and ask you questions before you had time to wake up. So I used not to sleep at night. I used to doze off if I could during the day for a little time.

So you know, it happens to you once and you have survived that once. . . . And then you think, ah but, the next time it might be different. So you prepare yourself for the next time that may come or not come – in my case it did come. And then you survive that and then you think, oh well, I don't know when the third time is going to come and you never know. Never, ever. So that you spend all of your time, as much as is possible, trying to be ready for it. I don't know how to explain it. You have your great moment of almost despair if one day you will not be prepared enough. At the same time you cannot live in despair permanently because it will kill you. So you have a little hope.

But hope was hard to come by, not just because of what the Germans had done to her but because of what Bleicher now told her. One day during these summer weeks, Bleicher came to see her and invited her to guess who had been in his flat the previous night and that morning. When Odette said she had no idea, Bleicher triumphantly told her that it was Bodington. He had stayed the night in his flat, Bleicher said, and had left this morning. He was probably back in London now, continuing his work.

This information shattered Odette. She tried to disbelieve it but she could not: it explained too many discrepancies; there was too much which fitted into place around it. And believing it, she felt her grip on life waver: up until now she had been sustained by the belief that even if she died, other F Section agents would go on to strengthen and arm the Resistance; she had been able to bear her isolation, fear and the prospect of her death because her silence allowed others to remain free. But now it appeared that F Section was rotting from within, and that the efforts and sacrifices of agents in the field might be wasted, worse – they might be twisted to help the Germans.

Odette had a storm of reactions. They overwhelmed her carefully nurtured defences and brought her to the edge of despair. Nearly fifty years on, the sense of betrayal still haunts her – together with the burden of the promise she has made, not to make that betrayal public.

The very first thing Odette said to me when we met was to do with this revelation: she told me that she had been given it during captivity, that she had lived with it, painfully, throughout the rest of the war. She also told me that when she returned to London and took her knowledge to the SOE authorities, they asked her to bury it. She had gone away to consider and she had agreed: the matter was past healing; exposure would mean terrible loss of prestige for the organization and distress for many people; so she had kept silent then and has maintained her silence ever since. But the knowledge had not gone away, nor lost its poison. She would not name the name to me, because she had promised, but she wanted me to understand, before we began talking, that the knowledge of this betrayal hung at the back of all her memories, and all her emotions.

I didn't know then as much as I do now about Déricourt and Bodington and what happened to F Section agents in 1943. But during this first and my subsequent conversations with Odette, I became aware that this betrayal, this hollowness at the heart of her experiences, continues to deny her peace. The fact of it comes up again and again in Odette's conversation; sometimes it seems to undermine everything she did and experienced during the war: 'It was a dirty job in a sense,' she said to me once. 'It was a very complicated job, very. I couldn't do it now, knowing what I know.'

It was a loss of faith and of innocence which many of the Prosper agents must also have been suffering at the same time, locked into different parts of Fresnes prison and different cells in the Avenue Foch.

So the summer of 1943 wore on, with Odette living a kind of nightmare solitary existence in her cell, fighting to come to terms with fear and betrayal. Bleicher had reappeared in Fresnes after her official sentencing to death: he had told her that he'd been unable to stop her torture, and had appeared to want some kind of absolution from her.

Odette, like all other prisoners, also found her way into the prison grapevine by tapping on walls and pipes to her neighbours, and by finding the occasional visiting priest or sympathetic guard who would take messages to other prisoners. News of the progress of the war filtered in; so did news of new arrests and new arrivals in Fresnes. Odette was aware that other F Section women had arrived, though she didn't know who they were.

In late summer, the interrogation sessions with Bleicher stopped. By now, Odette's health was suffering badly: she developed pleurisy and a gland on her neck swelled up to the size of an orange. And though a long time had passed since her last summons to the Avenue Foch, she still lived under sentence of death. It was possible that on any day they would fetch her to carry out the sentence. And Odette wanted to go on living. She had three daughters waiting for her in England; she had Peter Churchill locked up in another part of Fresnes; she had, as she put it, 'a little hope'. But she was adrift in a sea of helplessness. With no power left to determine whether she lived or died, she had to struggle to keep her identity from one day to the next.

> When you are condemned to death, you know very well that they are going to put an end to it because let's face it, they have the right to do so. So every day you prepare yourself for the ordeal.
>
> I'll show you a little sidelight: I had no stockings left at the end of this period, they had suffered a lot, so I decided that I would keep them and wear them as curlers – if you do that [twist] with a stocking, they used to roll up like a rubber ball. So I kept them and I used to put them on every evening religiously in case they would fetch me the next morning to put me to death. I wasn't going to be seen going to my death without my curls.
>
> And I couldn't put my shoes on because of what they had done to my feet so whenever I was on the move I would carry them. Again I would not have gone to my death without shoes no matter how painful it would have been to put them on.
>
> Silly little things to keep your pride and your personality.

By November 1943 Odette had become so ill that she was allowed out of solitary confinement. She was moved to a warmer cell with two cell-mates – a mother and daughter, in prison for the daughter's Resistance activities. It was difficult for Odette to adjust to company after her solitude, especially when the mother was released and a prostitute moved in to take her place. From then on there was a constant stream of new arrivals and departures in the cell and Odette fell sick again. She was allowed out of the cell and into the sewing-room for part of every day: the German authorities wanted to keep her alive a while longer.

There now came another trip to the Avenue Foch, and an interrogation all about Peter Churchill. Odette repeated her story that she was the main figure in the Resistance partnership; she was allowed back to Fresnes without being tortured. And she had one last meeting with Peter himself: she was sent one day in a convoy of prisoners to the Gestapo administrative headquarters at the Rue des Saussaies. In the bedraggled, malnourished crowd of prisoners, she was waiting to be fingerprinted and photographed when she saw Peter Churchill. They shuffled their way over to one another; talking was forbidden but a young woman whom Peter would later describe as slim and strikingly English-looking saw them looking at one another and understood. She moved to stand in front of them, shielding their faces from the nearby guard, and turned her back on them so they could speak together in private. It was Diana Rowden.

That was the last time Odette saw Peter in Fresnes. The long winter continued with its unending cycle of days, nights, bad food, sickness and the continuous struggle within Odette to find some kind of peace. For much of it she was too exhausted to think; she had become very ill again. In February 1944 – ten months after her arrest – she was given an illicit pencil by a fellow prisoner, and used it to write a note to Peter which she smuggled to him via a guard. But when news came back it was not a message from him: she heard he had been removed, taken away to Gestapo headquarters in Berlin.

In May 1944, a full year after she had come to Fresnes, it was Odette's turn to leave. Outside in the country, much had changed. Sabotage attacks were almost daily events; battles flared between *maquis* and the occupying forces, and resistants were preparing frantically and hopefully for D-Day. But for Odette and thousands of other prisoners, the surging up of Resistance brought only a change for the worse. In preparation for the invasion, the Germans were clearing many of their political prisoners out of French jails; they sent them into Germany and the concentration camps.

On 12 May, Odette was told that she was going to Germany. She was taken to the usual van, carrying her shoes because it was still too painful to put them on her feet, and was shut in to her tiny compartment. She heard other passengers through the partitions, and when the van arrived at 84 Avenue Foch they were all led into a room and locked in together. They looked at one another: there were eight of them, all women, and as they began to talk they realized that they were all agents. Yolande Beekman, Andrée Borrel, Madeleine Damerment, Vera Leigh, Eliane Plewman, Diana Rowden and Odette met face to face for the first time. The last woman was not an F agent, recruited from London, but she was from an F *réseau*: her name was Sonia Olschanesky and she had been recruited in France to work for the Prosper-linked *réseau* Juggler. For several months in 1943 she had worked closely with Juggler agents and Prosper resistants, and she had been arrested as part of the Prosper downfall. These eight women were now going to Germany together.

They talked, eagerly and yet cautiously, while they were left alone. Was it a good or bad sign that they were moving on? At this stage, no one knew about the mass killings taking place in the camps. It was feasible that they were going to labour camps, as men had been sent under 'STO'. But then, to be in Germany was to be farther away from the liberating Allies when they came. They exchanged questions and news, about people believed to be captured, about information gathered from the outside. Odette was horrified by the appearance of some of them: Diana Rowden looked grey and haggard, a different person from the woman Odette had seen in the Rue des Saussaies at the start of her captivity. But then, Odette wondered what she must look like to them, shoes in hand.

That evening, handcuffed in pairs and under heavy guard, the eight women were taken to the Gare de l'Est and put on a train for Germany.

It was the start of another period of transition for Odette. In Germany they were all taken to Karlsruhe prison and separated from one another. For the next eight weeks Odette was locked into a cell with three German women; the cell had a window overlooking an exercise yard and every so often Odette saw one or another of her fellow agents walking round the exercise yard on her own.

But after a while they vanished. Odette did not know where they had gone or why.

Odette was herself moved on in mid-July. It was a reminder of her journeying after her arrest, except that this time she was constantly in the company of others. First she travelled on a train packed with captive men to Frankfurt, and stayed six days there in a prison cell with two other women. Then she was moved to Halle and a communal attic cell crowded with women and filth. She stayed there just one night, suffocating with the smell and lack of air, and the next morning she and the other women were taken in a convoy to Fürstenberg station. From here, they walked the three miles – Odette carrying her shoes – to where Ravensbrück concentration camp was built high on a hill.

Ravensbrück was a collection of wooden huts, with its own industrial buildings and crematorium, enclosed by walls and electric fences on three sides, and falling away in a steep drop on the fourth. As Odette trooped in through its entrance with the others, she saw the armed guards and the neatly kept huts but only fleetingly: the crowd of women was ordered into a 'washroom' – a wooden hut with rows of showers, and there they were shut in and left for the night. The next morning, Odette heard the sound of the hooter at dawn, and the

established women prisoners assembling outside for '*Appel*' (roll-call).
But that was to be the extent of her participation in the everyday life
of the camp. Soon afterwards she was called out of the washroom
and taken to see the camp commandant, Fritz Sühren. He told her
that as Odette Churchill, related by marriage to the British Prime
Minister, she was to be locked in an underground punishment cell.
She was to have reduced punishment food rations and nothing else,
no privileges such as exercise or books. She was to go there straight
away.

Odette was led to the block known as the 'Bunker'. After going
through a short passage with rooms on either side of it, she was taken
through a barred gate, down a flight of stairs, along an artificially lit
corridor and into a cell. Apart from a plank to sleep on there was
nothing in it: no bed, no chair, no blankets, no light. And of course,
no window. She was shut into the darkness and left there.

For weeks, no one came near her. But long before any interruption,
time had already lost all the meaning left to it. Not knowing day from
night, she existed in a pit of nothing. Food in tiny 'punishment' rations
was put through a hatch in the door. Now and then she could hear
women being brought into the next door cell and horribly beaten.
But apart from that, nothing.

Physically, Odette was sinking but mentally she had already touched
bottom. At some point during the previous year she had crossed a
line after which she knew she would stay sane. It was not that it was
more of the same; it was that she was learning that there was always
something more to draw on inside her, however little.

> The first year I had to learn a lot of things. But the
> second year – I had to learn other things. Being left in
> darkness – I think it would have been a tall order for
> somebody else. But you see, what they did not know was
> that as a little girl I was blind for three and a half years.
> And therefore I just said to myself, well all right, I have
> been blind in the past. I'm not frightened of being in this
> darkness. My door used to open once a month and the camp
> commander would stand there and say, 'Have you anything
> to say?' And I couldn't see you know, I would be peering
> like this, and I would say, 'No', and the door would shut
> again. So I think for someone normal if you like, it would
> have been hard but it was more easy for me to accept that.
> So you see one thing helps another.
>   I had TB and I'd read a book written by a Belgian

doctor before the war – I don't know why I had read that book – which said the treatment for TB is all wrong; you should starve yourself and clean your body and all that sort of thing. And I thought well, I am starving all right! I've got nothing to do – there's not even a bed but a plank and I can stretch myself on it all day long, twenty-four hours a day and not move. And that's what I did, and by the time I came back there was a scar on my lungs but no active TB.

You learn. You learn. You can be very – I don't know if you can call it pride or vanity or whatever but in a sense I never felt wasted. I thought maybe I was taking the place of someone else who was doing the work much better than I could have done. Also I felt it almost a privilege to share the suffering of the people around me.

I consider I was very fortunate to be in solitary: it gave me time to learn to suffer and you have to learn to hold yourself up. You don't get there in one day: you have to work at it.

And she thought about her children.

I thought about them all the time. All the time. It made me stronger. It's a mistake when people say that in the camp I was courageous. It wasn't then that I was. It was the day I left this country. I left it with a broken heart. And I knew that nothing else that happened to me would ever be that painful, and it never was. Physically yes, but inside me, never. Never. It was the greatest sacrifice of all; the rest was nothing compared to it. And it gave me the strength . . . to battle on, in more than one way because when I was terribly ill – and I was terribly ill in prison – maybe it would have been easy to let go, but I could never let go until it was not my choice. It definitely helped me to fight on. I used to think, if I have to stay in this cell ten years just to earn one day of freedom, I'll battle on.

It was in the middle of August, when she had been in darkness for several weeks, that Odette became seriously ill again. It was no accident that sickness struck now – it was brought on by the fact that the heating in her cell was turned up sickeningly high. This was part of her 'punishment' – the Bunker had special facilities for artificially heating and chilling its cells and this was retaliation on Odette for the fact that on 15 August the Allies had successfully landed on the south coast of France, in the very area where Odette and Peter used to work. The heating was left to mount for a week and no food was brought in at all. Odette became very ill with dysentery, scurvy and her old chest trouble. At the end of a week, the heating was turned off and her punishment rations resumed but Odette continued to grow sicker and sicker.

Odette did not know that it was the end of September, and that almost all of France was liberated, when the door opened one day, or night, and she was told to come to the hospital block. She could hardly stand; she had to be half-carried out of her cell and up into the open. She discovered that it was day – the light blinded her and the fresh air made her retch. In the hospital block she was examined; the doctor gave her treatment for scurvy, and some eyedrops, and she was sent back to her underground cell again. But while she had been in the hospital block, a nurse had whispered to her the news of the liberation.

And on the way back to her cell, she saw something which seemed to her a symbol of hope: it was a leaf, still green, lying on the ground. But there were no trees in Ravensbrück; this leaf must have drifted in from outside. Odette bent down and picked it up, smuggling it back into her cell. For the rest of her captivity she was to keep it by her, touching it to remind herself of the free world now coming closer, carrying it with her when she changed cells.

For Sühren had decided to keep his important prisoner alive. Weeks more passed – another timeless stretch in the darkness – and at the end of October, Odette was taken out of her pit and through the searing light of outdoors to a new cell on ground level.

And there the solitary confinement continued. For the next six months Odette lived alone in this cell. She had light from the window and she was given exercise – officially a few minutes' walk each day round the small Bunker yard, though days often went by without it. She had her leaf to give her hope and she needed it to bear what was happening; for although she was strictly segregated from the rest of the prisoners, she could still hear from her cell some of what went on.

What went on was terrible, and grew daily more so. Until now, Odette's lot had been one of the hardest of the captive women. From now until she was released, in May 1945, she was relatively fortunate. She was not to suffer the mass degradations, nor to die in the atrocities; but she had to live with them.

TWENTY-TWO

Captivity

Ravensbrück was built on an area of high marshy ground, about fifty miles north-east of Berlin. It was near a lake and in the summer the air was sultry and hot. At night, though, a cold mist rose from the water-logged soil and covered the camp.

Every morning at 4.30 a.m. a hooter sounded throughout the camp and at 5 a.m. women stumbled out of the rows of wooden huts for '*Appel*' or roll-call. The *Appel* was not just a method of checking on their presence; it was a way of reinforcing discipline and demonstrating the prisoners' subjugation. The women stood in lines five deep, each with her arms stretched out on to the shoulders of the woman in front. They remained there long after the needs of roll-call had been met; unprotected from the freezing air by their thin camp issued clothes, they had to keep standing and motionless for two hours.

When the hours were up they would be dispatched to their day's work, or sent back to their wooden huts.

These huts were the prisoners' accommodation. Within Ravensbrück's perimeter wall and electric fence they stood in rows, separated by squares of grass and flower beds. A Third Reich flag fluttered from a flagpole. At the back of the camp was an industrial compound and beyond that lay an auxiliary camp for men; at the front, pressed up against the wall and overlooked by guards, were a kitchen block and a crematorium.

When women first arrived at Ravensbrück, they were sent to the shower hut, stripped and bathed in the communal showers. Their clothes were taken away and they lined up naked to be examined by SS doctors and dentists. Most of them were already weak and undernourished from their time in prison, but the doctors were less interested in general health than in certain catching complaints – like head lice, which meant immediate head shaving. Once the long process of examination was over, the women were given camp clothes, tattered rags of various origins (some had been seized from Jewish shops; some had belonged to former, dead prisoners), and camp shoes: wooden shoes which were kept on with a strap around the heel. They were then usually put into a hut and kept shut up there for several weeks, to give any infectious diseases time to show themselves.

The conditions were cramped – there were not enough bunks to go round; there was often scarcely enough floor to hold everyone. Rations were very meagre – mostly bread and soup – and by the time the quarantine was over, almost all the women were in much worse health than when they had arrived. They were then put into huts according to nationality and were assigned work. They laboured in the hospital and the crematorium; they worked in the industrial compound making machine parts; they dug vegetables, kept the camp grounds, worked in the houses of the camp staff, knitted clothes for the German army and civilians.

From time to time, groups of women were sent off on working parties. They would leave Ravensbrück to work in labour camps elsewhere in Germany, doing intensive work in factories or on roads and communications, sometimes for months at a time. Conditions encountered by working parties were harsh – they worked usually twelve hours a day – but sometimes the food was better than in Ravensbrück. When the project was completed or the work party members were worn out by the labour, they would come back to Ravensbrück.

This round of work and deprivation would have been bad enough in clean conditions, and under a humane administration. But though Ravensbrück camp looked neat and tidy from the outside, the prisoners lived in conditions of growing squalor and the regime was brutal. In September 1944, prisoners received food only once a day, in the evening. They could expect half a loaf of bread and a bowl of thin soup; as extras, distributed throughout the week, they might get a single piece of sausage, two tablespoonfuls of jam, two tablespoonfuls of sugar and a small piece of margarine. Bronchitis, incipient TB and dysentery were widespread. Prisoners had to have a temperature of 102°C before they were admitted into the '*Révier*' or hospital block and three days off work was the maximum allowed. Prisoners who worsened, as many did in the overcrowded hospital, were usually removed and put in 'the tent', a half-finished building covered with tarpaulin; here they were left to die. The hospital block was run by

SS doctors and nurses and the menial tasks were carried out by prisoners; equipment such as thermometers, and drugs, were in extremely short supply and were rarely used to relieve prisoners' suffering. Instead SS doctors at the camp carried out medical experiments on the inmates – they took muscles from the legs of some women to see what effect it would have on them; they sterilized others.

Sickness was endemic in Ravensbrück. So was brutal discipline. In the 'Bunker' where Odette was held were other underground punishment cells which could be heated or chilled artificially. Women were locked into these cells for all kinds of offences, trivial and major: from smoking to insubordination to sabotage. In the 'Bunker' also, women were beaten for such offences. The beatings were extreme; up to seventy-five strokes could be given and were. Women would emerge from these beatings bleeding and unable to stand; such punishments were often staggered with intervals of several days in between, and sometimes women would kill themselves rather than face the next time.

Under these conditions, thousands of women were held for months, some for years. Inside the huts, lined with tiers of bunks, women formed little groups of friends for comfort and solidarity. One such group contained three F agents: Violette Szabo, Denise Bloch and Lilian Rolfe. And among the mass of prisoners there were other agents too: Cecily Lefort, Yvonne Rudellat, Yvonne Baseden, and Didi Nearne.

From the moment she found herself in the Rue des Saussaies under interrogation, Didi Nearne had refused to give up hope. She had entered Fresnes that evening under the name of Jacqueline du Tertre, her real identity as a British agent still undetected, and throughout her time in Fresnes, in Ravensbrück and on working parties she sustained herself by a determination not to give in.

Before she even reached Ravensbrück, she had tried to escape. Unlike Odette, she was not in solitary confinement in Fresnes; she shared her captivity with other women and it was not long before they were put on a convoy for Germany. They were crammed into overcrowded carriages for the journey, with stops at different points along the line. They left Paris in the morning, and at 4 p.m. that afternoon they stopped in Alsace-Lorraine to change trains. The women were led out under guard.

Didi longed to escape; she had thought continually about the possible ways of doing it, and now, as she looked out of the stationary train and saw open fields, fringed with woodland, she realized that this was a chance which might not come again. The distance across the open field was dangerous, but if she could reach the trees beyond she might be able to hide.

She said to the woman beside her, 'I'm escaping.'

'Oh, don't do that!' her companion said. 'You'll be shot.'

But Didi felt under a compulsion to try; she could not let the chance slip away.

'I am going,' she said, and as her group of women filed out of the door, at the orders of the German officer, she broke away from the line and ran towards the trees. She heard a scream from behind her and then a German soldier's voice shouting at her to stop or he'd shoot. She looked round and saw the soldier aiming straight at her; she had no chance of getting away. She stood still and let herself be seized and put back in line, but while the officers shouted at her and threatened her, her mind still ran with the possibilities of escape.

She was loaded on to the next train, along with all the others, and while the carriage swung and rattled along the tracks she held on to the hope of another chance. One would surely come, and the next time she might succeed. There would be other stops; now and then Red Cross parties were permitted to enter the carriages and offer medicines and first aid to the prisoners . . . .

It was the voice of a German officer which stopped these thoughts. He was moving along the train making an announcement. 'Someone has tried to escape,' Didi heard. 'If that person tries it again not only will she be shot but the whole convoy will be shot with her.'

Didi felt the other women look at one another and at her. Now she could not go.

It was bitter for Didi to feel so helpless. The journey wore on and there was another stop, for Red Cross representatives to come on board. They came in uniform, holding special passes, and Didi saw something amazing taking place beside her. The woman next to her was handed a parcel by a member of the Red Cross; she opened it and inside was a nurse's uniform and a pass. Didi watched incredulously as the woman struggled quickly into the uniform, smoothed down her hair and fell in behind real nurses about to leave. With them, she passed by the guard at the door, holding up her pass, and vanished into the safety of the Red Cross party.

Didi watched with a mixture of disbelief, joy and hopelessness.

'I saw that and couldn't believe it. And I wanted so much to escape.'

So miracles did happen. And much later Didi was to learn that her own attempt to escape had not been fruitless: while the guards' attention was turned to her in the fields of Alsace-Lorraine, two other women had slipped out of the line and dropped into the river. By the time their absence was noticed, they could not be found.

It was night when the convoy arrived at Ravensbrück. In darkness they were led into the camp, put through a roll-call and sent into the shower hut to bathe. The next morning as they left the hut they saw the camp in daylight, and at the sight of the tall chimney by the main entrance Didi heard a horrified whisper go round: 'the crematorium, the crematorium.' They were taken past it to the '*Rêvier*', where they now lined up for the long numbing periods of medical inspection, examination and clothes issue. In inexorable stages, they were embarking on the life of the camp.

Once examinations and confinement were over, Didi was put in a hut with French women. There were hundreds of them in the camp as far as she could see, probably more, among a mass of women of other nationalities including Russians, Poles, Swedes and German women convicted of crimes. It was disorienting to be among so many people, and the filthy conditions and poor food quickly sapped the newcomers' strength. They were put to work immediately; Didi was doing hard labour in the grounds, growing vegetables, and within a few weeks she noticed that she and others who had arrived with her were living and working in a daze. And they were debilitated psychologically as well as physically, by the brutality they encountered. They saw and heard about savage punishments: a *maquisarde* who worked with Didi on the vegetables stole a potato and was locked underground in the 'Bunker' with no food. There was a camp warder who walked round with a whip, whipping exhausted prisoners where they had fallen to force them back on their feet. One day Didi passed a woman she didn't know stretched out naked on the freezing ground in punishment for some unknown misdemeanour.

> 'The conditions were very bad. We had clear soup, it was like water, with a piece of dry bread. For soap we had a piece of stone. And we were all dazed, like drugged. It was bitter cold and we had to work and as I was walking up and down the camp I met Violette Szabo and another girl, called Denise. "Oh!" she said. "You too!" '

Didi warned Violette that she was passing herself off as French. Violette asked her what the Gestapo had done to her, and when Didi told her about the '*baignoire*' in the Rue des Saussaies, she was horrified. She told Didi that neither she nor Lilian nor Denise had been tortured, and she advised Didi to change her story and admit her British nationality.

'She said, "You should have said you were English. English girls are better treated than the French," but I said, "No, I'm sticking to my story." '

Didi could see that Violette was in good spirits. Denise looked weak and ill but Violette was convinced that they would be rescued eventually. Didi admired her courage but she was wary of being seen with the British women; her alias of Jacqueline du Tertre was important to her as a way of protecting her SOE knowledge, and it was as Jacqueline that her fellow prisoners knew her.

Didi's main friend in the camp was a young French resistante, Geneviève Mathieu. She slept in the bunk above Didi and had a strong, stubborn personality. She was always looking for little ways to thwart the camp rules without being caught, collecting forbidden things like pencils and scraps of material, and where Didi was a natural loner she was a mixer and entertainer. Younger than most of the women around them, they talked together a lot, but like everyone else Geneviève knew Didi only as Jacqueline.

In the autumn and winter of 1944, the Third Reich was under seige. The Allies had reached the Rhine, and though the German army held them there, the effort was fast draining the last of the nation's resources. Germany could no longer import requisitioned goods and labour from its neighbouring countries; it was thrown back inside its national boundaries, and here it was reeling under the Allied 'carpet bombing' raids which wreaked terrible devastation on towns and cities as well as on military targets. Germany now relied increasingly on the slave labour of its prisoners to keep up the production it needed. Concentration camp prisoners were made to work until they dropped; men and women who had the remnants of strength left in them were sent on work parties to build roads and manufacture machines and produce food and clothing for the German army.

Didi and Geneviève, Violette and Denise and Lilian were among the women sent from Ravensbrück to nearby Torgau, a camp where they farmed vegetables, dug roads and worked in machine factories.

They did not stay in Torgau all the time; Didi and Geneviève were moved from there to a nearby camp at Abteroda; periodically they went back to Ravensbrück. In the middle of winter they went on another working party to Markleburg, near Leipzig.

Didi's memory of these months is confused – confusion, and a loss of perspective, was something which afflicted most prisoners in these camps. The regime was so harsh, and the realities of exhaustion and hunger, sickness and fear, so relentless, that the passage of time was easily lost among them.

But Didi still nursed a fierce desire to escape. One day in Torgau she saw Violette Szabo again and chanced a few words with her.

'I said, "Look, I'm dying to escape; I've got to escape." She said, "So do I, and the other two, we want to escape." '

And Violette, it turned out, had the beginnings of a plan. Torgau was less strongly guarded than Ravensbrück; the washroom was a hut inside a barricade, and beyond the barricade there was a wall with a door in it. Beyond the wall was an open field. If they could get hold of the key, they might be able to plan an escape.

For the first time in months, Didi had something to hope for. She wanted to go at once, but Violette said no, she couldn't get the key so quickly. Ten days later, Violette came to Didi in the hut and said that she had the key. But before they could put their plan into action, someone talked. Next time Didi saw Violette, she heard that Violette had had to throw the key into a gutter in order to clear herself. And in any case, the women were being separated: the English women were leaving the camp and soon Didi was on the move too, in a group of women bound for the factories at Abteroda.

In the factories, rumours reached Didi that the English women had escaped and been shot. She had no way of knowing if it were true nor if the women were Violette, Denise and Lilian. But she had to live with the fact that she had once more lost the opportunity to escape.

Didi was now in a working party being forced to make parts for German aeroplanes; but although she could not escape, she could rebel. Her stubborn streak sustained her when she might have despaired: she refused to work the machines. As an overt rebellion it was hopeless: the guards dragged her off to have her head shaved as a punishment and then took her back to the machines at gunpoint. If she didn't start work in twenty minutes, they told her, she would be shot. So she started work, going as slowly as possible and contriving to break parts here and there. When challenged, she defended herself by saying she wasn't used to the work: Jacqueline du Tertre emerged again, the clumsy, gauche young girl from the South of France who could not be held responsible for her actions.

As a strike it had limited success: the guards threatened to lock her in a tower if she continued, and forbade the other women to talk to her. She had to get on with the work, as slowly as she dared. But it had raised her morale; it had also roused the suspicions of the camp's commandant. She put Didi through another interrogation about her nationality, saying that she had heard Didi was English. Speaking in English to display her (completely unaffected) French accent, Didi replied that she had never said she *was* English, only that she *spoke* English. She spoke quite rudely; it cheered her and she felt that it unnerved her captors.

But meanwhile, Didi's health was worsening. The winter brought her chest pains and she felt increasingly weak and tired. She and the other women worked crushingly long hours, often under bombardment from Allied planes. One day as they were working in the factory, an air raid began and they all had to leave their machines and take cover. Didi was so exhausted that despite the noise of the planes and the bombs falling, and the panic around her, she fell asleep. Geneviève was with her; she watched Didi sleeping and when the raid was over, wakened her. Didi was confused and didn't know where she was: for a moment she had forgotten all about the concentration camp and captivity.

'Where am I?' she asked Geneviève. 'Am I in England?'

For Geneviève it was one of the worst moments of all her time in the camps. Didi had no idea where she was and her face, though bewildered, was momentarily unhaunted. Geneviève had to watch understanding come back into it as she told Didi, as gently as possible, that no, she was not in England nor at home in France but in a German concentration camp.

Didi was beginning to feel her strength ebb away. And in midwinter they were on the move again, back to Ravensbrück and then on to another working party at Markleberg, near Leipzig.

In the Markleberg camp the women were plunged into another regime of working in factories. By now the food was a mere bowl of thin soup a day with a scrap of bread; in Markleberg as in Ravensbrück and other camps, disease – especially dysentery – swept through the ranks of the prisoners. Didi fought not to give in to it: unable to martial her physical strength, she held on to her will-power.

'The will to live. Will-power. That's the most important. You should not let yourself go. It seemed that the end would never come but I have always believed in destiny and I had a hope. If you are a person who is drowning, you put all your efforts into trying to swim.'

It was Didi's good fortune not to be in Ravensbrück during the first few months of 1945. Life there had become increasingly hellish: more and more women were arriving there so that the camp was full to bursting; dysentery raged out of control, so that by February hundreds of women died of it daily. And those who did not fall ill with dysentery were in danger of another kind of death – mass killings were taking place regularly in the death camps.

The Ravensbrück death camp, known officially as the 'youth camp' had been started in 1944. It was a mile away from the main camp at Ravensbrück and it was described to the women in Ravensbrück as a superior kind of camp where conditions were much better. Prisoners could volunteer to go there if they wished, and many prisoners did. It was only gradually, as some of the Ravensbrück prisoner-nurses and workers accompanied convoys to the camp and returned, that the truth began to filter back. Conditions in the so-called youth camp were very bad – rations were even more meagre than those in Ravensbrück; the lavatories were an open trench; prisoners stood for five or seven hours every day for roll-call. And about 100 or 150 were taken away from the main part of the camp every day and didn't return. Rumours began to circulate Ravensbrück that the youth camp was really an extermination camp.

But these rumours, or at least any proof of them, came too late for many of the women. In any case, when the Germans were short of volunteers for the youth camp they simply rounded up the weaker prisoners and took them there. Cecily Lefort was one of them. After a few days in the bewildered, panic-stricken atmosphere of the youth camp she was put into a party of other women and taken to the gas chambers.

At the same time, mass executions began in Ravensbrück itself. In early spring 1945, with the Allies breaking through on the Rhine and defeat for the Third Reich just weeks away, the German authorities began a systematic process of killing prisoners who might bear witness to the concentration camp atrocities. They also killed prisoners who were considered 'important' or dangerous to the German state. From her ground-level cell opposite the crematorium, Odette heard groups of women being herded alive and screaming into the building. Thick smoke now poured from the chimney for hours at a time; and there were spates of gunfire from different directions, signs that another batch of women had been executed by shooting.

Among the first to die in this wave of killings were Violette Szabo, Denise Bloch and Lilian Rolfe. Despite Didi's hopes, these three friends had not escaped from Torgau. Instead they had been sent on another gruelling working party until February, when they returned to Ravensbrück. They were there only a few days, very much weakened now, so that ideas of escape were beyond them. Violette had all along believed that their British nationality protected them, but as Didi put it, 'The Germans feared so much the English and hated them so much more.' Staring defeat in the face, the Berlin

High Command decided to dispose of most of the British agents still in their camps. Execution orders were sent from Berlin to several of the men's camps, naming F and RF agents; an order was also sent to Ravensbrück for the immediate execution of Violette, Denise and Lilian.

When the guards came to fetch them Denise was so ill that Violette and Lilian had to hold her up. They were taken past Odette's cell to a small courtyard and shot in the back of the neck.

The death toll at Ravensbrück was mounting every day, and last humiliations and terrors were inflicted on many Ravensbrück prisoners before they died. A grotesque fitness parade now took place every few days in the camp, with women being called out into the open and made to stand for a physical inspection by Dr Winkelmann, a camp doctor, and a man named Pflumm. The women were made to strip to the waist and run past the men: they were all emaciated, and all sick, but from them the men would pick out the oldest and weakest and send them on to a convoy. They would be taken straight to the gas chambers. As the women realized the purpose of the parades they frantically rubbed mud on to their heads to disguise grey hairs and tried to force back their thin shoulders. But each time more women were taken to their deaths.

Women were also taken out of Ravensbrück and sent to other camps, moved on by the immutable logic of the concentration camp system which was now processing prisoners as if they were raw material in some vast factory complex. Among the women who left Ravensbrück in February was Yvonne Rudellat. She had passed as a Frenchwoman in the camp; her time in Blois hospital just after her arrest, had kept her away from the other Prosper agents, and had made it possible for her to erect a cover story. With so many key Prosper agents in the Avenue Foch, the SD had been disinclined to make a great fuss over the middle-aged Frenchwoman helper. She had eventually been sent to Ravensbrück as 'Madame Gauthier' and, like Didi, she had kept up this cover.

Now she was part of a convoy of prisoners on the move between camps: she arrived in Belsen at the end of February. Belsen was a huge camp holding tens of thousands of prisoners; Yvonne Rudellat joined them. She had kept herself in reasonably good spirits so far, but disease in Belsen was even more widespread than in Ravensbrück and she soon fell ill with both dysentery and typhus.

In April, as Russian troops advanced on Berlin, the concentration camps entered the last phase of their existence. In some concentration camps, guards were ordered to turn their guns on prisoners, to speed up the rate of executions; mass evacuations were also underway, with thousands of the surviving prisoners being moved from one camp to another, as camp commandants tried to obtain orders from Berlin. Huge piles of carefully maintained camp records were burned as staff left. Prisoners who lived through those last few weeks describe scenes of unbelievable panic and brutality.

As news reached Ravensbrück that the Russians were approaching from one side and the Americans from another, the prisoners saw barrels of oil being brought into the camp. Many of the women, all illusions about the regime now gone, believed that they would be shot or burned to death within the sound of the Allies' guns. But the Red Cross was at the gates before the Allies: rescue parties from various nations came and took away their own nationals, and word came that the Swedish Red Cross was about to remove British prisoners.

Yvonne Baseden, now very seriously sick with TB, was put on to this Red Cross convoy by another British woman in the camp, a former escape-line organizer Mary Lindell. Yvonne was driven away from Ravensbrück, to safety.

This left just one F Section woman in Ravensbrück: Odette, still in solitary confinement.

And now Odette's 'Churchillian' bluff paid off. One day at the very end of April, the commandant of Ravensbrück, Fritz Sühren, came into her cell and told her to get ready to move. Believing that her execution was at last here, Odette followed him out of her cell, but instead of leading her to a courtyard or to the crematorium, he took her to his car. The camp was in a state of hysteria and uproar all around them as they drove out of the gates.

There followed a series of journeys around neighbouring camps, a nightmare journey during which Odette had no idea where they were going or why. They passed columns of prisoners marching on the roads; they were stuck in convoys of trucks and lorries full of dying prisoners and guards. German troops in retreat passed them.

Sühren drove Odette into various camps and compounds, shutting her in a cell or room for a night and then, after he had done whatever he had come for, moving her on again. After several days, Sühren drove not to a new camp but into a forest. Odette looked at the trees and wondered if this were finally the moment; Sühren had a gun – had she been driven into the woods to be shot?

But Sühren explained that the American troops were stationed here. He was not going to shoot her; he was going to hand her over to them. For Sühren had decided to cash in his insurance policy: as commandant of Ravensbrück he would inevitably be tried by the Allies. He had spent the last few days trying to put his affairs in such order as he could, destroying the worst of the evidence against him. But there would be plenty of witnesses to the Ravensbrück regime. He hoped to gain some credibility by personally safeguarding a member of Winston Churchill's family.

They stopped the car some distance from the Americans and walked to the first group of them. Approaching an officer, Sühren said to him briefly and formally that the woman with him was Mrs Churchill, a relation of the British Prime Minister. She had been a prisoner of his and now he was releasing her to the American troops.

The American officer took Sühren's gun and Odette stumbled away. She still had her leaf with her: she had brought it on all the recent journeys, believing that she might be taking it to her death. It was curling round the edges now and she held it gently; it was a symbol of everything she had survived and everything she had hoped for throughout the last two years.

Odette was free, but what of the women she had last seen in Karlsruhe prison, the previous July? What had happened to Yolande Beekman, Andrée Borrel, Eliane Plewman, Diana Rowden, Vera Leigh, Madeleine Damerment and Sonia Olschanesky? And what of Noor Inayat, who – unknown to the others – had been in chains in the nearby prison of Pforzheim when they arrived?

They were all dead.

The first to die were Andrée Borrel, Vera Leigh, Diana Rowden and Sonia Olschanesky. They had been in Karlsruhe just two months when, early in the morning of 6 July, prison staff woke them in their cells and told them to prepare for a journey. They were put into a van, with Gestapo guards, and were driven west, back into Alsace, the borderlands of France. The van entered the gates of Natzweiler concentration camp and set them down. They were marched across the camp, past a team of men laying a pipeline, and were shut into separate cells. Natzweiler was a men's camp; among the prisoners held there were Brian Stonehouse and Albert Guérisse, *Pat*. They both saw the women arrive and, like everyone else, wondered who they were and why they had been brought there. By evening it was rumoured among the prisoners that the women were English and had come from Fresnes, and some of the men had managed to talk to them briefly through their cell windows. But that night the men were ordered to their huts earlier than usual and were told to keep doors shut and curtains drawn.

At about 10 p.m., two of the camp's officers went to the cells and took out the women one by one, walking them to the crematorium. They were told that they were going to receive innoculations against typhus and they were taken, again one by one, into a small room and each was injected in the arm. At least one of them argued and struggled against being injected, suspicious and afraid. The injection was of the poison phenol, and the women died within a few minutes, their heart muscles and lungs paralysed. Their bodies were put into the ovens and burned.

The truth about their deaths was not discovered until after the war, when Vera Atkins went to France and Germany to trace what had happened to the agents who had not returned from captivity. At that time, Sonia Olschanesky's identity wasn't known and there seemed no very clear reason why Andrée, Diana and Vera should have been taken to their deaths first, in the company of an unknown woman. Then, during Elizabeth Nicholas's research into her book,[1] the unknown woman emerged as Sonia Olschanesky, a member of the Jean Worms and Jacques Weil Juggler *réseau*, and linked through this to Prosper.

Of the eight women who had travelled to Karlsruhe together, these four were directly linked to the Prosper *réseau* and its downfall. Andrée, Sonia and Vera had all worked in Prosper or with Prosper contacts in and around Paris; they had all been known to the SD through Déricourt's agency. Diana Rowden too had been under SD surveillance courtesy of Déricourt. In the eyes of the SD (and of Berlin, which had taken such interest in the Prosper drama) these four women were players in the same game. And so they were killed together, tangled in the same net until the very end.

Yolande Beekman, Madeleine Damerment, Noor Inayat and Eliane Plewman were killed in September. Noor Inayat was taken out of Pforzheim on 11 September, and was put into nearby Karlsruhe with the other three. They were told to be ready to leave the prison the next morning and they were duly driven to the station and put on to a train. They travelled under guard but they were allowed to talk to one another during the long journey; the German officer with them thought they seemed in good spirits. The train stopped in a station late at night and they were walked in the darkness to a new camp: Dachau. For the rest of the night they were locked into separate cells and early in the morning they were taken out in a group and led into a yard. They were told to kneel down; they knelt in pairs, holding hands and were shot one by one in the back of the neck.

But what of Didi? She had survived the ordeals of Fresnes, Ravensbrück and various working parties and in April 1945 she was in

[1] *Death Be Not Proud*, Elizabeth Nicholas, Cresset Press, 1958

Markleberg when the order came to move. The camp commandant announced to the prisoners that they would be leaving Markleberg and travelling through the night to another place eighty kilometres away. Panic, excitement and fear prevailed: the prisoners knew that the Allies had advanced so that they were near Leipzig, which was just seven kilometres away. The towns and roads around the camp were thick with people getting away, but it was in these last desperate stages of a camp's life that the prisoners were in greatest danger.

The women were assembled in a line and marched out of the camp under guard. They walked along the roads in the darkness, patrolled by armed guards who shouted orders and threats into the mêlée. Didi knew she would never get a better chance than this: at about 11 p.m. the party's route passed through a forest and Didi waited for a moment when there was no guard looking at her and ducked out of the procession. She ran into the trees, dodging around them and heading further into the forest, away from the road. She heard no cries or shots from behind her: so far so good.

She slowed down when she felt she was far enough away from the road, and hid behind a tree. She saw no pursuers: she moved on more slowly, pausing often to listen. After about ten minutes she heard a rustling noise; someone was walking on the fallen leaves. She shrank behind the nearest tree and peered round it into the darkness. Two figures were threading their way through the trees – they were not Germans but two more women from the working party, escaping like herself.

Didi joined the other two women: they were French women about her own age, named Renée and Yvette. They greeted one another quickly in whispers and Renée told Didi that they thought they had been missed: after she and Yvette had dropped out of the line and hidden behind a tree they had seen flashes of light as the guards shone their torches around. They had still been so close to the line that they could hear the footsteps passing on the road, an almost endless procession of them. But no one had come to find them and eventually the whole column had passed them by.

The three women walked through the woods and across fields, trying to head in the direction of Leipzig. Although it was April it was a freezing night and they were already weakened by their escape. Eventually they came to a deserted house; it had been bombed and there was a hole in it a few feet above ground level. Yvette clambered up first; she reached down to help up Renée. Renée was so small that it took both Yvette pulling and Didi pushing her from behind to get her up to the hole. Then Didi herself climbed in and they slept the rest of the night there. In the morning when light came they woke and looked around them: they were amazed to see the hole through which they had climbed – it was scarcely big enough to take a dog.

They hid out in the house most of that day, but by the evening they were faint with hunger. They went out to look for food and came to a farm. They dared not ask openly for food in case it had been requisitioned by Germans, so they crept towards the chicken coop, hoping to steal a bird. They were disturbed by a loud, angry barking – the farm dog had heard them. They abandoned the idea of food and ran away. They were on the edge of the town of Markleberg by now, and they decided to make for Leipzig. As they walked along the road, they turned a corner suddenly and saw a German patrol ahead. Renée whispered to leave it to her, as she spoke German. They were stopped and their papers demanded. In German Renée explained that they had no papers as they were *travailleurs libres*, French volunteers for work in Germany. They were on their way to a new working party. The Germans let them pass.

After that they left the road whenever they heard anything coming. Once a German car drove past and they stayed hiding in some bushes for a long time. They were terribly cold and weak now; snow had fallen and they were suffering from exhaustion. They found a church and crept into its churchyard to sleep. Early in the morning they awoke, too cold to sleep longer, and took to the road again. Soon, through the darkness, they could make out the shapes of buildings ahead. It was still before dawn when they reached Leipzig.

There was no sign of American troops, but they knew they could not press on further. They were too exhausted and hungry; they would have to take a risk and find shelter here. Reaching a church, they decided that they would enter it and ask the priest for help.

They couldn't be sure that the priest would help them but it was possible: many priests would help resistants and fugitives from the Nazi regime. Didi's own strong Catholic faith gave her confidence that they would be well received and besides, they really had no choice. They couldn't stay in the open; they had to take the risk.

They went into the church and found the priest. He was a practical man; horrified at the state of the three half-dead women, and only too aware of the German soldiers roaming in disarray through the town, he hurried the fugitives upstairs into the belfry and settled them there. They were to stay there quietly, he told them and he would bring them food and drink.

For Didi, the few days and nights in the belfry had a dream-like quality. She lapsed into a fever; afterwards she remembered food arriving at intervals, and a woman doctor leaning over her, and the priest appearing and vanishing again.

After about three days, her trance was penetrated by the sound of guns. Didi, Renée and Yvette went downstairs and looked out at Leipzig; there were white flags showing on many of the buildings: the Americans had arrived.

The women wanted to go to meet them, but the priest warned them against it, saying they would risk being shot. So they waited and after a while American soldiers burst into the church and aimed their guns at the priest, ordering him to lie down on the floor and demanding to know if anyone else was in the building. Didi, as the English speaker, told the Americans that she and the other two were fugitives, that they had been in the Resistance and that the priest had been hiding them from the Germans. The Americans allowed the priest back to his feet and held a discussion about the women. Eventually it was decided that Didi had better go with them, while Renée and Yvette would be taken to French camps. Didi, Renée and Yvette embraced one another and parted. After all, Didi had escaped.

All over Germany camps were being liberated and prisoners released. But it came too late for Yvonne Rudellat. Belsen was liberated by British troops on 15 April, just as the Americans arrived in Leipzig. The scenes which greeted the British troops stunned and horrified them – just as other Allied troops looked in disbelief at what they found in other concentration camps. So many of the prisoners were starved and sick beyond recovery, and now the long process began of trying to save them and of realizing the cost of the Nazi camps – over 12 million people dead. Yvonne Rudellat was alive when Belsen was taken, but she was gravely sick with typhus and dysentery and she could not respond to the efforts of the rescue teams. Within ten days she died. She died as Madame Gauthier and no one knew her real name; she was buried in a mass grave with thousands of other Belsen victims.

On 7 May, Germany surrendered. During the next three weeks, the three F Section women who had survived the camps, Odette, Didi and Yvonne Baseden, were taken back to England. The last of the women agents had finally returned. Their experiences had left them deeply marked in body and mind, yet it is true to say that they were the lucky ones: they came back.

TWENTY-THREE

The End of SOE

For the women who had seen the liberation of France, the autumn months of 1944 were full of events, homecomings and adjustments. Their work in the French Resistance was finished, but the process of acknowledging that work and bearing witness on their struggles, helpers and betrayers was just beginning.

In September Buckmaster arrived in France (Bodington and de Guélis had already been brought in to take part in the liberation), and embarked on a mission known rather portentously as 'Judex'. This was a mission to recognize those people who had helped F agents. Already the French communities were riven with accusations of collaborating and *ad hoc* trials, some fair, some horribly unfair, were taking place. The Judex mission aimed to give some kind of recognition and thus protection to F Section's helpers.

Buckmaster toured through France, visiting different regions with agents who had worked there. Yvonne Cormeau had a few weeks' leave in England in September, to rest and see her daughter; later that autumn she went back to south-west France as part of Judex. Jacqueline Nearne, home since April, was also flown out and took Buckmaster round the old Stationer territory. Lise de Baissac had not yet left France by September: she had been gathering together what information she could in the Mayenne, as the liberation progressed east. Now Claude came to find her in a car and, once they had seen Buckmaster, the two of them drove off to look for Mary Herbert, a part of Judex which was especially important to them.

For Maurice Buckmaster, this Judex tour was an incredible experience. The names he had heard for years were at last transformed into real people: he was finally able to meet them, to walk into their homes, to see for himself the relationships and circumstances which had shaped the lives of his agents in the field. And if this was extraordinary for him, his arrival in the Resistance communities often provoked a mixture of delight and incredulity among the French. For years these people had put their faith in the mysterious British 'Organization' and risked their lives in order to receive its weapons and shelter its agents. Now the 'Organization' itself – or at least, the man the agents clearly regarded as their commanding officer – was revealed.

The reunions between agents and resistants were exhilarating and emotional. Relief, congratulations, sadness, comedy and grief were all tangled up together. Agents on Judex worked hard to get recognition for their Resistance friends, well aware of the angry accusations and counter-accusations beginning to fly among the French. The mission went on for months, with different agents making trips at different times. In London, agents continued to be interviewed for their final reports; the staff of Baker Street made copious verbatim notes, and took lists of names and recommendations to pass on to the Judex representatives.

Judex was not an unqualified success. France in the months after the liberation was a tumultuous place. General Eisenhower later paid tribute to the French Resistance, saying that its activities had hastened the end of the war in Europe by a considerable amount. But well before such official recognition, the people of France could see what had been achieved. Everyone now claimed to have been in the Resistance and it was not always easy for the old friends of SOE to get their rewards. They were sometimes shouted down by other people, claiming to have deserved more; they were sometimes missing – away seeking imprisoned relatives? Lost? Dead? There was also an unexpected threat to their security from General de Gaulle, now poised to form the new government of France. De Gaulle was not about to fête those French resistants who had worked with British and American agents; far from it – anxious to restore French pride, he had recently stated that any French national who had co-operated with non-French military agents – even those of Allied forces – might come under suspicion of collaborating with a hostile power. De Gaulle wanted France to be clear that she had liberated herself: SOE agents were not welcome to share honours and diplomatic pressure was now being exerted on SOE to get the Judex mission over with fast.

But it was a different story in the towns and villages and families which had known F Section agents. So, during the late months of 1944 and the early months of 1945, Yvonne Cormeau revisited her friends in the Gascogne; Jacqueline Nearne took Buckmaster round her old Stationer haunts; celebratory dinners were cooked and reunion parties given, and the wartime friendships were set on a new footing, to last through the peacetime years ahead.

In September 1944, Lise and Claude de Baissac finally found Mary Herbert. Trying to retrace her movements after she had left Bordeaux, they had followed the trail to Poitiers. The visit was a sad one: Lise's old flat was empty, and her good friends the Gateaux were gone. The family had been arrested, neighbours told them, and mother, father and son were believed to be in concentration camps. Lise asked among her old Resistance contacts if anyone had news of Mary and eventually she was directed to the farmhouse of the two old sisters, out in the country. Sure enough, there they found Mary and her baby daughter, cloistered where they had been for the last six months, in the care of the old women. They began to arrange their return to Britain.

The women's homecomings were many and different. No one went back from occupied France the same as she had gone in; no one went back unscathed.

In spring 1945, the concentration camp survivors came home. Maurice Buckmaster and Vera Atkins met most of them as they arrived: Didi, Odette, Yvonne Baseden. They were terribly sick. Didi could hardly walk; Odette was upright but Anna Buckmaster, Maurice's wife, remembered the emptiness in her eyes: 'They were like the eyes of an animal that's died.'

In autumn 1945, after the German surrender, Vera Atkins assigned herself a new task: she wanted to go to Germany and try to trace the F Section agents – over one hundred of them – who hadn't come back. She had to fight to be allowed to go but she insisted. She felt very strongly that SOE and the country owed it to the missing agents to find out what had happened to them. It was a massive job; it involved her in travels to numerous camps and prisons, and in interviews with the German officers who had been responsible for the British prisoners. But she spoke German and she was a formidable interrogator: she succeeded in tracing all 117 missing F agents: they had all been killed. When she returned to London, she brought back evidence which threw new light on many F Section events – she had interviewed Bleicher, for instance, and had heard him allege that Déricourt had worked for Boemelburg. She also brought back harrowing evidence of illegal executions (such as the killing of the four women in Natzweiler), which would later be used in the War Crimes Trials.

So, piece by piece, the journeys of the lost F Section women were traced and the news brought back to their families.

Meanwhile, SOE was wound up, with little ceremony. It had been created to answer the needs of a war of occupation; now the war was over and the existence of a secret network of subversives was a potential embarrassment for the government. The process of vetting records had already begun: all 'telegrams' – the term used to describe the texts of radio messages from agents – were sorted and many were destroyed. SOE's remaining files and records were handed over to MI6 for classification. And in January 1946 SOE was officially disbanded – in the same conditions of secrecy that had seen its birth. Few people outside its ranks knew that it had ever existed.

Epilogue

The war was over; SOE was no more and the women agents who had survived their F Section missions were slipping back into 1940s civilian life. The survival rate for agents had turned out to be much higher than the 50-50 chance they had been given at the start of their missions; in F Section, three-quarters of the total agents had returned. The rate of loss among F's women was slightly higher: 37 F agents had gone out and 24 had returned.

These twenty-four were now trying to adjust to a more normal way of life. They had given their final reports to Baker Street and been released from their duties. As SOE was being shut down for good, they scattered to their own lives. What became of them?

Four of the women, of course – Didi, Odette, Lise de Baissac and Yvonne Cormeau – have worked with me on this book; and the best way that I can end it is to let them speak about what they did after the war, and what those Resistance years have meant, and still mean, for them. But these last words of theirs come in a while.

Of the other women, I have tried to trace their post-war lives, but there are many of them and some now live far away on different continents; others have died; still others are almost certainly alive but no longer keep in touch with fellow agents and F Section staff. It is after all nearly fifty years since they were brought together by Resistance work. But I have been able to find out something of those women (such as Virginia Hall and Nancy Wake) whose Resistance adventures play a significant part in this book, even though I have never met the women themselves. This is what I know of them:

Virginia Hall married a man named Guillot, whom she had met

in the Resistance armies during her 1944 mission. They went to live in the USA where she continued to work for OSS after the war. When OSS became the CIA, she went on working there for a number of years. She was always discreet about her work, and refused to give interviews about it; she also discouraged journalists and writers from asking about her war-time Resistance work. She and her husband finally went to live in the mid-west of America, where Virginia died a few years ago.

Mary Herbert came back to Britain and brought up her daughter. She and Claude de Baissac married but they did not live together; it was, as Lise puts it, 'a friendly separation'. Mary helped support herself by giving private French lessons. She died a few years ago, and so did Claude. Their daughter, born to a British mother and French father under a false French name, now lives in America.

Jacqueline Nearne helped to look after her sister Didi immediately after the war and arranged a flat in London for her. Then she moved to New York where she worked in the protocol department of the United Nations. She kept up a long distance friendship with Lise de Baissac in France, visiting her every so often. In the 1950s her fellow former agent and friend Brian Stonehouse painted a portrait of her: it shows a slight figure sitting graceful and upright in a red dress, her face – startlingly vibrant – turned straight to the viewer. The portrait shows clearly what Maurice Southgate describes as her 'fascination'. She died in the early 1980s.

Francine Agazarian settled in England after the war. Her husband Jack did not come back from concentration camp. She had led a quiet life ever since; she finds it hard to honour the past and at the same time take part in the present: 'I have not been able to free myself entirely from grief.' In 1967 she went to Flossenberg concentration camp, where Jack had died, stood in the cell he had occupied and followed his steps to the yard where he had been executed. She feels it would be too painful for her to talk about her work in the war, but she is glad that all these years later, books should be written to remember the Resistance.

Julienne Aisner was married to Charles Besnard before the war ended and after the liberation they lived together in Paris. She died in the early 1980s; he died two years ago.

Pearl Witherington settled in France and married Henri Cornioley, her fiancé from pre-SOE days and, as it happened, also an agent. She worked in banking in Paris. Some years after the war Maurice Southgate was at a Resistance reunion dinner when he met a man who had come across Pearl in her professional capacity. 'By God,' the man said, 'what a capable woman!' She retired some years ago and now lives in Paris. She keeps in regular touch with her Resistance friends.

Elizabeth Devereux-Rochester was released from French gaol in the liberation. She lived in France until her death a few years ago.

Anne-Marie Walters wrote a book of memoirs shortly after the war, called *Moondrop to Gascony*.[1] Since then she has lived in France and Spain and married a Frenchman named Comert. I wrote to her via her memoirs' publishers but the address they had for her was an old one and she has since moved on.

Yvonne Baseden came back to England, married and went to live in what was then Northern Rhodesia. She later remarried and is now Mrs Burney. She now lives in Portugal and no longer wants to talk about her experiences in the war.

Paddy O'Sullivan settled in England, married Eric Alvey, a former SOE trainer, and had two sons. She lives in England.

Odette Wilen is now Mrs de Strugo and lives in South America.

Nancy Wake went back to Marseille after the liberation, and discovered that her husband Henri Fiocca had been killed in captivity. She later returned to England and then went back to Australia, where she stood for parliament and became something of a celebrity. She has co-operated with authors of books on her life and a few years ago a television mini-series was made about her Resistance adventures. She came back to England in the 1950s, married John Forward, and now they live in Australia.

Phyllis Latour married an engineer and moved to East Africa.

Marie-Thérèse Le Chêne was in England at the end of the war. I have not been able to trace her since.

Peggy Knight returned to England and soon afterwards married and had children. I have been unable to find out where she lives now.

Sonia Butt married ex-resistant Guy D'Artois and went to live in Canada, where she is still.

Blanche Charlet returned to England; I have been unable to trace her.

Krystyna de Gyzicka, (Christine Granville), Cammaerts' eleventh hour courier, came back to England after the war. She supported herself with a variety of jobs, such as working in shops and as a stewardess for a shipping line. On one of her working voyages a fellow steward became first her friend, then her obsessive suitor. He began following her and during one of her periods on land, in 1952, he stabbed her to death.

[1] *Moondrop to Gascony*, Anne-Marie Walters, Macmillan Ltd, 1946

Of the two other women who were not strictly F Section recruits but who worked with F *réseaux*: Yvonne Fontaine married a French man named Dumont; Madeleine Lavigne died in Paris in 1945.

And what of those male agents whose stories have fed into this book?

Maurice Southgate – the Stationer *réseau*'s *Hector* – survived torture and a year's imprisonment in gaols and in Buchenwald concentration camp. He was one of the few F Section agents who left that camp alive, and he still keeps in touch with the others. He remains proud of the fact that not a single arrest was made in his *réseau* as a result of his own capture. He went back to Paris after the war and returned to his career in commerce. His wife died and later he married again, another Frenchwoman. He is now retired and lives with his wife in the Lot. He goes to fewer Resistance reunions now but keeps in touch with his old comrades and fellow agents by letter and telephone.

Peter Churchill was freed from concentration camp by the Allies. Back in London, he and Odette got married. He wrote several volumes of memoirs and they became a celebrated SOE couple. But Peter became increasingly bound up in his memories of the war and eventually he and Odette separated, with him going to live in France. They divorced and he remarried, as did Odette. When he fell ill in the 1960s, he asked for Odette and she travelled to France to be with him, staying with him and his wife until he died.

Arnaud was executed in concentration camp. So was France Antelme. So too were Bernard and *Laurent*, Eliane Plewman's comrades; Yolande Beekman's chief, Biéler, and Noor Khan's chief Garry. All Prosper captured male agents were executed, except for Pierre Culioli. When he was freed at the end of the war, he returned to England and had a struggle to clear himself of collaborating with his German captors in the matter of surrendering the arms. He requested an investigation into his part in the affair and he was cleared. He went back to France where he still lives.

Hilaire, George Starr, came back to England and took up his old job as a mining engineer. He kept in close touch with his Resistance comrades of south-west France and visited them regularly. He moved to France on his retirement and lived there until he died a few years ago.

Francis Cammaerts returned to England and teaching after the liberation. He lived for many years in London's Isle of Dogs, paying regular visits to his Resistance friends in the Drôme, who all still know him – with great friendship and pride – as *Roger*. Now he has moved to south-east France.

Then there are the two members of F Section staff who figure so prominently in this book.

Colonel Buckmaster went back to civilian life and work at the Ford company. He lived in southern England with his wife Anna and in 1960 he became public relations officer for the champagne producers' professional body, the *Comité Inter-professionel du Vin de Champagne*. Ever since the war he has kept close links with former F agents and French resistants. He is retired now; sadly his wife died in 1988, but he still attends Resistance reunions and keeps in touch with many F Section friends.

Vera Atkins became Secretary of the Central Bureau of Educational Visits and Exchanges. She too is retired but is endlessly applied to for help by writers and researchers of Resistance affairs. She lives in London and Winchelsea and is a friend to innumerable F Section people.

There are many local resistance associations in France, which bind together agents and resistants. These associations keep records of the people who worked together, organize reunions, act as unofficial post offices for people who want to get in touch with long lost comrades or their descendants. Each F Section *réseau* had a *liquidateur* after the liberation – a resistant from the *réseau* who gathered together information, addresses, records of resistance activity. Today there are still a number of *liquidateurs*, not always the original people any longer, but people who hold the information in trust for others. Among the scores of Resistance associations in France, there are many '*Amicales Buckmaster*'; associations for resistants and agents of the various F *réseaux*.

The women and men who were once agents of F Section have their different ways of remembering the war, and their Resistance comrades. Some of them have close links with French Resistance associations; some keep in touch with their Resistance friends outside the association circuit. Others do not go in for clubs and reunions but most still have the addresses of individual resistants stowed away and exchange the occasional letter, phone call, or visit.

As for F Section itself, there is one organized way in which former agents and members of staff can keep in touch: through the Special Forces Club in Knightsbridge.

The four women agents who have helped me so much with this book, Didi Nearne, Lise de Baissac, Odette Hallowes and Yvonne Cormeau, are not all frequenters of the club.

Didi is the only one of them I have met there. When she wrote back in reply to my first letter, she said that she would be glad to talk about her mission and suggested that we meet there soon: 'These things live with you,' she added. And with Didi they do indeed, often more vividly and arrestingly than what goes on today. Didi continues to live her experiences in Paris and Germany, and most of all the memory of her interrogation is still powerfully alive in her.

She was very ill when she was brought back to England in 1945, and for months she was in a state of physical and emotional collapse. When she began to recover physically, she was still too weak to work, and she took to painting, producing violent, terrible pictures, which expressed the horror of her captivity and the camps. When she was well enough, she took up working as a nurse. Didi has lived in London ever since the war, and still does nursing work from time to time.

She keeps in touch with friends from SOE days – Maurice Buckmaster and Vera Atkins, certain other agents, the pilots who flew her out on that bitter cold March night in 1944. She is also in touch with French friends she met in captivity – particularly with Geneviève Mathieu, who had the bunk above hers in Ravensbrück, and with Renée Bernet, one of the women she escaped with. Over the years she has gone regularly to France to see them: they have lunches and reunions at the Club de la France Libre in Paris, which is Renée's second home.

The Special Forces Club is not Didi's second home, though: she is comfortable there but in the club as everywhere else she is an independent, rather solitary figure. Her Resistance work is still overwhelmingly important to her; she replays aspects of her mission in her mind – especially the interrogation and her attempts to escape. Her time as an agent has had a profound effect on her life: its impact is of course partly due to what she went through after her arrest, but it is not just the horrors of captivity which have impressed themselves on her personality. For Didi, solitary and intense since childhood, the SOE mission was a chance to forge meaning and moral strength out of those natural inclinations.

'It was a life in the shadow but I think maybe I was fitted for it. I could be a bit hard and secret. I could be lonely. I could be independent. No, I wasn't bored – I liked the work. After the war, I missed it. I even tried to find a job doing radio operating but it wasn't the same.'

It seems very characteristic of Didi that she should have tried to return to radio operating after the war, hoping to approximate the feelings of Resistance in this way. It was a seeking for the fulfilment she had temporarily known during those months of 1944, and if the four women agents I met have anything in common now, it is that they all share some similar sense of loss. It has its positive aspect, of course: pride in their achievements and the memories of certain acts of bravery and generosity which others made towards them.

Didi, for all that she lived and worked so much alone, felt a fierce respect for the Resistance people she knew.

> There were very strong feelings between the people who worked together in Paris. We were together, there was danger, the Germans were there. My chief was a Frenchman of great courage and I was very proud to be working for him. When I was arrested I used to think, what will he say when he knows what's happened? I wanted to continue with the work. I was so very, very disappointed not to finish it. But then it's selfish to think that, because so many people have died. Maybe I took it too much to heart.

Maybe, but it's hard to see how else one could take it. Didi still has anxieties about whether she did well enough as an agent. She doesn't express them overtly; rather, she brushes by them in musings like that just quoted. So many agents who were arrested feel this unease: was it their fault? Could they have done anything to hold off arrest or even just postpone it? Would more caution have saved them or would it have made impossible the work they did?

Didi reruns the circumstances in her mind, trying to answer these questions. She also reruns the circumstances of her inter-rogation because she is proud of her achievement in fooling the Gestapo and she wishes to remember exactly how it was done. She is anxious to remember all the incidents, large and small, and anxious that they should be recorded at last. Recently, she enlisted Vera's help in writing to various French and German authorities, asking them to find a copy of the statement she made in the Rue des Saussaies – that signed Jacqueline du Tertre. The enquiries unearthed a man who is making records of the Rue des Saussaies proceedings and personnel: he has asked to meet Didi on his next trip to London, and so all these years later she might be able to back up her memories at last with documents; she might be able to see photographs of the men who interrogated and tortured her, and for the first time learn their names. It might not sound a pleasant procedure, but it would restore to Didi a little bit more of a past which is vitally important to her, but which continues to elude her, scrambled as it is by trauma and the intensity of her feelings.

Still, Didi is not an unhappy person. On the contrary, her memories are precious to her. She continues the independent person she always was; she guards her privacy – hence being 'Didi' in this book, her nickname rather than her real name – and she goes on being a different figure in different circumstances. To her SOE friends she is Didi; to the French friends she met in Ravensbrück, and whom she still visits, she is always 'Jacqueline'. Now as then, she intertwines the various strands of her life and only she knows where one begins and another ends.

Lise de Baissac, by contrast, seems almost remote from her SOE past. After the Liberation, and once she and Claude had found Mary Herbert, she returned to Britain and embarked on a new civilian life. It was as busy and independent as her life had been before the war; for a while she was based in Britain, working as a translator, then she went back to France and – among other activities – married a French architect and old friend named Villameur. They moved to Marseille, a city which had seen much Resistance during the war, but which held no such associations for Lise. She still lives there, widowed now but surrounded by friends and leading a very active life.

She was mildly surprised that I should be so interested in the war years, surprised but ready to help. She was astonished to hear that some women had refused to see me. 'If somebody wants to find things out, why shouldn't you help them?' she said. She accepted all my questions with good humour, and made a conscious effort to evoke the memories I sought.

Lise's memories are selective ones – not in the sense that they have been consciously edited, but because over the years many of the details of her Resistance life have faded and she has been content to let them go. At the time, she saw her SOE work as a necessary task; she did not embrace it jubilantly – she could not, because she was always unhappily aware of what had created the need for it. The exodus of the French from the north, the fall of France, the hasty manoeuvrings of the Vichy government were things which cast a shadow over her spirit. The shadow still hovers today: she cannot remember this period of France's past with equanimity. While there are some aspects of her Resistance work which kindle happiness and pride in her, there are others – like safeguarding herself from collaborators – which it obviously oppresses her to recall.

Yet Lise has not shut out those days from her mind. It is rather that she chooses to keep these memories and emotions private. Certain Resistance friends, and particularly the Gateau family, occupy a place deep in her affections, but the emotions they stir are complicated: as well as gratitude and love, there is mourning for those who died, and the sense of a debt which she, as a survivor, owes them. Lise has her own quiet way of honouring these debts: reunion dinners and reminiscing speeches would make her uncomfortable.

Perhaps too she has a slight fear of being caught in the past. After all, the greater part of her life has been lived since the war and Lise is someone who likes to be active, and fully involved in life. Her life is full now, as it always has been.

'I enjoy living alone,' she says. 'I was very happy while I was married to my husband, but now I am alone again I don't mind. I have always been very well able to occupy myself and I like being independent.'

She has a sharp intellect and an appetite for ideas and discussions. She meets regularly with a group of friends to do readings of short plays – most of them in English. A friend of hers whom I met at an F Section reunion dinner – needless to say, Lise wasn't there – described the dinner parties Lise used to give after the war.

'They were very smart affairs, where you were expected to perform. The conversation wasn't idle chatter and gossip; oh no, you had to be right up to the mark. Lise has always liked to be challenged intellectually. She and Vera made a formidable pair.'

Lise feels no compulsion to tell new friends about her SOE work. Sooner or later, however, the subject of the war tends to arise and then she talks about her experiences as they seem relevant or interesting. There is an undeniable reluctance in her to elaborate, though: certain of her memories are perhaps more powerful and demanding than is quite comfortable. There were several times during the day we spent together when she was suddenly moved by a remembered emotion – touching the soil of France when she dropped by parachute; the succession of bleak winter days in Poitiers in 1942–3; the memory of the Gateaux's kindness and Monsieur Gateau's eventual death.

Her favourite links to the past are the light-hearted ones, which do not stir these emotions: a few years ago, quite unexpectedly, she received a letter from a man named Rémy Clément. He wrote to her that she might not remember him but back in 1943 they had spent a night in the hay together. His name then had been *Marc*.

'And it was quite true!' she said, smiling. 'This man had been arranging the pick-up for Claude and I to go back to England and we had had to stay overnight with him in a barn waiting for the aeroplane. But to get a letter from him out of the blue, after more than forty years, saying that we had spent the night together – I thought that was so funny. I wrote back, saying, "You are quite right, we did."'

Thus, with a light but unmistakably formidable touch Lise de Baissac deals with her Resistance memories.

Yvonne Cormeau is still known to all her French resistance friends and to many SOE people as *Annette*. Ever since 1944 she has kept in constant touch with the former Wheelwright resistants; she goes to France at least once a year to visit them and to attend a reunion dinner. Until his death in the early 1980s *Hilaire* went to many of them too. The reunions embrace large regions of France and take place in different locations every year, knitting together far-flung communities and families.

'Last year when we had our meeting – people who were really active are older of course and some of them die but the younger ones come with their wives and some of them come with their children and their children's children. There were 462 for the dinner last year so you see how they cling still.

'And the *préfet* came and the military colonel and the *gendarmerie* and a senator and a deputy. . . .'

Yvonne's friendships with Resistance families now span several generations. She is very close to the daughter of the house in Pujols where she sheltered on the night of her arrival, even though at the time the daughter was only sixteen. The father and mother were arrested shortly after her arrival: the father was killed in captivity; the mother came back from the camps in 1945 'pretty deaf from her treatment'. Ever since then, Yvonne has been going to see the mother and daughter. The bonds which hold them together are very strong – they are bonds of trust and respect and shared memory. A few years ago the mother died but Yvonne remains close to the daughter, so close that she is godmother to the daughter's eldest child – a girl, named Yvonne Annette.

Yvonne Cormeau is matter of fact when she talks about these friendships, and a touch competitive. She is proud of the depth of feeling between herself and the resistants she knows; she sets this depth against the more widespread acclaim which some of the other SOE figures enjoy.

> Don't forget that the Resistance itself was only about 8 per cent of the population. You didn't want to speak to too many people about it; it's bound to spread all the more. By keeping it smaller you had more devotion – pride also: 'We're in the know', you see. Then it was only after the D-Day messages came that those last minute people offered their services; we didn't trust them as much as the others. So one made a good many friends – but not friends on the surface. Buckmaster of course has

streets named after him. My friendships were far more
deep.

An *habituée* of Resistance reunions, Yvonne is quite casual about the
fact that she is a prestigious figure among the French, and one who
can be fought over.

> One time I'll try to see four *départements* over here,
> then I'll go and see the others down there. I can't do it
> all every year and I realize it makes a great jealousy but I
> just can't do it. It's usually the ones who've done the least
> who make the most fuss because I don't go and stay with
> them.
> I managed to get one woman – it was her husband
> who was in it more; she did practically nothing – but
> I managed to get her a certificate which says she has
> been a resistante and which gives her a little pension and
> possibilities of travelling cheaper and things like that. But
> she's not grateful at all! Last year she came to this lunch
> and she was furious because she wasn't put to sit next to
> me!

Yvonne Cormeau is not exaggerating when she tells these stories.
Last year I applied to a friend of hers, Monsieur Peré, holder of
information on Resistance in the Gers. I explained that I wrote at
Annette's suggestion to ask for contacts who had worked with her in
Wheelwright, and his answer made it clear that my main credential in
his eyes was that I came 'with the recommendation of our Madame
Annette'.

This respect and affection – devotion might be a more accurate
word – helps to compensate for what Yvonne feels is a lack of official
recognition here in Britain. It rankles with her that she did not get a
George Cross, despite being put up for it by SOE.

> At the end of the war we all got MBEs, except for Odette
> and Noor Inayat Khan who got the George Cross. Pearl
> and I were put up for it too, for working in the field for
> a long time, but no, 'we hadn't been caught'. It's a funny
> condition – as *Hilaire* said, you have to fail before you get
> it.

Through Yvonne Cormeau's conversation comes a lingering sense
of having been passed over, slightly ignored. Perhaps she regrets

that in the years after the war she returned to her quiet life with
her daughter and did not court recognition more. But then, after the
war she felt that the thirteen months in France had taken a great toll
on her.

> My time in France certainly aged me considerably. I had
> quite a bit of white hair at thirty-three. I suppose it was
> the tension. It was a strain, there's no doubt about that –
> you couldn't help it.
>   Still I was pleased when I got back and one of the
> codes and ciphers men said, 'Mm, 402 messages, jolly
> good! And only one I couldn't decipher.' Only one man
> beat my number of messages and he was out two years.

This mixture of introspection and pride is characteristic of Yvonne's
way of talking about her war. On the one hand she is a quiet,
self-contained woman who takes things seriously; on the other she
enjoys the knowledge of her own achievements. In the last few years
she has begun to speak more openly about her Resistance work: she
has given a few radio and newspaper interviews; she has advised on
the fictionalized SOE television series *Wish Me Luck* and has appeared
on television to discuss it.

Perhaps at last, she is beginning to claim for herself some of the
recognition which is overdue this side of the Channel. She has no
need to claim it in France of course.

Last year Yvonne Cormeau married; she is now Mrs Farrow
and has moved from the London flat – which has been her home
for many years – to Derbyshire. Her new neighbours may not know
what she did in France in the war, but this summer she will doubtless
be going back to France for a reunion with several hundred people
who have very good reason to know.

For Odette, one incident in particular sums up the bizarre experience of coming out of a concentration camp and into 1945 civilian
Britain.

> When I came back I had a terrible abscess in my mouth,
> enormous, and I had had that for fourteen months in cap-
> tivity, so I said to Vera the first thing when I got back, 'Oh,
> I must go to a dentist.' They said very kindly, yes, yes; they
> didn't say, well, you are not fit to be seen on the streets of
> London! The next day I was collected and I was taken to a
> dentist at Harley Street; he was terribly smart, I had never

seen a man looking so impeccable for years, and I thought, 'He's not going to touch me!' But he did say quietly, 'Do sit down,' so I sat in this chair and he started looking, and he said quietly, 'I understand you were a prisoner of war in Germany.' And then he said, 'How very tiresome for a woman.' I thought, this is perfect! It is the perfect definition of what has been! And I laughed and laughed; I left his room laughing away and Vera Atkins was with me and she said, 'Have you gone mad?' and I said, 'No, I know for the first time Vera, I'm truly back in England and the war has not existed!'

There was often a sense of absurdity and unreality about these early days back in Britain. Odette was weak and ill after her captivity; she also had to deal with the emotional intensity of reunions with her daughters and with Peter Churchill, who had also survived his imprisonment. On top of that, there was the matter of the 'traitor' in Baker Street; immediately on her return she told senior SOE figures what she had learned from the Germans, namely that Bodington had supposedly allowed agents to be arrested. As we know, she was asked to hold her peace about this, on the grounds that no good could be done by exposing what she knew. And she agreed.

But she was still encumbered by the knowledge, as she was by the memories.

In the few years after the war, Odette rejoined her children, married Peter Churchill and received widespread recognition for her Resistance work and her fortitude in the camps. The recognition came largely because a man named Jerrard Tickell, who had worked in the War Office and interrogated Odette on her return, wrote a book about her.[1] She told him her memories and he was allowed access to the files (a privilege given to no one else but M.R.D. Foot, the official F Section historian). The book was written as a popular war story and when it came out in 1949 it made Odette famous. A film was made of it – also called 'Odette' – starring Anna Neagle. When it opened, there was a royal *première* and a dinner in Britain, and a similarly lavish French *première* (at the Paris Opera) and banquet, in the presence of President Auriol. In the 1950s Odette Churchill, as she was almost universally known, was a celebrity.

The former agents are on the whole a competitive community; most are conscious of representing their own *réseaux* and comrades, sometimes an entire region of France. They like to have recognition

[1] *Odette*, Jerrard Tickell, Chapman & Hall, 1949

for what was done in their area, for their own work and that of their Resistance friends. Odette's fame has stirred jealousy in quite a few breasts and some people suspect her of courting publicity.

But she did not act like a star when the film opened, in a blaze of publicity and royal patronage. She attended the *première*, but not the dinner afterwards: instead she held a small dinner party for a few friends in the garden of her house. Vera Atkins was one of her guests, and she remembers that Odette was quiet and far from revelling in the occasion.

The making of the film had been an emotional experience for Odette, who was asked to come on set and act as adviser.

> One of the torture scenes we did fifty-four times in one day. The first week I thought, 'I don't know if I'm going to be able to go on with it.' And then I thought, 'I have to. I have to take myself away from thinking it's to do with me. It is to do with all the girls. I wanted it made for all of them. I must remove the emotional element.' From that moment it was all right. Some days it was a bit hard to take but it was all right.
>
> To this day, when I see it I am satisfied. It gave a true picture of what it was like. You can't ask for more than that. . . . I said to Jerrard Tickell, 'If you are fond of me as you say, don't let the film be done by the Americans. They will make it a Hollywood story and my story is a Hollywood story enough – if you knew the end of it.'

There again is a reference to the secret Odette was carrying; her thoughts about the war never take her very far without coming back to that. This sense of betrayal battles with her sense that she can honour the memories of the agents who died. She wants to remember these other agents and resistants; she wants their sacrifices to mean something. Yet she can't forget the evidence that they were sent to their death by someone within their own trusted organization – in which case, did some of them die pointlessly? These are thoughts which Odette struggles to keep at bay, nurturing in their place memories of the people themselves.

> I never wish to forget. I want to remember – all of it. I have to remember. You know we have a little memorial on the side of the church in Knightsbridge, for all the girls who did not come back. There is a plaque with the names

and whenever I am there I can imagine my name on that plaque, and for no reason that I know of, it isn't there. But the others are there. And I see faces. No, I don't wish to forget. As long as I am alive, they are alive.

I don't specially want to see the people who are alive. I want to keep faith with the ones who are not because it is easy to forget them. It is easy to forget the girls. It is easy to forget *Arnaud*. It is easy to forget a number of people like that. I can't forget and I don't want to.

For all this, ever since her return in 1945 Odette has taken care to have a life independent of SOE memories. She set about rebuilding a family life with her daughters, and with Peter Churchill, now her husband. For Odette, despite the publicity surrounding her, life moved on into a new rhythm. But Peter found that he could not leave the war behind. He wrote a volume of memoirs about his Resistance work, then another about his captivity. He gave talks about his experiences. Odette hoped that through these means, he might come to terms with what had happened but he remained obsessed with it.

Sadly enough, it was the war that broke up Peter Churchill and me. I loved him very much and he loved me but we were so very different in the way that we thought about it. He wanted to go on with it, writing about it and lecturing about it. He did not want to leave it behind. The war had been for him the best part of his life – he had led a very privileged life before the war but in the war he was very good at his job and he had to try. He discovered what he could do and for him it was a great thing.

Peacetime life did not stretch Peter in the same way; he grieved for the qualities he felt were now gone from his life – the courage, the loyalty, the willingness to sacrifice himself. He tried to recapture them by reminding himself constantly of war-time conditions:

'Every time we sat in front of food, he would say, "How marvellous it is to have this food." And I would say, "No, it's not marvellous, it's normal." '

Odette believes that their shared fame was a bad thing for Peter.

'After the war he liked being the romantic couple with me and he turned down all the very good offers of a job. In the end I couldn't stand it any more and I said, "We must stop living like this." '

After ten years, they parted and Peter asked a good friend of his, Geoffrey Hallowes, to keep in touch with Odette and help her if need be.

'Then he met someone else who wasn't involved in the war and married her and I thought, that will save him. But he did what he always wanted to do, he went to live in the South of France where he had worked and went on writing and lecturing.'

And Odette married Geoffrey Hallowes. But she kept up a close friendship with Peter and when he was dying in the 1960s, he asked for her to go to him. She visited him in France several times and finally stayed with him and his wife until he died. He died still absorbed in the events of the war, the time when he felt he had lived at his best.

This sense that they had touched something special during the war, that they had encountered better things than any they were to meet again, lingers with most of the agents I have met. It helps them to live with the unhappier memories – the loss of friends, the suffering of others. It has been a lifeline to sanity for those who were in concentration camps, like Didi or Odette, and for those who (like Francis Cammaerts in the Vercors) saw terrible atrocities during fighting. But the great danger is that peacetime life can seem petty by comparison. Perhaps it's in recognition of this danger that Lise de Baissac has always chosen to look forward instead of back.

> 'I very often feel lonely,' Odette acknowledges. 'I feel lonely for the feeling that it was. How can I put it? A lot of things seem to me irrelevant, meaningless, when I know other ways. I have a desire for quality and I find it very difficult to have it in ordinary life. I'm not great enough. . . . . You know, I am like somebody who has been lucky enough to have a belief in God and has lost it. That's the way it is. And I should think people who have had faith and lost it – may be like that, a bit lonely for what they once had and have got no longer. I have memories and people – nothing like that is lost. But you have this little bit of loneliness that sets you apart.'

Yet Odette and Didi, who both talked about this sense of isolation, succeeded in remaking their lives. It was perhaps easier for women agents than for men to adjust back to peacetime. Men are still conditioned today to aspire to acts of bravery and daring; in the 1920s and 1930s, when most of the male agents were brought up, the mythology of the 'Great War' had given this conditioning a special edge. For some of the male agents, like Peter Churchill, their work in the Resistance fulfilled a yearning long since instilled into them by their education. It was hard for them to go quietly back to civilian life, especially given the public fascination with their exploits.

Women might have been frustrated as they went back to their peacetime lives but in 1940s terms they at least were spared the public expectation of what they would do next. And as women, they were used to taking a back seat: most of them had done so even in their Resistance days. Odette was an exception; the fame established for her after the war has followed her right down the years, but both she and the other women know that the famous 'Odette Legend' shows only a very little of the real women's stories. For the most part, these have rested untold.

But now, nearly fifty years later, their stories are emerging on their own terms. So long afterwards, the women's memories of events are confused in places, but their memories of people, and of their feelings for those people have kept all their power.

Francine Agazarian feels that the honouring of these memories is her *raison d'être*. She honours them alone. Yvonne, Didi and Odette like to gather with others from the past; Lise goes her own way in Marseille, but her mail includes regular letters from Vera Atkins and, while she isn't to be seen at parties, she knows much of what is happening to her fellow agents. Among the women like Yvonne Baseden and Pearl Witherington who declined to see me, and those others still living in this country or abroad who I could not trace, I imagine that Odette's words will touch a chord:

> I don't think you will find anybody who has been through these experiences who will say they have put it aside, they have forgotten. . . . If you have been fortunate enough to witness the most wonderful sides of some human beings you are left with a desire for what is the best. And in ordinary life there is no reason for people to manifest this. But you know it exists.

Bibliography

Amouroux, Henri *La grande histoire des Français sous l'occupation*, vols 1, 2, 3, 4, 5, 6, Robert Laffont, Paris
La vie des Français sous l'occupation, Fayard, 1961
Andrew, Christopher *Secret Service: The Making of the British Intelligence Community*, Sceptre, 1986
Beevor, J.G. *SOE: Recollections and Reflections, 1940–5*, Bodley Head, 1981
Bernard, Henri *La Résistance 1940–5*, La Renaissance du Livre, 1968
Braddon, Russell *Nancy Wake*, Cassell, 1956
Buckmaster, Maurice *Specially Employed*, Batchworth Press, 1952
They Fought Alone, Odhams Press, 1958
Chauvet, Maurice *D-Day, 1er B.F.M. Commando*, Amicale des Anciens Parachutistes S.A.S. & Commando, 1974
Lancelot, Soldat de la France-Libre, L'Association des Anciens Combattants Français Évadés et Internés en Espagne, 1964
Churchill, Peter *Duel of Wits*, Hodder & Stoughton, 1953
The Spirit In The Cage, Hodder & Stoughton, 1954
Cowburn, Benjamin *No Cloak, No Dagger*, Jarrolds, 1960
Foot, M.R.D. *SOE in France: An account of the work of the British Special Operations Executive in France, 1940–4*, H.M.S.O., 1966
SOE: An Outline History of the Special Operations Executive 1940–6, BBC, 1986
Six Faces of Courage, Eyre Methuen, 1978
Gellhorn, Martha *The Face Of War*, Virago, 1986
Gleeson, James *They Feared No Evil*, Corgi, 1978
Howarth, Patrick *Undercover: the Men and Women of the Special Operations Executive*, Routledge & Kegan Paul, 1980

King, Stella *'Jacqueline': Pioneer Heroine of the Resistance*, Arms and Armour, 1989

Le Chêne, Evelyn *Watch For Me By Moonlight*, Eyre Methuen, 1973

Lheureux, Danièle *Les Oubliés de la Resistance 'Sylvestre-Farmer'*, Editions France-Empire, 1988

Lorain, Pierre *Armément Clandestin, France 1941–44*, Paris, P. Lorain, 1972

Maloubier, Bob *Plonge Dans L'Or Noir, Espion!*, Robert Laffont, 1986

Marshall, Robert *All The King's Men*, Collins, 1988

Michel, Henri *The Shadow War*, History Book Club, André Deutsch, 1972
Les Courants de pensée de la Résistance, Presses Universitaires de la France, 1962

Millar, George *Maquis*, Heinemann, 1945

Miller, Russell *The Resistance*, Time-Life Books, 1979

Minney, R.J. *Carve Her Name With Pride*, Newnes, 1956 & Fontana, 1989

Nicholas, Elizabeth *Death Be Not Proud*, Cresset Press, 1958

Noguères, Henri *Histoire de la Résistance en France de 1940 à 1945*, vols 1–5, Robert Laffont, 1967–81

Overton Fuller, Jean *Madeleine*, Gollancz, 1952
Double Webs, Putnam, 1958
Double Agent?, Pan, 1961

Ruby, Marcel *F Section SOE, The Story of the Buckmaster Network*, Leo Cooper, 1988

Salvesen, Sylvia *Forgive – But Do Not Forget*, Hutchinson, 1958

Tickell, Jerrard *Odette*, Chapman & Hall, 1949

Walters, Anne-Marie *Moondrop to Gascony*, Macmillan, 1946

Webb, A.M. (Ed.) *The Natzweiler Trial*, Hodge, 1949

Wynne, Barry *No Drums, No Trumpets*, Barker, 1961

Young, Gordon *In Trust and Treason*, Hulton, 1959

Index

Abwehr
  Carte documents, theft of 91, 118, 129
  Donkeyman réseau, surveillance of 152
  objectives 117
  role in occupied France 2, 39
  SD, rivalry with 117
  Spindle réseau, destruction of 117-28
Acolyte (réseau) 259
Acrobat (réseau) 158
Agazarian, Francine
  arrives in France 67
  de Baissac, Lise, processed by 78
  post-war life 15, 330, 344
  Prosper, role with 63-4, 66, 109, 110, 132
  return to London 135
Agazarian, Jack
  arrest of 155
  Déricourt, Henri
    contact with 108, 113
    suspicions about 143
  Dutch agents, arrest of 135
  execution of 148, 330
  Prosper, role with 63, 65, 66, 78, 110, 156
  torture of 147
Air Intelligence 105
Air Movements
  Déricourt, Henri, trains for 104
  foundation of 58, 59, 76, 108, 145
  role of 76-9, 152, 176
  SD surveillance of 111
  termination of 146
Aisner, Julienne
  Bodington, Nicolas, contact with 143
  Déricourt, Henri, recruited by 108
  Farrier réseau, role with 131
  marries Besnard, Charles 146, 330
  post-war life 150, 330
  training in England 113
Albert 182, 187
Alice see Lefort, Cecily
All the King's Men (Marshall) 99, 100
Alphone see Brooks, Tony

Ambroise see Bloch, Denise
'Amicales Buckmaster' 333
Amps, Jean 55
Anastasie 274
Annette see Cormeau, Yvonne
Antelme, France
  arrest of 217-18, 224, 232
  arrives in France 57, 74
  D-Day, economic preparations for 57, 223-24
  de Baissac, Lise, and 74
  Inayat, Noor, and 154, 158, 215-16
  Phono réseau, compromise of 158, 215-18
  post-war life 332
  returns to London 77, 109, 155
  Savy and 155, 224, 232
Archambaud
  Agazarian, Francine, and 64
  arrest of 138
  arrived in France 55, 56
  Borrel, André, and 65
  Déricourt, Henri, and 67, 113
  execution of 148
  interrogation of 139, 140, 141, 147
  power station, attack on 114
  Prosper, role with 55, 63, 66, 110, 132, 135
  radio controlled by SD 143, 215, 218
  torture of 147
Archdeacon (réseau) 218-20
Arends, Robert 148
Armand 234
Armistice Army, Vichy 19, 90
arms drops 46, 49, 73-4, 77-9, 110, 130, 131, 132, 133, 134, 174, 182, 191, 211, 213-15, 228, 235, 241, 242-43, 270
Arnaud see Rabinovitz, Adam
Arnault, Claude 190
Artist (réseau) 68-79
Atkins, Vera
  background 26
  F Section, role with 24, 29, 48, 64, 106
  Kieffer, interrogation of 157
  on Colette 191

Atkins, Vera *contd*
  on Déricourt affair 150
  on Fontaine, Yvonne 227
  on Southgate, Maurice 165
  post-war interrogations 157, 321, 327-28
  post-war life 332
  trusted by agents 25
Autogiro (réseau) 18, 19, 50, 118

Baker Street
  F Section HQ 24, 26, 27
Bardet, Roger
  Arnaud, suspected by 127
  background 96
  Bleicher, Hugo, and 120, 127
  D-Day and after 262, 272, 289
  Donkeyman réseau, infiltration of 152, 196, 253-54
  Frager, Paul, and 144
  Odette and 96-7, 127
  Spindle, role with 96
  trial of 150
  Yonne crisis 257-58
Base Signals Station 229
Baseden, Yvonne
  arrives in France 224
  background 224
  escape from prison camp 319, 324
  post-war life 331
  Ravensbrück, captivity in 311
  training 230, 239, 274, 293
Bastien see Clech, Marcel
BBC (British Broadcasting Corporation)
  Messages Personnels 28-9, 61, 77, 115, 125, 223, 233, 236, 260, 261
Beaulieu
  SOE training schools 32, 38, 39, 40, 43, 154, 164-65, 182
Beekman, Yolande
  arrest of 205
  arrives in France 203
  background 202
  death 321
  description 202, 203
  imprisonment 304
  interrogation 205
  Musician réseau, role with 203-5
Bégué, George 18, 28
Belson 148, 293
Benoist, Robert 221, 222, 260
Bernard 197, 198-99, 200, 201, 202
Besnard, Charles 143-44, 146, 150, 330
Biélier, Gustave
  arrest of 149, 205
  Beekman, Yolande, and 203
  Buckmaster, Maurice, on 204
  death 332
  description of 204
  interrogation of 205
  Musician réseau, role with 57, 110, 203-5
  Prosper, links with 66, 132, 141
blackmarket
  Côte d'Azur 84
  Marseille 86
  Paris 59
Bleicher, Sergeant Hugo
  Bardet, Roger, and 120, 127
  Churchill, Peter, arrest of 294

Donkeyman réseau, infiltration of 152, 196, 253-54
Frager, Paul 144, 149, 253, 258, 272
  Odette, interrogation of 294-302
  post-war 150, 327
  Spindle réseau, infiltration of 118, 119, 120, 127
Bloch, Denise
  arrest 274
  arrives in France 221
  background 221-22
  captivity
    in Ravensbrück 311
    in Torgau 314
  Clergyman réseau, role with 222-25, 260
  death of 317-18
Bloom, Marcus 81
Bob see Starr, John
Bodington, Nicolas
  arrives in France 142-43, 238
  background 100-1
  Boemelburg, Karl, and 100, 101
  Dansey, Claude, appointment supported by 102
  Déricourt, Henri, and 100-7, 113-14, 130, 142-46, 149
  double agent 123-24, 140, 142-46
  F Section, role with 24, 85, 102
  Hall, Virginia, recruits 10
  Inayat, Noor, and 155
  MI6 and 102, 103, 106, 107
  Political Warfare Executive 145
  post-war career 150
Boemelburg, Karl
  Bodington, Nicolas, and 100, 101
  death of 150
  Déricourt, Henri, and 100, 104, 107, 108, 109, 110, 130, 152
  Prosper réseau, infiltration of 108, 109, 111, 112, 113, 114, 124, 130
  SD, role with 101, 327
Bomber Command 27, 228
Bony-Lafont gang 111, 112, 113, 131, 152, 154, 160, 161, 198
Bordeaux
  Scientist réseau 57, 70, 73, 76, 132
Borosh, Henri 259
Borrel, Andrée
  arrest of 98, 138, 139, 147
  arrives in France 50, 70, 129
  background 53
  captivity 304
  cover story 56
  death of 148, 320-21
  Déricourt, Henri, and 67, 108, 113
  PAT escape line, role in 53
  Prosper réseau, role with 55, 61, 62, 64-5, 66, 80, 107, 110, 135, 321
  Suttill, Francis, and 183, 189
Bourne-Patterson, Robert 25
Bricklayer (réseau) 216, 220
Brisse, Irene *see* de Baissac, Lise
Brooks, Tony 163, 175, 239, 241
Browne-Bartroli, Albert 197
Buchenwald 293
Buckmaster, Anne 14, 327
Buckmaster, Maurice
  'Aimicales Buckmaster' 333
  background 25-6

Buckmaster, Maurice *contd*
  D-Day misinformation and 134
  F Section, role with 25, 26, 28, 34, 103
  Judex, role in 325-26
  loyalty to agents 106
  on Bielier, Gustave 204
  on Beekman, Yolande 202
  on Déricourt, Henri 99, 113, 149
  on Inayat, Noor 154
  on MI6/SOE rivalry 106
  on Nearne, Jacqueline 164
  on Sansom, Odette 83
  on Southgate, Maurice 165
  on Starr, George 181
  on Suttill, Francis 132
  on Szabo, Violette 246
  Phono réseau, compromise of 215
  post-war life 14-15, 332
  Prosper réseau, destruction of 142
  Specially Employed 132, 165, 181, 202
  women agents, support of 45
Bureau, Jacques
  arrest of 141, 147
  captivity of 148
  Carte réseau, role with 117
  interrogation of 147
  on Suttill, Francis 135
  post-war life 150
  Prosper réseau, role with 61, 62, 65, 66
Butler (réseau) 63, 79, 110, 132, 149, 216
Butt, Sonia 259, 331
Byck, Muriel 245, 248, 259

Calais Line 16
Cammaerts, Francis
  arrives in France 116
  Bardet, Roger, suspicions about 120
  description 116
  Granville, Christine, and 273
  Jockey réseau, role with 159-60, 163, 211, 212,
    248
  Lefort, Cecily, and 136, 153
  post-war life 15, 332
  Sansom, Odette, and 298
  SOE assessment of 43, 165
  Spindle réseau, role with 121
  Vercors massacre 343
  Wake, Nancy, and 273
Cannes
  conditions in 1942 83-4, 86, 87
Carte (réseau)
  Churchill, Peter, investigates 19, 85
  destruction of 90, 94
  Frager, Paul, leadership battle 92
  F Section, value to 50, 54, 56
  Girard, André 19, 61, 85, 90, 92
  records, theft of 91, 118, 129
  security lapses 85, 91
Carve Her Name With Pride (Minny) 245
Canaris, Rear Adm Wilhelm Franz 117
Castres prison 207
Céline see Sansom, Odette
Cesar see Ree, Harry
Chalon-sur-Marne
  foundation of Juggler réseau 63
Chantraine, Octave 165, 176
Charisse, Suzanne 207
Charlet, Blanche

  arrest of 22
  arrives in Lyon 21
  Castres prison, escapes from 207
  post-war life 331
Chestnut (réseau) 155
Chicago Times 226
Churchill, Peter
  arrest of 128, 220
  betrayal of 123
  captivity of 293-305
  Carte réseau, investigation of 19, 85
  Donkeyman réseau, foundation of 112
  interrogation of 294-96
  maquis, links with, 174, 205
  post-war life 332
  returns to England 97, 115, 116
  Sansom, Odette, and 84, 97, 126, 342-43
  Spindle réseau, role with 87, 90-1, 95
Churchill, Winston
  aircraft, allocation of 212-13
  Bodington, Nicolas, and 146
  Churchill, Peter, and 296
  D-Day misinformation 134
  London Controlling Station, creation of 133
  radio broadcasts 1, 28
  SOE, creation of 102
  Suttill, Francis, recall of 132
cigarettes, shortages of 188
Cinema (réseau) 136
Clech, Marcel 131, 151, 152, 156
Clément see Liewer, Philippe
Clément, Remy
  de Baissac, Lise, and 238, 337
  Déricourt, Henri, and 108
  Farrier réseau, role with 77, 108, 113, 146, 153
  post-war life 150
  SD surveillance and 137, 154
  Suttill, Frances, and 66
  training 176
Clergyman (réseau) 221-25, 260, 274
clothes, 'authentication' of 25, 47, 187-88
codes, use of 36, 37, 184-85
Colette see Walters, Anne-Marie
Combat, resistance group 193
communists
  Francs-Tireurs et Partisans 174, 193, 234, 249
  Prosper réseau, links with 64
Cormeau, Yvonne
  arrives in France 180
  background 178-79
  Beekman, Yolande, and 202-3
  D-Day and after 268-69, 288, 290
  post-war life 11-12, 337-40
  radio operator, role as 35, 182-85, 191-92
  returns to England 323
  Sansom, Colette, and 190-91
  SOE assessment of 43-4, 178, 179
  Starr, George, and 180, 189-90
  training 179, 187-88, 202
  Wheelwright réseau, role with 163, 178-92, 211,
    224, 248
Cornioley, Henri 330
Côte d'Azur
  blackmarket 84
  conditions in 1942 83-4, 86
  North Africa, after invasion of 87
Cottet, Jean 95, 122, 125, 128, 220

Cottet, Simone 95, 125
couriers
  cut outs, use of 40
  dangers facing 88-9
  role of 34, 41
  training of 35-6
cover stories 30, 47-8, 56, 71
Cowburn, Ben
  Hall, Virginia, and 20, 22
  Prosper réseau, links with 67, 110
  Southgate, Maurice, and 165-66
  Tinker réseau, role with 227
  training 38-9
Culioli, Pierre
  arrest of 138-39, 141, 218
  arrives in France 51
  Gaspard and 52, 130
  Lefort, Cecily, and 160
  Monkeypuzzle réseau, role with 131, 132, 134, 136, 137
  post-war life 332
  Prosper réseau, role with 55, 56, 75
  Suttill, Francis, and 135
  torture of 147
'Cut-outs'
  réseau cell structures and 40, 66, 88, 160
cyanide pills 49

Dachau 293, 321
Damerment, Madeleine 216-18, 304
Dandicole, Jean Renard 242, 267, 291
Dansey, Claude
  Bodington, Nicolas, and 102, 103
  Déricourt, Henri, and 102-7, 113
  description 102
  London Controlling Station 133-34, 146
  MI6, role in 102-3
  post-war career 150
  Prosper's destruction, celebration of 142
  SOE, conflict with 102, 124
D-Day
  arrests prior to 240
  communications networks and 259
  Jedburghs, role of 267-68, 287
  misinformation operation 133-34, 146, 147, 148
  mobilization, réseaux 260-75
  preparation for 192, 222-23, 237, 242, 260-61
  Scientist réseau, role of 242-43
  targets, réseaux 260-61
Death Be Not Proud (Nicholas) 53
de Baissac, Claude
  arrest of 98
  Artist réseau, links with 76, 77
  Buckmaster, Maurice, and 208
  Déricourt, Henri, and 108, 109
  description 208
  France, escape from 69
    returns to 239
  Herbert, Mary, and 208, 330
  Judex and 325
  recalled to London 145, 155, 238
  Scientist réseau, role with 57, 70, 75, 81, 174, 207-8, 242-44
de Baissac, Lise
  arms drops, organization of 74, 242-43
  arrest of 98, 208-9
  arrives in France 50, 70

Artist réseau, role with 57, 68-79, 80
  background 69
  cover story 71
  D-Day and after 261-62, 267-68, 286-87, 290-91
  Déricourt, Henri, and 76-79, 108, 109
  description 54, 69
  France, arrives in 50, 70
    escape from 69
    return to 239
  Judex and 325
  maquis, links with 243, 244, 286
  Pimento réseau, role with 239-44
  post-war life 13-14, 335-37
  recalled to London 145, 155, 238
  Scientist réseau, role with 242-44, 261-62, 267-68
  SOE assessment of 44-5, 238
  SOE recruitment of 69-70
  training 164, 238-39
de Gaulle, General Charles 28, 249, 290, 326
de Guélis, Jacques 24
de Gyzicka, Krystyna *see* Granville, Christine
demarcation line 1, 18, 21, 22, 38, 87, 169-70
Déricourt, Henri
  arrest of 149
  arrives in France 58, 100, 107
  background 100, 106
  Bodington, Nicolas, and 100-7, 113-14, 130, 142-46
  Boemelburg, Karl, double agent for 105, 109, 110-11, 112, 113, 118, 152
  death of 150
  Farrier réseau, role with 76-9, 104, 107, 109, 146, 151, 176, 196, 203
  Frager, Paul, suspected by 112, 127, 129, 144, 146, 253
  F Section, recruited by 100, 104
  impressions of 67, 77
  MI5 and 104, 113-14, 129-30
  MI6, contacts with 103-4, 105
  PAT escape line 104
  Prosper réseau, betrayal of 130-41
  recalled to London 146
  SOE, investigated by 146, 327
  training 104
  trial of 98, 99, 149-50
  Vichy, pilot for 101
detector vans (D/F) 22, 27, 35, 161, 182, 205, 227, 235, 236, 276
Devereux-Rochester, Elizabeth 205-7, 331
de Vomécourt, Jean 18
de Vomécourt, Philippe 18, 21, 63, 154, 239, 245, 259
de Vomécourt, Pierre 18
DF Section 226
D/F vans *see* detector vans
Digger (réseau) 270
Diplomat (réseau) 196
Director (réseau) 224, 225
Dominique see Rafferty, Brian
Donkeyman (réseau)
  foundation of 112, 144, 151, 221
  infiltration of 152, 196, 253-58
  Jockey réseau and 160
  maquis, links with 264, 289
  Yonne crisis 255-57
  see also Frager, Paul
Double Webs (Fuller) 99, 100

Duel of Wits (Churchill) 84, 126
du Terre, Jacqueline *see* Nearne, Didi

Ecole Nationale d'Agriculture 65, 113, 135, 137
El Alamein 246
Elie see Jones, Sidney
Elizabeth see Devereux-Rochester, Elizabeth
escape lines
    Borrel, André, and 53
    Calais line 16
    Charlet, Blanche, and 207
    DF agents and 193
    Lyons 17
    PAT line 53, 104, 216, 250
    Var line 159
'Eucalyptus', role of 272-73

FANY 164, 229
Farmer, John 250, 251, 259, 267, 270
Farmer (réseau) 57, 110, 174, 196, 204, 225
Farrier (réseau)
    see Air Movements: Déricourt, Henri
Félix 182, 183, 187
Files de Calais see Calais line
Fiocca, Henri 331
Fireman (réseau) 225
Flossenburg 293
Fontaine, Yvonne 9, 227, 331
Foot, MRD 9, 116, 123, 126, 142
Forces Françaises de l'Interieur (FFI) 249
Frager, Paul
    arrest of 149
    Bleicher, Hugo, and 144, 149, 253, 258, 272
    Carte réseau, role with 92
    D-Day and after 262, 272
    Déricourt, Henri, suspicions of 112, 127, 129,
        144, 146, 253
    Donkeyman réseau, role with 112, 144, 152, 196,
        221, 255, 256
    England, leaves for 97, 115, 116
    Périgueux operation, role in 93-4
    Yonne crisis 257
Franc-Garde 170
Francs-Tireurs et Partisans (FTP) 174, 193, 234, 249
Freelance (réseau) 252, 267
Fresnes prison 147, 152, 205, 218, 283, 296-97
F Section
    Baker St HQ 24
    D-Day misinformation campaign and 133-34
    Déricourt, Henri, and 98-9
    foundation of 19
    Judex 325-26
    MI6, conflict with 102-4
    objectives 26-7
    radio procedures 27-9
    recruitment 29-31, 81-2
    resistance, co-ordination of 193
    structure and administration 25-31
    training 32-45, 47, 82
    women agents, advantages of 35
    see also Atkins, Vera; Buckmaster, Maurice; SOE
Fuller, Jean Overton 99

Gabriel see Young, John
Gaby see Plewman, Eliane
Garel, François 63
Garry, Henri 154, 155, 156, 158, 217, 332

Gaspard (Flowers) 51-2, 55, 56, 77, 109, 130
Gaspard (*maquis* leader) 250, 251
Gerson , Giliana 9
Gestapo
    Bony-Lafont gang, use of 111, 112
    D/F vans, use of, 22, 27, 161, 182, 205, 227, 235,
        236, 277
    Lyons assassinations 227
    Monk réseau, infiltration of 201
    Montlucon, raid on 271
    Phono réseau, compromise of 215-18
    role in occupied France 39
    Vichy, operations in 20-21
    Wheelwright, infiltration of 201
Gilbert see Déricourt, Henri
Girard, André *see* Carte
Grand Nouvel Hotel (Lyon) 18, 21
Granville, Christine 9, 273, 289, 331
Gubbins, Colin 133, 134
Guérin, Germaine 16, 19
Guérisse, Albert 250
Guerne, Armel 65, 66, 138, 141
Guy see Biéler, Gustave

Hall, Virginia
    background 10, 16-17
    CIA, role with 17, 330
    D-Day and after 290
    France, arrives in 10, 16-17
        escapes from 23
        returns to 225
    F Section, early role with 16-23
    Heckler réseau, role with 227, 245, 289
    maquis, links with 226-27, 250, 270
    post-war career 329-30
Harratt, PJ 159
Headmaster (réseau) 171, 259, 265
Heckler (réseau) 227, 245, 289
Hector see Southgate, Maurice
Hellet, Jean 199
Herbert, Mary
    arrest of 209
    arrives in France 81
    background 76
    de Baissac, Claude, and 208
    description 84
    Judex and 325-27
    post-war life 330
    recalled to London 208
    Scientist réseau, role with 76, 207-9
    training 70, 164
Heslop, Richard 205, 206
Hilaire see Starr, George
Himmler, Heinrich 39
Historian (réseau) 245, 275
Hitler, Adolf
    intelligence services and 117, 118
Hot Club (Montmartre) 65
Humphreys, Leslie 102-3

identity papers, problems with 47-8, 60, 63, 89, 169
Inayat, Noor
    arrest of 157, 215
    arrives in France 136, 149, 151-53, 203
    Bodington, Nicolas, and 155
    death of 321
    description 153-54

Inayat, Noor *contd*
  escape attempts 157-58
  interrogation of 157-58, 159
  MBE awarded 339
  Phono réseau, role with 154-55, 156, 178
  security lapses 156, 157
  SOE assessment of 154
  training 339
interrogation
  cyanide pills 49
  training for 41, 230
Inventor (réseau) 131, 151, 152, 198
Italy
  Allied invasion of 177

Jacqueline see Rudellat, Yvonne
Jean-Marie see Frager, Paul
Jedburghs, role of 267-68, 287
Jepson, Capt Selwyn 30-31
Jews, persecution of 59-60, 171
Jockey (réseau) 159-60, 163, 174, 175, 196
Jones, Sidney 131, 151, 152, 198
Judex 325-26
Juggler (réseau) 63, 132, 136, 141
Julien 240, 241, 242
Jullien, Ginette 9
Jura mountains
  Acrobat réseau 158, 161
  resistance in 198

Karlsruche 321
Khan, Noor Inayat *see* Inayat, Noor
Kieffer, Josef 136, 150, 152, 157
Knight, Marguerite
  arrives in France 253, 254
  background 252
  Bardet, Roger, and 255
  D-Day and after 262-64, 271-72
  Donkeyman réseau, role with 255, 256, 258, 262-64
  maquis, links with 264
  post-war life 331
  SOE assessment of 252
  Yonne crisis 255-57
Koenig, General Pierre 249

La Grande see Devereux-Rochester, Elizabeth
Lancastria 165
Landsell 255, 256, 257, 258
Larcher, Maurice 242, 267, 291
Latour, Phyllis 242, 244, 286, 331
Laurent 197, 199, 200, 201, 332
Lavigne, Madeleine 9, 259, 331
Le Chêne, Henri 20, 81, 176
Le Chêne, Marie-Thérèse 20, 81, 84, 176, 331
Lee, Lionel 216, 217, 218
Lefort, Cecily
  arrest of 160
  arrives in France 151, 154, 203
  background 159
  captivity, Ravensbrück 311, 317
  death of 317
  Jockey réseau, role with 136, 153, 159-60, 162
  training 179, 202
Leigh, Vera
  arrest of 152
  arrives in France 131, 151, 198
  background 151

captivity 304
death of 320-21
Les Baumettes prison 202
Les Tissots
  Spindle réseau, transmissions from 96, 122
Libération, resistance group 193
Liéwer, Philippe 196, 247-48, 274
Lille
  Farmer réseau 57, 109, 283
London Controlling Section
  D-Day misinformation operation 133-34, 146, 147, 148
Lucien 224, 274
Lyon
  Gestapo assassinations in 227
  Grand Nouvel Hotel 18, 21
  Pimento réseau 239
  Plane réseau 20, 81, 176
  resistance groups in 17, 81
  security of réseaux in 20, 21

Macalister, John 136-39, 218-19
Madeleine see Innayat, Noor
Mainguard, Amédée 172, 177, 259, 270
Maloubier, Robert 197
Marks, Leo 25
Marksman (réseau) 196, 205, 214-15, 224, 228, 289
Maquis (Millar) 206
maquis
  arming of 115, 116, 126, 127, 213-15, 226-27, 228, 235, 241, 242-43, 250, 251
  Churchill, Peter, and 174, 205
  community, role in 211
  D-Day mobilization 265
  de Baissac, Lise, and 243, 244, 286
  'Eucalyptus', role of 272-73
  foundations of 58, 172-74, 193, 210
  Hall, Virginia, and 226-27
  Haute-Savoie, attacks in 199-200
  Jedburghs, role of 267-68, 287
  Marksman réseau and 205
  Morel, Anton 95-6, 116, 126, 127, 228
  Plateau de Glieres, battle of 228
  reprisals against 227, 228, 265-66
  Stationer réseau and 173-74, 175
  Toulouse, liberation of 288
Marc see Clement, Remy
Markleberg 314, 316, 322, 323
Marsac, André
  arrest of 117
  Bleicher, Hugo, and 118-19, 120, 121
  Carte documents, loss of 91, 129
  Spindle réseau, role with 94, 116
Marseille
  conditions in 1942 86, 87, 170
  conscription rafles in 22
  Monk réseau 163, 176, 196, 197, 221
Marshall, Robert 99, 100
Mathieu, Geneviève 314-16
Mayer, EP 225
Mayer, PE 225
Menzies, Stuart 102
Messages Personnels 28-9, 77, 115, 125, 223, 233, 236, 260, 261
MI5
  Déricourt, Henri, and 104, 113-14, 129-30, 146

MI6
  Dèricourt, Henri, and 103-4, 105, 146, 149
  SOE, conflict with 102-4, 106, 117, 124
    dissolution of 327
    training 32
  see also Dansey, Claude
milice
  role in Vichy 35, 39, 170-71, 185-86, 193, 199-
    200, 210, 228
Millar, George 206
Mimi see Fontaine, Yvonne
Minister (réseau) 227
Minny, RJ 245
Monk (réseau) 163, 176, 197-202, 221
Monkeypuzzle (réseau) 52, 57, 131, 132, 134, 136,
  137
Moondrop to Gascony (Walters) 331
Morel, Anton 95-6, 116, 126, 127, 228
Morel, Gerry 25, 217
Moulin, Jean 196
Mulsant, Pierre 227
Musician (réseau)
  foundation of 57, 110, 196, 221
  objectives 203
  Prosper réseau, links with 66, 110
  sabotage and 174, 203, 204

Nantes
  Clergyman réseau 221-25, 260, 274
Natzweiler 293, 320
Nearne, Didi
  arrest of 277
  arrives in France 223, 224, 229, 231
  background 229
  captivity 293, 311, 314-16, 322
  escape 322-24
  interrogation of 278-84
  post-war life 11, 330, 333-35
  radio operator, role as 231-35, 276
  Spiritualist réseau, role with 234, 235-36, 275
  training 230
  Wizard réseau, role with 232
Nearne, Jacqueline
  arrives in France 166-67
  background 163-64, 229
  cover story 168, 172
  description 168
  FANY interview 164
  Judex 326
  post-war life 330
  recalled to London 234, 239
  SOE assessment 164-65
  Stationery réseau, role with 163, 168, 171-73,
    213, 244
  training 70, 164
Nelson, Sir Frank 102
New York Post 16
Nicholas, Elizabeth 53, 321
Noel 253-56
North Africa
  Allied invasion of 58, 81, 87, 177

Odette (Tickell) 82, 123, 341
Olive 18, 19, 85
Olschanesky, Sonia 304, 320-21
Oradour massacre 265-66, 274, 286
Orchard Court, Portman Square
  F Section planning centre 25, 48, 64

OSS 226
O'Sullivan, Patricia 225, 331

parachute drops 46, 49, 58-9, 74-7
Paris
  blackmarket in 59
  conditions in 1943 59-62; 1944 232
  Gestapo HQ 39
  liberation of 290
  Prosper réseau, foundation of 54-55
Parson (réseau) 216
passwords, use of 40-41
PAT escape line 53, 104, 216, 250
Paulette see Latour, Phyllis; Rowden, Diana
Périgueux operation 92-4
Pforzheim prison 159, 320
Philibert 182
Phono (réseau) 154, 155, 158, 215-18
Pickersgill, Frank 136-39, 218-220
Pierrot 248
Pimento (réseau) 163, 175, 196, 239, 265
Placke, Joseph 219
Plane (réseau) 20, 81, 176
Plateau de Glieres, battle of 228
Plewman, Eliane
  arrest of 201
  arrives in France 197-98
  background 197
  captivity 205, 304
  death of 321
  description 197
  Monk réseau, role with 163, 176, 197, 199-201
Poitiers
  Prosper arrivals centre 67, 68-79, 109
  Political Warfare Executive 145
  Prosper (réseau)
    arms drops 62, 110
    arrests of agents 137-39, 149
    communists, links with 64
    D-Day misinformation leaked to 133-34
    Déricourt, Henri, and 98-114, 129
    destruction of 65-6, 98-114
    Farmer réseau, links with 110
    foundations of 52, 75
    Gaspard, role of 51-2, 56
    interrogation of agents 139, 147-48
    Musician réseau, links with 66, 110
    objectives 50-1, 57-8
    overview 50-67
    power station attack 114
    recruitment 56, 57
    Scientist réseau, links with 67, 110
    SD raids 137
    security 66
    Spindle réseau, links with 91-2, 117
    training recruits 65
    see also Suttill, Francis

Rabinovitz, Adam (*Arnaud*)
  Bardet, Roger, suspicions about 120, 121, 127
  Cammaerts, Francis, and 117, 159
  Carte réseau, collapse of 94
  death of 332
  Gestapo, evades 219-20
  Les Tissots, transmissions from 96
  Sansom, Odette, and 89, 90, 123, 298, 342
  Spindle réseau, role with 85, 87, 88, 89, 93, 116,

Rabinovitz, Adam (*Arnaud*) *contd*
    122, 125, 126
radio transmissions
    bluff security checks 38
    codes, use of 36
    Gestapo interception 22, 27, 35, 161, 182, 191,
        205, 227, 235, 236, 276
    interpretation of 28
    Messages Personels 28-9, 77, 115, 125, 223, 233,
        236, 260, 261
    radio operators, role of 34, 182-85, 191-92, 231-
        32, 233-35
        training of 36-8
    radios, concealment of 89-90
        design of 36, 185-86
        security and 37-8
Rafferty, Brian 171, 175
rafles, conscription 22, 60, 86, 181, 265
Rake, Denis 251, 267, 270, 271
rassenschande 292
Ravensbrück 148, 160, 202, 205, 293, 303-309, 316-
    18
Rechenmann, Charles 165, 167, 168, 221
recruitment
    F Section agents 29-31, 81-2
    resistants 56, 72, 210-11
Rée, Harry 161, 172
reprisals 227, 228, 265-6, 273-4, 286, 287
réseaux
    Acolyte 259
    Acrobat 158, 161
    Artist 68-79
    Autogiro 18, 19, 50
    Bricklayer 216, 220
    Butler 63, 79, 110, 132, 149, 216, 218
    Chestnut 155, 221
    Cinema 136
    Clergyman 221-25, 260
    Digger 270
    Diplomat 196
    Director 224-25
    Donkeyman 112, 144, 196, 253, 260-61, 289
    Farmer 57, 174, 196, 203, 204, 234
    Farrier 58, 59, 76, 108, 111, 145, 196
    Fireman 225, 265
    Freelance 252, 267, 289
    Headmaster 171, 259, 265
    Heckler 227, 289
    Historian 245, 275
    Inventor 131, 151, 152, 198
    Jockey 159-60, 174, 175, 196
    Juggler 63, 132, 136, 141
    Marksman 196, 205-7, 224, 228, 289
    Minister 227
    Monk 163, 176, 196
    Monkeypuzzle 52, 57, 134, 135
    Musician 57, 110, 132, 141, 174, 196, 203, 234
    Phono 154, 155, 234
    Pimento 163, 175, 196, 239-42, 265
    Plane 20, 81, 176
    Rover 221
    Salesman 196, 246
    Satirist 63, 218
    Scholar 274
    Scientist 57, 67, 70, 75, 76, 163, 174, 207-9,
        242-44, 259, 261, 267
    Shipwright 259, 270, 284
    Silversmith 274

Spiritualist 221, 234
Stationery 163-77, 196, 221, 225, 228, 239, 240,
    245, 248-49, 250
Stockbroker 161-62, 196
Tinker 110, 174, 196, 227
Urchin 85
Ventriloquist 21, 265
Wheelwright 163, 174, 175, 178-92, 196, 248,
    260
Wizard 223, 224, 232
Wrestler 259, 270
    see also Carte; Prosper; Scientist
resistance movement
    arming of 213-15, 228, 235, 242-43
    Combat 193
    D-Day and after 260-75
    Françaises de l'Interieur, links with 249, 250
    Francs-Tieurs et Partisans 174, 193, 234
    ideological disputes 240, 244, 249
    Libération 193
    maquis 58, 115, 116, 126, 127, 172-74, 193,
        199-200, 203
    mobilization of 210-36
    security and 210-11
    splits within 193
    training of resistants 212, 242
RF Section 193, 196, 205, 249, 252, 266
Roger see Cammaerts, Francis
Roland 187
Rolfe, Lilian 243, 275, 311, 314-15, 317-18
Roun
    Salesman réseau 196, 247-48
Rousset, Marcel 63, 149
Rover (réseau) 221
Rowden, Diana
    Acrobat réseau, role with 161, 162, 172
    arrest of 162
    arrives in France 136, 151, 153, 160, 203
    background 161
    captivity 304, 305
    death of 320-21
    SD surveillance of 161
Royal Air Force (RAF)
    air raids on France 235
    Bomber Command 27, 213, 228
    F Section recruitment and 29-31
    Lyon, escape networks in 17
    Périgueux, surveillance of 92-4
Rudellat, Yvonne
    arrest of 98, 138-39, 147-48, 218
    arrives in France 50
    background 51
    captivity 311, 318
    death of 148, 324
    Monkeypuzzle réseau, role with 52, 57, 134, 135
    power station, attack on 114
    Prosper réseau, role with 55, 56, 67, 75, 80, 110,
        136, 137, 138, 160
    sabotage work 114, 131, 132
sabotage 114, 131, 132, 151, 174, 175, 193, 200, 203,
    208, 211, 212, 221-22, 227, 228, 241, 244, 248,
    260-61, 262-63, 264, 304
Salesman (réseau) 196, 246-47
Samuel see Maingard, Amédée
Sansom, Odette 80-97, 293-308
    Arnaud and 89, 90, 123, 298, 342
    arrest of 128, 205

Sansom, Odette *contd*
  arrives in France 81, 83
  Bardet, Roger, suspicions about 97-8, 120
  background 81
  betrayal of 123
  captivity 293-308
  Churchill, Peter, and 84, 88, 97, 126
  courier, role as 86, 87
  cover story 83
  escape, from Ravensbrück 319-20
  F Section, recruitment by 81-2
  interrogation of 139, 145, 294-302
  maquis, links with 174, 205
  MBE awarded 339
  post-war life 12-13, 340-44
  Ravensbrück 293, 303-8
  SOE assessment of 82-3, 164
  Spindle réseau
    betrayal of 115-28
    foundation of 87
    organizational problems 90-1
    St Jorioz base 95
  training 70, 82, 164
Satirist (réseau) 63, 67, 218
Savy 155, 223, 224, 231, 232, 233-34, 239
Scholar (réseau) 274
Scientist (réseau)
  Artist réseau, links with 73, 76
  D-Day targets 261
  maquis, links with 267, 286
  Prosper réseau, links with 67, 110, 132
  role of 57, 70, 75, 174, 207-9, 259
  sabotage 208
SD (Sicherheitsdienst)
  Abwehr, rivalry with 117
  Archdeacon réseau 218-20
  Bony-Lafont gang 111, 112, 113, 131, 151, 154,
    157, 160, 161, 198
  Prosper réseau
    arrest of agents 137-39
    infiltration of 105, 109, 110-11, 113, 118
    interrogation of agents 139, 147
    raids on 137
  recruitment, pre-war 101
  role in occupied France 39
  see also Bardet, Roger; Bleicher, Hugo; Bodington,
    Nicolas; Boemelburg, Karl; Déricourt, Henri;
    Sansom, Odette
security, of réseau
  arrests and 20, 27, 40
  bluff security checks 38
  Carte 85
  cell structure, importance of 40
  codes, use of 36, 37
  cover stories 30, 47-8, 56, 71
  cut outs 40, 66, 88, 160
  messages, concealment of 41
  passwords 40-1
  Phono 156
  Prosper 66
  radio transmissions 37-8
  Stationer 169, 175
Simon, André 105
Simon, Octave 63, 67
Skepper, Charles 136, 153, 163
SOE (Special Opereations Executive)
  Base Signals Station 229
  D-Day misinformation and 133

  dissolution of 327-28
  foundations of 20
  Hall, Virginia, role of 16-23
  Judex 325-26
  MI6, conflict with 102-4, 106, 117, 124
  RF Section, co-operation with 249
  Spanish Section 226
  Vichy, early operations in 16-23
  see also F Section
SOE in France (Foot) 116, 123, 126, 142
Southgate, Maurice
  arrest of 259
  arrives in France 166-67
  background 165
  Buckmaster, Maurice, on 165
  Nearne, Jacqueline, and 168, 330
  post-war life 15, 331-32
  recalled to London 176
  security and 168-69
  Stationer réseau, role with 163, 165, 168, 171-77,
    213, 225, 228, 239, 245, 248
  Witherington, Pearl, and 270
Special Forces Club 11, 333
Specially Employed (Buckmaster) 132, 165, 181, 202
Spindle (réseau) 87, 90-1, 95, 115-28, 174
Spiritualist (réseau) 221
Sporborg, Harold 99, 133, 134, 146
SS (Schutzstaffel)
  role in occupied France 39
Stalingrad 177
Starr, John 158, 161, 220
Starr, George
  arrives in France 81
  Buckmaster, Maurice, on 181, 189
  Cormeau, Yvonne, and 178, 180, 189-90, 191
  cover story 183
  D-Day and after 268-69, 288, 290
  post-war life 332
  security and 185, 210-11
  Wheelwright, role with 181-82, 187, 224, 248
Stationer (réseau)
  development of 168-69, 171, 173, 196
  Headmaster réseau, links with 171
  maquis, links with 173-74, 175, 228, 248
  objectives 165
  role of 163-77, 221, 239, 250
  security and 168-69, 175
St Jorioz 95-7, 115-28
Stockbroker (réseau) 161-62, 196
Stonehouse, Brian 21, 22, 330
St Quentin 57, 66, 110, 132, 196, 203-5
Suhren, Fritz 306, 308, 319-20
survival courses 36
Suttill, Francis (*Prosper*)
  arrest of 139
  arrives in France 55
  background 55
  Borrell, Andrée, and 183, 189
  Churchill, Winston, recalled by 131-34
  cover story 56
  D-Day misinformation and 133-34
  death of 148
  Déricourt, Henri, suspicions about 129, 134
  description 55, 63
  interrogation of 139, 140, 147
  Prosper, destruction of 135, 155
    foundation of 50

Suttill, Francis (*Prosper*) contd
   security lapses 65-66
Szabo, Violette
   arrest of 274-75
   arrives in France 245
   background 245-46
   Buckmaster, Maurice, on 246
   captivity of 157, 311, 314-15
   Carve Her Name With Pride 245
   death of 317-18
   description of 246
   MBE awarded 339
   Salesman réseau, role with 247-48
   training 239

Tambour, Germaine 544, 61, 65, 92, 114, 117, 119,
   135-36
Tambour, Madelaine 54, 61, 65, 92, 114, 117, 119,
   135-36
Théodore 204
Tickell, Jerrard 82, 123, 341
Tinker (réseau) 110, 174, 196, 227
Toulouse, liberation of 288
Tours 51, 52
training
   assessment of agents 34, 42-3
   Beaulieu 32, 38, 39, 40, 43, 154, 164, 182
   couriers and 35-6
   cut outs, use of 40-1
   for French life 38-9, 47, 82, 187
   interrogation, preparation for 41, 230
   overview 32-45
   passwords, use of 40
   resistants and 65, 212, 242
   survival courses 36
   Wanborough Manor 32, 33
   women agents and 33
Trotobas, Michael
   arrives in France 57
   death of 149, 204
   Farmer réseau, role with 109-10, 132
   security and 141
Troyes 110, 227

Urchin (réseau) 85

V1 rockets 232
Vecors massacre 273-74, 286, 343
Ventriloquist (réseau) 21, 245, 265
Verity, Captain Hugh 113
Vichy France
   Armistice Army 19, 90
   conditions in 1941 1, 2-3; 1943 169-70
   Jews, persecution of 60, 71
   milice, role of 35, 39, 170-71, 185-86, 193, 199-
      200, 210
   rafles, conscription 22, 60
   Service Travail Obligatoire (STO) 58, 60
Villevielle, Julien 200, 201

WAAF (Women's Auxiliary Air Force)
   F Section recruitment and 29
Wake, Nancy
   arrives in France 250-51
   background 250
   description 250-51
   D-Day and after 270-71, 289, 290
   Freelance réseau, role with 267, 270-71, 289

   maquis, links with 251-52
   PAT escape line, role with 250
   post-war life 331
   Southgate, Maurice, and 250-51
Walters, Anne-Marie
   Arnault, Claude, and 190
   Corneau, Yvonne, and 190-91
   D-Day and after 268
   Moondrop to Gascony 331
   post-war life 331
   security lapses 191
   Wheelwright réseau, role with 224
Wanborough Manor
   SOE training school 32, 33
Watt, André 146, 150, 176
Weil, Jacques 63, 136, 141
Wheelwright (réseau)
   air drops 182, 191
   cell structure 181, 187
   D-Day targets 260-61
   gendarmerie support 185
   Gestapo infiltration of 186
   role of 163, 174, 175, 178-92, 196, 224
Wilen, Odette 245, 331
Wish Me Luck 339
Witherington, Pearl
   arrives in France 176
   D-Day and after 269-70
   maquis, links with 269
   Shipwright réseau, role with 289
   Southgate, Maurice on 270
   Stationer réseau, role with 177, 244, 248, 259
   Wrestler réseau, role with 259, 265, 270
Wizard (réseau) 223, 224
Worms, Jean 62-3, 107, 141, 148
Wrestler (réseau) 259, 265, 270

Xavier see Heslop, Richard

Yonne
   crisis of Donkeyman réseau 255-57
Young, John 161-62, 172
Yvonne see Beckman, Yolande